THE ROAD TO SENECA FALLS

WOMEN IN AMERICAN HISTORY

Series Editors
Anne Firor Scott
Nancy A. Hewitt
Stephanie Shaw
Susan Armitage

A list of books in the series appears at the end of this book.

The Road to Seneca Falls

Elizabeth Cady Stanton and the First Woman's Rights Convention

JUDITH WELLMAN

UNIVERSITY OF ILLINOIS PRESS
URBANA AND CHICAGO

Manufactured in the United States of America
1 2 3 4 5 C P 5 4 3 2 1

∞ This book is printed on acid-free paper.

Library of Congress Cataloging-in-Publication Data
Wellman, Judith.
The road to Seneca Falls : Elizabeth Cady Stanton and the First Woman's Rights Convention / Judith Wellman.
p. cm. — (Women in American history)
Includes bibliographical references and index.
ISBN 0-252-02904-6 (Cloth : alk. paper)
ISBN 0-252-07173-5 (Paper : alk. paper)
1. Stanton, Elizabeth Cady, 1815–1902.
2. Woman's Rights Convention (1st : 1848 : Seneca Falls, N.Y.)
3. Feminists—United States—Biography.
4. Women's rights—New York (State)—Seneca Falls—History.
I. Title. II. Series.
HQ1413.S67 W45 2004
305.42/092 B 22—pcc 2003017060

To the people of Seneca Falls and Waterloo,
especially to local historians,
the Elizabeth Cady Stanton Foundation,
the National Women's Hall of Fame,
the Seneca Falls Historical Society,
and the Women's Rights National Historical Park,
who keep the home fires burning for all of us.
And to women and men everywhere
who work toward respect for themselves,
each other, and the earth.

CONTENTS

ACKNOWLEDGMENTS

Everything has a history, including the writing of this book. For help and support throughout this process, I owe many thanks to many people. My first appreciation goes to the keepers of the records, for without them this work would not have been possible. Thanks to librarians and archivists at the American Antiquarian Society, American Baptist Historical Society, Boston Public Library, Cornell University, Douglass College at Rutgers University, Harvard University, Haverford College, Ithaca College (especially William Siles), Johnstown Historical Society, Library of Congress, National Archives and Records Service, New Hampshire Historical Society, New York State Archives and Records Administration (especially James Foltz), New York State Library (especially James Corsaro), New York Yearly Meeting of Friends (especially Elizabeth and Roy Moger), Radcliffe, Rochester Public Library, Seneca Falls churches, Smith College, Smithsonian Institution (especially Edie Mayo), State University of New York at Oswego (where Mary Bennett and Shirley Omundsen generously helped with interlibrary loan services), Syracuse Public Library, Syracuse University, Friends Historical Library at Swathmore College (especially Bert Fowler and Christopher Densmore), University of Massachusetts (especially Pat Holland and Ann Gordon), University of Rochester (especially Mary Huth), Vassar College, and the Waterloo Library and Historical Society.

Special thanks to the Seneca Falls Historical Society and its many staff members and volunteers (including Anne Ackerson, Ann Hermann, Lisa Johnson, Philomena Cammuso, Jesse Watkins, Ethel Bishop, and Frances Barbieri) who made me feel so consistently welcome; to Betty Auten, Seneca County Historian, who generously shared her files with me; and to the many, many local historians and citizens in Seneca Falls, Waterloo, Johnstown, and central New York who took an interest in this project (including John Genung, Waterloo; Howard Van Kirk, editor of the *Seneca Falls Reveille,* and Lewis Decker, Fulton County historian). I hope they will consider this work a small repayment for their many kindnesses.

Particular thanks to Pat Holland, Ann Gordon, and the staff of the Elizabeth Cady Stanton and Susan B. Anthony Papers at the University of Massachusetts in Amherst and later at Rutgers, with whom I spent some of the most enjoyable times of my academic career. In a labor of both scholarship and love, they have done an extraordinary job. With the assistance of the National Historical Publications and Records Commission, they have created both a microfilmed edition of these papers (with fourteen thousand documents) and selected documents printed in hard copy: *Papers of Elizabeth Cady Stanton and Susan B. Anthony: Guide and Index to the Microfilm Edition,* ed. Patricia G. Holland and Ann D. Gordon et al. (Wilmington, Del.: Scholarly Resources, 1991); *The Selected Papers of Elizabeth Cady Stanton and Susan B. Anthony,* ed. Ann D. Gordon, vol. 1: *In the School of Anti-Slavery, 1840 to 1860* (New Brunswick, N.J.: Rutgers University Press, 1997) and vol. 2: *Against an Aristocracy of Sex, 1866 to 1873* (New Brunswick, N.J.: Rutgers University Press, 2000). These are an immeasurable gift to every scholar of U.S. history in general and of the U.S. woman's rights movement in particular.

Time off from ordinary responsibilities and a chance to interact with lively colleagues are priceless gifts to any historian, and I wish to thank several institutions for providing me with these. The assistance of the National Endowment for the Humanities has been irreplaceable. With NEH support, I attended the Family and Community History Program (directed by Richard Jensen at the Newberry Library), spent a summer of research at the Newberry Library, attended a seminar on social history at Brandeis University (led by David Hackett Fischer), and received a summer fellowship for intensive writing on Seneca Falls.

The State University of New York has provided essential assistance for this project. Thanks to the University Awards Committee for funding an early stage of this research and to the State University of New York at Oswego for granting me sabbatical leaves to work on this book. No project of this size would be possible without such strong institutional support.

Thanks also to the Social Science History Association, the Organization of American Historians, the New York History Conference, the Upstate New York Women's History Organization, the Berkshire Conference on Women's History, the National Park Service, and the National Council on Public History, as well as to Brandeis, Syracuse University, and Binghamton University for opportunities to present papers.

Thanks to the New York State Historical Association for allowing me to use my article "Women's Rights, Republicanism, and Revolutionary Rhetoric in Antebellum New York State," originally published in *New York History* (July 1988), as the basis for chapter 6 in this book.

Many thanks to superintendents and staff of the Women's Rights National Historical Park in Seneca Falls. Judy Hart, one of the people to whom Women's Rights Park owes its very existence, became the first park superintendent and hired Corinne Guntzel and me to collect materials relating to Elizabeth Cady

Stanton in Seneca Falls. She also gave me the privilege of working with a dedicated group of rangers and volunteers as the first park historian in the summer of 1982. Linda Canzanelli, Joanne Hanley, Josie Fernandez, and Nancy E. Watts succeeded Judy Hart. Vivien Rose and Mary Ellen Snyder, Chiefs of Interpretation; Anne Derousie, Historian; and Dwight Pitcaithley, Chief Historian of the Park Service, have provided vital encouragement and dialogue.

I have been lucky, as well, to find students, friends, and colleagues who offered ideas, moral support, and, most important, criticism. Special thanks to Teresa Bales, Amy Cardamone, Al Cope, Mary Curry, Elisabeth Dunbar, Paul Grebinger, Connie Hasto, Elinore Horning, Mary Kelly Black, Carrie Lavarnway, Joni Massiucca, Elizabeth Moger, Ron Myers, Betsy Patsos, Claire Putala, Lawrence Rainey, Carolyn Stefanco-Schill, Caroline Wright-Dauenhauer, and Nan and Russ Yerkes for their assistance in research or their willingness to read pieces of this work. Students in my women's history and local history classes have provided continuing inspiration and energy. Friends at Syracuse Quaker Meeting, including Marjorie Banks, provided the definition of love as "taking care of ourselves, each other, and the earth," that I have adapted in the dedication. Colleagues Robert Schell and John Kane are especially appreciated for their willingness to spend long hours dealing with data banks and statistics. Their generosity, good cheer, and amazing expertise left me awed.

Thanks also to feminist colleagues and friends on the Board of the Elizabeth Cady Stanton Foundation in Seneca Falls, in the Upstate New York Women's History Group, and in the Women's Studies Program at SUNY Oswego. I will not name you all, but I hold you in my heart. I think of each one of them as part of the energy that sustains the world.

Rosemary Agonito, Margaret Hope Bacon, Nirmala Bidani, Stefan Bielinski, Lois Banner, Suzanne Cusick, J. Douglas Deal, Ellen DuBois, Harlene Gilbert, Paul Grebinger, Nancy Hewitt, Hans Kuttner, Suzanne Lebsock, Margaret McFadden, Beverly Palmer, David Rowe, Loretta Schmidt, William Siles, Dorothy Sterling, and the late Mary Kay Tachau have shown friendship and support over the years. Carroll Smith-Rosenberg and Linda Kerber were inspiring early role models. Betsey Griffiths's emphasis on the importance of Elizabeth Cady Stanton's personal relationships has deepened my appreciation for the ways in which Stanton's own connections with family and friends in turn connected her to larger networks of reform. Carol Burdick at Alfred University Summer Place and Frank and Sandy Ellis at Blue Heron Point provided the great gift of special habitats for concentrated writing. Sally Roesch Wagner has been an inspiration to me ever since I first discovered her work on Matilda Joslyn Gage. Through her, I have been influenced by the wisdom of both Audrey Shenandoah and Jeanne Shenanoah. Christopher Densmore has been a pleasure to work with as a colleague, friend, and Quaker historian *par excellence.* He is the world's expert on Quakers in western New York, and his spirit shines through this whole book. Corinne Guntzel is as much a part of this book and of the story of Seneca Falls as anyone I know. Her untimely death has left a void that none can fill.

Rhoda B. Jenkins, John Barney (two of Elizabeth Cady Stanton's great-grandchildren), and Coline Jenkins-Sahlin, Stanton's great-great-granddaughter, generated enthusiasm and good cheer for me, as they have for so many others. Amy Post Foster and other descendents of Amy Post, and several descendents of Lucretia and James Mott have given very helpful family information to the park. Special thanks to Roy and Elizabeth Moger for pointing me in the direction of the Syracuse Monthly Meeting of Friends, where I have had a chance to share Quakerism in action. Deep appreciation for Gerda Lerner, who has truly been both an intellectual and a personal mentor and who has offered her work and her self as a role model for all of us who follow her in writing women's history. In particular, as the first woman president of the Organization of American Historians in 1982 (which also happened to be the first year of operation for the Women's Rights National Historical Park), Gerda Lerner supported the Women's Committee of the OAH in its attempt to bring national attention to Seneca Falls. Norman Graebner, my thesis advisor at the University of Virginia, provided a context for this work by his willingness to extend his mentoring skills to a novice graduate student working on the burned-over district of upstate New York.

No author can long survive without editors, and I have had the immense benefit of working with several. Nancy Hewitt, Kathryn Kish Sklar, Grey Osterud, and Howard Kirschenbaum remain valued friends as well as colleagues. Laurie Matheson has kept me on track through the whole process. Their willingness to balance thoughtful and incisive editorial suggestions with kindly encouragement has been a great gift. Nancy Hewitt's organizational ideas were nothing less than brilliant.

My family has provided the crucible for what I am and for what I might become. They deserve more than the small thanks I can give them here. I honor my husband, a renaissance man, for being there, always, a writer, a scholar, an editor, an architect, teacher, parent, and best of all, a friend; my children, Mark and Amaliya, for deepening my understanding of joy, compassion, and unconditional love; my mother, Marguerite Carpenter Wellman Matteson, who has been part of my life longer than anyone, and who has shared discussions of writing as well as children through the long period of development for each; the memory of my grandmother, Mary Irish Carpenter, whose growing up as a Seventh Day Baptist in rural upstate New York in the nineteenth century shaped my own worldview; the memory of my father, Silas Harold Wellman, whose hardscrabble boyhood in upstate New York shaped him into a most loving and scholarly Dad, a very uncommon common man; and the continuing affection of my brothers, Kendall and David Wellman, and their families.

THE ROAD TO SENECA FALLS

PROLOGUE

The following is an imaginative re-creation of what Elizabeth Cady Stanton might have seen if she had taken the shortest route from her house to the convention at the Wesleyan Chapel. This description is based primarily on maps, newspaper advertisements, village minutes, memoirs of local residents, and photographs.[1]

* * *

Elizabeth Cady Stanton, hair in curls, arms laden with law books and carefully guarded manuscripts, stepped off the front porch of her frame house on the outskirts of the village of Seneca Falls, New York. It was July 19, 1848, a warm, bright morning. Alongside walked her sister Harriet Cady Eaton and Harriet's eleven-year-old son, Daniel. All were excited. This was the opening of the world's first woman's rights convention, and Mrs. Stanton, only thirty-two years old, was the convention's main organizer.[2]

The Stantons' own house stood on the high ground west of the village. People called this place Locust Hill. In the wintertime, when the trees were bare, Mrs. Stanton could look from her front yard along the river and canal, past the noise and dirt of the mills, to the town itself, strung out along the river's high banks. White spires of village churches punctuated both sides of the river.[3]

If Mrs. Stanton took the river road to the village, as she often did, she would have turned right at the end of her drive onto Washington Avenue. So grandly named, this street was only a dirt track, muddy in spring and dusty in summer. Ordinarily, such dirt was distressing to her sense of order. Today she barely noticed it.[4]

At the bottom of the hill, just a few yards from her house, Washington Avenue ended at the Seneca Turnpike. This, too, was a dirt road, but a very important one. Not too long ago, before canals and then railroads had made travel easier, this turnpike had been the main route from Albany and Utica west to Buffalo. Several times a week, even now, Mrs. Stanton could see the heavy red

Map 1. Village Plat of Seneca Falls, 1852. *Plat-book of Topographical Maps, Seneca County, New York.* Ovid, N.Y.: W. E. Morrison and Co., 1852.

Concord stages roll into town, drawn by teams of horses, all in a hurry. If the coach were one of the twice-weekly mail stages, the driver would blow a long blast on his horn at this very corner, to let the villagers know that he was now at the edge of the village. These coaches carried mail and passengers from New York City in six to eight days.[5]

The Seneca Turnpike was a toll road. If you came from the east, you had to pay your toll at the mile-long bridge that crossed Cayuga Lake. In spite of that, some travelers still came through this way. So did local farmers. At harvest time, their wagons, laden with the prized Genesee wheat, thronged this road. Drovers, too, with great herds of cattle, sheep, swine, and horses and flocks of geese and turkeys still came along, filling the road with noise and dust from fence to fence for half a mile or more. Just the winter before last, somebody had tried to take a large drove of cattle across the lake on the ice, to avoid paying the bridge toll, and fifty head drowned when the ice broke.[6]

More and more, however, long-distance shippers and travelers preferred the Cayuga and Seneca Canal. Running between the turnpike and the river, just at the bottom of the Stantons' hill, the canal connected Seneca Falls with the Erie Canal and then with ports in the whole northeastern United States. Canal travelers took the slender packet boats, the *Heron* or the *Red Bird,* with their hawkers, crying for business, and the banners, flags, and blaring brass bands they carried to attract a crowd. The packets, two every day from the east and two from the west, blew their horns as they entered the village, just below the Stanton house. Clumsy cargo boats, with straighter sides and deeper drafts than the packets, clogged the canal, filled with produce such as lumber, potatoes, or apples, and with the heavy barrels of flour produced by the nine grist mills of Seneca Falls. Stanton's sons liked the excitement of the canal, and she had to keep a constant watch lest they fall in.[7]

Mrs. Stanton and her sister and nephew followed the turnpike as it ran below the high bank, covered now, in high summer, with weeds. On their right, between the road and the waterfront, diagonally across the intersection from the Stantons' house, stood the Chamberlain family's long white house, with a row of Lombardy poplars in front. The Chamberlains had lived here for the past five years, ever since Jacob Chamberlain took over the lower Red Mills, just behind their house.[8]

Farmers liked Jacob Chamberlain. They counted him as one of themselves, and they always thronged his mill. The Chamberlains had nine children. Their oldest daughter, Mary, had been a head teacher at the Seneca Falls Academy. All the rest of the children, down to the littlest one, Charles, still lived in the Chamberlain house.[9]

Mrs. Stanton expected Mr. Chamberlain to come to the woman's rights meeting, and she was glad of it. Not only was he one of the most respected men in town, but he was also, like her husband, Henry, involved in the new Free Soil movement. Mr. Chamberlain had, in fact, been elected president of the first Free

Soil meeting in Seneca Falls, just a month ago. This new Free Soil Party was drawing people out of both the Democratic and Whig Parties, to work against the extension of slavery in the territories. That was all fine, as far as it went. But if these men were serious about all this talk about equality, they would come to the woman's rights meeting today.[10]

Mrs. Stanton's husband, Henry, had been stumping New York state for Free Soil for a month now. He had conveniently managed to be out of town for this woman's rights convention, Mrs. Stanton thought ruefully. Well, too bad for Henry. She hoped Mr. Chamberlain, at least, would come and bring as many other Free Soilers as he could.[11]

On their right, as they walked along, the river was usually filled with logs at this time of year. Hemlock, whitewood, oak, ash, and elm, brought as rafts through the canal, were waiting to be cut into lumber at William Kline's sawmill. Kline had a good business, because most local bridges, buildings, and boats were built of wood, as were the pumps made by John Cowing and Henry Seymour.[12]

High above them to the left, they could see the spire of the small frame Episcopal Church where Mrs. Stanton took her boys on Sunday mornings. It was one place, she would say, where they had to sit still, and where she could just sit in peace for an hour and enjoy the organ.[13]

View of Seneca Falls looking west from the south bank of the Seneca River near the Stanton house, c. 1840. Church spire on the left belongs to the Episcopal Church. From John W. Barber and Henry Howe, *Historical Collections of the State of New York* (New York: S. Tuttle, 1842), 526. Courtesy of Special Collections, Penfield Library, State University of New York at Oswego.

She expected several people from the church to come to the woman's rights meeting. She hoped that fourteen-year-old Susan Quinn would be there. The Quinns were an Irish family, originally Catholic but now members of the Episcopal Church. Though Patrick Quinn, Susan's father, had come here without money or education (he still could not read), he had done very well for himself. Mr. Quinn did a good business as a gardener, and the family owned their own home on Garden Street.[14]

As they swerved right to cross the turnpike bridge, they could see the broad river below them. Mills were strung out along the islands and the edges of the water for almost a mile, from the lower Red Mills all the way west to Bridge Street. There were grist mills, sawmills, and pump factories, some of wood, some of stone. There were also two woolen mills. Just to their right stood the old carding and fulling mill, newly enlarged with weaving machines to bring it up to the standards of the Seneca Woolen Mills farther up the river. Just last week, Mrs. Stanton had read an advertisement in the newspaper: "Cloth Manufactory! Joel W. Smith, manufacturer of cloth, wishes to exchange cloth for WOOL, or manufacturers, or shares, or by the yard. He is prepared to do wool carding and cloth dressing with neatness and despatch." Girls who might have made good servants were going to work in these mills, adding to Mrs. Stanton's housekeeping problems.[15]

Near the textile mill, Mrs. Stanton could see the Old Red Shop, where Henry Seymour made hand pumps. This pump-making business was an unstable one, with manufacturers changing partners and going in and out of business so rapidly that it was hard to figure out which company was which. But after ten years, pump making seemed finally to be catching on in Seneca Falls. Now there were three different pump companies in town.

On Mrs. Stanton's left stood Dey's Mills, the first ever built in Seneca Falls, two and a half stories high above a stone basement. Originally painted with deep red paint, it was still called the upper Red Mills. Next to these mills was Whiting Race's lumber yard where Mr. Race, now president of the village, sold pine lumber for carpenters and joiners.[16]

Looking farther west, Mrs. Stanton glanced quickly at the other mills along the river. The Stone Mills, on the north bank, produced five hundred barrels of flour a day, and some people thought this was the most prosperous business in town. Farther west stood smaller flour mills—the City Mills, Clinton Mills, and the Empire Mills and Distilling Company. Finally, a large stone textile mill stretched along the canal on the south side. Built in 1844, it was the largest textile mill in the village.[17]

The road took Mrs. Stanton across the river, past Haskell's boat yard, up a steep bank and then onto Fall Street, the main business area on the north side of the river and the oldest part of town. As they crossed the Ovid Street bridge, Mrs. Stanton looked briefly behind her, across the river to the south side. When the canal had been built twenty years before, that side had grown quickly.

At the very end of the bridge, she could see the Seneca House and the brick stores built by Ansel Bascom. Woodworth's general store was there. So was Miss Gilbert's millinery shop. Miss Gilbert, it was rumored, would soon be married to S. E. Woodworth, in spite of his bankruptcy last winter. Woodworth and his brother, "the People's Agent," were the young merchants of the village. They sold everything: ready-made clothing (sewn on the premises by William R. Goetchius with thirty assistants), dry goods, groceries, carpets, boots and shoes, hats, crocks, "candies, toys, and Yankee notions," even books. It had been a long time since Mrs. Stanton had had leisure to read, but perhaps she would stop in someday (definitely not today) to see what they had. They advertised as the "cheapest bookstore in the United States," with the most competitive prices in town. "Farmers, Mechanics, Laborers, Men, Women and Children, young and old, draw near with pockets full of *rocks,* and you will not be permitted to go without purchasing, if you are satisfied to buy goods cheap," they claimed.[18]

At the west end of the village, also on the south side, Gary V. Sackett had built another hotel, the Franklin, and another business block to take advantage of the canal trade, at the corner of Bayard and Bridge Streets. These two southside hotels and business areas had managed to capture not only the canal trade but also most of the stage traffic from northside taverns. Lang's and Carson's, who groomed horses and trimmed carriages across from Sackett's block, were advertising, "Hold Your Horses! Hurrah for the South Side of the River!"[19]

But now southside merchants had cause to worry. The north side was beginning to grow again. Since the railroad had come through a few years before, business on the north side had picked up. The railroad brought noise and more dust into town, but still, most people were happy to see it come. Now businesses on the two sides of the river were about even, with keen competition between them.

Charles Hoskins welcomed the north side's rejuvenation. He was the best-established merchant in town, and his store was straight ahead of Mrs. Stanton now, literally a cornerstone of the northside business district. Hoskins had been at the same place at the corner of Fall and Cayuga Streets for twenty years, since the canal had come through. This was his second store on the same spot. His customers knew him, and he felt no need to write profuse newspaper copy, as Woodworth's did. "Have no time to write advertisements," he noted. "The public are respectfully informed that my stock of FALL and WINTER goods is now complete. P.S. My goods were bought *this Fall, not last Summer,* when none but old goods were in Market."[20]

Charles Hoskins felt no need to change much at all, in fact. He still priced his goods in shillings and pence. Country folk came to Hoskins's store every day. Cash was scarce, and Hoskins kept good accounts, so people could trade farm goods for store goods. The women exchanged their butter and eggs and fruit for dry goods, boots and shoes, tinware, drugs, and groceries. Only the new Empire Cash Store refused to take goods in trade.[21]

The men, as often as not, came to pick up the *New York Tribune* when it arrived twice a week in big bundles. While doing errands, everybody came to catch up on the latest village gossip. In the wintertime, men would gather around the stove to talk politics and tell stories. Jacob P. Chamberlain was a regular at Hoskins's store. Young William Burroughs, that country lawyer from Varick, would be there. So would the Latham brothers, builders and contractors, red-haired, red-faced, and loud. Somebody said that "when Obadiah Latham expressed his mind, Sidney Watkins held his breath and clung to the counter with both hands." Hoskins's store was "a capital place to fire up and let off steam," thought William A. Sackett. But another one of the group remarked that "when intellectual gas was too feeble to go through a meter there wasn't much chance for illumination."[22]

Most of the Hoskins crowd were Whigs. Edward Mynderse, whose speech impediment allowed him to speak only in a loud whisper, was one of the few Democrats—"politically lonely," remembered a friend. Whigs or Democrats or Free Soilers, it made little difference to Mrs. Stanton. None of them paid much attention to women.[23]

Still, Mrs. Stanton liked Charles Hoskins. As she passed his store, she may have peered inside to say hello. Mr. Hoskins had been active in the Free Soil meetings, and he had been sympathetic to her ideas about a woman's rights convention. He should be sympathetic. After all, he had five daughters of his own. But would Mr. Hoskins come to the meeting? What if no one at all came, except the handful of committed women? Well, they would hold this convention anyway, no matter who did or did not come. Mrs. Stanton would not back down now.[24]

From Hoskins's store, Mrs. Stanton could see all the way down Fall Street. The Globe Hotel stood on the opposite corner of Fall and Cayuga. With its broad front steps, its wide veranda, and its tall columns, it was, in spite of its age, an elegant building. People still remembered when General Lafayette himself, hero of the Revolution, had stayed there almost twenty-five years ago.[25]

Yet, thought Mrs. Stanton, in spite of a few cosmopolitan connections, this town still had the look of a country village. Most of the stores and shops were made of wood, no bigger than ordinary houses. Even the few brick buildings were only two stories high. There were no gas lights. The stores fronted on narrow board walks, which kept your feet out of the mud and manure but did little to cut down on the dust. In dry spells, people had to spray the road with water.[26]

It was true, Mrs. Stanton admitted to herself, that people could buy almost anything here. All the merchants brought back the latest goods from New York City, either on the canal or the railroad. There were shoemakers and dentists and tailors and milliners in town, and one barber, Thomas James, an African American. With her three sons to provide for, Mrs. Stanton made good use of them all. It was true, too, that there was talk of macadamizing Fall Street. She had seen advertisements in the village paper for contractors.[27]

But Seneca Falls was not at all like Boston. The Stanton family had left Boston more than a year ago, but she still missed it. Seneca Falls had few trained servants. Hardly any lectures or concerts. And barely a committed reformer in town. Boston had all of those, especially reformers, such as Oliver Johnson, John Greenleaf Whittier, William Lloyd Garrison, Margaret Fuller, and Theodore Parker.[28]

Well, maybe Ansel Bascom counted as a real reformer in Seneca Falls. He was a thorough temperance man and staunch abolitionist. He had certainly done his share for legal reform, with his local reform paper and his work at the state constitutional convention two years ago. She knew that, though he had refused to come out publicly and say so, he even agreed with her about a woman's right to vote. Not everybody felt comfortable with Mr. Bascom. He was, thought some of his neighbors, too "anxious to dig up the hatchet," "a mercurial citizen," "rather a poor follower," "peculiar," and even "obnoxious." Everybody agreed, however, that Mr. Bascom did like a controversy. They usually admitted, too, that he was "public spirited," "a good talker," and "a fine leader." Such controversy was the price he paid for being the most enthusiastic reformer in town. Mr. Bascom would be a candidate for office on the new Free Soil ticket. At least he would come to the woman's rights meeting, if for nothing else than to drum up votes.[29]

As Mrs. Stanton hurried along the boardwalk, arms full of books, pleased and a little frightened that this woman's rights convention was actually going to happen, George Milks, proprietor of the Clinton House, might have been standing on the front porch of his establishment at the west end of the village, very near the Wesleyan Chapel that was Mrs. Stanton's destination. The Clinton House had been built in 1827, as a stage stop, and Mr. Milks still kept a livery stable as well as a hotel. The smell of warm horses frequently mingled with the smells of supper, and the clip-clop of horses' feet added to the noise of the street.

One of Mr. Milks's predecessors had been Mr. Thompson, whose motto had been "attention, good cheer, and civility," and Mr. Milks still dispensed all that at the Clinton House along with wines, liquors, and (for the temperance minded) root beer. He also served strawberries, bullheads, oysters, and blackberries in season; milkshakes, ice cream, and mince pie any time; and onion suppers on Sunday nights.[30]

The morning was warm and bright, and the day promised to be a hot one. Mr. Milks idly watched the street. Horses and wagons passed by, kicking up dust as they went, and Mr. Milks nodded to the drivers. One wagon stopped just down the street in front of the Wesleyan Church. Oh yes, today was that woman's rights convention. Seemed like kind of a fool idea, but maybe there was something to it. Most of that Hoskins bunch would probably be there, and judging from the group that was gathered on the boardwalk outside the church, they would not be the only ones.

Henry Stanton's wife, they say, was the one that had thought up the idea. That Mrs. Stanton, she was a lively one, all right. She was pretty well-known in town, because she used to visit here eight to ten years ago, before she was married.

If Mrs. Stanton was going to get to that woman's rights convention on time, she would be coming along here any minute. Mr. Milks leaned over the railing and could just see Mrs. Stanton herself, coming along in front of the Globe Hotel. Who was with her? Oh yes. He had heard that her sister was visiting. That other woman must be Mrs. Eaton, and one of the children had come along, too. They were all carrying papers and books. Mr. Milks watched them coming, said good morning as they passed his porch, and, curious, saw them approach the Wesleyan Chapel. As Mr. Milks went inside, back to work, he may have wondered what in tarnation people would think of next.

Mrs. Stanton, Mrs. Eaton, and Daniel Eaton stepped onto the new boardwalk in front of the Wesleyan Chapel. Although they were early, a crowd had already gathered. Wagons drew up alongside the road and in the yard beside the church. The door was locked, and no one from the church had yet arrived. They hoisted Daniel through an open window to unlock the door and entered the building.[31]

Meanwhile, on the same sunny morning, near Geneva, about fifteen miles west of Seneca Falls, Rhoda Palmer stepped into the carriage, adjusting her skirts as she sat alongside her father, Asa. Thirty-two years old, Miss Palmer had already traveled widely, from Philadelphia, New York City, and New England to Michigan and Chicago. In her own lifetime, she had seen the country change from a wooded landscape (laced with rivers and trails), to cleared, open fields (tied together with bumpy dirt roads), to an expanding world of cities (linked by canals, steamboats, and railroads). She had seen Indians fishing from bark canoes; European settlers—among them her own family—who plowed the land with oxen; African Americans, many of whom had escaped from slavery; and urban dwellers, who had poured into America's cities from rural areas all over Europe and the United States to walk on plank sidewalks and shop for machine-made cloth.[32]

Rhoda Palmer was part of a great transition in the United States: from rural to urban; from agricultural to industrial; from handmade objects to machine-made things; from the power of wind, water, wood, and muscles to the power of oil, coal, gas, and steam. She was part of a quantum shift in the way people related to the earth, a shift that would affect almost every aspect of almost every person's life. It would make some people rich and others poor. It would change the ways that men and women related to each other, to their children, and to their neighbors. It would transform what they thought about themselves and the world.

As Rhoda Palmer and her father drove away from their house that summer day—the house that Asa Palmer had built forty years before, where Rhoda had been born and where she would live almost until the end of her long life—they drove from an older, rural world into the future. It was their intent to bridge the old and the new, to make sure that values they had placed at the center of their own lives would also be at the center of this emerging urban, industrial system. In particular, they believed that each person had access to the Light of the Spirit, and that everyone had a responsibility to act on God's leadings. As

Quakers, they acted on those beliefs every day. They tried to make them real in their families, in their Quaker meeting, in their dealings with their neighbors. And they wanted to make them real in the larger world. They believed that God existed in every person. That belief led them to act against slavery. Today they would consider what this meant for women.

When Rhoda and Asa Palmer reached the Wesleyan Chapel in Seneca Falls, they tethered their horse, entered the building, greeted their friends, and settled themselves in one of the pews.

In front of the pulpit, Mrs. Stanton carefully put her law books and her manuscripts in her seat. With relief, she saw that Lucretia Mott had arrived with her sister Martha Wright. Mrs. Mott lived in Philadelphia, but she and her husband, James, were visiting her sister Martha Wright in Auburn, New York, fifteen miles east of Seneca Falls, just as they did almost every summer. Although Mrs. Wright was seven months pregnant, she had accompanied Mrs. Mott on the cars from Auburn. They would be staying overnight at the Stanton home.[33]

Mrs. Stanton was also very glad to see the M'Clintocks. The M'Clintock family, Mary Ann and Thomas and two of their four daughters, had helped Mrs. Stanton get the convention organized. Around their parlor table in Waterloo, they had worked together to write the Declaration of Sentiments. Mrs. Stanton knew that she could count on Mrs. Mott and Mrs. Wright and the M'Clintocks to keep things going.

It was 11 A.M., an hour after the scheduled time of convening. The women moved to the front of the church. Today was a planning day for women only. Tomorrow they would present their ideas to the public, men and women both. Mary Ann M'Clintock Jr. agreed to be secretary. Mrs. Stanton, walking forward to explain the object of the meeting, felt like "suddenly abandoning all her principles and running away." But it was too late to back out now. The Seneca Falls woman's rights convention had begun.[34]

* * *

In 1848, one hundred women and men met in Seneca Falls, New York, to hold the first woman's rights convention in the United States. They asserted that "all men and women are created equal, that they are endowed by their Creator with certain inalienable rights, that among these are life, liberty, and the pursuit of happiness." Sound familiar? It should, for this declaration closely resembled the U.S. Declaration of Independence. It reminded Americans that no democracy could be real without respecting the rights of all its citizens. Appealing both to older republican ideas of corporate responsibility and to newer liberal values of individual rights, it challenged the country to put into practice its own egalitarian ideals. In so doing, it helped create what Elizabeth Cady Stanton, the convention's main organizer, called "the greatest revolution the world has ever seen."

Locally inspired, the Seneca Falls woman's rights convention attracted immediate national attention. Like a magnifying glass, it transformed widespread but unorganized public sentiment into a focused movement for change. Seneca Falls inspired other meetings, first two weeks later in Rochester, then in small groups throughout the northeastern United States, and then, beginning in Worcester, Massachusetts, in 1850, national conventions, held annually except for 1857 until the Civil War. Seneca Falls initiated a crescendo of activism on behalf of women, based on the conviction that women, too, were citizens of the United States, and that they, too, had every right to "life, liberty, and the pursuit of happiness." Woman's rights activists demanded nothing less than respect and equality of opportunity for women in every area of life—politics, jobs, education, marriage, the law, the church, the home, and popular custom. The Seneca Falls woman's rights convention represented an intellectual, social, and political revolution that left its mark on the minds, hearts, and institutions of the country down to our own time. As journalist Arch Merrill noted, "[T]he Seneca Falls and Rochester meetings were the Lexington and Concord of the women's 'revolution.'"[35]

Any story of the Seneca Falls convention must begin with Elizabeth Cady Stanton, the convention's main organizer. Stanton powerfully captured the personal drama inherent in the public event, and her account has dominated historical narratives ever since. Using her own life as a lens, Stanton connected everyday events, grounded in personal relationships, with the meaning of American democracy itself. In so doing, she validated not only her own experience but the experience of women everywhere, not simply in their roles as daughters, wives, and mothers but as individual human beings. More than a mere historical document, Stanton's story is so compelling that it has assumed the status of a myth, and Seneca Falls itself has assumed mythical proportions.

To call Stanton's story a myth is not to say that it is untrue. It is, however, simplified and larger-than-life. Beginning in the 1880s, it functioned as a kind of origin story, unifying Stanton and her allies (and distinguishing them from their opponents) by affirming their connection to each other and to the central ideals of the country through one event (the Seneca Falls convention) and one document (the Declaration of Sentiments).

After 1920, when the country passed the Nineteenth Amendment giving women the right to vote, a generation of scholars, many of whom were also members of the National Woman's Party, reflected both the gains of the woman's rights movement and renewed interest in its roots. In 1922, two of Stanton's children, Harriot Stanton Blatch and Theodore Stanton, published a new version of Stanton's autobiography as well as a much-edited collection of her letters and diaries. Alma Lutz published a solid and still useful biography of Stanton in 1940, while Mary Ritter Beard used Seneca Falls as a foil for her own argument that women had always been "a force in history." Finally, in 1959, Eleanor Flexner's influential *Century of Struggle* provided a mature and concise account of the convention itself and a bridge to later scholarship.[36]

From the 1970s on, fueled by a revitalized women's movement, women's history became one of the largest fields of historical study, and historians looked once more at Seneca Falls. Lois Banner, Estelle C. Jelinek, and Elisabeth Griffiths treated the convention as part of Stanton's biography. Margaret Hope Bacon viewed it from the perspective of Lucretia Mott, while James Livingston and Sherry Penney looked at it through the eyes of Martha Wright. Ross Evans Paulson, Keith Melder, Suzanne M. Marilley, and Nancy Isenberg looked at it in terms of the emerging woman's rights movement. Others referred briefly to Seneca Falls in the context of local studies of reform, the post–Civil War woman's rights movement, woman's rhetoric, comparative studies of nineteenth- and twentieth-century feminist movements, or international women's activism. Two excellent collections of documents presented the early woman's rights movement in its historical context. Popular interpretations included a video by Ken Burns and accompanying book by Geoffrey Ward. Future scholars will rejoice in the enormous amount of documentary evidence made available by *The Selected Papers of Elizabeth Cady Stanton and Susan B. Anthony* (edited by Ann D. Gordon and based on a microfilmed edition by Pat Holland and Ann Gordon) and the *Selected Letters of Lucretia Coffin Mott,* edited by Beverly Wilson Palmer.[37]

If we focus on the Seneca Falls convention from the perspective of social and community history, however, we ask new questions and gain very different perspectives. Why, for example, did the convention happen in Seneca Falls, New York, instead of in Boston, New York, or even Washington, D.C.? What was Stanton's own relationship to her community in the years before the convention? Who were the other ninety-nine signers of the Declaration of Sentiments? And why did they come to the convention?[38]

This book argues that, in time and place, Seneca Falls was at a fulcrum point. Between the Revolution and the Civil War, Americans experienced changes so dramatic that we can rightly call them revolutions—in industry, society, and culture. Caught in dramatic change, people searched to define the core meaning of citizenship. What did it mean to be an American? What did it mean to be "created equal"?

Because of its geography, upstate New York became a particular focus for these revolutions. Lured by rich lands, abundant waterpower, and the country's most important access routes to the west, people poured into the region from various parts of the eastern United States and western Europe. Seneca Falls and its neighboring community of Waterloo were right in the middle of this turmoil.

Among those who poured into these villages in the 1830s and 1840s were three key groups of reformers, linked by thirty-two-year-old Elizabeth Cady Stanton. Legal reformers, whom she met through work in her father's law office, identified the connection between woman's property ownership and woman's political rights. Political abolitionists, represented most immediately by her husband, Henry, and her cousin Gerrit Smith, stressed the power of voting to create social change. Egalitarian abolitionists, personified by a network of

Quaker reformers (most notably by Stanton's friend, Lucretia Mott) embodied their commitment to the equality of every human being.

Representatives from all three of these groups signed the Seneca Falls Declaration of Sentiments. Although strongly influenced by abolitionist ideals, most were European American. Frederick Douglass was the only known African American signer.[39]

As a uniquely gifted leader, Stanton acted as a catalyst, enlisting the energies of these local abolitionists and legal reformers to claim the Declaration of Independence as a document that spoke for women as well as men. In so doing, they gained immediate national attention. They bound the woman's rights movement to the central debate over the meaning of citizenship, in the United States and around the world.

By looking at the woman's rights convention from the perspective of families, communities, and the larger context of reform, we can begin to understand Stanton's significance, not only as an individual but also as a product of her own family, community, and culture. We can test Stanton's own recollections against evidence from her contemporaries. In so doing, we can broaden our understanding of what caused the convention to happen, of why it happened in Seneca Falls, and of why so many local people supported ideas "of the kind called radical."[40]

Because the ideas expressed at Seneca Falls remain so central to our own lives, we may approach this book not entirely as outsiders, as dispassionate observers. We may deal with Seneca Falls in some sense from the inside out, as if we, too, were part of that world (as in some sense, we are), as if we, too, knew the Stantons, the Motts, the M'Clintocks, the Posts, and the Wrights (as in some sense, we do).

Living simultaneously in the 1840s and in the 2000s has its perils. For one thing, such a double vision forces us constantly to shift focus between our current world, both material and cultural, and a world long past, constructed in our own minds from traces only, from wisps of memory braced and bounded here and there by physical remains—a newspaper, a letter, a house, the intersection of streets in a village, a locust tree, just where it ought to be, descendent (just as we are) of generations past. We are sometimes truly if temporarily missing from our own times, captive in a time warp, from which we can be called back only with conscious effort.

On the other hand, mentally walking the streets of Seneca Falls, or anywhere else, in a different time brings its own rewards. We recognize that historical characters lived their own lives, on their own terms, less aware of us than we are of them. For us today, they may serve as models and instruments for us to use as we search for solutions to our own problems. They, however, acted to resolve their own dilemmas. Sometimes, as at the Seneca Falls woman's rights convention, their actions reverberated so powerfully that the sound echoed deeply into the past and far into the future, making our world in some sense a continuum of their own. When that happens, it behooves us to pay attention, to understand such an event first on its own terms and then for what it may say to us, on our own terms.

Once, the Seneca River roared through Seneca Falls, forming the falls that gave the village its name and bringing economic, social, and cultural change. Today, however, the tallest dam east of the Mississippi River has quieted the noise of the river. Instead of a torrent, a tranquil pool lies in the heart of the village. Quiet eddies along the shore invite us to pause for reflection. Leaning over the edge of the water, we first see our own faces shimmering back at us among green trees and blue sky above. Looking deeper into the water, with our mind's eye now, we see far below the dim outlines of a long-ago world—houses, factories, and streets that once stood solid in the sunlight, the economic and physical heart of the village, flooded by the same dam that created the lake.

Once a year, the lake is lowered, and we can see, with ordinary vision, the foundations of the factories and homes that lined the banks of the Seneca River. Perhaps by telling the story of Seneca Falls, we can re-create that lost world more vividly in our minds than we will ever see it again in its physical form. Perhaps we can drain the waters of time to reveal once more the village of Seneca Falls as it stood in 1848, to see once again the people of Seneca Falls as they struggled to harness the currents of change that raced through their town and through themselves, eroding the world they had known but at the same time revealing how very deeply, how tenaciously, the roots that held the forest along the banks of the river—the roots of an older world—shaped and contained the energies of change.

PART 1

The Context: Converging Paths

CHAPTER 1

Elizabeth Cady Stanton: Growing Up, 1815–35

In July 1848, at the Seneca Falls convention, Elizabeth Cady Stanton began her life's work as a public agitator for the rights of women. What Stanton was and would become had its roots in her childhood. She grew up in a world where wealth was based on land; where people recognized their places in an orderly, communal world; and where her neighbors continued to value citizens who placed the good of the whole group above their own personal gain. Such a community was predominantly hierarchical, but people balanced their strong sense of hierarchy with a corresponding sense of mutual responsibility.

In 1815, the year Stanton was born, the northeastern U.S. country stood poised between two ways of life. Fading into the past was a world dominated by slow communications, by local allegiances, and most of all by the land. More than 90 percent of Americans were farmers. Looming ahead lay a period of change so rapid that even historians, normally the most cautious of observers, would label this a time of revolutions—in transportation, industry, city growth, family life, and personal values. Transportation, restricted in 1815 primarily to country roads, turnpikes, and sailing ships, would be revolutionized, first by the construction of canals and then by the application of steam power on both water and land. Manufacturing, still mainly small-scale, local, and organized into a craft-apprenticeship system in 1815, would be transformed by new machines, new systems of transportation, new sources of workers, and new markets into a factory-oriented, industrialized economy. Americans, drawn by opportunities for trade and manufacture in new urban areas, would move from farms into cities in what would become proportionally the largest rural-urban migration in the country's history.

Moving physically, Americans would also face major changes in traditional social structures and traditional values. Old systems of order based on hierarchy and deference would crack. People would salvage what they could of old ideas, and they would weave them into safety nets to bridge the chasm between the old order and an often threatening new world.

At the time of her birth, Elizabeth Cady's family reaffirmed its commitment to values that were, even then, growing out of fashion. As society changed dramatically in almost every way, the Cady family did not. In a time of industrialization, they continued to invest in farmland. In a time of urbanization, they stayed in the country. As others began to have fewer children, Elizabeth's parents continued to produce offspring, ten in all. As ideas of free will began to dominate Protestant religious expression, the Cadys clung to their Calvinist belief in predestination. As voters abandoned the old Federalist Party, Elizabeth's father retained his commitment to it. By almost every measure, the Cady family found itself out of step with the new world.

Because of this pronounced conservatism, few would have predicted that Elizabeth Cady would grow up to be a reformer. Stanton herself recognized the irony of it. As a judge, her father was, she remembered, "a conservative of the conservatives." Her mother, born into the landed Livingston family, was "blue-blooded socially as well as physically." "When I became an Abolitionist and a woman suffragist," Stanton recalled, "I outraged the family traditions."[1]

Certainly, Stanton's economic and cultural background seemed antithetical to her reform ideals. What interest had her mother's family, the Scottish and Dutch Livingstons from the Hudson Valley, in woman's rights? They were, after all, landed gentry, the aristocrats of New York. Her father identified even more strongly with conservative values. As a Congregationalist-Presbyterian in religion and a Federalist turned Whig in politics, he upheld a hierarchical order in society and found himself completely at odds with his daughter's adult commitment to abolitionism and woman's rights.

Yet strands in this family culture intertwined to support Stanton's reform interests. While Stanton's family was part of an elite, their status as one of the first families was based only partly on wealth. Although Daniel Cady was at the top of the social scale, he was virtually a self-made man. What identified this family as "blue-blooded" and "conservative" was not so much the amount of money they held as the fact that their resources were based on land and the law rather than on manufacturing. Their money did not compare with that of rich urban families, nor did it rival the fortune they might have made by investing in canals, railroads, or factories.[2]

More importantly, both parents shared a commitment to republican ideals and the American revolutionary tradition. They balanced a sense of order and community responsibility with ideals of liberty and independence. Her mother brought stories of parents and grandparents honored for their service in the revolutionary cause. Her father provided her with a clear personal example of republican values. Honest, incorruptible, and unassuming in his dealings with highborn and poor alike, oriented all his life toward community service and personal benevolence, Daniel Cady balanced material success against spiritual and civic virtue. Money was less important to him than character. He judged himself a success not because he was wealthy but because he was a man of integrity, respected by his fellow citizens.

Finally, Margaret Livingston Cady emerged from a family who showed relative respect for woman's property rights. In Margaret's family, Scottish Livingstons had intermarried with Hudson River Dutch families, and their descendants inherited a tradition of Dutch law, based on Roman rather than English tradition, which gave women rights to hold property.

Within the Cady family, Elizabeth's parents seemed almost polar opposites. Daniel was slight of build, brilliant, extremely conscientious, and painfully shy. Contemporaries would call him "one of the most generous and gifted men of his time," a man of "sweetness" and "refinement," "exalted worth and strict integrity," and "unsurpassed ability." Said one colleague and former student, "his name has been for years, throughout the State, almost a synonym for 'honest man,' a bye-word by which to denote uprightness and purity of character."[3] His daughter Elizabeth echoed these contemporary descriptions. He was, she wrote, a man of "firm character and unimpeachable integrity," yet "sensitive and modest to a painful degree," "truly great and good,—an ideal judge; and to his sober, taciturn, and majestic bearing, he added the tenderness, purity, and refinement of a true woman."[4]

Margaret Livingston, Stanton's mother, was quite different. She was almost six feet tall, extremely sociable, and (so her daughter remembered) stern—an imposing, dominant, and vivacious figure who controlled the Cady household with a firm hand. Stanton would later describe her as "the soul of independence and self-reliance,—cool in the hour of danger, and never knowing fear," "inclined to a stern military rule of the household,—a queenly and magnificent sway." At the time of Elizabeth's birth, wrote another commentator, Margaret Livingston Cady was "a young lady of high spirit, dash, and vivacity," qualities she retained until her death.[5]

In later life, Elizabeth Cady Stanton always emphasized her father's formative influence. Like her father, she pursued intellectual interests, legal studies, and persuasive public speaking. In personality, however, although she did not acknowledge it, Elizabeth more closely resembled her mother—lively, sociable, fun loving, and efficient. And like her mother, she would derive much of her adult sense of identity from her role as mother of a large family. Much of her success as a public figure would come, in fact, because Elizabeth made motherhood, normally a private role, the basis of her public career.

Johnstown, the village in which Daniel and Margaret spent most of their lives, had an ethnically diverse population. English, German, Scots Highlanders, Dutch, and New Englanders farmed the land. More than five hundred African

Americans, many of them enslaved, also lived in Montgomery County. Interspersed among these newcomers, Mohawk people retained remnants of their homelands. Local people still pointed out "a few hundred acres of excellent meadow" as the former home of Hendrick, a famous Mohawk sachem. As a child, Stanton would hear Iroquois legends told by the Presbyterian minister. Ethnic divisions remained prominent for many years. One observer noted in 1802 that Montgomery County "appears to be a perfect Babel, as to language. . . . The articulation even of New-England people, is injured by their being intermingled with the Dutch, Irish, and Scotch." Its five churches served different ethnic groups. Even the shape of the village reflected its ethnic origins. Its town square suggested New England influences, but many dwellings still incorporated Dutch and German patterns. Long double houses opened directly onto the street from the broad side, with small porches in front and gardens and porches toward the rear. As one visitor noted in 1830, most of the houses were "neatly painted white with green venetian shutters, which gives the whole town a charm and prettiness of appearance."[6]

Within the context of this ethnically and racially diverse population, Johnstown developed as a prominent legal and cultural center. At the center of the village stood the courthouse and jail. Built in 1772, they reflected the village's importance as the county seat for Tryon County, which encompassed all of New York west of Albany. Daniel Cady added his name to the long list of eminent jurors who debated their cases here. The two-story academy, built in 1798, was one of the best secondary schools in the state of New York. Observers described Johnstown at the end of the eighteenth century as "a marked intellectual center," "the most important place in the State west of Albany."[7]

The Cady children grew up in the middle of the village, bounded by home and courthouse, church and school. Elizabeth Cady's maternal grandparents, James and Elizabeth Simpson Livingston, were the first to climb the hills north of the broad Mohawk Valley. As land agent and merchant, James supported his growing family on what he described as "comparatively . . . small" means. When Elizabeth Simpson Livingston died on June 10, 1800, at age forty-nine, she left James alone to cope with a household containing five children under fifteen; two enslaved people; and two young women, including their fifteen-year-old daughter Margaret.[8]

Elizabeth Cady's father, Daniel Cady, was born in Chatham, New York, in 1773 and came to Johnstown in 1798. Although he grew up in eastern New York, Daniel shared the political and religious values of his transplanted Yankee neighbors and kin. Church, state, and family all stood for right order and proper authority.[9] He shared with the Federalists a strong sense of community responsibility and moral concern, buttressed by his religious upbringing. Presbyterians and Congregationalists shared a belief that "no mortal man [or woman] and no human institution can be regarded as infallible," and that, therefore, "the church must be limited in power." Individual conscience acted as a centripetal force, eroding attempts to centralize human institutions. Daniel Cady embodied this commitment to conscience and passed it on to his daughter Elizabeth. It would be the wellspring of her own commitment to woman's rights.[10]

Daniel Cady was community minded, but he was also personally ambitious. He tried out careers as a shoemaker and teacher before he finally settled on the law. In 1795, when he was about twenty-two years old, he became an attorney in his own right. In 1798, he moved to Johnstown. On July 15, 1801, twenty-eight-year-old Daniel Cady married sixteen-year-old Margaret Livingston. After a brief career as a Federalist member of the U.S. House of Representatives (1815–17), he retreated to his law practice and his family. "There were but two places in which he felt at ease," wrote his daughter Elizabeth, "in the courthouse and at his own fireside." Margaret, outgoing, gregarious, balanced Daniel's shyness, and Daniel's tenderness modified Margaret's inclination to control those around her. For the rest of her life, she and Daniel would nourish their children in the home that became the emotional center of both their lives. Within their household, Margaret Livingston Cady presided over their growing family. People recognized her central importance by referring to this household as "Mrs. Cady's."[11]

Daniel Cady had come to Johnstown with very little capital, but he amassed a considerable fortune from land speculation. He thought of himself, justifiably, as "much of a financier," and he owned farms and undeveloped tracts all over central New York. Throughout his life, he loved farming, especially "the reclaiming of waste lands."[12] Cady made his most important mark not in land speculation or politics, however, but in the law. He earned a distinguished reputation, rivaling that of the best-known lawyers of his time. At his death, he was hailed as "the very image and personification of justice," "a model lawyer and a model man."[13]

Every week, in all kinds of weather, the Cady family also attended church. "When the thermometer was twenty degrees below zero on the Johnstown Hills," Stanton recalled, "we trudged along through the snow, foot-stoves in hand, to the cold hospitalities of the Lord's House, there to be chilled to the very core by listening to sermons on 'predestination,' 'justification by faith,' and 'eternal damnation.'" As one of Cady's former law students recalled, "probably there has scarcely been a Sabbath during the sixty years that he has resided in this village, when he was at home, that has not seen him [and his family] in his place in the house of worship." Founded in the 1740s by supporters of Bonnie Prince Charlie, the church was still called the Scottish Presbyterian Church. On ceremonial occasions, many members wore kilts and held communion in the Scottish way, seated around a common table. As late as 1830, one visitor could hardly understand Rev. Mair's sermon, so thick was his Scottish accent. Neither the building nor the service appealed to the young Elizabeth. The church, she remembered, "was bare, with no furnace to warm us, no organ to gladden our hearts, no choir to lead our songs of praise in harmony." Instead, "the chorister . . . intoned line after line of David's Psalms, while, like a flock of sheep at the heels of their shepherd, the congregation, without regard to time or tune, straggled after their leader."[14]

On November 12, 1815, while Daniel Cady was serving in the U.S. House of Representatives, Margaret Cady gave birth to Elizabeth, her seventh child. Elizabeth's first strong memory was of the birth of her sister Catharine in January 1820. So many friends kept saying, "What a pity it is she's a girl!" that the four-year-old Elizabeth regarded the new baby "with a kind of compassion."[15]

Though she endured the usual childhood diseases of chicken pox, whooping cough, measles, and scarlet fever, Elizabeth seems in general to have been a healthy child. She was "a plump little girl, with very fair skin, rosy cheeks, good features, dark-brown hair, and laughing blue eyes." She credited herself with "strong self-will," "a good share of hope and mirthfulness," "a vigorous constitution and overflowing animal spirits," which saved her from becoming "a mere nullity."[16]

In spite of her genetic assets, which certainly included a cheerful personality and remarkable intelligence, Elizabeth found the world a fearful place. When she recalled her childhood in later years, words such as "tyranny," "fear," "dread," "gloomy," and "solemn" filled her descriptions. "I well remember the despair I felt in those years, as I took in the whole situation, over the constant cribbing and crippling of a child's life."[17]

Stanton associated fear with authority, which she often equated with tyranny. And authority figures were everywhere, especially in home and church. "Fear, rather than love, of God and parents alike, predominated," she recalled, reinforced by her "dread of the ever present devil." At home, she viewed her father with "fear rather than affection." Her mother she saw as a "military" figure. And for her, the devil was an ever-present reality. "I early believed myself," she recalled, "a veritable child of the Evil One, and suffered endless fears lest he should come some night and claim me as his own. To me he was a personal, ever-present reality, crouching in a dark corner of the nursery."[18]

Much of Stanton's later rebellion against women's place in the larger world had its roots in her fight against the repressive authority and strict discipline of her childhood. All through her life, she struggled with a tension between her own needs for growth and the demands of institutionalized authority. Living at the margin in her childhood years helped her develop a critical perspective that would become part of her core personality. With it, she could function successfully in a world she would at the same time try to change.

By 1820, when Elizabeth was five years old, nine people lived in the Cady family. At age forty-seven, Daniel was already middle-aged. Margaret herself, at thirty-five, had already birthed nine of their ten children. She had also seen three of them die. Still living were two teenagers, Tryphena and Eleazer, aged sixteen and fourteen; ten-year-old Harriet; and the three youngest, all girls, Elizabeth, Margaret, and Catharine, aged five, three, and one. In addition, many other people lived and worked in the house—three African American men as well as four Scottish nurses and a cook. A Catholic chambermaid named Margaret remained with the family from about 1810 until the 1860s. Daniel Cady's law office was also connected to the house, and law students came and went every day. There is no indication that these students lived with the Cady family. They may well have boarded with other local families or at the hotel next door.[19]

The family lacked no material comforts. By any measure, they were affluent. They lived in a large frame dwelling, which a later visitor described as "an elegant great house." It was painted white, two stories high, with shuttered windows. The front door opened directly onto the street from the gable end of the house. Flanked by two windows on the left and one on the right, the door opened into a central hallway with rooms on each side. Judge Cady noted in November 1816 that he had been "surrounded and tormented with joiners, carpenters and masons," and the Cadys may have built or remodeled their house at that time.[20]

Larger than most of its neighbors, the house had a commodious attic, a cellar that included a store room and two large kitchens, and "a large back building," "with grounds on the side and rear." Lilies of the valley filled June days with their sweet smell. Over the back building was their nursery, with "three barred windows reaching nearly to the floor." A veranda with a gently sloping roof opened onto a garden, which connected with Rev. Simon Hosack's back yard. Barns and carriage houses, full of driving and saddle horses, carriages and sleighs (including an old cutter built in 1770), stood either on or near this land and completed the family homestead.[21]

Its location as well as its size made the Cady house special. It sat right in the middle of town, on the other side of the square from the county courthouse, next door to a fancy goods store and the Cayadutta Hotel. At the corner stood the town water pump. Here the Cady family lived in the center of village life. Daniel Cady and his law students found it convenient to move easily from the Cady law office to the courthouse and hotel. Just as importantly, Margaret Livingston Cady enjoyed being in the middle of village life. When the Cady family debated later whether or not to build a new house in the country, it was Mrs. Cady who vetoed the move.[22]

Food was abundant, supplied in great quantities by farmers "who paid interest on their mortgages," according to Stanton, "in barrels of pork, headcheese, poultry, eggs, and cider," all of it stored in the Cady cellars, which were "well-crowded for the winter, making the master of an establishment quite indifferent to all questions of finance." Barrels of hickory nuts, cakes of maple sugar, and bunches of dried herbs filled the attic. Butter and eggs were plentiful, and turkey was always on the Christmas dinner table.[23]

The family spared no expense in furnishing their home. Sallie Holley, a visitor to the house in 1854, noted with pleasure the comfortable surroundings. Delicate side chairs, a lamp with gold fluted Doric column, and a Chickering piano of mahogany or rosewood remain as testimony to the family's ability to purchase the latest fashions. Her parents gave the piano, reputedly worth $1,500, to Elizabeth on her sixteenth birthday. They sent a sample of wallpaper to England to have its pattern replicated in a cover to lay across the new instrument. Books were also abundant. Daniel Cady willed his famous law library to the first of his namesake grandsons to enter the bar. When the Cady mansion was finally sold in the mid-1880s, Tryphena and Harriet donated a large bookcase, with more than two hundred volumes in it, to the Johnstown Public Library.[24]

Just as Daniel Cady was absorbed in a traditional, land-based economic world and lived his life according to traditional republican values, so this family maintained social and cultural patterns common to a rural, preindustrial world. Margaret and Daniel believed in maintaining proper order, so Margaret ran her household with very strict rules. She had, said Stanton, "the military idea of government," and she controlled her children's behavior as much as she could. Every season, the family purchased new clothes for each child, but it was Margaret who chose the outfits. In the wintertime, she dressed the three littlest girls, Elizabeth, Margaret, and Catharine, all in red cloaks, red hoods, red mittens, and red stockings, along with bright red flannel dresses, black alpaca aprons, and starched and ruffled collars. Stanton hated these dresses, both for their color and for their uncomfortable collars.[25]

Margaret, along with their Scottish nurses and their teachers, regimented not only the children's time but their space as well. When they were small, the children had dinner in the nursery, out of sight of adults. At school, they were expected to remain in their seats until they recited, standing with their toes on a crack in the floor. Places of delight were forbidden, including the attic and the Cayadutta Creek, which flowed through the village.[26]

Stanton's attitude toward the physical space of the Cady house reflected her ambivalent relationship to people in authority. The only interior spaces that Stanton described in detail in her autobiography were the nursery, which she associated with strict discipline, and the attic and cellar, both spaces on the periphery of the house, which she viewed as places of escape. Stanton called these "our favorite resorts."[27]

She and her sisters would go to the attic to play among dried nuts, herbs, and artifacts of the past—spinning wheels, cloth, and old clothing. Their sense of adventure was keener because they knew this was "forbidden ground." Once in a while, they were caught. One little sister, standing with her head in the attic and her feet on the stairs, once exclaimed, "By the holy pokers, what if mother should catch us?" She was startled to feel a firm grasp on her legs, accompanied by a familiar and decisive voice saying, "By the holy pokers, here I am!"[28]

Stanton had her fondest memories of the cellar, where they played hide and seek, blind man's buff, and other games, and where they sang, danced, and ate hickory nuts, sweet cider, and *olie-koeks* (the Dutch name of a donut with raisins inside), often accompanied by violin or banjo music, especially during winter evenings.[29] Her sense of freedom extended to areas outside her house as well. Even as a very young child, she found release through outdoor activities. She and her sisters made snow forts, climbed up and down ice-covered piles of wood in winter, sailed on the mill pond, explored the woods, and picked up stones in the creek in summer.[30]

Stanton found allies in these youthful escapades. Just as she carved out spaces for herself on the physical periphery of her house, so she chose allies who were at the margin of her social world. Her most important friends in these years were either young or, if adult, African American. Her earliest friend was her sister Margaret. Although two years younger than Elizabeth, Margaret was, as Stanton remembered, "larger and stronger than I and more fearless and self-reliant." And it was Margaret who plotted their strategy for liberation. Stanton recorded a version of their conversation, told to her by their nurse Mary Dunn many years later. As Margaret one day proposed: "I tell you what to do. Hereafter let us act as we choose, without asking." "Then," said I, "we shall be punished." "Suppose we are," said she, "we shall have had our fun at any rate, and that is better than to mind the everlasting 'no' and not have any fun at all."[31]

Stanton's other primary ally was Peter, probably enslaved in the Cady family. Peter was "black as coal and six feet in height," a man of princely bearing, and "the only being," she wrote, "visible or invisible, of whom we had no fear." "Like Mary's lamb, where'er he went we were sure to go. His love for us was unbounded and fully returned." Peter's protection, his love for the children, and his interest in village affairs opened up the world for the girls. "No questions were asked when we got to the house, if we had been with him," Stanton remembered, and "through his diplomacy, we escaped much disagreeable surveillance."[32]

It was Peter who made the kitchen such a welcome spot for Stanton and her sisters. Peter was nurturer, protector, and promoter of the children's adventures. It was Peter, too, who expanded their world outside the Cady house, protecting them from punishment as they went to Fourth of July celebrations, militia training, sleigh rides, and visits to the jail and courthouse. Peter was, happily for Stanton, "overflowing with curiosity" and "very fond of attending court." As Stanton's daughter Margaret described the scene, Peter would carefully explain "the merits and demerits of the suits to his young charges before entering [the courthouse], then with one on each knee and the third standing beside him they would sit contentedly and listen." Peter was also an active participant in the Episcopal Church, although he was forced to sit in the "negro pew" and to take communion alone. When the Cady children attended, however, they all sat with Peter.[33]

Stanton never abandoned either her hostility toward her nurses or her love for Peter. In her old age, she turned these feelings into stories she told over and over again to her own children. One of their favorites was "Polly and the Pounding Barrel," in which "the hated Scotch nurse met her Nemesis through the beloved black Peter imprisoning her in the big barrel in which laundry was pounded."[34]

Throughout her life, Stanton pronounced herself well-satisfied with her youthful rebellions, and she described them in political terms. Her tantrums she labeled "justifiable acts of rebellion against the tyranny of those in authority." Her escapades with Margaret became for her a source of pride.[35]

But Stanton paid a price for her childhood pleasures. Unlike Margaret, who apparently wholeheartedly enjoyed her forbidden escapades, Elizabeth's fun was dampened by her strong fear of punishment, even though punishment in the Cady family seems to have been relatively mild. The only specific reprimands Stanton remembered were having her hands slapped (for trying to keep her ruffled collar away from her neck) and lengthy lectures. "I am so tired," she wrote, "of that everlasting no! no! no!" Even as Stanton chose growth over repression, she felt guilty about it.[36]

Elizabeth's early life was shadowed by death. Five of Daniel and Margaret's ten children died, including one daughter and all four of their sons. In August 1826, when Elizabeth was eleven years old, her oldest brother, twenty-year-old Eleazer, died after a lengthy illness. Anticipating his death, his parents took their own way of filling his place. Although Margaret was then forty-one years old and Daniel was fifty-three, they conceived one last child in the spring of 1826. He survived less than two years.[37]

Eleazer's death was a defining experience not only for Daniel and Margaret but also for Elizabeth. Daniel Cady was devastated. "Well do I remember," wrote Stanton, "how tenderly he watched my brother in his last illness, the sighs and tears he gave vent to as he slowly walked up and down the hall, and, when the last sad moment came, and we were all assembled to say farewell in the silent chamber of death, how broken were his utterances as he knelt and prayed for comfort and support." On August 17, Daniel Cady wrote tersely to Gerrit Smith: "This afternoon at three O'clock I am to follow an only son to his grave. The ways of God are just, but to us unscrutable." Stanton herself never forgot the "sad pageantry of death, the weeping of friends, the dark rooms, the ghostly stillness, the exhortation to the living to prepare for death, the solemn prayer, the mournful chant, the funeral cortege, the solemn, tolling bell, the burial. How I suffered during those sad days!"[38]

Eleazer's death highlighted Elizabeth's inner conflicts between acceptance and rejection of parental control. Of all the people Elizabeth loved, Daniel Cady would be least sympathetic to her work for woman's rights, yet, ironically, in his grief, Daniel Cady sowed the seeds for his daughter's life work. Stanton, ever the dramatist, recalled one moment that crystallized a whole worldview. She walked into the "large darkened parlor" to view her brother in his casket. There she found "casket, mirrors, and pictures all draped in white, and my father seated by his side, pale and immovable." "As he took no notice of me," Stanton recalled, "after standing a long while, I climbed upon his knee, when he mechanically put his arm about me and, with my head resting against his beating heart, we both sat in silence, he thinking of the wreck of all his hopes in the loss of a dear son, and I wondering what could be said or done to fill the void in his breast. At length he heaved a deep sigh and said: 'Oh, my daughter, I wish you were a boy!' Throwing my arms about his neck, I replied: 'I will try to be all my brother was.' "[39]

Her father's sigh struck her profoundly, and she spent the rest of that long day thinking about "the problem of boyhood." "The chief thing to be done in order to equal boys," she concluded "was to be learned and courageous. So I decided to study Greek and learn to manage horses." In her small world, these two activities most distinguished boys from girls. These were "resolutions never to be forgotten—destined to mold my character anew." These were not idle fantasies. She began the very next morning to study Greek, convincing Simon Hosack to teach her. Throughout her life, she would repeat this pattern: instead of succumbing to adversity, she would overcome it.[40]

Eleazer was buried under two tall poplar trees in the old graveyard, and for two months or more, Daniel Cady went every evening to throw himself on the grave, "with outstretched arms, as if," remembered Stanton, "to embrace his child." Months later, Daniel Cady still spoke of the "deep wound upon my heart."[41] Such abandon, in a man known for his extreme reserve, must have reinforced the intimacy between father and daughter.[42]

In those difficult days, Stanton began to recast her childhood battle into a new form. Stanton now saw herself through her father's eyes, and she did everything in her power to fulfill his wishes. Her own struggle against parental authority now became a struggle to please that authority. She knew how desperately he wanted a son. She knew she could never be that son. But she also knew that, if she tried, she could do everything that boys could do, and often she could do it better.

In return for working so hard to please him, her father gave her a double message. On the one hand, he gave her love, affection, and most of all respect. He validated her emerging sense of herself as a person of worth, intelligence, ability, and humor. As a result, Stanton gained new confidence in her own judgment and growing awareness of her own power to influence others and create change. On the other hand, Daniel Cady profoundly believed that maleness was a prerequisite for public power, and he lamented that his daughter, as a woman, could never inherit his own position in the world. It was Stanton's genius ultimately to reconcile these conflicting messages.

As a mature woman, Stanton would recall Eleazer's death as "one of the bitterest experiences a girl can experience." Yet it also "deepened and glorified" her whole life and gave her "an unspeakable tenderness for all human suffering." Most importantly, it led to Stanton's single most important feminist insight, that her failure to please authority figures was not a personal failing but a function of her sex. By reaffirming his affection for her, while he rejected her as a replacement for his son, Daniel Cady unwittingly helped transform his daughter's personal unhappiness into a political movement for the liberation of all women. Because gender was an ascribed characteristic, not under her control, Stanton could externalize it. She was freed to attack the problem of sex discrimination without attacking her own core self.[43]

Eleazer's death coincided with an easing of the strict discipline of Elizabeth Cady's childhood. Shattered by his losses, Daniel immersed himself in his work. Margaret, physically and emotionally exhausted, withdrew some of her energies from her older children. Their places were filled in part by Elizabeth's oldest sister, Tryphena, and her new husband, Edward Bayard, one of Daniel Cady's law students. Edward had been a classmate of Eleazer's at Union College, and the Cady family saw him in part as a replacement for their beloved son and brother. Both Edward and his brother Henry were fun loving, thoughtful, and affectionate. Their coming, wrote Stanton, "was an inestimable blessing to us." With the Bayards "came an era of picnics, birthday parties, and endless amusements; the buying of pictures, fairy books, musical instruments and ponies, and frequent excursions with parties on horseback."[44]

Added to her new freedoms at home were new experiences in her father's law office, where Elizabeth studied her father's law books, acted as his clerk, and listened to clients' stories. She paid particular attention to the plight of women. Daniel Cady's reputation for benevolence brought more than one destitute widow to his office. "Old Sarah" was a prime example. Her husband had died and left their farm, Sarah's own father's farm, to their son and his young wife, who wanted to evict Sarah from the house in which she had lived all her life. "Sarah," noted Stanton's daughter many years later, "always supplied the Judge's family with eggs, butter, chickens and other good things, so that Elizabeth looked upon her as a kind of lady bountiful when she appeared at the week ends." Her plight gave a personal face to what might otherwise have been an abstract legal problem.[45]

Aware of Elizabeth's interest in the law, her father's students teased her with examples of legal discrimination against women. One Christmas morning, Elizabeth proudly showed them her new coral necklace and bracelets. Henry Bayard pointed out that "if in due time you should be my wife, these ornaments would be mine; I could take them and lock them up, and you could never wear them except with my permission. I could even exchange them for a box of cigars, and you could watch them evaporate in smoke."[46]

Bayard's teasing would not have been as effective a year or two earlier. In 1828, New York passed the *Revised Statutes of the State of New York,* which undercut one kind of legal protection that had existed for women in the state. These *Revised Statutes* emerged from a debate between those who emphasized the power of appointed judges and those who emphasized the authority of a democratically elected legislature. The *Revised Statutes* dealt a major blow to judge-made law. They abolished equity courts, whose judges had often administered trust funds for women, through which parents could ensure inheritances for their daughters. After 1828, no one knew whether such trusts remained legal. Like other lawyers and men of property, Daniel Cady struggled to sort out the implications of such a major change.[47]

Stanton, ignoring legal complexities, decided simply to cut out from her father's law books all those laws which oppressed women. She turned down the corners of all the appropriate pages and put the volumes back on the shelves upside down, so she could find them again, but she never accomplished her purpose, for "dear old Flora Campbell," remembered Stanton,

> to whom I confided my plan for the amelioration of the wrongs of my unhappy sex, warned my father of what I proposed to do. Without letting me know that he had discovered my secret, he explained to me one evening how laws were made, the large number of lawyers and libraries there were all over the State, and that if his library should burn up it would make no difference in woman's condition. "When you are grown up, and able to prepare a speech," said he, "you must go down to Albany and talk to the legislators; tell them all you have seen in this office—the sufferings of these Scotchwomen, robbed of their inheritance and left dependent on their unworthy sons, and, if you can persuade them to pass new laws, the old ones will be a dead letter.[48]

It is possible, of course, that Stanton invented this story, to justify her own life's work. Why, after all, would her father have thought that she, a woman, could testify before the legislature? Whether this incident actually happened or not, however, the story suggests the powerful influence that Daniel Cady had on his daughter. In her perception, she carried on his legacy. Her life posed not a contradiction but a continuity to her father's wishes. She spent her life trying to win his approval.

Her world expanded beyond the village, too. Immediately after Eleazer's death, the family traveled to visit her Cady grandparents in Canaan, twenty miles east of Albany. The three youngest sisters had never before left Johnstown, and they were enthralled with all they saw. The journey took them through Schenectady, where they embarrassed their parents with their wild delight at the biblical scenes on the dining-room wallpaper in their hotel. Their grandmother's large farm and their numerous relatives kept them "in a whirlpool of excitement." Though they afterwards took many excursions, Stanton remembered, they were "never again so entirely swept from our feet as with the biblical illustrations in the dining room of the old Given's Hotel."[49]

Stanton's world also expanded at school. She entered the Johnstown Academy soon after her brother's death. There she interacted freely not only with girls but also with boys. "In running races, sliding downhill, and snowballing," she remembered, "we made no distinction of sex." Instead, "there was an unwritten law and public sentiments in that little Academy world that enabled us to study and play together with the greatest freedom and harmony." In 1818, a conscientious schoolmaster, Phil. R. Frey, reflected Stanton's comments in the "Rules and Regulations, To Be Observed in this School." Throughout, he referred to students as "he or she," and equal rules applied to them all. "To prevent the necessity of leaving seats," for example, ". . . every pupil is required to furnish him or herself with every necessary book or implement which he or she may want."[50]

Stanton's experience in the Johnstown Academy gave her a chance not only to emulate boys but also to compete with them. In part, she viewed her academic success as a way to atone for the loss of her brother. In a class otherwise made up entirely of boys, she studied Latin, Greek, and mathematics. For good measure, she studied chess on the side. When she received a prize in Greek, she had only one thought, "'Now,' said I, 'my father will be satisfied with me.'" He recognized her accomplishment, but he mourned the limitations of her gender. "Ah" he said, "you should have been a boy!"[51]

The years from 1827 to 1831 were "the most delightful" of her girlhood. Her new relationship with her father, the new prominence of Edward and Henry Bayard, the more relaxed discipline in the family, and greater freedom in the world beyond the household helped Stanton work through her earlier fears. She began, for the first time, to feel confidence and joy.[52]

When she graduated from Johnstown Academy at age sixteen, however, she received another blow. She wanted desperately to go to college, to Union College, thirty-five miles away, in Schenectady, New York, just as her brother Eleazer had done, just as many of the boys she had grown up with were doing. But Union was for males only. Her "vexation and mortification knew no bounds" when she learned that attending Union College would be impossible. Once more, she confronted institutional distinctions based on gender alone. Once more she felt her own growth stunted by an encounter with authority.[53]

The most suitable place for their intellectually precocious daughter, her parents concluded, was not Union College but Troy Female Seminary. Run by the impeccably respectable Emma Willard, it was the finest girls' school in the region and perhaps in the country. Founded in 1821, Troy Female Seminary reflected the views of its founder, who believed that "women should cultivate to the fullest their intellectual, moral, and physical potential so they may be the greatest possible use to themselves and others." Willard offered to women those collegiate courses usually taught only to men, including sciences, geography, history, and classical languages. She also believed, however, that women had a special duty to perform as wives and mothers, and she cultivated womanly manners and social graces as well as intellectual growth.[54]

When Stanton went to the seminary in the spring of 1831, she entered a school with more than three hundred other students. One-third of them, like herself, were boarding students. She shared her room with a roommate, made her own bed in the morning, and heard weekly talks on proper Christian behavior.[55]

During the first term, beginning March 2, Stanton took classes in botany, writing, Euclid, and probably history. The following September, she enrolled in courses in criticism, arithmetic, and chemistry, as well as French and music. Judging from the bills that her father paid for the following year's work, from March 14 to August 8, 1832, Stanton continued her courses in French and music (both piano and singing). She recalled in her later life that she especially enjoyed courses in dancing, as well as French and music, because these were the only courses she had not already taken in Johnstown. Dancing lessons cost more than the regular tuition, and her father said he was less than willing to spend money to educate her heels, although he was prepared to spend any amount to educate her head. Young Elizabeth retorted quickly, "Thank you, dear father, your epistle shows great ignorance: dancing is not done on the *heels* but on the *toes*, so send me the cash by return mail." And, so family tradition recorded, he did.[56]

While she was in Troy, Stanton had a confrontation with evangelical religion, personified by the greatest revivalist of the age, Charles Grandison Finney. Among the crowds who filled Finney's protracted meetings in Troy was one young, very susceptible Elizabeth Cady. Her childhood experience with an unflinching Calvinism had left her fearful and depressed. Her exposure to the revivalist version made her no happier. Stanton, with her "gloomy Calvinistic training" and her "vivid imagination," counted herself "one of the first victims" of Finney's revivals. "We learned," wrote Stanton, "the total depravity of human nature and the sinner's awful danger of everlasting punishment. . . . The most innocent girl believed herself a monster of iniquity and felt certain of eternal damnation."[57]

For sinners who reached this state, only one alternative presented itself. Stanton remembered it well: "repent and believe and give our hearts to Jesus, who was ever ready to receive them." Stanton, however, never quite figured out how to do this. Confronted with a renewed vision of herself as a hopeless sinner, doomed to damnation, she struggled hard to be saved. But her logical mind was tormented. She neither felt herself to be utterly depraved nor found release in the formula of repentance. Caught up in fearful visions, she was too honest to pretend a transformation she did not feel. For Stanton, the new Calvinism might just as well have been the old Calvinism. Suffering, she returned home and "often," she wrote, "roused my father from his slumbers to pray for me." Significantly, she chose her father rather than her mother, one of her sisters, or Edward Bayard to share her fears.[58]

This religious struggle brought her to one of the great turning points of her mental and spiritual life. She resolved her dilemma by taking one more step toward rejection of Calvinism. With her father and Edward and Tryphena Bayard, she took a long trip to Niagara Falls. On the way, traveling in their own carriage, they talked not at all of religion. Instead, they dwelt on a new topic, phrenology. Phrenology was nothing less than a new "science" of human behavior. Human skulls, phrenologists argued, revealed human personalities. Ridges on skulls revealed as many as thirty-seven separate faculties, including "alimentiveness" (hunger), "amativeness" (a propensity to love), spirituality, self-esteem, and combativeness.[59]

Phrenology offered Stanton a solution to her old dilemma. Human beings were not, after all, innately evil and doomed to destruction. In their essence, people were good. If they acted out God's laws, perhaps they could even become perfect. Stanton embraced this optimist philosophy with enthusiasm. "After many months of wandering in the intellectual labyrinth of 'The Fall of Man,' 'Original Sin,' 'Total Depravity,' 'God's Wrath,' 'Satan's Triumph,' 'The Crucifixion,' 'The Atonement,' 'Salvation by Faith,' I found my way out of the darkness into the clear sunlight of Truth," she remembered.[60]

Stanton had at last found her conversion experience, and it influenced her powerfully as she began to develop her convictions about woman's rights.

Stanton spent the next few years in relative freedom at home, riding horseback, playing chess, and helping her father in his law office. She spent hours arguing with Daniel Cady's students. She was "a match for any of them," she remembered, and she read their law books and played their chess games less for her own enjoyment than "to make those young men recognize my equality." At times, she acted as her father's clerk, especially when rheumatism made his own writing difficult.[61]

Daniel Cady represented those old values that Stanton struggled against. Yet in spite of his generally aloof manner, he loved her dearly. Though he often disagreed with his daughter, he continued to talk with her and to take her seriously. In some measure, then, he validated her ability to think for herself. This was to be a valuable lesson, for it would allow her to think freely, to follow her own visions as far as they would take her, knowing at some deep level that her father would continue to love her.

Edward Bayard, an "inestimable blessing" to Stanton, was the person most responsible for her growing sense of freedom and self-confidence. With Bayard, she and her sisters entertained friends from school; engaged in "intellectual fencing" on topics in "law, philosophy, political economy, history, and poetry"; read serialized novels by Scott, Bulwer, James, Cooper, and Dickens on winter evenings; gave recitations, musical recitals, danced, and played games; and took long walks and horseback rides, winter and summer. Just as importantly, she found personal acceptance from Bayard, and through his rational ideas and inquiring mind, she found a way out of her religious dilemma. By imitating his skills of logical analysis, as well as her father's, she forged a weapon with which to fight for women's equality, first in debates with her father's law students and ultimately in debates with the world. No wonder Stanton called these "the most pleasant years of my girlhood." For the first time, in a powerful way, "the old bondage of fear of the visible and invisible was broken and, no longer subject to absolute authority, I rejoiced in the dawn of a new day of freedom in thought and action."[62]

Stanton's relationship with Edward Bayard may have been more than that of beloved brother-in-law. Although the evidence is skimpy, family tradition suggested that Stanton and Bayard were in love. In her autobiography, she remembered this period as a "dream of bliss," "the period when love, in soft silver tones, whispers his first words of adoration, painting our graces and virtues day by day in living colors in poetry and prose, stealthily punctuated ever and anon with a kiss or fond embrace." This may be a an oblique tribute to Bayard. Many years later, Stanton's daughter, Harriot Stanton Blatch, agreed that "yes, no doubt my mother was as much in love with Edward Bayard as he was with her."[63]

Certainly, in her father's law students, Stanton had plenty of young men to woo her. "A succession of them," she recalled, "was always coming fresh from college and full of conceit." Indeed, she had "the usual number of flirtations." But she emerged from all of them "in a more rational frame of mind." She and her sisters knew too much about boys to idealize them, she explained. But Bayard, "wishing to save us as long as possible from all matrimonial entanglements," quite willingly pointed out any defects she might have missed. Whatever the reasons, Stanton delayed her own marriage far beyond the age when her older sisters had taken husbands. She was twenty-four and a half years old when she married.[64]

Even as she assumed male roles in her father's law office and absorbed a broad-ranging education from Bayard, Stanton also learned proper housewifely tasks from her mother. "We were required," she recalled, "to keep our rooms in order, mend and make our clothes, and do our own ironing." They shortened the time spent on ironing by smoothing out their underwear and sitting on it during their French lessons, a trick shared with them by their young tutor, Margaret Christie. Thanks to Margaret Livingston Cady, none of her daughters would be ill-prepared for housekeeping.[65]

Stanton forged the basis for her adult personality within the confines of her parents' traditional world view. As an adult, she emphasized equality rather than hierarchy, social change rather than the status quo, and scientific rationality over religious dogma, but she also incorporated much that she had learned as a child into her life's work.

She struggled through the first half of her life with a tension between her own needs for growth and the demands of institutionalized authority. She rightly emphasized the importance of her interaction with both her sister Margaret and her father. From Margaret, she learned to express her optimistic nature. Throughout her life, she would choose deliberately to look on the cheerful side, even in the most unlikely situations. "I never encourage sad moods," Stanton told her daughter in 1880.[66]

Her relationship with her father was more complicated. He certainly provided her with legal training. He also brought her into contact with men who would be important sources of future support. Most importantly, however, although lamenting her femaleness, he ultimately validated her remarkable gifts as a scholar and as a person. In so doing, he created a tension in Stanton between self-acceptance and self-rejection. By framing her concerns as legal questions, he helped her to understand that oppression was external, part of the social structure, not part of herself.

Stanton's legacy from her mother was complicated as well. In her adult writings, Stanton discussed Margaret Livingston only briefly, and then she emphasized her mother as a negative force, trying to control her children's desires for self-expression. Yet Stanton resembled her mother strongly. Her vivacity, sociability, and wit came from her mother, not her father. And her mother, in turn, was more sympathetic to her daughter's concerns in her adult life than was her father. Sallie Holley, a lecturer for abolitionism and woman's rights, visited the Cady household in 1854 and contrasted the attitudes of Daniel and Margaret toward reform. "The judge is not a 'woman's rights' man," she noted. "Mrs. Cady is more in sympathy with reforms generally. She and Mrs. Stanton seem more alike."[67]

Just as Stanton remained profoundly influenced throughout her life by the personal dynamics within her birth family, she also never forgot her class background. Like being female, her identity as part of America's landed gentry was ascribed, not achieved. She could not escape it, nor did she wish to escape it. Economically, she and her household would base their survival on law and the land, just as her own parents had done.

Her class standing set her apart from most other reformers. "When I became an Abolitionist and a woman suffragist," she recalled, "I outraged the family traditions. . . . I suppose there were hardly a dozen representatives of the 'first families' among the reformers."[68] Even her good friend Susan B. Anthony always referred to her as "Mrs. Stanton," in part a tribute to Stanton's class standing.

Her class status brought her a certain confidence. By accident of birth, Stanton gained access to families and social situations that were denied to other reformers. When she moved to Seneca Falls, for example, she listed the people she knew locally. The list read like a who's who of wealthy Whig families. No matter what her personal situation or political views, she was always a part of elite society. Her mother had been, as Stanton recalled, "at her ease under all circumstances and in all places." Stanton acquired this gift as a birthright.[69]

She repudiated, however, much of the elitist and exclusionary values that might have accompanied her social standing. Throughout her life, she chose to associate with people outside of her class. Just as in her childhood she had enjoyed sitting with Peter in the pew reserved for African Americans in the Episcopal Church, she would always thrive on her ability to get along with ordinary people. She married a reformer who had no wealth at all and who found it difficult to deal with material concerns. In Seneca Falls, she organized "conversationals," which deliberately included people from various backgrounds. By the end of her life, she had become a socialist, affirming that "the few have no right to the luxuries of life while the many are denied its necessities."[70]

In terms of her own experience with marriage and family, she departed clearly from her own upbringing in one key area. Influenced in part by Andrew Combe, she adopted flexible discipline and an egalitarian style. She talked of "trying to secure equal rights to all in the home as well as in the nation," and she respected her children's desires so completely that she would often refuse to impose her own will. When her son Theodore refused his piano lesson, for example, his mother would say only "Theodore, be a reasonable being."[71]

In other ways, however, she was her mother's daughter. Like her mother, she married a man many years her senior, and she had a large family. While middle-class couples around her were choosing to limit their children to four or five, the Stantons had seven. Ironically, given her parents' intense desire for a living son, five of the seven Stanton children were boys. When others were choosing children's names from a variety of sources, Elizabeth and Henry named their own offspring after family members.

Throughout her life, Stanton rebelled against childhood religious teachings. Paradoxically, in their effort to win Stanton's conformity to church doctrine, the Presbyterian preachers of her youth had done just the opposite. They had taught her to think for herself. But religious values had been so powerfully imprinted on her that she could not ignore them. Throughout her life, she lectured and wrote about religion almost as often as she talked about woman's rights. Childhood habits died hard, however. In spite of her thorough rejection of Calvinist doctrines, her attendance at Unitarian churches in the 1840s, and her affiliation with reform-minded Quakers in the 1850s, she retained her membership in the Johnstown Presbyterian Church into her old age.[72]

Finally, Stanton felt a clear ideological and familial connection with the American Revolution. Republican ideals of community responsibility sustained her work as a reformer and provided a context for converting her personal concerns into a political movement. All of her life, she worked to develop herself fully, but she also recognized that personal change required change in social institutions. She expressed these ideas in the language of the American Revolution, applying words such as *tyranny* and *oppression* to both personal and public events.

Stanton played out her childhood tensions as the world around her changed. The America of her childhood was not the one she confronted as an adult. The grand transformation from a preindustrial to an industrial and from a rural to an urban society eroded the cohesive hierarchical, Calvinist, Federalist worldview that had sustained her parents' sense of self and order. A world in transition allowed Stanton to deal creatively with her own conflicts about self and authority. In so doing, she spent her life trying to create a new order, one based on autonomy, respect, and equality for women.

CHAPTER 2

Entering the World of Reform: Antislavery and Woman's Rights, 1835–40

Stanton's parental home was a congenial place in the 1830s. "There is always a freedom at home which it is impossible for us to feel elsewhere," Stanton wrote about 1835. During this decade, however, she used her home as a launching pad to propel herself into the larger world. As she did so, she found new role models and friends. Most important were her cousin Gerrit Smith; her husband, Henry B. Stanton; and her friend Lucretia Mott. Intertwined with her identities as daughter, sister, wife, and friend, she also began to define her own life's work as a reformer.[1]

Beginning in the mid-1830s, Stanton made frequent visits to the home of her cousin Gerrit Smith and his wife, Ann Fitzhugh Smith, of Peterboro, New York. Six feet tall, with long, brown hair and an expressive, musical voice, Gerrit Smith would be a major influence on Stanton throughout her life.

The Smiths were famous for their hospitality. People of all classes, races, and ideas were welcome to enjoy "the feast of (sanctified) reason and the flow of soul." The Smiths often added a table in the hall to seat the overflow from the dining room. Ann's southern relatives came to this house. So did Gerrit's wealthy land-owning family. So did the Smiths' Oneida Indian neighbors, along with freedom seekers leaving slavery on their way to Canada. Moral adventurers of all kinds joined this assemblage. One guest gave a detailed assessment:

> I have seen eating in peace, at one time, at dinner, in his house—welcome guests—an Irish Catholic priest, a Hicksite Quakeress minister, a Calvinistic Presbyterian deacon of the Jonathan Edwards school, two abolition lecturers, a seventh-day Baptist, a shouting Methodist, a Whig pro-slavery member of Congress, a Democratic official of the "Sam Young school," a south-

> ern ex-slaveholder and a runaway slave, Lewis Washington by name, also his wife, one or more relatives, and "Aunt Betsy" Kelty. And he [Gerrit Smith] managed them all.[2]

With such a varied company, one might expect the Smith household to be a volatile one. Indeed, people debated their views on the most explosive issues thoroughly and often passionately. So far-ranging were the debates that guests often felt that once a topic had been discussed at the Smiths, it had been settled forever. Yet such was the calmness and sympathetic concern of Ann and Gerrit that their household seemed close to paradise to Stanton. "Their warm sympathies and sweet simplicity of manner," she recalled, "melted the sternest natures and made the most reserved amiable. There never was such an atmosphere of love and peace, of freedom and good cheer, in any other home I visited."[3]

Partly because they made their guests feel so at home, Gerrit and Ann Smith created a major center of reform in upstate New York. Motivated by his religious commitment, Gerrit, with Ann's full support, contributed to Bible, religious tract, and Sunday school societies. He supported temperance work, abolitionism, and land reform. He worked against debtors' prisons; religious sectarianism; and for equal rights for everyone, including the right of suffrage for African Americans and women. In the Smith household, Stanton developed her passion for equal rights, and through their circle, she found kindred spirits.[4]

Significantly, the Smiths, like the Cadys, derived their wealth not from factories or commerce but from land. Gerrit's father, Peter Smith ("a man of purely Holland blood") had begun as a fur trader but made his real fortune from land speculation. When he died in 1837, he held about 556,000 acres of land, much of it acquired from the Oneida Indians, in all but six of New York's counties, plus land in Vermont and Virginia.[5]

Like many other wealthy New Yorkers, Peter Smith owned African Americans in slavery. Until the Revolution, New York state had the largest proportion of enslaved people (12 to 15 percent) of any state in the North. Smith bought seven people and sold all but one of them before 1827, when all enslaved people in the state of New York were declared free.[6]

Even as a boy, Gerrit Smith was a thoughtful person. When Peter Smith refused to give one mortgage holder a day's extension to raise eleven dollars still remaining on his debt, Gerrit persuaded his mother to lend the man the money. No one ever told Peter the source of his mortgagee's sudden wealth. Peter did, however, know enough about Gerrit to complain that if Peter Skenandoah Smith, his older son, did not spend all of his money, Gerrit would give it away.[7]

After Gerrit graduated from Hamilton College in 1818, he began to manage his father's investments as well as his own. Most lucrative was his purchase, in 1827, of land, port facilities, and water rights in Oswego, New York. By the early 1830s, he owned almost one million acres of land, and his income averaged sixty to one hundred thousand dollars per year.[8]

In 1822, after the early death of his first wife, Gerrit Smith married seventeen-year-old Ann Carroll Fitzhugh, daughter of a Maryland slave-owning family. Ann brought warmth and cheerful serenity to her new home, and she and Gerrit had a very loving marriage. "Heaven has broke loose!" Gerrit once exclaimed when his wife entered the room. The Smiths had several children, but only two of them survived to adulthood.[9]

They lived in a large frame house facing the village green. A central hall ran from front to back, with parlor and conservatory on one side and library, dining room, and kitchen on the other. Plain bookshelves held fifteen hundred to two thousand volumes. Thirty outbuildings completed the estate, including a small brick land office, stables, and farm buildings.[10]

Every aspect of Gerrit and Ann's life together reflected their commitment to equality, simplicity, and intellectual and spiritual concerns. Furnishings in their house were plain, so that not even the poorest visitor would be made uncomfortable by an ostentatious display of wealth. They had no mirrors, no heavy draperies or expensive carpets, no lounges or upholstered chairs. A few inexpensive prints decorated the walls, but the only oil painting in the main rooms of the house was of cattle on a Dutch farm. At dinner, they served no wine. After 1835, they never served food grown with slave labor. That same year, Gerrit Smith became a vegetarian.[11]

Key to all the Smiths' reform activities was their spiritual life. In 1826, they joined the Presbyterian Church. By the mid-1830s, however, they began to shift from traditional Calvinist theology toward "perfectionist" or "ultraist" beliefs. Believing that humans were essentially good, they began to live as they envisioned the earliest Christians might have lived, expressing religious values in every moment of every day. By 1839, Gerrit began to support the Christian Union movement, which welcomed all Christians. He started a Free Church in Oswego in 1839 and another in Peterboro in 1843. In the late 1840s, the Smiths went even further in their attempts to live out a biblical Christianity. They were baptized by immersion in August 1848, and by the following year, Gerrit, at least, began to keep Saturday as the Sabbath, much like his Seventh Day Baptist neighbors in nearby DeRuyter. Their religious practices alienated them from many traditional Christian believers. In 1852, Gerrit noted that "in my own county I still pass for a christian—though a very queer sort of one in the eyes of the many."[12]

By the mid-1830s, the Smiths were becoming more radical in their reform interests as well. They abandoned their support of African colonization and wholeheartedly embraced the total abolition of slavery. Immediate abolitionism was new in the United States in the 1830s. It emerged from developments within both black and white communities in the late 1820s. In 1829, David Walker's *Appeal* alarmed conservatives by advising enslaved people to take any measures necessary for their freedom. That same year, Samuel Cornish edited the first African American newspaper while European American editor Benjamin Lundy promoted antislavery in Baltimore. Nat Turner, enslaved preacher from Southampton County, Virginia, led a rebellion 1831, in which more than 120 people (both black and white) died. In 1831, William Lloyd Garrison began to publish the *Liberator.* "I will not retreat a single inch, I will not equivocate, and I will be heard," promised Garrison. Two years later, abolitionists from Boston, New York City, and Philadelphia organized the American Anti-Slavery Society.

Gerrit and Ann Smith at first held back from this new crusade. On October 21, 1835, they attended the organizational meeting of the New York State Anti-Slavery Society in Utica. Intending only to observe, they were amazed when local citizens (among them Samuel Beardsley, a "gentleman of property and standing" and a future judge of the New York State Supreme Court) rushed into the Bleecker Street Presbyterian Church, shouting abuse and threatening violence. Gerrit Smith, jolted into outrage, sprang to his feet and did what he could do best: he invited everyone to reconvene the meeting in Peterboro the next day, where they could talk in peace.[13]

Ann and Gerrit rushed home in the middle of the night in the rain and roused their household to begin baking bread and pies, grinding coffee, and preparing other food for an unknown number of visitors. At 3:00 A.M., Gerrit came into the kitchen to get a candle and stand so that he could write resolutions and a supporting speech for the day's meeting. Nearly four hundred people came to the Peterboro gathering, and the Smiths fed a hundred of them at tea, served seventy or eighty at dinner, and provided sleeping space for forty of them at night. Not incidentally, the experience convinced Gerrit to commit his considerable resources to the antislavery cause. Elizabeth Cady reported in 1838 that "[e]very member of their household is an abolitionist even to the coachman."[14]

Ann and Gerrit Smith's famous hospitality extended, from the mid-1830s on, to people who had escaped from slavery, and the Smith home became a very active station on the Underground Railroad. One day in October 1839, Elizabeth Cady was visiting the Smiths when one of their most famous fugitives arrived, a young woman named Harriet Powell. Gerrit Smith summoned Elizabeth and her friends from their parlor conversation to a large third-floor room. There sat Powell, who had just escaped from her owners.[15]

Casual observers would certainly not have labeled Harriet Powell as enslaved. Her complexion was almost white, and she wore expensive clothes. When she escaped, she had disguised herself with a man's coat and hat. Underneath these rough clothes, however, she wore a black printed poplin dress, small earrings with stones, and three gold rings on her fingers. For two hours, Powell told her white peers the story of her life. She had been sold in the New Orleans slave market when she was fourteen years old. When she arrived at the Syracuse House with her owners, Mr. and Mrs. J. Davenport of Mississippi, Tom Leonard, an African American waiter at the hotel, convinced her to escape. Two European American abolitionists in Syracuse had brought her to Peterboro. In a handbill offering $200 for her return, her owners asserted that they had refused offers of $2,500 for her purchase because they did not want to separate her from her mother and sister.[16]

Powell left the Smith house in the evening, dressed as a Quaker. Driven by one of Smith's clerks to the shore of Lake Ontario, she took a ship for Kingston, Ontario. The next day, her owner arrived. Gerrit Smith entertained him affably and offered to let him search the house. When Smith was sure that Powell was safe with Canadian friends, he published an open letter to her owner in the *New York Tribune.* Mr. Davenport, he noted, "would no doubt rejoice to know that his slave Harriet . . . was now a free woman, safe under the shadow of the British throne. I had the honor of entertaining her under my roof, sending her in my carriage to Lake Ontario, just eighteen hours before your arrival; hence my willingness to have you search my premises."[17]

Gerrit and Ann Smith's commitment to abolitionism quickly brought them into contact with the most active reformers throughout the northeast. In 1836–37 and again in 1839, Ann accompanied her daughter Elizabeth to Philadelphia, where Elizabeth went to a Quaker school. Their sojourn took them into the circle of reformers around Lucretia and James Mott, where they met African American abolitionists such as Sarah Douglass, who ran a school in Philadelphia, and her brother, a sign painter, who copied a picture of Gerrit Smith for Ann. They met Robert Forten, a wealthy African American sailmaker, several times. Forten's daughter Charlotte was even then keeping a diary, which later become one of the earliest published works by a black woman. So impressed was Robert Forten with the Smith family that he named one of his sons after Gerrit Smith. In Philadelphia, the Smiths also met European American abolitionists such as C. C. Burleigh and Mary Grew. Mary Grew would accompany Lucretia Mott in 1840 to the World Anti-Slavery Convention in London. With several black women teachers in Philadelphia, Ann and Elizabeth Smith also taught a Sunday school for black children.[18]

Gerrit and Ann Smith's commitment to a broad spectrum of reforms won approbation from some and opposition from others. In spite of personal attacks, Gerrit and Ann's enthusiasm for abolitionism never wavered, and they spread their concern to visitors. Describing a visit to Peterboro in the mid-1830s, Stanton noted that "Mr. Bayard and cousin Gerrit argued all the time upon the subject of *abolition.* I enjoyed it very much as they both argue well and without the least impatience either in word or manner."[19]

Even conservative Daniel Cady was drawn into the debate. Although he probably did not attend the antislavery meeting held in Johnstown in February 1838, he certainly gave thought to antislavery arguments. Slavery could not be abolished without force, he argued, unless a majority of whites in the slave-holding states became Christian or slavery itself became unprofitable. He knew his own mind, and for him the choice was clear: "I go for slavery rather than a civil war."[20]

Gerrit and Ann Smith did not abandon their abolitionism, no matter what pressures they faced. And they confronted many, both personal and economic, in the late 1830s. Their five-year-old daughter, Ann, died in April 1835 of scarlet fever. Twelve-year-old Fitzhugh died in 1836. As a result of Fitzhugh's death, Gerrit fell into depression in early 1837. Ann tried to understand the loss of her children as part of God's plan. "We ought to rejoice my dear husband," she wrote to Gerrit in January, "for He does love us, and all our afflictions have been so many proofs of his love." Smith himself had continual trouble with what seemed to be piles and frequent illness, enduring surgery in 1836 and 1839.[21]

Adding to their family problems were economic woes. The real estate boom of 1835–36 had collapsed, leaving the country in a severe depression. When Peter Smith died in April 1837, he left Gerrit with half a million dollars of debt. Although debtors owed him $600,000 by 1840, he could not collect and was forced to borrow money at 20 percent interest simply to keep himself financially afloat. He wrote despairingly to Ann in 1839 that "never, my dear wife, have I been reduced to such straits in money matters." In 1842, the Smiths advertised the mansion house for sale, moved to a cottage just outside the village, and fired two of Gerrit's three clerks. Ann and their daughter Elizabeth clerked in the land office.[22]

In spite of their financial difficulties, Gerrit and Ann purchased and freed the enslaved family of Harriet Russell. Russell had been Ann's personal servant in Maryland. The Smiths brought the whole family—Harriet, her husband Samuel, their children, and her father—to Peterboro in 1841, where they lived for the rest of their lives.[23]

In the midst of all of this, Stanton regularly visited the Smiths. One of the most compelling attractions for her was the company of Gerrit and Ann's daughter Elizabeth. Both young women were full of fun and enjoyed what Stanton remembered as "the wildest hilarity in dancing, all kinds of games, and practical jokes carried beyond all bounds of propriety."[24]

Most importantly, in October 1839, Stanton met her future husband. Henry Brewster Stanton was conducting a series of antislavery conventions in the Peterboro area, and Elizabeth Cady was enthralled. Here she experienced her real conversion to abolitionism. "I had never had so much happiness crowded into one short month. . . . I felt a new inspiration in life and was enthused with new ideas of individual rights and the basic principles of government, for the antislavery platform was the best school the American people ever had on which to learn republican principles and ethics," she remembered. "These conventions and the discussions at my cousin's fireside I count among the great blessings of my life."[25]

Part of her enthusiasm had to do not only with Henry Stanton's message but with Henry himself. What began as a friendship turned into a love affair. Elizabeth believed at first that Henry was already engaged. She could treat him, she thought, as she treated Edward Bayard, more as a brother than as a potential marriage partner. How wrong she was! Henry turned all his charm on Elizabeth that fall, and the season of long horseback rides, good conversation, "bright autumnal days" and "bewitching moonlight nights" ended with their engagement at the end of October.[26]

Ten years older than Elizabeth, Henry B. Stanton was charismatic, idealistic, humorous, and very persuasive. He was born June 29, 1805, in Pachaug, Connecticut. His father, Joseph, was a trader with the West Indies. If his cargo resembled others of the time, he would have dealt in foodstuffs, rum, and slaves. The Stantons themselves enslaved a man who often took care of young Henry. When the War of 1812 disrupted West Indian trade, Joseph Stanton, like many other New England merchants, shifted his energies to manufacturing. He invested in both a woolen factory and a cotton mill and later added a machine factory and three stores.[27]

At age thirteen, Henry began working in his father's factories. At twenty-one, he became a journalist for the *Monroe Telegraph,* Thurlow Weed's Rochester newspaper. Weed, even then a major power in New York state politics, considered Stanton to be "intelligent, bright, sagacious and efficient." Stanton served for three years as deputy county clerk of Monroe County, where he gained considerable experience with the law. Sometime during this period, he also attended a lecture on African colonization for freed people. The orator? None other than Gerrit Smith.[28]

In 1830, Charles Grandison Finney came to Rochester and changed Henry Stanton's life forever. Finney failed to convert Elizabeth Cady, but he was spectacularly successful with Henry B. Stanton. Finney's rational approach to religion appealed especially to young men, and Henry was captivated. "It was in the afternoon," he remembered. "A tall grave-looking man, dressed in an unclerical suit of gray, ascended the pulpit. Light hair covered his forehead; his eyes were of a sparkling blue, and his pose and movement dignified. I listened. It did not sound like preaching, but like a lawyer arguing a case before a court and jury. . . . I have heard many celebrated pulpit orators in various parts of the world. Taken all in all, I never knew the superior of Charles G. Finney."[29]

Under Finney's powerful influence, Henry Stanton decided to abandon journalism, the law, and public office and to enter the ministry. He enrolled first in the Rochester Manual Labor Institute, but in 1832, he went to the new Lane Seminary, in Cincinnati, Ohio. Lane Seminary was designed to save the American West from Satan, and Henry took the message personally. When his eighteen-year-old brother, George, lay dying of cholera, Henry badgered him mercilessly (and unsuccessfully) to accept salvation and avoid hell. Brother Robert Livingston Stanton became a model Lane graduate. Ordained by the Presbytery of Mississippi in 1839, he spent much of his life in the South, serving as pastor, university president, moderator of the General Assembly of the Presbyterian Church, editor, and author.[30]

Henry Stanton, however, took a different path. In 1834, newly converted to abolitionism, he was expelled from Lane Seminary for organizing antislavery debates. By 1839, he was a seasoned abolitionist speaker and organizer. He had organized hundreds of antislavery societies, endured mob violence, and spearheaded an antislavery petition campaign.

After her engagement at Peterboro, Elizabeth Cady returned home to Johnstown, but not before receiving a long and serious lecture from Gerrit Smith "on love, friendship, marriage, and all the pitfalls for the unwary, who, without due consideration, formed matrimonial relations." Following Smith's advice, Elizabeth seems to have announced her engagement to her father by letter, hoping to deflect his wrath. Such was not to be. Daniel Cady was extremely upset. Much as he disagreed with Henry's abolitionism, his formal objections had more to do with Henry's dismal financial prospects. In a letter to Gerrit Smith, Daniel Cady expressed his strong reservations about "your friend H. B. Stanton." "I understand," he wrote, "he has no trade or profession[,] that he is not now and never has been in any regular [employment] and if so—and he willing to marry—he cannot in my judgment be overstricken with prudence—or feel much solicitude for her whom he seeks to marry."[31] Daniel expressed himself forcefully in a lecture to his daughter "on domestic relations from a financial standpoint." "These were two of the most bewildering interviews I ever had," remembered Elizabeth. "These two noble men, who would have done anything for my happiness, actually overweighted my conscience and turned the sweetest dream of my life into a tragedy."[32]

Henry well knew that Daniel Cady's influence could prevent their marriage, and he asked Gerrit Smith to intervene for him. "I feel very intense solicitude as to the result of that affair," he wrote to Gerrit on Christmas Day in 1839. "My first visit to your house may be productive of great happiness or great misery to me. . . . A word fitly spoken by you," Henry noted, "may be a word in season."[33]

Henry was a persuasive and enthusiastic lover, and every mail brought "tender missives" to Elizabeth. In a New Year's Day letter to his "own beloved Elizabeth," Henry glowed with all his charm. She was "cheerful & brilliant," he wrote, "the loveliest correspondent I ever had." Addressing her with the Quaker term of "thee," he quoted Irish poet Thomas Moore:

> The heart that loves truly, love, never forgets,
> But as truly loves on to the close,
> As the sun-flower turns to her god as he sets,
> The same look that she turned when he rose.[34]

His reference to Elizabeth as a sunflower must have impressed her, for she would take this as her pen name for newspaper articles she wrote in the 1850s.

A few days later, he responded to Daniel Cady's arguments. He had been financially self-supporting since he was thirteen years old, he argued. He had gone to school eight years, assisted two brothers with their education, spent money on books and reform causes, and been sick one whole year, yet he had still managed to save $3,000. Never, he said, had he accepted aid from anyone:

"I was aware that if I would be a man, I must build on my own foundation with my own hands." "You may ask," he concluded, "by what means I obtained the necessary funds to do this. I answer, by the hands, the tongue, the pen, and the ingenuity of a New Englander, trained up by a mother who is the great-great-great-grand-daughter of a man who set his foot on Plymouth Rock in 1620."[35]

Swayed by her father's objections, Elizabeth broke off their engagement. She spent several weeks with Tryphena and Edward Bayard in Seneca Falls, where Edward worked as a lawyer. Edward Bayard opposed Elizabeth's marriage, and Henry "dreaded" his influence.[36]

Elizabeth still had clear hopes, however, that she and Henry would marry. She wrote to Ann Smith on March 4 that her "engagement with S. is dissolved and I know you wonder and so do I. Had anyone told me at Peterboro that what has occurred would come I would not have believed it, but much since then has convinced me that I was too hasty. We are still friends and correspond as before, perhaps when the storm blows over we may be dearer friends than ever. The oak stands straight though the winds rage fierce and the rains beat heavy upon it—for it has the strength to oppose them all—not so the gentle flowers they droop their heads, and when the storm is passed they rise again."[37]

Elizabeth's premonition was right. Gentle flower though she thought (uncharacteristically) that she was, she quickly recovered her resolve. By mid-April, she had decided once more to marry, and soon. Henry was scheduled to go to London in early May, to the first World Anti-Slavery Convention. Elizabeth made up her mind to marry Henry before he left, secretly if necessary, no matter what the family's objections. Henry wrote to Gerrit Smith in confidence, asking if he would be at home on May 2, since he and "a very dear friend of yours" might visit that evening. "We may come *in chains*—& much as you abhor thralldom, we shall totally dissent from any proposition of emancipation, immediate or gradual, present or prospective!" Don't tell even Ann, Henry cautioned, "All will be disclosed in due time. I am not at liberty to say anything now—&, the peace of one of my friends is involved in keeping all your suspicions closeted till you hear from me again. . . . Is your organ of cautiousness & secretiveness, *large*?"[38]

And so, on Friday (an unlucky day for beginnings, some said), May 1, 1840, in a simple white evening dress, Elizabeth Cady married Henry Stanton, without the word *obey* in their marriage vows. In spite of the haste, her family and friends managed to find "shining silver presents" for her, which they displayed "to admiring eyes." Among them were twelve silver spoons, which Elizabeth would use to serve chocolate, coffee, tea, and desserts throughout her married life. Everyone, even close friends, was surprised at the match. "Only think of it," wrote John Greenleaf Whittier, "H. B. Stanton it is rumored, will get married and go out with his woman to Europe!"[39]

Elizabeth's marriage to Henry plunged her right into the middle of both personal and political conflicts. Henry believed that men should dominate marriages. For a time, at least, Elizabeth herself seemed to accept this model.

Her reference in early March to the (male) oak and (female) flower certainly would have met with Henry's approval. In its earliest days, their marriage intensified Henry's sense of mastery and personal possession. On May 10, he wrote exuberantly to Gerrit Smith, hardly daring to believe that Elizabeth was, in fact, a real person, that "I need not say one word in praise of my newly acquired treasure; for, you esteem it very highly." Then, perhaps recognizing that something seemed a bit wrong in this boasting, he added, "I speak this, not because Elizabeth is now *mine:* but because of her intrinsic excellence."[40]

In the years to come, both Henry and Elizabeth had to work hard at their marriage. They were physically very compatible. Emotionally, they shared not only a commitment to reform but also a spirit of good cheer and an appreciation for witty repartee. In other ways, however, they found themselves at odds. Ironically, their very similarities created considerable tension between them. Henry never did feel comfortable with a stable routine. Nor did he put a priority on making money. He loved the excitement of politics, public speaking, and travel. So did Elizabeth. Someone, however, had to stay home to tend to their increasing brood of children ("chicks" or "chubs," as Henry called them). As the responsible parent, Elizabeth must have been doubly infuriated when Henry occasionally tried to parent *her.* Certainly, Henry was forced, again and again, to deal with Elizabeth as a strong personality in her own right.[41]

Henry also brought Elizabeth directly into the middle of a major controversy within the antislavery movement. The main issues were two: women and politics. Painful confrontations and frantic behind-the-scenes jockeying for power led to a formal split in the American Anti-Slavery Society in 1840. And Henry was right in the middle of the turmoil.

After the formation of the American Anti-Slavery Society in 1833, abolitionists devoted their whole energies to what they called "moral suasion." They based their efforts on an appeal to the consciences of white Americans, both North and South. In this phase of the movement, they tried three main tactics: mass mailings throughout the southern states, grassroots organization of antislavery societies in northern states, and a petition movement to sway congressional opinion. When moral suasion proved slow, some abolitionists turned to politics. After 1837, they began to organize antislavery political parties. Henry Stanton was at the forefront of each phase of this movement.

In 1834 and 1835, abolitionists sent thousands of pamphlets, churned out cheaply on the new rotary printing presses, to post offices across the nation. Incensed citizens in such places as Charlestown, South Carolina, burned this literature in huge bonfires. When President Andrew Jackson upheld the decision of the U.S. Post Office not to deliver antislavery literature through the mails, abolitionists shifted tactics.

In the fall of 1836, the American Anti-Slavery Society trained a team of antislavery lecturers, a "holy band" of seventy. Their task was to convert northerners to the antislavery cause and to organize antislavery societies wherever they could.

Theodore Weld, Henry Stanton, and John Greenleaf Whittier (a young Quaker poet) trained these speakers. Weld, Whittier, and Stanton would remain friends for life.[42]

The American Anti-Slavery Society had chosen its agents well. By 1838, they had organized about 1,350 antislavery societies all over the Northeast. Both Stanton and Weld were preeminent speakers. People said that Stanton could make an audience cry, which even the great orator Wendell Phillips could not do.[43] Their work, however, was not easy. Mobs disrupted antislavery meetings all across the North. Routinely, rowdies pelted windows with stones, drove people from buildings with smoke, and let greased pigs loose among audiences. As a reward for his labors, Stanton received his share of angry attacks. Although Weld became known as "the most mobbed man in America," Henry Stanton earned a close second. By 1840, he had been mobbed 150 times. Opponents in one New York village even burned down the local church rather than let Stanton speak in it.[44]

Facing severe financial difficulties after the depression of 1837, the American Anti-Slavery Society shifted its energies toward a third, and cheaper, tactic, an antislavery petition campaign. Stanton, Weld, and Whittier mailed out thousands of petition forms from the executive offices of the American Anti-Slavery Society. Stanton's exceptional organizational and oratorical abilities made him, said William Lloyd Garrison, "worth his weight in solid gold a million times over," the "Napoleon of our cause."[45]

Petitioners were careful to ask the federal government to do only what it was clearly constitutionally able to do. They did not ask that Congress abolish slavery everywhere, within the boundaries of every state, since they conceded that slavery within state boundaries was a state issue. Instead, they focused on two basic requests, which they often separated into several different petitions: (1) that Congress abolish slavery and the slave trade in the District of Columbia and the territories, and (2) that Congress admit no new slave states (including Texas) to the Union.[46]

To justify their requests, abolitionist petitioners invariably relied on two basic arguments. On the one hand, slavery was incompatible with the Declaration of Independence, which stated that "all men are created equal." On the other hand, slavery was incompatible with Christian ideals. An 1835 petition from Rochester, New York, reflected the general view. "As members of a Republic professedly based on the principles of equal rights and impartial law," it stated, "your petitioners . . . understand the government of the country to have been founded upon the broad ground laid in the memorable Declaration of our Independence, viz. 'That all men are created equal, that they are endowed by their Creator with certain inalienable rights, that among these are life, LIBERTY and the pursuit of happiness.'"[47]

Through this petition campaign, abolitionists hoped to recruit every church, school, neighborhood, and family in the northern United States. In some areas of the Northeast, they almost succeeded. Certainly, this petition campaign became one of the largest grassroots reform efforts in U.S. history.[48]

Petitioning was an ideal activity for local groups. It educated and empowered thousands of ordinary people. It was relatively inexpensive and took pressure off national organizations to raise money for agents and publications. In the depression of the late 1830s and early 1840s, this was especially important. Most significant, petitioning was amazingly effective. Simply by signing and sending petitions to Congress, neighborhood activists made abolitionism the topic of national debate. By 1838, abolitionists in hundreds of communities across the North had sent enough petitions to Congress to fill a room twenty feet wide by thirty feet long, floor to ceiling.[49]

Upstate New York proved particularly susceptible to antislavery agitation. By 1836, New York state counted 104 local societies, second only to Ohio's 133 and ahead of the 87 societies in Massachusetts. Almost all of these were in small upstate towns. Underground Railroad networks also emerged by the 1830s, and many villages organized local "Vigilance Societies" to move self-emancipated slaves more quickly to Canada. Upstate New Yorkers sent more than three hundred antislavery petitions to Congress in 1838–39 alone.[50]

Fearing that debates over slavery would lead to dissolution of the Union, Congress tried to minimize the issue. From 1836 to 1844, it passed a series of "gag" rules prohibiting any discussion of antislavery. For several years, only former president John Quincy Adams (the son of assertive, fair-minded Abigail) continued to try to submit these petitions to the House of Representatives. Gag rules rejuvenated the antislavery movement. Suddenly, the rights of free white citizens became entangled with the rights of enslaved African Americans. By refusing to accept antislavery petitions, Congress turned abolitionists into heroes. Now they fought not only for freedom for enslaved people but also for the right of petition, guaranteed in the Constitution, for free people.

In this phase, when abolitionists defined slavery essentially as a moral issue, women were very active. Scottish-born Frances Wright had worked with the Working Men's Party in New York City in the late 1820s, speaking out against slavery, women's oppression, and class divisions. In 1832 and 1833, Maria W. Stewart, an African American woman, had spoken in Boston on education for free blacks, the first American-born woman to speak to mixed audiences of men and women. Boston women, centered around Mary S. Parker (sister of Theodore Parker) and the brilliant and sophisticated Maria W. Chapman, formed the Boston Female Anti-Slavery Society. Lynn, Massachusetts, boasted an extremely active group of women abolitionists. Philadelphia women organized the biracial Female Anti-Slavery Society in 1833. And in 1836, Sarah and Angelina Grimké, two Quaker sisters from South Carolina, struck the abolitionist movement like lightning, igniting the bonfire of woman's rights from the kindling of egalitarian ideas they cherished as Americans and as abolitionists.[51]

At first, these women's groups grew up separately from male abolitionist societies. When abolitionists from Boston, New York, and Philadelphia met in Philadelphia in December 1833 to form the American Anti-Slavery Society, women were not officially listed among the more than sixty delegates. At least one woman, however, Lucretia Mott, spoke at the initial meeting.

Since 1821, Mott had been a recognized Quaker minister, small in stature but powerful in spirit and intellect and very effective in public speaking. Some would characterize her as "a regular ultra Barn Burning kind of a woman." She herself would urge people to call her "a radical of radicals and a heretic among heretics." She tried to live always by her favorite motto: "Truth for authority and not authority for truth."[52]

Mott had been born of Quaker parents in Nantucket in 1793. Both her birthplace and her religion laid the basis for her lifelong sense of respect for all people, especially for her commitment to woman's rights. "Being a native of the island of Nantucket," she recalled, "where women were thought something of, and had some connection with the business arrangements of life, as well as with their domestic homes, I grew up so thoroughly imbued with woman's rights that it was the most important question of my life from a very early day."[53] At Nine Partners, a Quaker boarding school, Lucretia Coffin met and married fellow teacher James Mott. They moved to Philadelphia in 1814, and there they lived through the death of one child and the growing up of five others.

In 1833, the Motts hosted a house full of guests for the American Anti-Slavery Society meeting. On the opening day, Lucretia invited about fifty of them, including William Lloyd Garrison, to tea. The next day, they asked her to attend the meeting itself. Although she had not intended to speak, she (along with three other women) ended up taking an active part in the meeting, urging those present not to wait for prominent men to approve of their course but to follow their own sense of right and wrong. "If our principles are right," she declared, "why should we be cowards?" When people still hesitated, they heard Lucretia's voice clearly: "James put down thy name!" The convention itself adopted a resolution of thanks to "our female friends for the deep interest they have manifested in the cause of antislavery." In his later reflections, Samuel J. May, one of the delegates, recalled "the mortifying fact, that we *men* were then so blind, so obtuse, that we did not recognize those women as members of our Convention, and insist upon their subscribing their names to our 'Declaration of Sentiments and Purposes.'" If they had shown such forethought, much of the later history of both abolitionism and woman's rights might have been very different.[54]

Although not officially included in the founding meeting of the American Anti-Slavery Society, women themselves took action. On December 9, three days after the national meeting ended, Lucretia Mott called a meeting to organize the Philadelphia Female Anti-Slavery Society. This small band included black women as well as white. Most of them were Quakers. Mary Grew, Sarah Pugh, the Fortens, and Sarah Douglass joined Lucretia Mott and a handful of others to promote not only antislavery but also the rights of African Americans to education, jobs, and citizenship. Unfamiliar with constitutions, resolutions, or voting, Mott asked James McCrummel, an African American minister, to act as chair at the first meeting. It was the last time they would need a male leader. From then on, this small group became a crucible not only for antislavery but also for woman's rights, "a springboard," as historian Margaret Hope Bacon called it, for the woman's rights movement. When Stanton met members of this group at the World Anti-Slavery Convention in London in 1840, her life, and theirs, would be forever changed.[55]

Philadelphia Quakers also nourished two more women who would become beacons for the woman's rights movement. Sarah and Angelina Grimké, of French Huguenot background, had been born into a prominent South Carolina family in 1792 and 1805, the sixth and fourteenth children of John Faucheraud Grimké (judge, plantation owner, and slave owner) and Mary Smith Grimké. Sarah, as Angelina's godmother, took over most of Angelina's care from their mother, who was exhausted by constant childbearing. A serious young woman and a dedicated student, Sarah also studied law with her brother Thomas. She could not follow him to college at Yale, however, where mere girls, no matter how brilliant, were not welcome.[56]

In 1819, Judge Grimké asked Sarah to accompany him to Philadelphia in search of health. He never returned home, and only Sarah was with him when he died. During this visit, Sarah first came into contact with Quakers. In 1821, she moved to Philadelphia, and two years later, she joined the Society of Friends. Angelina followed her sister north in 1829, and she, too, became a Quaker. Neither sister would ever again live in Charleston. During her Philadelphia years, Sarah fell in love with Israel Morris, a Quaker widower, and she herself felt a call to Quaker ministry. Neither marriage nor ministry, however, were to be Sarah's lot in life.

Instead, caught in the middle of a split between Orthodox and Hicksite Quakers, both Sarah and Angelina Grimké found themselves on the periphery of Quaker life. They began to read antislavery newspapers and, in 1835, Angelina joined the Philadelphia Female Anti-Slavery Society. In August, Angelina took a step that would have historic consequences for herself and the world. Moved by the justice and logic of antislavery appeals, Angelina, daughter of a well-respected slaveholder, wrote a letter to William Lloyd Garrison, preeminent radical abolitionist. Garrison recognized what an impact such a letter could have on the whole movement. Without asking her permission, he published her note in the *Liberator,* and suddenly, abolitionists had a new and powerful ally.

By the fall of 1836, abolitionist women in Boston were discussing the organization of a national female antislavery society and the appointment of female agents. Encouraged by such talk and buoyed up by her sister's newfound abolitionist commitment, Angelina Grimké felt as if she were "given up to travel in the Cause." She feared her new path would lead to disownment by the Society of Friends, but she was ready to face even that, "for I do consider the restrictions placed on our members as so very anti christian," she confessed, "that I would rather be disownd than to be any longer bound by them." By November, both Sarah and Angelina found themselves attending Theodore Weld's training sessions, the only two women among the "Seventy." "I felt," reported Angelina of Weld, "as tho' he was a brother indeed in the holy cause of suffering humanity, a man raised up by God." "I am very comfortable, feeling in my right place, & Sister seems so too," she concluded, "tho' neither of us see much ahead."[57]

What lay ahead was a short two years of intense, trail-blazing public activity on behalf of abolitionism, as they had planned, and of woman's rights, which they had not planned. As abolitionist agents who happened to be female, the Grimké sisters were forced by circumstances to also become pioneers for woman's rights. In December 1836, they began speaking to groups of women in New York City in private parlors. By the middle of the month, they began meeting in a Baptist church. Gerrit Smith feared that people would call the gathering "a Fanny Wright meeting," but Weld encouraged them "not to fear, but to trust in God &c."[58]

On December 16, the inevitable happened: a man appeared among their otherwise female audience. Angelina and Sarah were addressing three hundred women at the Baptist Church when "a warm-hearted Abolitionist . . . found *his* way into the back of the church." Someone escorted him out. Weld thought it "extremely ridiculous" that a man should not be allowed to hear a woman speak," but Sarah and Angelina merely smiled.[59] In February, another man appeared and refused to leave, "& so there he sat," wrote Angelina, "& somehow I did not feel his presence at all embarrassing & went on just as tho' he was not there." By April, in spite of themselves, they found themselves talking to a "mixed" audience of three hundred African American women and men in Poughkeepsie, New York. "For the first time in my life," wrote Angelina, "I spoke in a promiscuous assembly, but I found that the men were no more to me then, than the women." Ironically, Gerrit Smith himself, initially so skeptical about women lecturers, shared the platform with them. On June 21, 1837, the Grimkés spoke in Lynn, Massachusetts, to "our *first large mixed* audience, about 1000 present." "It is wonderful to us how the way has been opened for us to address mixed audiences," reported Angelina, "for most sects here are greatly opposed to public speaking for women."[60]

Conservatives were shocked. Catherine Beecher, not for nothing the daughter of conservative Congregational minister Lyman Beecher, criticized the Grimkés in her *Essay on Slavery and Abolitionism.* In 1837, Congregational clergy in New England brought their own charges against the Grimkés in their *Pastoral Letter.*

The Grimkés defended themselves. Angelina responded to Catherine Beecher in a series of letters, published in antislavery newspapers between June and December 1837. "The investigation of the rights of the slave has led me to a better understanding of my own," Angelina asserted. "I have found the Anti-Slavery cause to be the high school of morals in our land—the school in which *human rights* are more fully investigated, and better understood and taught, than in any other." In 1838, Sarah wrote *Letters on the Equality of the Sexes and the Condition of Woman,* first published as a series in the *New England Spectator.* "Men and women were CREATED EQUAL," she asserted; "they are both moral and accountable beings, and whatever is *right* for man to do, is *right* for woman." For the Grimkés, as for the woman's rights advocates who followed them, this belief would form the bedrock of their lives.[61]

The Grimkés found allies within the abolitionist movement. Henry B. Stanton himself proved to be one of the earliest and staunchest champions of the right of the Grimké sisters to speak in public. In August 1837, when Sarah reported that "Brothers Whittier & Weld are anxious we should say nothing on the woman question," Angelina noted that "brother Stanton . . . was sound on the subject of woman's rights. He says he wants very much so to arrange some meeting so that *we & he* may speak at it together. This would be an *irretrievable commitment.*" Six months later, Stanton persuaded Angelina Grimké to speak before a committee of the Massachusetts legislature, the first woman ever to do so. Stanton proposed "half in jest & half in earnest" that Angelina speak in support of the presentation of abolitionist petitions, since the petitions included thousands of women's names. A few days later, Stanton seemed to back off from the suggestion, but not before Angelina had already decided to try it. Even the Boston radicals, including Garrison himself, were lukewarm about the idea. When Angelina sought their support, she reported that, "except for one, they all flinched."[62]

John Greenleaf Whittier, writing from the American Anti-Slavery office in New York City, wondered why Sarah and Angelina Grimké wanted to write about woman's rights, but he applauded their public speaking. "You are now doing much and nobly to vindicate and assert the rights of woman," he wrote in August 1837. Although Whittier would oppose what he saw as the confusion of woman's rights with abolitionism, Elizabeth Cady Stanton remembered that Whittier had advocated women's right to vote as early as the 1830s.[63] Certainly, woman's rights suddenly became a major public issue. A debate in Boston in January 1838 expanded the discussion to include the right of women to vote, to join the army, and to be active in government.[64]

As for Theodore Weld, he did, indeed, object to Sarah's and Angelina's publications about woman's rights, not on principle but because he feared that such debates would draw them away from the antislavery cause. He claimed, however, to be a thorough woman's rights man himself. He even believed, he said, that a woman had as much right to propose marriage as a man did. "I have never found man, woman or child," he boasted, "who agreed with me in the 'ultraism' of woman's rights." The Grimkés, however, were not convinced that he really understood the issue, and they wrote him scathing letters defending their own point of view.[65]

Three national women's antislavery conventions, in 1837, 1838, and 1839, highlighted the debate over woman's rights and heightened tension over the role of women, both European American and African American, within the abolitionist movement. In May 1837, 71 women delegates and 103 "corresponding members" (among them Ann Smith) gathered in New York City to promote women's abolitionist activity. Lucretia Mott, one of the organizers of this meeting and a vice president, played a prominent role. Angelina Grimké wrote one of the pamphlets published by the convention, *An Appeal to the Women of the Nominally Free States;* Sarah Grimké wrote another, *An Address to the Free Colored People of the United States.*[66]

Both pamphlets and convention resolutions reflected the conviction of women abolitionists that all Americans—women as well as men, northerners as well as southerners, whites as well as blacks—were implicated in American slavery and racial prejudice and were therefore responsible for working against it. Women have "*human rights* and human responsibilities," and "*all moral beings have essentially the same rights and the same duties,* whether they be male or female," argued Angelina in her *Appeal to the Women of the Nominally Free States.* A human being who happened to be a woman was not thereby absolved from her responsibilities as a citizen of her country and of the world. "Are we aliens because we are women?" asked the *Appeal.* "Are we bereft of citizenship because we are the *mothers, wives,* and *daughters* of a mighty people? Have women no country—no interest staked in public weal—no liabilities in common-peril—no partnership in a nation's guilt and shame?"[67]

Their goals were not modest. They intended, as Sarah Grimké suggested, to "establish a system of operations throughout every town and village in the free states, that would exert a powerful influence in the abolition of American slavery." The *Appeal* suggested five courses of action: 1) organize antislavery societies; 2) read and discuss antislavery literature; 3) refuse to use slave-grown products; 4) wipe out in themselves the sin of prejudice and identify with "our oppressed colored sisters"; and 5) send antislavery petitions to Congress. They decided, in fact, to collect one million signatures on antislavery petitions.[68]

More than any other activity, petitions challenged women as well as men to take a personal and very public stand against slavery. They also challenged traditional gender roles. As women were well aware, antislavery petitions bridged the gap between moral suasion and political action. As a moral campaign, abolitionism attracted large numbers of women. To sign a petition, however, was a political act. It was, declared women at the third national convention of antislavery women in 1839, "our only means of direct political action." Under the headline of "PETITIONS! PETITIONS!! PETITIONS!!!," the *Friend of Man,* the newspaper of the New York State Anti-Slavery Society, echoed this invitation, urging Americans to send "the petitions of men, women, and children, on behalf of men, women, and children!"[69]

Nowhere did women take such advice more seriously than in upstate New York. Almost 70 percent of the antislavery petitions sent to Congress from upstate New York between 1837 and 1839 carried women's names, either alone or in conjunction with the names of men. By 1837, New York women had formed twenty separate female societies. Among the most active was the Farmington Female Anti-Slavery Society, which in July 1838 urged women in western New York to work more actively against slavery. An address published by the society went right to the heart of the problem: some people, some husbands, thought that the only duty of women was in the home. "Undoubtedly," they acknowledged, "the duties of domestic life appropriately belong to our sex, but have we no other object to claim our affections? . . . Rest assured, dear sisters, that he who would chain you exclusively to the daily round of household duties, is at least in some degree actuated by the dark spirit of slavery, and that this feeling is a relic of barbarism, having its origin in countries where woman is considered emphatically the *property* of another." A blow struck for the slave would be a blow struck for women's freedom, too.[70]

Meanwhile, in their personal correspondence, Angelina Grimké and Theodore Weld vociferously debated questions of woman's rights, peace, and nonresistance throughout the fall of 1837. Grimké never backed down. She continued to act on her convictions, as well as to debate them with Weld. In February, she spoke to a committee of the Massachusetts legislature. In March and April, she gave a series of lectures on woman's rights, sponsored by the Boston Female Anti-Slavery Society. By that time, however, she had moved on to another more personal topic—marriage to Theodore Weld. In February 1838, Weld wrote to Grimké that "for a long time, *you have had my whole heart.*" She responded that "your letter was a great surprise, My Brother, & yet it was no surprise at all." From the time she had first met Weld in New York, she confessed, she found "that my happiness was becoming bound up in you." Sarah approved. "Since our first meeting," she wrote to Weld, "I have felt you were kindred spirits."[71]

Friends thought that Weld showed "great moral courage" in committing himself to Angelina Grimké. "*No man,*" thought Boston abolitionist Anne Weston, "would wish to have such a wife." But neither Grimké nor Weld had second thoughts. In a simple Quaker ceremony, without minister, attendants, wedding cake, or wine, they married each other in Philadelphia on May 14, the evening before the second convention of abolitionist women. Theodore, Angelina, Sarah, and several others spoke as the Spirit moved them. Theodore, reported Sarah, "alluded to the unrighteous power vested in a husband by the laws of the United States over the person and property of his wife, and he abjured all authority, all government, save the influence which love would give to them over each other as moral and immortal beings." William Lloyd Garrison was there. So were Henry B. Stanton and Gerrit Smith. Angelina and Theodore had also invited several African Americans, including two people who had once been enslaved. Thus they could "bear our testimony against the horrible prejudice which prevails against colored persons, and the equally awful prejudice against the poor."[72]

Such "amalgamationist" ideas enraged many Philadelphians. A huge local mob soon turned the symbolic fires of reform into a physical conflagration. On the morning after the wedding, Sarah and Angelina attended the opening meeting of the Anti-Slavery Convention of American Women. They were the first group to meet in the brand new Pennsylvania Hall, all decorated with gas lights and painted with blue-and-white interiors. The convention attracted an angry mob of several thousand people, incensed to see black and white women meeting in the same place. The women saved themselves from harm by leaving the hall arm-in-arm, black and white together. But the hall itself was doomed. On the night of May 17, the mob broke into the building, piled all the papers they could find into a bonfire, and opened the gas jets to make sure their work would be thorough. Within a few hours, the $40,000 hall was completely gutted. The mob rushed on to destroy a church and an orphanage for black children.[73]

Not to be deterred, the women met the next day in a small schoolhouse and vowed to invite the convention back to Philadelphia the following year. Nor would they give up their "amalgamated" meetings. Instead, they passed a resolution urging even more "social intercourse" between blacks and whites. Such proceedings, reported Lucretia Mott, "have greatly aroused our pseudo-abolitionists" and alarmed the "timid" ones. Such a "rich feast," Mott concluded, "was not seriously interrupted even by the burning of the Hall."[74]

Among the women who spoke during the 1838 convention was Abby Kelley, a twenty-seven-year-old Quaker woman from Lynn, Massachusetts. "I have never before addressed a promiscuous assembly," she shouted above the noise of the crowd outside, amid the thud of rocks and bricks against the windows. "Nor is it now the maddening rush of those voices nor the crashing of those windows, the indication of a moral earthquake, that calls me before you. . . . But it is the still small voice within which may not be withstood, that bid me open my mouth for the dumb; that bids me plead the cause of God's perishing poor." Theodore Weld was so impressed that he told her emphatically that she must become an abolitionist lecturer. "If you don't," he declared, "God will smite you!" Encouraged by Sarah and Angelina as well as by Theodore, Kelley decided to follow her leading. "She has a call to lecture which she will obey," reported Anne Weston from Boston.[75]

When the third convention of antislavery women met in Philadelphia in May 1839, however, Kelley did not attend. She faced a logical dilemma. If it was not right for men to meet separately, why was it right for women? The 1839 meeting was, in fact, the last separate national women's antislavery convention. At the local and regional level, women began to join existing antislavery organizations. Kelley herself had accepted a position on a committee of the New England Anti-Slavery Society in 1838. In January 1839, the Pennsylvania Anti-Slavery Society appointed Lucretia Mott as an officer. The same integration occurred in upstate New York, too, perhaps modeled after existing black abolitionist societies. The Anti-Slavery Convention of Western New York, held in Penn Yan in late February 1839, resolved that "every Abolitionist, whether male or female, who shall be in regular attendance at this convention, be requested to enrol his or her name."[76]

Differences revolved not only around woman's rights but also around political action. Conflict focused on the provocative public voice of William Lloyd Garrison. Garrison, with his clean-shaven face and wire-rimmed glasses, looked mild indeed, but his words shot through the men and women of America like thunderbolts. In the late 1830s, Garrison redefined his motto of "Universal Emancipation" to include not only the abolition of slavery but "the emancipation of our whole race from the dominion of man, from the thraldom of self, from the government of brute force, from the bondage of sin—and bringing them under the dominion of God, the control of an inward spirit, the government of the law of love, and into the obedience and liberty of Christ, who is '*the same,* yesterday, *to-day,* and forever.'"[77]

Specifically, Garrison began to advocate the causes of peace and woman's rights. He interpreted peace to mean not only nonresistance to violence but also total nonsupport of human institutions, including governments and churches. He attributed his antisectarianism to the influence of James and Lucretia Mott. Theological ideas which he "once regarded as essential to Christianity" he now repudiated as "absurd and pernicious." Religion, wrote Garrison to his wife, Helen, in 1838, "is nothing but love—perfect love toward God and toward man—without formality, without hypocrisy, without partiality—depending upon no outward form to preserve its vitality, or prove its existence."[78]

As late as the spring of 1838, abolitionist leaders remained, at least outwardly, a cohesive group. In June, however, disagreements over woman's rights erupted at the annual meeting in Boston of the New England Anti-Slavery Society. The convention opened warmly enough. "Before the meeting was called to order," reported delegate Charles C. Burleigh, "I had an opportunity to see & shake hands with several dear friends whom I had not seen in a year. There was S. J. May, & there was Stanton & H. C. Wright & N. P. Rogers . . . all warm with good feeling, & rejoicing in each other's presence & sympathy." Garrison himself boarded at the home of Mary S. Parker. Such cordiality quickly deteriorated, however. When the convention voted to enroll women as members, with full privileges, Abby Kelley found herself part of a committee to write a memorial on slavery to the clergymen of New England. "This startled some of the sober ones," reported Burleigh, "who think woman is in great danger of getting out of her sphere." When opponents attempted to remove her, Kelley spoke "with much feeling, force, & propriety. It was genuine eloquence," thought Burleigh.[79]

Many people within the abolitionist movement joined conservatives outside of it in opposition to women's equality. "Our *womanhood*—it is as great offense to some as our abolitionism," noted Angelina Grimké Weld in 1837. When the New England Anti-Slavery Society admitted sixty-five women to its ranks in 1838, seven ministers signed a "Protest," arguing that admitting women was "injurious to the cause of the slave" because it raised "an irrelevant topic." Massachusetts abolitionists antagonistic to woman's rights formed a new society, the Massachusetts Abolition Society, which excluded women as members. British abolitionist Charles Stuart (Theodore Weld's mentor and friend) reflected the passion of these opponents in a letter to Gerrit Smith in 1841. He could not assent to women's activism, he told Smith, without "trampling my conscience in the dust."[80]

Within a year, Henry B. Stanton found himself completely cut off from most of those who supported women's equality. Garrison, May, Wright, and Rogers all lined up one side. Henry Stanton found himself on the other. Although he supported woman's rights, he believed in promoting abolitionism through political action. There, without voting rights, women could be of little use.

In the summer of 1838, the break deepened. This time, the question of woman's rights was subsumed in the larger issue of no human government, a denial of the right of any human being to control another. Garrison incorporated his most radical egalitarian ideals into a Declaration of Sentiments for a newly organized peace group, the New England Non-Resistance Society. "I put into it," Garrison reported, "all the fanaticism of my head and heart. . . . It goes against every human government, all human politics, all penal enactments." Much to Garrison's amazement, the society accepted this document by a vote of five to one. "It will make a tremendous excitement in this country and Great Britain," predicted Garrison. And indeed it did. In terms of woman's rights, Garrison proclaimed his new goal. "As our object is *universal* emancipation," he declared, "to redeem women as well as men from a servile to an equal condition,—we shall go for the RIGHTS OF WOMAN to their utmost extent."[81]

By 1839, many abolitionists, including Henry Stanton, thought that Garrison's tactics would destroy the abolitionist movement entirely. Garrison's willingness to espouse issues such as nonresistance and woman's rights, they believed, truly endangered the cause. From his own perspective, Garrison explained, "The Lord is my witness that, in seeking to undo the heavy burdens & let the oppressed go free I have never been unwilling to associate with any man on any pretence whatever. . . . Our friends abroad will lament, perhaps marvel at the division which now prevails. I am filled with as much grief as any of them." Garrison's opponents were just as adamant as he was. "Garrisonism and Abolitionism in this State, are contending for the mastery," Henry Stanton wrote. "Love to God and love to the slave *impell* me to stand and battle for the Right and the True."[82]

Lucretia Mott placed herself firmly in Garrison's camp. The words of "truth & soberness" that emerged from nonresistant meetings were "of deep interest" to her, she reported. "*Women* were there by right, and not by sufferance, and stood on equal ground." For their part, Boston abolitionists reciprocated Mott's admiration. Maria Weston Chapman called Mott "a woman of a thousand."[83]

Mott's political stance did not prevent her from maintaining contact with Henry Stanton, who stayed with the Motts while he gave antislavery lectures in

Philadelphia in December 1839. Mott reported that "he bore very well an allusion to their wrong-doings in New York & Mass." "We hope," she confessed, "they begin to see the error of their ways. What a pity to waste any of our precious time—& devote any of the valuable space in our Abolition papers—in childish quarrellings among ourselves!"[84]

Debates about woman's rights and no human government were enmeshed in disagreements about political action. Moral suasion did not seem to be working. In spite of energetic and whole-hearted appeals to the consciences of Americans in both North and South, slavery seemed more entrenched than ever. In particular, congressional refusal to accept antislavery petitions led many abolitionists to wonder why they should continue to support proslavery politicians. Beginning in 1838, upstate New Yorkers took the first tentative steps toward political abolitionism, when voters in several central New York counties began to query candidates. By 1839, supporters of political abolitionism met in Warsaw, New York, to organize a national party, the Liberty Party. In 1840, they ran their first candidates for national office.

Most powerful of all the anti-Garrison abolitionists were those who made up the Executive Committee of the American Anti-Slavery Society. After the Society's annual meeting in 1839, both sides began to fight in earnest for control of the whole organization. By early 1840, political abolitionists realized they were likely to lose. To pay their debts (as they explained) or to rob the national organization of its assets (as the Garrisonians believed), they transferred the society's newspaper into the hands of a New York City antislavery society and sold all of the society's books, papers, and office furniture. Wendell Phillips thought this was "an abuse of power which I call swindling." "Stanton and Birney, both members of the Comee," reported Phillips, "may make black *appear* white, but it is one of those things which require almost impossible proof to make one believe it honestly done."[85]

Henry Stanton was one of those most deeply involved. From his perspective, he was saving the antislavery cause from certain ruin. In February 1840, in the middle of his courtship of Elizabeth Cady, he wrote to Gerrit Smith, noting that "You probably have read the Manifesto of the Massachusetts Board against our E. Com. I am astonished at their course—& yet, not astonished. . . . From all I hear, I presume they will make a violent effort to overthrow & displace the Ex. Com. in the Spring." Stanton wrote more urgently to Charles Torrey, "We must save the National Society, if possible, & through it, the *Cause.* Rally, then all the friends of Constitutional Abolitionism, to be at the Annual meeting. Begin in season. Don't say that I have written a word to you about [it]. *Burn this letter!*"[86]

At the annual meeting of May 1840, after Henry and Elizabeth Stanton sailed for London, disputes between Garrisonians and political abolitionists culminated in the final break-up of the American Anti-Slavery Society. Garrisonians successfully packed the convention by sending their own supporters (many of them women from Lynn, Massachusetts), who elected Abby Kelley to the executive committee. About three hundred political abolitionists, all male, walked out to form the new American and Foreign Anti-Slavery Society. Bitterness over the break-up, especially on Garrison's part, would last for years. During the 1840s, many abolitionists were divided into two camps, the "old organizationists," who embraced nonresistance, come-outerism, and woman's rights, and the "new organizationists," who espoused political action and put most of their energies into the Liberty Party.

Such a two-fold division, however, did not reflect the complex reality of abolitionism in upstate New York. There, many abolitionists refused to take sides. Instead, they formed a third group, combining commitment to radical reform, including woman's rights and nonsectarianism, with a willingness to use pragmatic methods, including political action. Meeting at Penn Yan in March 1839, the Western New York Anti-Slavery Society, for example, saw no inconsistencies in supporting woman's rights and political action at the same time. They enrolled women as members, and they also pledged themselves to faithful and conscientious political action.[87]

Many other abolitionists felt the same way. The whole Grimké-Weld family felt "*impelled,*" reported Theodore Weld to Gerrit and Ann Smith in June 1840, "to stand *aloof* from both of the National A.S. Societies." Gerrit Smith agreed. "Like yourself," he replied, "I can go neither with the Old nor New Antislavery Organization *at the present.* I am sick, heart sick, of the quarrels of abolitionists between themselves."[88]

For Henry and Elizabeth Stanton in 1840, these political questions immediately assumed personal form. On their wedding journey, they first visited Gerrit and Ann Smith. Then they spent several days with Theodore Weld, Angelina Grimké Weld, and Sarah Grimké. "We were very much pleased with Elizabeth Stanton," Angelina wrote to the Smiths, ". . . and I could not help wishing that Henry was better calculated to mould such a mind." Henry must have been proud to show off his witty and fun-loving bride. For her part, Elizabeth was delighted with the Grimké-Welds. "Dear friends how much I love you!!" she wrote shortly after their visit. "What a trio for me to love. You have no idea what a hold you have on my heart. The two green spots to me in America are the peaceful abodes of cousin Gerrit and Theodore Weld."[89]

But her introduction to abolitionism was only beginning. For their honeymoon, Henry took Elizabeth to the World Anti-Slavery Convention in London. He had a hard time raising money to pay for their trip. He may have saved $3,000, as he had told Daniel Cady, but it was mostly in notes due him. He wrote frantic letters to his antislavery friends, begging them to pay his back salary so that he would have money to finance his marriage. In April, he wrote to Whittier that he had had "a squally time in arranging the debt the Society owe me—but, finally, I have got it secured. Tho' some of it I do not get into cash till Sept. 1841! I have had to screw & dodge & scamper to raise the wherewithal—& shall barely make out—leaving some money behind which will be sent out. I have made close calculations & shall but just rub & go."[90]

Their main companion on the voyage to London was James G. Birney, a former Alabama slaveholder turned abolitionist, soon to be nominated for president of the United States on the Liberty Party ticket. They sailed on May 11 in the packet ship *Montreal.* They did not wait to attend the annual meeting of the American Anti-Slavery Society, which Henry expected to be "wretched, doubly wretched." "I am glad to escape from it," he confided to Gerrit Smith.[91]

Elizabeth Cady Stanton thought Birney was "a polished gentleman of the old school," "excessively proper and punctilious in manner and conversation." For his part, Birney found this young woman far too unladylike for his taste. She even called her husband "Henry," instead of "Mr. Stanton," in public. When she accepted the captain's dare to ride to the top of the mast in a chair, Birney was "quite disturbed." When she was not poking fun at Birney's stuffiness, Stanton spent much of her time reading about antislavery.[92]

In London, the Stantons shared a boardinghouse with Birney and Nathaniel Colver, from the American and Foreign Anti-Slavery Society, as well as with several key delegates from the American Anti-Slavery Society, including James and Lucretia Mott; Emily Winslow and her father, Isaac; Abby Southwick; and others. William Lloyd Garrison and Nathaniel Rogers soon joined them.[93]

Around the boardinghouse dinner table, the main topic of conversation was woman's rights. Except for Birney and Colver, everyone hoped that the seven American women delegates, including Lucretia Mott, Sarah Pugh, Mary Grew, Abby Kimber, and Elizabeth Neal from Philadelphia and Abby Southwick and Emily Winslow from Massachusetts—would be easily seated on the floor of the convention.

Such a hope was not to be realized. When the women, Elizabeth Cady Stanton among them, arrived at Freemason's Hall, they were escorted to low, curtained seats behind a bar. Rather than taking their seats as delegates, they listened to a lengthy and impassioned debate over woman's place. Wendell Phillips touched it off on the first day of the convention. He called for a committee to prepare "a correct list of the members of this convention," such list "to include all persons bearing credentials from an Anti-Slavery body." "We do not think it just or equitable," argued Phillips in defense of his motion, ". . . that, after the trouble, the sacrifice, the self-devotion of a part of those who leave their families and kindred and occupations in their own land, to come three thousand miles to attend this World's Convention, they would be refused a place in its deliberations." Not for the first time, Phillips drew parallels between the position of African American men in a white-dominated world and the position of women in a male-dominated world. "It is the custom there in America," he argued, "not to admit colored men into respectable society; and we have been told again and again that we are outraging the decencies of humanity when we permit colored men to sit by our side. When we have submitted to brickbats and the tar-tub and feathers in New England rather than yield to the custom prevalent there of not admitting colored brethren into our friendship, shall we yield to parallel custom or prejudice against women in Old England? We cannot yield this question if we would, for it is a matter of conscience."[94]

American abolitionists—both old organizationists and new—fought not only for or against the seating of women delegates but also for the support of British abolitionists. As Kathryn Kish Sklar noted, "Garrisonians had committed themselves to the full incorporation of women within their ranks. Now they had to defend that choice before a jury of their British peers." British abolitionists were fascinated but confused. Even Garrisonian sympathizer Richard D. Webb, from Dublin, confessed that "I am often so puzzled that I don't know what to think."[95]

Complicating issues of gender and politics was another question, that of religion. The Motts and their friends belonged to that branch of the Society of Friends known, after 1828, as Hicksite. British Friends recognized as legitimate only those American Friends who called themselves Orthodox. William and Mary Howitt were British Quakers, poets, and abolitionists who thought that the Motts' religious views were the real reason for Lucretia's exclusion. "You were actually excluded as heretics," William confided. "That is the real ground of your exclusion." Mott herself recognized the religious factor. Women were kept out of the convention because of "English Usage, American New Organization, & sectarian proscription," she acknowledged. And it was clear to Elizabeth Cady Stanton that "the Quakers here have not all received her [Lucretia] cordially, they fear her heretical notions."[96]

Debate over the admission of women dominated the first day of the convention. Maria Waring, a British abolitionist sympathetic to the Garrisonians, described it as a discussion that "lasted for hours." "Part of the time it was quite impossible," she noted, "to know what was said. Cries of 'order, order,' 'Divide, divide,' 'No, no, no, no, no,' 'Vote, vote, vote,' 'Chair, chair,' were ringing in our ears. It was extremely interesting. It was just like a House of Commons uproar." After all this shouting, the convention voted by a large majority not to admit the American women.[97]

Elizabeth Cady Stanton, feeling "humiliated and chagrined," contemptuous of the "narrow-minded bigots" who opposed seating women, could nevertheless be proud of her own husband, who (along with Wendell Phillips) had been chosen one of six secretaries of the convention. Garrison reported to his wife on June 29 that "Stanton voted right in Convention on the question." Henry also voted for the protest introduced on the last day by Lucretia Mott's husband, James, and others. "H. B. Stanton . . . plead[s] for the right," noted Mott in her diary. Elizabeth remembered, more dramatically, that "my husband made a very eloquent speech in favor of admitting the women delegates."[98]

Barred from their seats at the convention, the women "kept up a brisk fire morning, noon, and night at their hotel on the unfortunate gentlemen who were domiciled at the same house." James G. Birney, affronted, left after the first day. Nathaniel Colver stayed, protected, thought Stanton, by his own sheer physical bulk and by the Bible he brandished. The Stantons stayed, too. Elizabeth found herself clearly allied with the women, and "in spite of constant gentle nudgings by my husband under the table, and the frowns of Mr. Birney opposite, the tantalizing tone of the conversation was too much for me to maintain silence," she recounted many years later. "Calmly and skillfully Mrs. Mott parried all their attacks, now by her quiet humor turning the laugh on them, and then by her earnestness and dignity silencing their ridicule and sneers. I shall never forget the look of recognition she gave me when she saw by my remarks that I fully comprehended the problem of woman's rights and wrongs."[99]

William Lloyd Garrison, Nathaniel Rogers, Charles Lenox Remond, and William Adams arrived in London on June 18, six days late. They brought a resolution from the American Anti-Slavery Society, expressing the hope that the World Anti-Slavery Convention would "fully and practically, recognize, in its organization and movements, the *equal brotherhood* of the entire Human Family, without distinction of color, sex, or clime." When Garrison discovered that the convention had refused already to seat women as delegates, he and his fellow representatives declined to take their own seats or to enroll their names as delegates. "This created much uneasiness," he reported to his wife, Helen, "and no pains were spared to seduce us from our position; but we remained inflexible to the end—looking on as silent spectators, from the galleries, from day to day." Remond, an African American delegate, was particularly distressed. "In few instances through life have I met with greater disappointment," he noted, "especially in view of the fact, that I was almost entirely indebted to the kind and generous members of the Bangor Female Anti-Slavery Society, the Portland Sewing Circle, and the Newport Young Ladies' Juvenile Anti-Slavery Society, for aid in visiting this country."[100]

Supporters called Lucretia Mott the "*Lioness* of the Convention," but Mott felt rather more like a "*sheep* for the slaughter." Still, the convention was a turning point for Mott. Her experience "unleashed her; thereafter she did not attempt to hold back either anger or commitment," wrote her biographer, Margaret Hope Bacon. "By opening herself thus to her own feelings as well as to the demands of the times she ensured that she would continue to grow decade after decade."[101]

Elizabeth Cady Stanton, too, was indelibly marked by this convention, especially by Lucretia Mott. With strong ideas about woman's rights, disillusioned with traditional religion, Stanton had few role models. Mott filled this void as no one else had ever done. "I have had much conversation with Lucretia Mott and I think her a peerless woman," Stanton reported to Angelina Weld and Sarah Grimké. "She has a clear head and a warm heart. Her views are many of them so new and strange. . . . I find," she concluded, "great delight in her company."[102]

Throughout her life, Stanton emphasized the importance of her encounter with Lucretia Mott. Mott, she recalled, "opened to me a new world of thought.

Lucretia Mott and James Mott. Quaker minister Lucretia Mott was an early advocate of woman's rights. Her visit to Seneca Falls in 1848 inspired the first woman's rights convention, and James Mott chaired part of the Seneca Falls convention. From a daguerreotype by Langenheim about 1842. Reprinted by permission of Friends Historical Library, Swarthmore College.

As we walked about to see the sights of London, I embraced every opportunity to talk with her. It was intensely gratifying to hear all that, through years of doubt, I had dimly thought, so freely discussed by other women, some of them no older than myself—women, too, of rare intelligence, cultivation, and refinement." Others echoed Stanton's view. "You have no idea of what important characters the Am. women have become . . . or of the overwhelming attention which we receive," reported Mary Grew.[103]

For her part, Mott reported that Stanton was "gaining daily in our affections." Stanton is a "bright, open, lovely" young woman, Mott wrote to Richard and Hannah Webb. "We had not seen her till we met in England & I love her now as one belong to us." The Webbs were also impressed. Richard D. Webb reported that "Mrs. Stanton is one in ten thousand—I have met with very few women I considered equal to her—such eloquence, such simplicity of [manner?]—such naivete, clearsightedness, candor, openness, such love for all that is great and good, so much of the spirit of old organization." Hannah Webb reinforced her husband's enthusiastic comments: "Elizabeth Stanton, with whom we were highly delighted," she noted, "is a brave upholder of woman's rights."[104]

Garrison himself praised Stanton as "a fearless woman," who "goes for woman's rights with all her soul." In her turn, Stanton was less impressed with at least one of Garrison's speeches. "Last evening," she wrote to the Grimké-Welds, "he opened his mouth, and forth came, in my opinion, much folly."[105] Garrison himself was not happy with Henry Stanton. He viewed his defection to political abolitionism as a betrayal of the cause. Mott viewed Henry with more forgiving eyes. "I never could regard her Henry," Mott reported to the Webbs, "quite as a New Organizationist, altho' he has acted improperly in some instances. He & Whittier & Birney ought to leave that clan and return to their first love."[106]

Though the supporters of woman's rights lost the battle, they won the war. By strengthening female networks and challenging women to confront their own oppression, the London convention became a major event in the development of the American woman's rights movement. "The action of this convention," recalled Stanton, "was the topic of discussion, in public and private, for a long time, and stung many women into new thought and action and gave rise to the movement for women's political equality both in England and the United States." As the convention adjourned, many people agreed that "it is about time some demand was made for new liberties for women." In retrospect, Stanton argued, "the movement for woman's suffrage, both in England and America, may be dated from the World's Anti-Slavery Convention."[107]

Forced to sit together behind the bar, these intelligent and articulate women in London carried their arguments back to their boardinghouse, through city streets, into the homes of English radicals, and deeper, indeed, into their own hearts. On the very first evening, Mott and Stanton walked home down Great Queen Street, arm-in-arm. It was obvious, they agreed, that men needed to be educated on woman's rights. And so they "resolved to hold a convention as soon as we returned home, and form a society to advocate the rights of women."[108]

The London convention created a broad network of American woman's rights advocates to support this resolve. When they returned home, rejected Philadelphia delegates forged a strong "binding tie of affection" that would help sustain their reform work for many years.[109] Stanton herself developed direct ties, almost completely independent of Henry's own network, to Quakers from Philadelphia and Garrisonians from New England. Perhaps it was in London that she began to call herself a Garrisonian. In 1841, she began to subscribe to the *Liberator* in her own name, and she continued to do so for several years.[110]

By 1840, then, Stanton had been thoroughly introduced to questions of legal reform, abolitionism, and woman's rights. In each area, she had developed personal networks. Her father's law students and legal connections formed one network. Her husband's ties with political abolitionism, reinforced by Gerrit Smith's involvement, formed a second network. And her own ties to woman's rights abolitionists, especially Lucretia Mott, formed a third.

For eight years, in spite of continued discussions, neither Stanton nor Mott actually organized the woman's rights meeting they had suggested in London. Instead, Stanton found herself engrossed, enthusiastically, in her new duties as wife and mother. Intellectually, she deepened her knowledge both of law and of reform. Personally, she began to make connections, drawing ideas from her father, her husband, her cousin, and her female abolitionist friends, to create a mosaic that she would make uniquely her own.

When the first woman's rights convention finally occurred, it would not be in Philadelphia, where Mott lived. It would not be in Johnstown, where Stanton had grown up. It would not even be in Boston, where the Stantons lived from 1843 to 1847. Instead, it would be in a place in western New York that neither Stanton nor Mott considered in 1840: the village of Seneca Falls.

CHAPTER 3

Communities in Transition: Seneca Falls and Waterloo, 1795–1840

The Seneca Falls woman's rights convention was rooted in economic and social instability affecting much of the Western world in the nineteenth century. Revolutions in transportation, industrialization, urbanization, and technology amounted to an economic earthquake, and out of them came a new market economy based on large-scale manufacturing and trade, competition, and consumerism.

These changes hit with particular force in the northeastern United States. Transportation routes and waterpower acted like magnets for new people and new capital. In New York, such changes transformed both the landscape and the people. Upstate New York straddled the main route between New England, New York City, and the West, and it encompassed rich agricultural land and abundant waterpower. When entrepreneurs rushed to buy land near waterpower, close to turnpikes, canals, and railroads, they discovered that Seneca Falls and its neighbor, Waterloo, had it all. Here, and in other places like them, Americans created a new economic order.

Accompanying deep economic changes were vast social and cultural dislocations. People moved from farms to cities, from Europe and Africa to America, from the eastern United States to lands formerly controlled by Native Americans. When they moved, they confronted challenges to traditional institutions—churches, schools, and families—and to traditional values. As they struggled to define the relationship between institutions and individuals, they argued over the meaning of the Declaration of Independence: "that all men are created equal, that they are endowed by their Creator with certain inalienable rights, that among these are life, liberty, and the pursuit of happiness, that government derives its just powers from the consent of the governed."

Forced to redefine themselves, they redefined the meaning of America. What was the real meaning of democracy in this new United States? Were poor citizens equal to rich ones? Could democracy coexist with slavery? Were women, half the population, citizens?

Economic change was rooted in the land and shaped by the land. Four different forms of transportation marked four different economic phases. In central New York before 1780, Haudenosaunee (also called Iroquois) villagers used rivers and trails to sustain a society based on agriculture, hunting, fishing, and gathering. From 1780 to 1828, European Americans built turnpikes and used waterpower to process farm products, especially flour. In the 1820s, canals brought new people, new markets, and astounding economic expansion. The bubble burst in 1837, when the country experienced its worst depression. Economic recovery in the mid-1840s, accompanied by railroad development, transformed many villages into industrial, urban, immigrant cities.[1]

In each of these stages, relationships to the land and its resources were intertwined with the way that people worked, lived, and thought. Shock waves from economic changes reverberated through the country. This time of transition—economic, social, and cultural—provided rich nourishment for the first roots of the woman's rights movement.

Along the Seneca River, before the American Revolution, Haudenosaunee hunting and fishing parties traveled by foot through woods rich with game. At Waterloo, they set up a permanent settlement of about eighteen houses, which they called Scauyes or Skoiyase. There they kept fish ponds and probably also planted acres of corn, beans, and squash, as well as orchards of apple and peach trees.[2]

The Revolution brought disaster to Haudenosaunee people. In 1779, George Washington ordered Generals John Sullivan and James Clinton to destroy every Indian village, orchard, and field in western New York, about forty in all. As they traveled, American soldiers were astonished to find frame houses and rich farm lands, full of apples, peaches, and all kinds of vegetables. And they proceeded to destroy them all. Cayugas and Senecas were forced to flee to British protection at Fort Niagara, where they endured extreme cold, hunger, and sickness.[3]

For U.S. soldiers, this glimpse into the richness of Haudenosaunee farms awakened visions of wealth for themselves and their families. The end of the American Revolution gave them their opportunity. Both the United States and the state of New York negotiated (often with threats, intimidation, and bribery) a series of treaties—beginning with the Treaty of Fort Stanwix in 1784 and ending with the Treaty of Canandaigua in 1794—that left Haudenosaunee people confined to ten small reserves, with European Americans in control of all the remaining territory of upstate New York.[4]

In the area around Seneca Falls and Waterloo, Cayugas formally ceded their land to New York state in 1789, with the exception of a one-hundred-square-mile reservation at the north end of Cayuga Lake. Between 1795 and 1807, Cayugas sold all this land to white settlers for as little as five dollars per square mile, but evidence of Seneca and Cayuga villages remained well into the nineteenth century. Often, Native American men, women, and children filled the lawn behind Charles Hoskins's house. Native American apple and peach orchards survived long after white settlers arrived—one around Ansel Bascom's house on the corner of Bayard and Ovid Streets in Seneca Falls and another on the Elam farm east of the village. By the 1830s, whites had revived and expanded these old orchards, selling the fruit as one of Seneca County's first commercial crops.[5]

European Americans, however, dominated the future of upstate New York. In 1790, New York state distributed former Indian lands in north-central New York as bonuses to veterans of the Revolution. They called this land the New Military Tract, and the white villages of Seneca Falls and Waterloo were located right in the middle of it. Some of the lots on the New Military Tract went directly to individual settlers. Ironically, one of the very first veterans to take advantage of this offer locally was "Indian John," an Oneida who had fought on the Patriot side.

In what became the village of Seneca Falls, Lawrence Van Cleef, a soldier in Sullivan's expedition, built a tavern in the early summer of 1789. On his ox-drawn sled, he portaged boats and cargoes (for six shillings apiece) around the falls, a full mile from one landing to the other. In Waterloo, European Americans built the first grist mill on the site of the old Cayuga village.[6]

Beginning in 1794, land speculators bought much of the best property at the place they called Seneca. By 1816, the Bayard Company owned 1,450 acres surrounding the falls. Here, they hoped to make their fortune from water-powered industries. And the village of Seneca Falls emerged, incorporating parts of the New Military Tract and the West Cayuga Reservation.[7] Wilhelmus Mynderse, who owned one-fifth interest in the Bayard Company, moved to Seneca Falls in 1795, where he lived for thirty years. Colonel Mynderse was a tall Dutch American from Albany, "a gentleman of enterprise." With his courtly manners and his "long, low mansion, with a broad verandah," he set an example for the whole village.[8]

The arrival of the Van Cleef and Mynderse families signaled the end of Native American dominance in Seneca Falls and Waterloo and the rise of a new European American culture, economically similar to the Native American world but very different in social structure and values. In the 1840s, almost everyone in Seneca Falls and Waterloo, as in upstate New York generally, was a migrant or the child of a migrant. They or their ancestors came from four major culture hearths: New England, eastern New York, Great Britain, or southeastern Pennsylvania. Yankees formed the dominant cultural base throughout upstate New York. They burst out of overcrowded, rocky New England farms and followed the route west from Albany along the Mohawk River, taking the Seneca Turnpike, the Erie Canal, or the railroad directly into Seneca Falls and Waterloo. Other immigrant groups challenged Yankee hegemony. Eastern New York supplied native-born people of English, Scottish, and Dutch ancestry. Some immigrants came directly from Europe, especially from England and Ireland. Finally, moving north along the Susquehanna River valley and the Finger Lakes, Quakers, African Americans, and others came from Pennsylvania and New Jersey.[9]

Some communities in upstate New York were relatively homogeneous. Settlers re-created a matrix of institutions, language, and value systems that virtually duplicated the social and cultural world of the villages they left. Most upstate villages and towns, however, contained people from several different ethnic, racial, religious, or cultural groups. Such were the villages of Seneca Falls and Waterloo. They lay at the intersection of the major east-west corridor (formed by the Seneca Turnpike, the Erie Canal, and the railroad) and the main north-south route along the Susquehanna River and Finger Lakes, so they attracted immigrants from many different places of origin. Synergism among these cultural groups, especially between Yankees from New England and Quakers from eastern New York and Pennsylvania, provided fertile ground for reform.

The completion of the Seneca and Cayuga Canal in 1828 and of the Auburn and Rochester Railroad in 1841 reinforced the east-west migration route. Irish-born Patrick Quinn came to Seneca Falls in the early 1830s, probably by canal. In 1838, Elizabeth M'Clintock traveled from New York City to Albany along the Hudson River by water, from Albany to Utica by railroad, and then from Utica to Waterloo by canal packet boat. In 1847, Stanton herself arrived in Seneca Falls by rail.[10]

African Americans had been part of the population of Seneca County since at the least the 1770s. Sometime during the Revolutionary War, Dr. Silas Halsey arrived from Long Island with one enslaved person. David B. Lum, hatter, held at least one person in slavery when he came to Seneca Falls from New Jersey in the early 1800s. By 1810, 101 people lived in slavery in Seneca County. Eighty-four remained enslaved in 1820. After 1827, however, all African Americans in New York state were free people. Some of the fifteen blacks in Seneca Falls and the sixty-three in Waterloo in 1850 may have been freeborn. Others were likely immigrants from the South seeking freedom from slavery.[11]

The coming of European Americans and African Americans marked the beginning of a new stage of development. At first, however, these new settlers used the land much as Native Americans had done before them. Like the Haudenosaunee, they used rivers and roads for transportation and relied on agriculture, supplemented by hunting and fishing, for food.

Farmers needed access to markets if they were to be successful, and turnpikes were among the first results of white expansion. The state of New York built the Great Genesee Road in 1797 and chartered the new Seneca Turnpike Road Company in 1800. Unable to build a road through several thousand acres of marshland north of Cayuga Lake, the company constructed an engineering marvel, the mile-long Cayuga Bridge. By 1800, travelers could take a stage line west from Utica directly to Seneca and Waterloo, connecting each of these villages to major cities both east and west.[12]

Stagecoaches were relatively slow. Mail took four days to reach Seneca Falls from Albany and six to eight days from New York City. But service was regular—twice a week for mail—and traffic was heavy. In the heyday of the stagecoaches, from the late 1820s until the railroad came through in 1841, as many as thirty-six great red Concord coaches crossed the Cayuga Bridge in a twenty-four-hour period. Tolls often came to $25,000 per year. Until the late 1840s, farmers also used these roads to drive cattle, sheep, swine, and horses to market. One resident remembered that "some of these droves would fill the road from fence to fence and would be a half a mile or more in length."[13]

Powerful rapids—a forty-three-foot drop of water at Seneca Falls and a fifteen-foot drop at Waterloo—earmarked these sites for manufacturing, not agriculture. The Bayard Company built two mills, both painted red, at Seneca Falls, one in 1795 and the other, near the future Stanton house, in 1807. These mills attracted the business of farmers for miles around. Robert Troup, one of the investors, reported in 1810 that two men paddled from Cross Lake, almost thirty miles away, "to the Seneca mills for flour."[14]

Easy access to these mills helped to draw settlers to the area. By the early 1820s, travelers along the Seneca Turnpike could have a "charming view" not only of the great blue expanse of Cayuga Lake but also, as Horatio Gates Spafford noted in his *Gazetteer* of 1823, a countryside "speckled with farms, copses of wood, fields of cattle, grain, grass, orchards, etc."[15]

Much of this agricultural development was based on wheat. Fine wheat it was, too—Soles, Hutchinson, and White Flint—the best in the country. In the 1820s, before Americans had settled the great Midwest, the Genesee country of western New York was the breadbasket of the nation, and wheat was its most famous product. In many areas of western New York, wheat production dropped precipitously by the 1830s. Wasteful agricultural practices had leached out the richness of once-virgin soil. Newer lands had opened farther west. And the wheat fly hindered the growth of large wheat crops.[16]

In Seneca County, however, wheat remained the largest crop. Oats and corn were poor runners-up. Potato crops were in decline, suffering from the same blight that brought such misery to Ireland after 1847. Farmers in Seneca County in the 1840s actually increased their production of wheat per acre. In 1848, they sent to market 644,960 bushels, almost double the number they had sent eight years before. In 1850, farm families sowed 35,000 acres in wheat, one-quarter of the total cultivated land. Charles Eliot Norton summarized the situation in his address to the Seneca County Agricultural Society in 1850: "This is a wheat county."[17]

Farmers continued to raise cattle and sheep for meat, milk, butter, cheese, and wool, but these were of secondary importance in terms of farm income. Farm women produced over five hundred thousand pounds of butter from Durham and Devonshire cattle in Seneca County in 1850, about twenty-six pounds per county resident. Most of this was for domestic use, but women traded some of it in village stores. Sheep production was in decline in the 1840s, although farmers could find a ready market in Seneca Falls and Waterloo, where two woolen factories used 325,000 pounds of wool a year in 1850, more than double the production of Seneca County itself.[18]

Agricultural prosperity brought relatively rapid population growth to the countryside around Seneca Falls and Waterloo. By 1840, more than three-quarters of the adult males in Seneca County were farmers. By 1845, 72 percent of the land in the county was improved acreage. In 1840, with 73 people per square mile, 24,874 people in all, Seneca County had almost reached its population peak. It grew only slightly until 1860, when its population stabilized at slightly more than 28,000.[19]

At first, very few people came to live in the village of Seneca Falls itself. The Bayard Company made a fair profit from its mills and had no desire to sell waterpower to competitors. Although they advertised lots for sale in 1817, they held on to their waterpower. By 1822, Stephen Bayard was unable to sell his property, because of a lien against it by creditors.[20]

In 1828, two events transformed these villages. First, people could finally buy Bayard Company lands. Second, New York state completed the Seneca and Cayuga Canal, a twenty-mile link connecting Seneca Lake to the Erie Canal, running straight through Seneca Falls and Waterloo. As one local historian suggested, "From the date . . . of the dissolution of the Bayard company, began the progress of Seneca Falls. Manufacturing establishments sprang up on every hand, and new life and activity were infused into all departments of trade, agriculture and business."[21]

The south side of the river, virtually undeveloped, grew especially fast. Large investments in land—one six-hundred-acre tract with water rights by Ansel Bascom, Gary V. Sackett, and Andrew P. Tillman, and another, smaller tract just east of it by Samuel and William Bayard—attested to hopes for rapid development. By 1832, Samuel and William Bayard had surveyed their land and were ready to sell. They had eight water lots for mills and factories, thirty village business lots, and one hundred home lots, which they advertised as "beautifully situated between Bayard and Seneca-streets, in the centre of which is a Park, or area for a public square. These are among the most desirable locations in the village for *private dwellings,* being on an elevated situation and commanding an extensive view of the village and adjoining country." Seneca Falls, they suggested, had every advantage: "extensive and uniform water power . . . its location on the Great Western Turnpike, in the heart of a fertile and Wheat growing country, and upon the Seneca Canal." The village, they predicted, would become "the most important village or city in western New York."[22]

If the Bayard brothers dreamed of getting rich from land sales, they were to be disappointed. By 1838, they managed to sell only seven lots, five of them along the river and the turnpike. They reserved the choicest site, where the Seneca Turnpike intersected the high bank overlooking the river, for their own use. This would later become Elizabeth Cady Stanton's home.[23]

Bascom, Sackett, and Tillman were even more determined to attract buyers.

They established low prices and easy terms, and their entrepreneurship paid off. Stephen Burritt, an early settler, contrasted the area in 1823, when "there was not a frame house on the south side of the river that could be seen from the north side," with the same spot from 1828 to 1832, when it "was built up very fast." Two new business blocks on the south side of the river testified to the growing prosperity. Three new hotels—the Clinton House on Fall Street, the Franklin House, and the Seneca House—reflected burgeoning travel.[24]

Canal transportation sustained this boom. The Seneca and Cayuga Canal gave shippers in both Seneca Falls and Waterloo unimpeded water access to eastern markets. Sleek packet boats joined heavier freight barges, connecting with the Erie Canal at Montezuma or with new steamboats on Cayuga Lake. Before 1828, said one local resident, "our village was indifferently connected with the outside world. . . . The packet . . . converted us into a canal town with something of cosmopolitan features." Passenger boats would go through Seneca Falls twice a day, west to Geneva in the morning and east in the afternoon. By the 1840s, two packet lines competed to provide spectacular entertainment. Bedecked with banners, brass bands, and uniformed captains, the old *Red Bird* or the new *Heron,* drawn by five or six horses with boy riders, slipped swiftly through the canal, leaving a high swell behind, each trying to outdo the other in speed and public display. Every day, the Stantons heard the blare of the packet horns announcing the arrival of the boats.[25]

But the canal brought more than passenger traffic. It also brought business. Through it came raw materials to be transformed into manufactured products in the new mills and factories of the village. Through it, most especially, came grain to be milled in Seneca Falls and Waterloo.

Seneca Falls exploded with people. In the early 1820s, the village had 200 residents, 40 houses, and one church. By 1835, it counted 3,786 people, 450 houses, and five churches. In 1831, Seneca Falls had a new cotton factory, a woolen factory, and sixteen other manufacturing enterprises, as well as seventeen dry goods stores and two each of hardware stores, druggists, shoe stores, and hat stores, plus five schools and five churches.[26]

It also had flour mills. The original two Red Mills expanded to five by the early 1830s, to seven by 1837, and to nine by the early 1840s. Most of these were on the north side of the river, near Bridge and Water Streets.[27] In the 1830s, these mills brought more wealth to the village than did any other single industry. In 1835, mill owners sold $252,350 worth of flour. More to the point, they had paid only $203,00 for wheat, making a value added by manufacture of $249,350. By 1850, Seneca Falls produced flour worth $453,290, more than four times the value of either pumps or textiles, the next largest industries.[28]

Along with flour mills, distilleries bought local grain and turned it into whiskey or "high wines." In Seneca Falls, one distillery in 1835 earned a value added by manufacture of $4,000. By 1845, another distillery had been added, to bring a $10,000 return.[29]

Millers and distillers in turn demanded barrel makers and boatmen. By the 1830s, millers needed one thousand barrels a day to ship flour to market. By the 1840s, they used double that number. Thus, coopers shared prosperity with millers. So did boat manufacturers. In 1823, Haskell's boat yard built the first canal boat in Seneca Falls. By the late 1830s, Asa Starkweather ran a second yard. Both businesses had plenty of work. All three industries—flour milling, barrel making, and boat manufacture—reached a peak in the early 1840s.[30]

So important was the canal to the success of the flour mills that many millers bought canal boats themselves, so they could better control access to raw materials and markets. Every few days, the son of one of these millers remembered, a fleet of canal boats, laden with grain, came in from the Finger Lakes, pulled by steamboats through the lakes and then drawn by mules along the canal. These boats traded grain for milled flour and feed, before they made their way down the canal to Syracuse, Rome, Utica, and other eastern markets. Even when farmers brought their grain by road to the mills, as they often did, millers such as Jacob P. Chamberlain personally traveled by canal to eastern New York to sell their flour.[31]

In the 1830s, only one other manufacturing establishment rivaled the flour mills in size and value of production. That was the cotton mill, built for one thousand spindles in 1830 just below the Bridge Street bridge on the south side of the river. By 1835, this cotton mill was spectacularly profitable, using only $10,000 worth of raw materials, principally cotton, to produce $35,000 worth of goods.[32]

More than flour, cotton was the seed that contained the future, for Seneca Falls and the country. Flour mills, despite their large size, used the same techniques that smaller mills had always used. In contrast, textile factories—in technology, size, and work force organization—epitomized the industrial revolution.[33]

Beginning in England in the mid-eighteenth century and extending to the United States by the 1790s, iron machines—large and expensive—installed in factories began to replace home production. At first, many cloth mills incorporated only carding machines. Carding wool at home—combing it between two brushes equipped with sharp metal teeth—was onerous and time consuming. Carding mills made that job easier, but spinning and weaving remained work for women at home. In Seneca Falls, Colonel Mynderse set up a carding and fulling mill as early as 1806. To this mill, women sent raw wool fleeces. From it, they received back long fluffy rolls of wool. At home, they spun this wool into yarn, and then they—or a neighbor who had a loom—wove this yarn into cloth, generally to be used by their own families rather than sold.

The War of 1812 freed American investors from English competition and encouraged the development of full-fledged factories, incorporating carding, spinning, and weaving machines under one roof. Men with money and an entrepreneurial spirit formed legal corporations to build brick or stone buildings, usually five or six stories high, along fast-falling waterways. These new factories employed not individual women in isolated households but large numbers of women, men, and often children. Workers operated large machines, counted their hours by clock time, and produced huge amounts of cloth, not for their own use but for sale to regional, national, and international markets.

Many of these factories were located in New England, but others emerged along fast-running streams in New York—at Cohoes (near Albany); New York Mills (near Utica); and at smaller sites such as Oswego, Seneca Falls, and Waterloo. These mills employed two different kinds of labor. The Rhode Island system, begun at the Slater mill in Pawtucket, Rhode Island, in 1790, employed whole families. By 1825, factories at Lowell, Massachusetts, employed mostly young women. These two systems became models for industrialists everywhere, including those in Seneca Falls and Waterloo.[34]

As cotton mills went, the Seneca Falls mill was relatively small. It did not compare with the great mills at Lowell. But it was part of a much larger movement, a movement that transformed personal lives, not only for those who worked in the mills but also for those who bought the new mass-produced goods. Industrialization was part of a great shattering of an older view of the world. Instead of harmony and order, it promoted competition, based on making money. Those who controlled the finances, the machines, and the buildings often found themselves at odds with those who contributed their labor. Economic transformations also promoted a clear division between the home (as a place for family life, for consuming the world's goods, for women and children) and the workplace (a place away from home, dominated by men, whose purpose was to make money). With its heavy capital investment, large-scale production, separation of workers and owners, and extensive employment of workers outside the home, the Seneca Falls cotton mill was a portent of industrial developments that would, slowly, subtly, but irresistibly, become the future for many Americans.

At the same time, the cotton mill tied Seneca Falls directly to slavery. Cotton, produced by enslaved people in the American South, became the country's most valuable export in the years before the Civil War. With the development of the Seneca Falls cotton factory, it also became an essential part of the local economy. From the 1830s on, people in Seneca Falls were inescapably and irrevocably tied to a national economic system based on slavery.

With the beginnings of factory-type manufacturing in Seneca Falls and Waterloo came a new system of transportation, the railroad. Like the trails, roads, and canals before it, the railroad in Seneca Falls and Waterloo paralleled the Seneca River. With it, life in general speeded up. Local residents contributed capital for the railroad in the boom year of 1836. Samuel Bayard, secretary of the Auburn and Rochester Railroad Company collected $122,900 from Seneca Falls in two days in October. Waterloo residents gave $40,000. Contracts were given to build the road in 1837. On July 5, 1841, an excursion train left Rochester for Seneca Falls, and by November, the last part of the road had been completed to Auburn. Citizens of Seneca Falls could then go all the way from Albany to Rochester by railroad. Passengers on canal boats traveled four to five miles an hour, maximum. On the new railroad, they could go five times that fast. Rochester used to be a day's travel away. Now it was only two hours.[35]

Boom times, however, could not last forever. Depression hit the whole country, Seneca Falls included, in the late 1830s. Businesses began to flounder. Marshall and Adams, for example, lost their clock-making shop in 1837, and Marshall reputedly committed suicide over it. But the worst effects of the depression seem to have engulfed the village after 1840. Jeremy Bement was forced to give up his thriving carriage-making business. The cotton factory closed in 1844. Samuel and William Bayard lost everything—land, investments, even their own homes. "I am in actual want," wrote Samuel Bayard. These "active and enterprising men," were forced to leave town, flat broke. Others were right behind them. Origen Stores, a dry goods merchant, lost his business and went to Lockport. James Gay lost his hardware store and moved to Cincinnati. Almost three hundred people fled the village in the early 1840s. It would take more than a decade before Seneca Falls recovered its population and its economic confidence.[36]

Waterloo could tell a happier story. Never as dependent as Seneca Falls on the milling of grain, Waterloo acquired a new woolen mill in 1836. Organized by Richard P. Hunt—who gained his fortune from the many farms he owned in Waterloo, as well as from his control of a downtown business block—the mill was based on a capital investment of $150,000. Hunt, a Quaker, deliberately created a wool mill rather than a cotton mill so that he did not have to buy raw materials produced by people in slavery. With carding, spinning, and weaving machines all under one roof, these Waterloo Woolen Mills were up-to-date in every respect. They emerged from the depression of 1837 and went on to become the second largest shawl factory in the United States.[37]

While Seneca Falls reeled under economic depression, Waterloo continued to grow, sustained by the success of its mills. In 1840, Waterloo had 37 percent more people than it had in 1835. During the next five years, while Seneca Falls was losing 7 percent of its people, Waterloo expanded by 19 percent. However, since Waterloo had considerable catching up to do, this spurt merely meant that by 1845 the two villages were almost equal in population, with 3,997 people in Seneca Falls and 3,634 people in Waterloo.[38]

In Seneca Falls, however, both grist mills and distilleries depended on wheat, and wheat production was under threat. In another ten years, the wheat harvest in Seneca County would be only one-third of what it was in 1845.[39]

The 1840s marked the real transition in Seneca Falls from an economy dominated by land and its products to an economy dominated by manufacturing. This was, as Walt Rostow suggested for the country as a whole, the "take-off" period of the industrial revolution. Investors were looking for new ways to make money. And in Seneca Falls they found it in two industries that were at the cutting edge of the industrial revolution: textiles and iron pumps.[40]

With money from milling and retail sales, a few men in Seneca Falls—including dry goods merchant Charles Hoskins, miller Jacob Chamberlain, and lawyer and land owner Ansel Bascom—pooled their capital to build the Seneca Woolen Mills, a fine five-story limestone building, 110 feet long and 50 feet wide, on the south bank of the river in 1844. If they hoped to emulate the success of the Waterloo woolen mill, however, they were disappointed. Production in the 1840s was never as impressive as the building itself. Neither were profits. This mill, and one other small woolen business, sold only 9,700 yards of cloth in 1845, compared with 122,000 yards produced by the Waterloo mill. In 1854, the company reorganized as the Phoenix Company, and its one hundred employees produced fine wool cashmeres for the New York City market.[41]

One other effort at wool manufacture in Seneca Falls emerged in the 1840s. Sensing a good opportunity, Joel W. Smith took an old carding and fulling mill, added weaving machines to it, and opened with a flourish in 1848. "CLOTH MANUFACTORY!" he advertised, "Manufacturer of Cloth wishes to exchange cloth for WOOL, or manufactures on shares, or by the yard." Like the Seneca Woolen Mills, however, Smith's mill, in spite of the celebrated quality of its "sheep's gray," was not successful in making money.[42]

One other modern industry emerged from the chaotic business conditions of the 1840s—the manufacture of a variety of metal products, the most important of which were pumps. The industry began in 1839–40, when three separate companies began to make wooden pumps. Five years later, they made their first iron pumps. At the same time, local people began to produce other metal products, including stove regulators, "thimble-skeins, pipe boxes, cast iron hand sleds, smoothing irons, jack screws, and a great variety of other useful articles." Iron manufacture proved to be highly profitable. In 1845, an investment of $4,372 in raw materials brought sales of $12,240. By the 1850s, two major iron factories began to produce even more iron products, including zinc washboards, clover-hulling mills, corn shellers, and knitting machines. "The amount of business transacted," wrote one local historian, "was simply enormous." Local entrepreneurs also developed the first fire engine pumps, the product that made Seneca Falls famous around the world. Gould's pumps eventually became one of the most important pump manufacturers in the world, maintaining its international headquarters in Seneca Falls into the late twentieth century.[43]

Marketing was a crucial part of the success of these businesses. Seneca Falls millers such as Jacob Chamberlain sold their flour primarily in eastern cities. Seneca Falls blacksmiths sold most of their axes in Pennsylvania. But Seneca Falls pumps relied on lands newly settled by farm families in the Midwest. Ironically, the migration of European American farmers to prairies of the West, while it proved to be ruinous competition to Seneca County wheat growers, ensured the success of Seneca Falls pump manufacturers. Farmers in the upper Mississippi Valley, a region of only seasonal rainfall, needed pumps if they were to survive at all.[44]

The transition to large-scale industrial manufacturing and to rail transportation brought profound changes in the way men and women organized their lives and in the attitudes they held about themselves. Conditions were chaotic; success was by no means assured. A core of men in Seneca Falls—inventors, mechanics, sales people, and capitalists—changed partners, tried out new products, and took new risks. In the process, they generated a sense of excitement and anxiety that set the stage for the woman's rights convention. Economic instability forced people into new ways of looking at the world.

In economic terms, the woolen mill in Waterloo and the woolen mills and pump factories of Seneca Falls represented deep shifts in the way men and women worked. In a world before factories, people made most of what they needed in or near their own homes. Working with their own children, apprentices, or neighbors, they made cloth, shoes, or furniture for their own use or for sale from their home shops. In the 1820s, as local historian Harrison Chamberlain noted, "the home and the store were so mixed up that you could not tell just where was the dividing line." Their work was small in scale, without complicated machinery or heavy capital investment money, embedded in a network of personal relationships.[45]

Factory-style production eroded this system. Many men and young women left their homes every day to go to work on a schedule set by someone else, in a building they did not own, operating someone else's machinery, making cloth or pumps they would not use, to be sold by total strangers to other total strangers. When and where they would work, how much they would make, how they would make it, were no longer under their own control.

Without payroll or personnel records, we may never know exactly who worked in the woolen factories of Seneca Falls and Waterloo. Extant millhouses in Waterloo suggest that many employees worked as families. Quite likely, however, many of them were also young women, unmarried, in their late teens or early twenties, like those in the Lowell, Massachusetts, mills.[46]

What workers—whether men, women, or children—brought home from a hard day's labor was money. But how much money? Industrial census reports by the state of New York in 1855 no longer exist for Seneca County. Similar records for mill workers in Oneida County, however, listed wages as twenty dollars per month for men, ten dollars a month for women, and even less for children. For males, these wages were comparable to what they earned as farm laborers, if room and board was calculated as part of their farm employment.[47]

People used this money to buy the goods they no longer made for themselves. Throughout the 1840s, local merchants used newspaper advertising to encourage consumption, promoting luxury items as well as staples. Men and women in Seneca Falls and Waterloo could buy all the latest things, most of them imported by canal or railroad directly from New York City. People bought their boots and shoes in town, along with hats and caps; wallpaper and paint; oil cloths for tables and floors; carpets; tea from India or China; sugar; and, if they could afford it, flowing blue crockery, stone ware, glassware, looking glasses, and clocks.[48]

Most important of all, they bought cloth. Not so long before, most people wore homespun clothes, made of linen or wool, rough in texture, simple in design. But factory-style methods found their earliest, most astounding success with cloth. First British and then American manufacturers produced fine cotton and woolen cloth, thousands of yards of it, for dresses and shirts and suits and sheets. And it was cheap. Women who used to grow their own flax and raise their own sheep (cleaning, carding, spinning, weaving, cutting, and sewing the wool) now found it economical simply to go down to the dry goods store and buy what they wanted in patterns and colors to match any mood.

As farms and factories produced more goods and as people began to have more money, women in the home found themselves spending less time making clothes and household articles. One measure of relative access to the market economy is simply to note the declining home production of cloth. This transformation occurred earlier in villages and cities than in the countryside. In 1813, for example, Horatio Gates Spafford reported in his *Gazetteer* that "much of the clothing is produced from household industry" in Seneca County. In the villages of Seneca Falls and Waterloo, however, that changed rapidly. By 1835, outside Seneca Falls and Waterloo, an ordinary adult woman aged sixteen to forty-five in Seneca County produced in her home, on the average, 25.6 yards of cloth per year. In Waterloo, such a woman made only 6.7 yards. And in Seneca Falls, she manufactured only 3.5 yards. Able to buy cloth rather than to make it at home, women found themselves inescapably part of a new economic order.[49]

It is easy to overestimate this transformation of homes from places of production to places of consumption. Clearly, most women—whether working class, middle class, or even upper class—continued to produce things at home. They grew, preserved, and cooked food; sewed and mended clothes; and kept house. Although home production of cloth dropped dramatically, women continued to make clothes for themselves and their children. If they could afford it, they would hire a dressmaker to work for several days a year. Such work, however, would still be home based, either in the seamstress's own home or in the home of her customers. The invention of the sewing machine in 1849 did not take dressmaking into factories as much as it brought mechanized production into individual homes.

Even in terms of home decoration, women acted not only as consumers but as manufacturers. They might buy a nice Brussels carpet or a fine white cotton bedspread, but they also made rag carpets and quilts. In fact, they probably increased their production of these, as rags from machine-made cloth became more readily available. They may have purchased store-bought wallpaper and paint, but they also continued to make their own brick dust and buttermilk stain. Catherine Beecher's *Treatise on Domestic Economy* was only one of many popular sources of ideas for what women could do to fix up their homes themselves, inexpensively.[50]

Most of what women made, they made for their own family. Some of it, however, they used instead of money, to trade for goods at Hoskins's or Woodworth's store. They might trade butter and eggs, wool stockings, cheese, or raspberry preserves. Because they kept very different accounts from the more formal ledgers that men preserved, women often lacked recognition—by historians, at least—for their economic role as manufacturers and traders. Such work, however, remained significant sources of income for many families in an increasingly cash-based economy.[51]

In Seneca Falls, cash was scarce, and trading was so common that only one store, the Empire Cash Store, refused to take anything but money. Hoskins's store was more typical. There, one resident recalled, "the country customers from far and near would come and rummage over the piles of shoe leather and rattle around among the tinware, have a smoke in the meantime, sit round in everybody's way, and go home at night, having had a nice visit, disposing of their eggs at 6c a dozen and their butter at 12-½c per pound, with their pay in what they ransacked the store for." Some local businesses even paid their employees in scrip. Hezekiah Kelley, owner of the cotton mill, issued shilling notes to his employees, which they could spend at the company store. Several store owners issued their own small-value bills, called shinplasters.[52]

Even as methods of production shifted toward factories, women's work at home remained indispensable. Women who worked outside the home could count on some other woman—a mother, sister, or aunt—to take care of the family and household. And most women, whatever the economic status they may have enjoyed through their husbands or fathers, were themselves members of the working class. Without capital of their own, they increased the value of their husband's holdings through their labor. Even middle-class women, who usually stayed at home and often had money to hire household help, were not only managers but workers.[53]

Nor did women's work allow for much leisure time. For most people, labor-saving devices did not save labor so much as raise standards of living. Sewing machines, for example, became important in many households, not to finish sewing tasks more quickly but to make more elaborate dresses in the same time, for the same labor cost, that simple dresses had once been made.[54]

For most men, too, the old order dissolved only slowly into the new. Village tailors, working and often living in their own small shops, continued to make men's clothes, at least their best suits. Henry Stanton and his sons patronized William Keith, on Ovid Street. True, they could also buy clothes off the rack. S. E. Woodworth's enterprising clerks, in the big store in Bascom's block, were making up large lots of ready-made men's garments. But Woodworth also provided more traditional service, advertising that he did "tailoring in all its branches executed with neatness and despatch." The same pattern was true for men's hats and shoes. People could buy either mass-produced items or locally made ones. David B. Lum, who owned the Seneca Falls Hat & Cap Store on Fall Street, advertised in 1840, "New York and London fashions just received," while Crandall Kenyon noted with pride that "[I] am a mechanic and manufacture all my hats and caps myself. I don't buy them in Albany and Ovid (as our neighbor in the 'row' does)."[55]

Many men, tailors and hatters included, still practiced the old craft system, training apprentices and making and selling their goods from the place where they lived. Barrel makers still had apprentices in the 1830s. So did boat builders. Joshua Martin bound himself out to Asa Starkweather as a boat builder in 1838 and ended up as foreman and then as manager. Shoemakers, saddlers, and shop owners still lived in the business section, over or behind their shops.[56]

In general, industrialization would affect men and women very differently, offering increased scope for men to work in the world while emphasizing that women's place (at least the place of relatively affluent women) was in the home. Stanton and other woman's rights advocates resisted attempts by the dominant culture to confine women's work and influence to home and family. They played upon the institutional, cultural, and personal instability of the 1840s to argue for equal access for all Americans, both men and women, to the opportunities and challenges of the world outside the home.

Economics and gender roles were not the only contested terrain in this changing physical, social, and cultural landscape. As surely as new migrants brought with them their worldly goods—oxen, wagons, furniture, and tools—they brought with them whole worldviews. Since they came from different parts of the country and the globe, they carried different value systems, different expectations of how their lives should function. They were also forced to confront each other in new ways. In Seneca Falls and Waterloo, they had to deal not only with a new physical place (a village, not a farm; America, not Ireland; the West, not the East) but also economic ups and downs, isolation from parents and family, and neighbors with very different values. Ties to family, familiar habits, and support networks stretched and sometimes snapped.

In times of dramatic economic and social change, people struggled to understand what was happening to them, to reconcile the values they knew as children with the world they confronted as adults, to create a new sense of place out of the splintered remnants of earlier worlds. As they lived and worked with people whose values were often different from their own, they tried to maintain what they could of their sense of right order. In the process, they created a new world out of the mosaic of the old, a cultural quilt bound together with new definitions of community. Some common denominators were relatively easy to establish: the right of individuals to make and spend money, to live in relative safety, and to maintain family relationships. Two issues were much more difficult: Who would represent the family in the world? How much diversity could be tolerated while still maintaining a stable political and social matrix?

Balancing community and diversity was not easy. In the process of trying, whole villages were engulfed in conflict.

Some people, of course, knew exactly what they wanted. A proper world should emphasize cooperation not competition; love not hate; order not chaos; and responsibility for oneself, one's family, one's friends. The jostling, competitive, and stressful demands of survival in a new land threatened these values.

Cultural tensions were often reflected in debates about religion and reform movements. To re-create an orderly, moral world, many people turned to religion. In Seneca Falls, five church spires punctuated the village skyline: Presbyterian, Baptist, Methodist, Episcopal, and Catholic. Waterloo included all but a Catholic church. For a few years, both villages also had Congregational churches. A German-language church at the Kingdom, halfway between the villages of Seneca Falls and Waterloo, was organized in 1826. Outside Waterloo, the Junius Friends meetinghouse reflected a Quaker presence. Nearby, Joseph Smith attracted many Seneca County people to the new Mormon religion.[57]

These churches reflected the cultural diversity of Seneca Falls and Waterloo. Catholics, organized in 1831 and serving primarily an Irish population, stood apart from the majority. As Catholics in a world dominated by Protestants, as Irish people in a world dominated by those of English descent, as people often unable to read or write, these immigrants were a cultural minority.

Yet Catholics and Protestants also shared a broadly common Christian tradition. They used a common vocabulary and maintained some consensus about individual obligations to the geographic community. Both Protestants and Catholics relied on Christian traditions to help communities of immigrants—whether from the east coast or Europe—adjust to their status as members of new communities and citizens of an emerging United States. They helped create a sense of order, stability, and meaning in the potentially chaotic conditions that existed in areas of rapid economic development. When Father Francis Donoghue gave the first Sunday mass in Seneca Falls in 1835, for example, he reminded his Irish congregation, "to be faithful to their religion and to their adopted country. He thanked God that America was the refuge for the oppressed of all nations and asked his hearers not to forget to pray for this country. He warned them against the evils of drink and to shun the dram shops; to avoid bad company, and to make their lives correspond to the teaching of their holy Faith." Protestant pastors would have added "Amen."[58]

Recognizing the importance of religious institutions in creating and defining community, civic-minded men in both Seneca Falls and Waterloo contributed money to build churches, even those they did not attend themselves. In 1835, Gary V. Sackett contributed land for the Seneca Falls Catholic Church and was duly recognized in the Catholic press as "a kind and liberal Protestant gentleman." About twenty more Protestants in town contributed fifty dollars to help the new congregation survive. Richard P. Hunt, Waterloo Quaker, gave money in 1843 to build the new Wesleyan Church in Seneca Falls. When the Methodist

Episcopal Church was incorporated in 1829, two of the five trustees, including Ansel Bascom, were not members. Nonmembers often contributed financially by purchasing pews (or "slips") for the use of themselves and their families.[59]

In their quest for ethical and moral order, people often grew exceedingly enthusiastic, both within churches and outside of them. Throughout upstate New York, many churches experienced religious revivals every two or three years. So frequently did the fires of revivalism burn, in fact, that some called this the "burnt district" or the "burned-over district." Beginning in 1825, Charles Grandison Finney, the same preacher who alienated Elizabeth Cady Stanton while enthralling Henry Brewster Stanton, traveled through the whole upstate region, bringing revivalism to new heights of effectiveness and power. In Oneida County in 1825, every Presbyterian church experienced a revival under Finney's influence.

Benevolent reform societies, all beginning with the name "American," expanded Protestant Christian energies beyond denominational lines, merging religious and political goals. The American Sunday School Union, the American Bible Society, and the American Missionary Society all promoted Protestant outreach to the larger population. Their goals were to set up Sunday Schools for every American, distribute Bibles to every home, provide Protestant Christian missionaries for every community, and create a Christian nation.[60]

Seneca Falls and Waterloo were not immune from this excitement. From 1817 to 1824, Waterloo Protestants held regular meetings of the General Missionary Society of Young People in the Western District.[61] Sunday Schools also found local promoters. In 1840, the Baptist Church in Seneca Falls reported an average Sunday school attendance of nearly three hundred children. Regularly, religious revivals swept through both villages, converting hundreds of people. In Seneca Falls, Methodists added seventy people to their membership in 1830–31. Noted Baptist revivalist Jacob Knapp spent five weeks in 1838 preaching to overflowing crowds. Methodists had another revival in 1841 and 1842.[62]

Whatever the issue and whatever the means, churches participated in the debate about the relationship between individuals and the community. Many religious people felt a sense of urgency about re-creating an orderly, Christian base in the chaotic and often cruel conditions of an emerging industrial village. People who joined churches found themselves in a relationship of mutual obligation, based on a commitment to Christian values. Churches, Sunday schools, and benevolent associations helped people re-establish relationships among themselves. Love, self-sacrifice, and a concern for the whole community challenged the individualistic, competitive model promoted by the emerging capitalist economy.

Women were particularly important in sustaining religious ideals. Most of Finney's converts were women. When Finney was criticized for allowing women to pray in church meetings, he defended himself by saying that he had not introduced this idea. Women already prayed regularly in public in these upstate villages.[63] In Seneca Falls and Waterloo, both men and women joined the Waterloo Missionary Society, although only men were officers. St. Paul's Episcopal Church formed a Female Sewing Society in 1837–38. Men were allowed to join this society, but women were its officers and the vast majority of its members. The St. Paul's Female Sewing Society, like many women's organizations, promoted both personal and public goals. On the one hand, they made and sold articles to support their church. On the other hand, they acted as a support group "to console each other in time of trouble, to strengthen in time of trial, to endeavor in every way consistent with the duty which they owe to their families & to themselves to advance the cause of Christ as identified with this Church."[64]

Christian ideals became the basis for reaffirming order not only in the private sphere of religion but also in the secular, public sphere. The Fourth of July became a religious as well as a political celebration. In 1840 and 1841, for example, Seneca Falls Sunday schools proclaimed the "Sabbath day of freedom." Four or five hundred Baptist and Presbyterian children joined a celebration on Saturday. Methodists and Episcopalians held a parade and picnic on Monday.[65]

Residents of Seneca Falls endorsed this alliance between religious and secular values. They merged the boundaries between themselves as Christians and citizens. "The establishment and prevalence of Sunday Schools in our country," noted the *Seneca County Courier,* "is one of those noble enterprises worthy the attention not only of the religious portion of community but also eminently worthy of the fostering care and encouraging approval of every patriot and sincere lover of his country. . . . It is in these schools . . . that the youth of our country imbibe their earliest and most enduring sense of the obligations and responsibilities which are soon to devolve upon them as the freemen of this free republic."[66]

The temperance movement reinforced this quest for moral consensus. One of the surest signs of salvation, argued temperance advocates, was abstinence from alcohol. Seneca Falls residents heard their first temperance lecture at the Presbyterian Church in 1828, when eighteen people signed the temperance pledge. By the late 1830s, the local temperance society had two hundred members.[67]

In the 1830s, temperance meant abstinence from distilled liquor only. By the early 1840s, however, a new, more passionate temperance movement—the Washingtonian movement—emerged. Promoted at first by six reformed drunkards from Baltimore, Washingtonians asked people to become teetotalers, that is, to pledge that they would never drink any alcoholic beverages, including wine and beer. When two of the Baltimore reformers held public meetings in Seneca Falls, local men and women enthusiastically took up the new banner. In July 1841, Seneca Falls men organized a Washington Independent Temperance Society. Women organized a ladies' temperance society soon after.

Temperance thoroughly took over Seneca Falls. It "produced a great sensation," noted Dexter Bloomer, editor of the *Seneca County Courier,* "almost revolutionizing public sentiment." By February 1842, the town supported a temperance newspaper, the *Water Bucket,* which took as its motto "TOTAL

ABSTINENCE FROM ALL THAT CAN INTOXICATE." Dexter Bloomer's new wife, Amelia Jenks Bloomer, sweetly refused to drink wine at her own wedding reception. "I cannot," she told her husband with a smile. "I must not." By May 1842, if we can believe the *Water Bucket,* 800 men and 700 women (not counting the children in the Juvenile Temperance Society) had joined these stalwarts, more than 37 percent of the entire village population. Waterloo was catching up. In March 1842, the Independent Temperance Society of Waterloo counted 310 members.[68]

So powerful blew the temperance wind in Seneca Falls that in April 1842, the town passed, by a majority of one hundred votes, a law prohibiting the sale of liquor within its borders. The town had granted twelve liquor licenses the year before. It granted none in 1842 or 1843. According to temperance advocates, the impact on poverty and crime was immediate. In the nine months before the organization of the Independent Temperance Society, assaults numbered seventeen. In the nine months afterward, they dropped to six. The number of petty offenses fell from twenty-four to three. Applications for relief dropped from thirty-one to two. "Examine it Taxpayers," advised the *Water Bucket,* "and then decide for yourselves."[69]

In Seneca Falls, temperance bridged lines of class, politics, religion, and gender. Perhaps because it seemed so manifestly good for business, businessmen took up the cause with gusto. Edward S. Latham, local builder, became treasurer of the men's organization. A. K. Townsend operated his blacksmith shop, he advertised, on the "tee total principle." J. C. Fuller ran the Seneca House as a temperance hotel.[70]

Workers also found it prudent to take the pledge. Employment, especially for unskilled laborers, might depend on temperance connections. Not only did workers join temperance societies but they also became officers. John Timmerman, a laborer in a local boatyard, was president of the Independent Temperance Society in 1841. When Edward Latham, "a truly valiant soldier in the great cold water army," became superintendent of the Seneca and Cayuga Canal in February 1843, the *Water Bucket* made clear its expectations. "We are sure he will allow no lock tender or person in his employ, to keep a rum shop along the Canal," the paper asserted, "from whence death and destruction may be dealt out for three cents a drink. Good Temperance laborers too, we are sure, will not be overlooked in selecting those in his employ."[71]

Temperance promoted alliances across class and ethnic divisions, based on personal character, integrity, and abstinence. Temperance thus posed a serious challenge to existing social distinctions. Many important men bitterly opposed the temperance movement, argued the *Water Bucket,* because "they fear their power is gone." Instead, "the *Reformed men*—and the men who have been saved from inebriation are destined to take a prominent stand in Society. . . . [They] are about to exercise the attributes of freemen and think and act for themselves." Temperance bridged political divisions, too. Josiah T. Miller, editor of the Democratic paper in Seneca Falls, joined Dexter Bloomer, editor of the Whig paper, in giving temperance speeches and reporting on temperance events.[72]

Nor did religious divisions prove a barrier to consensus on temperance. Christians refrained from pointing fingers at each other because every denomination recognized that its own members, too, suffered from alcoholism. In 1839, for example, even before the Washingtonian revival, Seneca Falls Methodists reminded themselves that "the sin of Intemperance prevails to an alarming extent, in the Methodist Episcopal Church," and brings "disgrace, & the loss of many who have been its most valuable members." In 1842, the Baptists agreed to use only unfermented wine in their services.[73]

Women, too, had a place in the temperance movement. They were advised not to drink, not to cook with wine or brandy, and not to associate with those who did. Sometimes, such sentiments took a radical turn. In Elbridge, New York, for example, just east of Seneca Falls, about one hundred local women promoted an oyster supper at the local temperance house. The meal left everyone feeling mellow. After-dinner toasts reflected their pride in themselves as women. Toasts to "The Washington Ladies. May their work of usefulness be prospered, and may they never forget the drunkard's home" led quickly to "May the union existing between the Ladies of Elbridge, at present be an ever endurable token of their independence." Not to be outdone in her commitment to the cause, someone else suggested "Temperance husbands or none." Another toasted "TO THE YOUNG MEN WHO REFUSE TO SIGN THE PLEDGE. May they be doomed to a life of single blessedness." And finally, there was a toast to "THE OLD MAIDS. We glory in our independence, an independence not from necessity, but choice."[74]

In Seneca Falls, challenges to female dependence were more muted. Temperance activities did, however, erode the walls between home and the world, and temperance women affirmed their responsibility not only to their husbands and children but also to the larger community. A few members of the Ladies' Temperance Society (which officially numbered several hundred) met on Friday afternoons each week through the winter of 1841–42 to repair and distribute clothes for poor families. Amelia Bloomer, who wrote for the *Water Bucket* under the pen name "Gloriana," answered skeptical observers who wondered what such charity would do for the temperance cause. "It *may do much*," she argued, and she phrased her appeal directly in terms of gender and class:

> The drunkard's wife is pleased with the notice taken of her, by those whose station in life is more fortunate. This is manifested, by the improved appearance of her house, on a second visit from one of the committee. She has not only set her house in order, but there is a tidiness about her person, and those of her children, which was not to be seen on the first visit. The wife communicates to her husband, in his sane moments, that fact, that Mrs. such-a-one, has called on her, and will call again. The husband too, is flattered by the no-

> tice of the lady (for in his sane moments the drunkard is still a man) and by the improved appearance of his wife and children. . . . And will not all this lead a man to reflect on what he has once been, and may still be, if he will but dash from his lips the "intoxicating cup?"[75]

In 1842, Seneca Falls temperance activities took over the Fourth of July parade, which Sunday schools had claimed the year before. Accompanied by banners and bands, rifle companies and revolutionary soldiers, fire engines and cannon, hundreds of temperance men, women, and children marched up one side of the river and down the other. John Timmerman, laborer, marched. So did "the ladies—in numbers, equal to all the rest of the line." They ended in Bascom's orchard, where the four hundred seats did not even hold all the women present. Altogether, about one thousand people sat or stood through the program. Josiah T. Miller, editor of the *Seneca Falls Democrat,* read the Declaration of Independence "in a full and distinct voice," D. Skidmore read the Washingtonian Declaration of Independence, and Dexter Bloomer, editor of the *Seneca County Courier,* gave the oration. At the end of the afternoon, two to three hundred people shared a picnic. By any definition, Seneca Falls had enrolled with gusto in the temperance army.[76]

Appropriately enough, this celebration reminded people in Seneca Falls of their clear and continued connection with the American Revolution. A common revolutionary experience bound Americans in the United States together; so did a common commitment to temperance. Revolutionary War veterans rode in the parade; the original Declaration of Independence was paired with a new temperance Declaration of Independence; and toasts, drunk with "clear cold water," reminded each group of their revolutionary legacy. No one was left out. All fit under the mantle of their common past, their shared present. I. H. Arnett, owner and operator of a local flour mill, recalled the "Two Declarations of Independence—the one framed by the Patriots of '76: the other by the Reformers of '42—May their existence, now parallel with each other, be identified together as one, and inseparable now and forever." Dexter Bloomer saluted "The Mechanics of Seneca Falls—Temperate, intelligent and public spirited—they not only know their rights, but they know how to maintain them." And someone exuberantly toasted "The Ladies—ever the champions of a good cause—they sent their husbands and their sons forth to battle in the days of the Revolution. Now they are the most faithful and consistent advocates of Temperance among us."[77]

The temperance movement brought a state of celebration and good feeling to all of its adherents in Seneca Falls. It created a unity of thought and action that bridged people of different classes, different political parties, and both sexes. To many, it seemed as if the Washingtonians had indeed triumphed with the only weapons they knew how to use, "kindness and love."[78]

Such euphoria could not last. In 1842 and 1843, the harmony of the temperance celebration disintegrated, as other religious and reform activities in Seneca Falls erupted into a raging bonfire, which residents could only with difficulty control. In many ways, these two years created a new Seneca Falls. In spite of considerable agreement on religion and temperance, the intensification of cultural and intellectual turmoil revealed seismic differences of opinion among the local population. Residents would have to learn once more to live with each other, recognizing their differences while building on what they had in common.

Fueled by organizers such as Bascom, the pace of radical reform escalated in the early 1840s. Transcendental philosophy—expounded by Ralph Waldo Emerson and Bronson Alcott—reached Seneca Falls in 1840 in the form of the *Dial,* a quarterly magazine edited by Margaret Fuller. The *Seneca Falls Democrat* hailed the *Dial*'s articles as "entirely original," promoting nothing less than "intellectual freedom and social progress," and hoped that such works "may be found on the 'centre table'—yes, on the plain pine table, of every American citizen," including presumably those in Seneca Falls. It is, noted the *Democrat,* "our favorite Magazine."[79]

H. G. Derby gave a series of lectures on phrenology, analyzing the heads of local residents in free "PUBLIC EXAMINATIONS!" to reveal their basic characters. (Disbelievers especially were invited to attend.) Local bookstores reflected the avid phrenological interests of area residents, advertising Orson Fowler's works, including the *American Phrenological Journal,* which gave advice on—among other topics—matrimony, memory, history, and tight lacing of corsets for women. The Seneca Falls Lyceum debated "Is phrenology a true science?"[80]

Homeopathy, too, created a furor in Seneca Falls, as local homeopaths challenged dominant members of the medical profession. Although not a doctor, Ansel Bascom became an honorary member of the Homeopathic Society of Western New York, when the group held its annual meeting in Seneca Falls. C. D. Williams and Edward Bayard, Stanton's brother-in-law, promoted homeopathy. After the Seneca County Medical Association ousted Williams in 1843, Bayard left the village to set up practice in New York City, where he became one of the country's most prominent homeopaths.[81]

Liberal religion also generated considerable discussion. Unitarians from Boston invaded the village, sensing good prospects for new members in Seneca Falls. Ansel Bascom hosted their lecture in August 1842.[82]

A passion for reform affected everyone. "This is a great age for reforming evils," noted the editor of the *Seneca Falls Democrat,* who quoted the ironic comment of a New York City newspaper that Bostonians had just organized a society "for the prevention of cruelty to piano-fortes," and that New York City needed an anti-bustle organization [to prevent women from wearing bustles, material drawn up on the backs of their dresses]. What we need in Seneca Falls, he added, is "an Anti-carrying-children-to-church-society." If that did not work to keep babies from crying during the singing of the choir, he recommended "the speedy formation of an Anti-marrying-society!" (The editor was a bachelor.)[83]

Debates erupted most dramatically in two interrelated areas: religion and abolitionism. In each case, individuals carried out their moral convictions by challenging established institutions. In each case, they also challenged existing gender roles. They based their challenge on both U.S. history and Christian belief, and they argued over the meaning of both the Bible and the Declaration of Independence. In each case, people focused on questions of moral and political authority within the community. Should individuals have the right to make decisions based on their own consciences? Or should they defer to institutions of family, government, and church? Should society be organized on the basis of equality among people or should power be distributed hierarchically? In this chaotic intellectual context, debates over the equality of women and men seemed a logical next step.

PART 2

The Movements: Parallel Paths

CHAPTER 4

Minding the Light: Quaker Traditions in a Changing World

It was Fourth Day, the twenty-sixth day of Third Month, 1845. Twenty-four-year-old Elizabeth M'Clintock sat quietly in the wooden, low-backed pew, hands folded in her lap, eyes closed. Outside, the day was chilly. Snow still covered the grass, but the sun shining brightly through the clear windows, combined with the heat of the wood stove, made M'Clintock warm, and she struggled against sleep. ("We believe sleeping and all other unbecoming behavior avoided," the meeting recorded that day.)[1]

A few other women sat around M'Clintock. They were dressed in a symphony of somber colors—grays, browns, and blues—reflecting their concern for simplicity in dress and speech. "Most friends are careful to keep themselves in plainness of speech behavior and apparel," they noted. Attendance was often sparse at these midweek meetings, but the stalwarts were there. Sixty-year-old Margaret Pryor had come to ask the meeting for a certificate of removal to Scipio Monthly Meeting, where she and her husband, George, lived off and on for several years. Deanna Dell Bonnel, thirty-six years old and descendent of two of the families who first organized this meeting in about 1803, was also there.[2]

The two-story wooden building in which they gathered was relatively large for a country Quaker meetinghouse. It was thirty-two feet wide by forty-two feet long, with a gallery overhead. It had been built in 1817 or 1818, two decades before the M'Clintock family became part of the meeting. One observer remembered "its plain seats and square galleries, void of all paint or ornament but scrupulously clean, its grassy yard and great trees, the carriages under the sheds and along the brown fences, the people coming from all sides, through winding roads and green lanes, from farmhouses where 'the glorious privilege of being independent' was won by honest toil, and where high thinking and plain living went together, making life rich and large."[3]

If the Spirit moved anyone in meeting, on the facing bench or in the pews, he or she could rise to speak. Sometimes many people spoke; sometimes the meeting ended as it had begun, in silence. On this day, someone shifted position, and a pew creaked. But M'Clintock centered down—focusing on the Light, listening intently with her inner ear—and sound and sense and time itself merged into a feeling of wholeness and well-being. She did not know how long she sat like this before she heard the clerk break the silence. Slowly, she opened her eyes. The monthly meeting for business of the women of Junius Monthly Meeting of Friends, Hicksite (otherwise known as Quakers), had begun.

Three years later, in July 1848, Quakers would form the single largest religious group at the Seneca Falls woman's rights convention. At least twenty-four Friends from Waterloo, Rochester, Wayne County, and elsewhere would attend the meeting. When they heard the call for a convention "to discuss the social, civil and religious condition and rights of Woman," they could respond so quickly because they had already created a strong reform network, small but efficient. Just as no woman's rights convention would have occurred in Seneca Falls in 1848 without Elizabeth Cady Stanton, so it would not have occurred without these egalitarian Friends. Stanton was the catalyst. Friends transformed the idea into action.[4]

Quaker woman's rights advocates were linked not by wealth but by a shared awareness of "that of God in every person." As one of them noted, "we are [not] all shoemakers or farmers but we 'mind the light.'"[5] Embracing a holistic worldview, these Quakers saw little separation between spirit, mind, and body. Minding the light therefore had immediate practical implications. As they followed spiritual leadings, they "let their lives speak" both inside and outside their homes. They defined their own families in egalitarian terms, incorporating parents and siblings as well as spouses and children. They also committed themselves to reform movements in the larger world, especially support for Native Americans, African Americans, and women.

These Quaker reformers consciously attempted to carry out the essence of Quakerism, as defined by its seventeenth-century founders. Yet, ironically, their commitment to practical philanthropy was part of a cataclysmic upheaval within Quaker meetings. Just as these reformers faced an economic crossroads between a preindustrial world and an emerging market economy, so they faced an institutional crossroads, between Quakers influenced by new evangelical ideas (who called themselves Orthodox Friends) and their own vision of equality. As they chose to mind their own ideas of the Light, many of them were forced to withdraw from existing Quaker meetings. That withdrawal infused energy into reform movements in the larger world, especially abolitionism and woman's rights.[6]

Three of these Quaker families—the Hunt-M'Clintock-Pryors in Waterloo, the Post-Hallowells in Rochester, and the Wright-Motts in Auburn, New York, and Philadelphia, Pennsylvania—would be key to the woman's rights movement in the 1840s. All of them had migrated to upstate New York in the 1820s or 1830s, not as individuals but as members of extended family groups, linked primarily by sibling ties.

Richard Pell Hunt was the first of the Hunt-M'Clintock-Pryor clan to arrive. In 1821, at age twenty-four, he moved from Westchester County, New York, to open a dry goods store in Waterloo. He quickly allied himself through marriage and friendship with Waterloo's two major landholders, Martin Kendig and Elisha Williams. By 1829, Hunt was wealthy enough to "retire" to a farm on the eastern edge of the village. To symbolize his new status as landholder, he built a large brick house that echoed in size and style both the Kendig and the Williams houses. The pedimented roof and Ionic columns of Hunt's new doorway, for example, duplicated the doorway of Elisha Williams's mansion.[7]

After the death of his first two wives, Richard P. Hunt married Sarah M'Clintock, a thirty-year-old Quaker from Philadelphia. Although some sources identify her as the sister of Thomas M'Clintock, she was most likely his niece and ward. In September 1837, Sarah married the forty-year-old Hunt, with Junius Monthly Meeting taking "the necessary Care . . . for her outgoing in Marriage."[8]

With her wedding, Sarah M'Clintock Hunt wove the M'Clintock and Hunt families into a large and complicated kinship network, linked by sibling ties. This network included not only their immediate families but also at least two of Richard P. Hunt's sisters, several sisters-in-law and brothers-in-law, and one of Mary Ann Wilson M'Clintock's sisters, as well.

The M'Clintock family was central to this network. Born in Delaware in 1792, Thomas M'Clintock, was forty-five years old when he moved to Waterloo. Thomas's wife, Mary Ann Wilson M'Clintock, was thirty-seven. Married since 1820, the M'Clintocks had five children aged six to sixteen at the time of their move.[9] Thomas M'Clintock was "a tall and slender man, with dark hair and eyes, finely expressive features, and an air of refined thought and benignant kindness." He had been a chemist and pharmacist in Philadelphia since 1808, and he followed the same profession in Waterloo. In December 1836, he advertised "a general assortment of Drugs and Medicines of the best qualities," as well as "an extensive assortment of BOOKS, STATIONARY, & PAPER HANGINGS, PAINTS, OIL, DYE GOODS and DRY GROCERIES (free from the labor of slaves) viz SUGARS, COFFEES, TEAS, SPICES, &c, &c."[10]

By 1839, Thomas M'Clintock had moved his store to the eastern end of a new brick business block, built by Richard P. Hunt, with large stone piers in the popular Greek Revival style. Here at No. 1 Hunt Block, Thomas M'Clintock, with the help of his daughters and his son, Charles, made a good living but never grew rich. R. H. Dun and Company considered him worth about $6,000 in 1845 and characterized him as "not w[orth] much . . . careful old Quaker," "business mod[erate] safe & prud[ent]." He earned a reputation, recalled a friend, "for the perfectness of his chemical preparations and for his strict integrity." A fellow druggist in Seneca Falls labeled him as "one of the best Druggists in Western New York." Ultimately, Thomas M'Clintock would be remembered for "the purity of his life and his single-hearted devotion to the cause of truth and practical righteousness."[11]

The M'Clintocks took education as well as business seriously. Above the store, Elizabeth M'Clintock opened a select school for girls in 1839. With Ruth Southwick, she taught chemistry, philosophy, botany, geography, grammar, astronomy, reading, writing, and arithmetic, charging her pupils three to five dollars for a twelve-week session. In 1844, Elizabeth, Mary, Julia, and Charles all attended the Waterloo Academy, a columned Greek Revival building whose "Library and Apparatus were purchased, not for *ornament,* but for *constant use.*"[12]

Through the yard behind the store, the M'Clintocks walked to the backyard of their own house, a brick building with a wooden addition at the rear, facing Williams Street. Like their store, this house belonged to Richard P. Hunt. Reflecting the mindset of the Hunts and M'Clintocks, the house embodied a transition between old values and new, between regional and national cultures. The square shape of the main house, with elliptical windows in the gables and narrow eaves, reflected vernacular, regional folk forms from southeastern Pennsylvania. But its trim incorporated new, nationally popular, Greek Revival details. Fluted Doric columns framed the front door, with sidelights and a transom to let light into the hallway. Window shutters, small window panes (nine on the top sash, six on the bottom), and four chimneys added to the house's integrity and style.[13]

A third nuclear family—George and Margaret Pryor—made up this Waterloo clan of Quaker abolitionists and woman's rights reformers. Margaret Wilson Pryor was Mary Ann Wilson M'Clintock's half sister. People often called her "Aunt Margaret," because she was literally an aunt to many of them. Born in Pennsylvania in 1785, Margaret and her husband, George, were spiritually rich, moving back and forth between Waterloo (where they were members of Junius Monthly Meeting) and Skaneateles (where they joined Scipio Monthly Meeting). They were, however, poor in wealth. According to the 1850 census, they owned no real estate. Although George had earlier been a teacher in a Quaker school in Skaneateles, by 1850 he was a farmer. Margaret ran a boardinghouse, which included a seventeen-year-old African American girl as well as seven European Americans.[14]

Like the Hunt-M'Clintock-Pryor clan in Waterloo, the Post-Hallowells in Rochester became key abolitionists and woman's rights reformers. Isaac Post and Amy Kirby Post had been born to Quaker families on Long Island (Amy in Jericho 1802 and Isaac in Westbury in 1798), and all their lives, they maintained strong connections with relatives there.[15]

Strong ties cemented this family. Isaac had first married Hannah, the oldest of the Kirby sisters. When Hannah died in 1827, he married the next oldest, Amy, who brought a third sister, Sarah, to help raise Hannah's two children as well as four more born to Amy and Isaac. In 1836, only shortly before the M'Clintocks arrived in Waterloo, Amy and Isaac Post, sister Sarah, and the children all moved to Rochester. Most of the rest of their lives, the Posts lived in a small frame house at 36 Sophia Street (later Plymouth Avenue North). When Isaac and Hannah's daughter Mary married William Hallowell, and Amy's sister Sarah married Jeffries Hallowell, the Posts extended their network to include these two additional nuclear families.[16]

Like Thomas M'Clintock, Isaac Post was a druggist. By 1840, he was doing a "smart business" at his store on Exchange Street, and took in Edmund P. Willis, his nephew, to work with him. Although the Dun and Bradstreet credit rating service feared in 1843 that Isaac Post was "too ready to endorse for his friends" and recommended "*Caution*" in dealing with him, they reported in October 1844 that he was "reputed a man of considerable prop., has just bo't a farm & we understand pd. for it." He had also amassed enough money to invest in woolen manufacture with daughter Mary's new husband, William Hallowell. By 1853, Dun and Bradstreet would call Isaac Post a "straight forward hon. man—char & hbts. unexcepble. w. 15m$ [fifteen thousand dollars] doing the largest bus. here . . . perfectly good for all wants."[17]

Amy Post was sociable, energetic, and strongly spiritual. Isaac was a steady, thoughtful, and generous man who shared both her religious and reform commitments. Together, they made their home a major center—along with the home of their friend Frederick Douglass—for radical reform in Rochester. As one local historian noted, the Post house "has ever been the hottest place in our reputed 'hot-house for isms'—so many reforms, agitations, and new questions have been furthered in its parlors."[18]

Martha Coffin Wright and her sister Lucretia Coffin Mott formed the core of a third extended, sibling-defined Quaker family. Martha was born on Christmas Day, 1806, the youngest of eight children, on the island of Nantucket. Her father, Thomas, was a ship owner and merchant, engaged in the China trade. Throughout his long absences at sea and then after his death in 1815, their mother, Anna Folger Coffin ran shops, schools, and boardinghouses. In 1824, Martha married Peter Pelham, an army captain from Kentucky. Committed to nonviolence, Quakers labeled marriage to a military man heresy, and Martha's Philadelphia meeting disowned her for it. "As thy marriage was accomplished contrary to the order of our discipline," they wrote, "thou canst not, consistently therewith, be continued in religious membership, unless thou should believe it thy duty to condemn the act." Martha acknowledged the decision in a brief note. "I do not feel willing to condemn the act of which you speak," she wrote to her Friends' meeting in Philadelphia, "but can truly say that I have much regretted the existence of a rule admitting of but one alternative." Such independent thinking would characterize her whole life.[19]

Martha followed her new husband to Pensacola, Florida, where she bore her first child, Marianna, in 1825. A year later, Peter Pelham died, leaving Martha a widow before she was twenty. To support herself and her daughter, she moved to Aurora, New York, where she taught painting and writing in her mother's school. In 1829, Martha married David Wright, a local lawyer, with whom she had six more children. In 1839, the family moved to Auburn, New York, where David practiced law.[20]

Among people she knew well, Martha Wright was an affectionate, lively, and witty person. Everyone noted her sense of humor, her "keen sense of the ludicrous." "Her pungent wit and satire," remembered Stanton, would "burst forth at unexpected moments to the surprise and delight of all of us."[21]

Throughout her life, Martha Wright had a special fondness for her older sister Lucretia. In spite of the thirteen-year difference in their ages, people often compared them. Martha was "a tall imposing woman, dignified, earnest and fine looking." Lucretia, on the other hand, weighed only eighty pounds. Lucretia was always self-possessed, never at a loss for words, while Martha was more "deliberate and reserved." Both sisters, however, "were alike earnest and sincere, accepting truth for authority and not authority for truth. I never knew," asserted Stanton, "more genuine, honest-minded women."[22]

In Auburn, neighbors considered Martha to be "an infidel" and called her "a very dangerous woman." She was never afraid to say exactly what she thought. She "went her dignified quiet way," remembered her daughter, "seemingly quite unmoved by any criticism, never deviating a hand's breadth from what she considered right."[23]

Like the economic position of these Quakers, their family patterns reflected transitions from older models to new. As Americans became increasingly urbanized, popular literature promoted a clear definition of family and gender roles. Families became places of refuge from an increasingly stressful and competitive world. While the husband-wife bond formed the essential basis of this new democratic family, the mother-child bond also became increasingly valued. Based on "companionate marriages," these were nuclear families (defined as husband, wife, and children), cut off, theoretically, from larger kin networks. Family functions were divided by gender. Outside the home, men worked in an increasingly cash-oriented economy to support their wives and children. Within the home, women, as mothers and nurturers, were central to family life, raising their children through love and persuasion, not coercion. If the family functioned well, a husband would affirm his wife's domestic decisions, and husband and wife would enjoy true companionship. In case of disagreement, however, it was the wife's duty to defer to her husband.[24]

Structurally, these Quaker families maintained characteristics more common in a preindustrial world. First, they continued to define their families as networks of kin, not as nuclear families. This allowed them to balance husband-wife and mother-child bonds—the primary family dyads in emerging urban middle-class families—with strong sibling and adult child-parent ties. Maintaining links between birth families and families created by marriage gave women as well as men a web of interlocking ties and a multiplicity of socially valued roles. No one relationship overshadowed all the others. Second, as people in the dominant culture began to separate private and public spaces, these Quakers continued to blur the boundaries between home and the world. Their homes were not refuges from the world but the basis for creating communities.

Such a definition of family reinforced respect for women. Inherently egalitarian, sibling bonds functioned outside the dominance-submission model of gender relationships promoted in the larger society. They were unregulated by law. Nor were they laden with sexual expectations. They might also be tempered by time and shared experience. An older sister might be respected in part because she had taken care of her siblings. Sisters or brothers who were good organizers (or good hosts or good letter writers) might become important family anchors.[25]

Children's names reflected the importance of families of origin. The M'Clintock family was typical. Their first child was a daughter, whom they named Elizabeth Wilson, after Mary Ann's mother. They named their second child after Mary Ann herself. When their son, Charles, was born in 1829, they gave him his mother's maiden name, Wilson, as a middle name.[26]

When these Friends moved into western New York, they used a pattern of chain migration, following their parents and siblings. The Post and Wright families illustrated this pattern. Amy Post followed her married sister Hannah to central New York. After Hannah's death, Amy married Hannah's widower, Isaac, and brought her younger sister Sarah to live with them. Later, Isaac's nephew Edmund P. Willis joined the Post household from Long Island. "He seems bound up with you," wrote his mother, "and no ordinary circumstance possesses power to shake his steadfastness." After Sarah's first husband died, she married Edmund Willis, making her not only Isaac's sister-in-law but also his niece-in-law.[27] Amy Kirby Post's parents, too, tried to sell their farm to be with their daughter. Her mother, Mary Kirby, was keenly disappointed when an auction produced no purchasers. She had hoped that "Sisters being Settled near together" might "blunt the keeness of our sepperation."[28] Martha Wright first came to central New York with her mother, Anna Coffin, and her cousin Rebecca Bunker. Their school did not succeed. Although Martha's marriage to David Wright kept her in Auburn, she spent weeks of every year with her sisters in Philadelphia, and Lucretia Mott spent more weeks each year visiting the Wrights.[29]

In their marriage patterns, too, these Quakers reinforced bonds between adult sisters and brothers and between parents and children. Before they married, adult children sought approval from their parents. Marriages of cousins, while not the norm, were nevertheless accepted. Martha Wright's oldest daughter, Marianna Pelham, married her cousin, Thomas Mott (Lucretia Mott's son) in 1845.[30]

These families also defined their boundaries in a way that differed from the emerging popular ideal. Unlike nuclear families, which incorporated only husband, wife, and children, these households had porous edges. They frequently took responsibility not only for extended family members but also for unrelated people. These might include servants, boarders, laborers, or children in need of care. The M'Clintocks counted two African American girls in their household in 1850, for example.

They also created networks among families, transcending individual households. Richard P. Hunt, for example, supported his nuclear family, including Jane Hunt, his wife, and six children, in one household, but he also gave at least some assistance to two sisters Lydia Mount and Hannah Plant and their four daughters.[31]

Often, Quakers seemed to think of their households as unlimited, embracing not only their own communities but the world. Reformers often referred, for example, not to the Post family but to "the Post circle." Even Martha Wright, so "retired and quiet" that Frederick Douglass "felt a delicacy about intruding," made their house a home for abolitionist speakers, people seeking freedom from slavery, and woman's rights advocates. "I never knew any one so hospitable," her daughter recalled, "except my Aunt Lucretia."[32]

The M'Clintocks, too, used their house as a dynamic reform center. Former critic Thomas Mumford, born into a slave-owning Episcopalian family in Beaufort, North Carolina, recalled that

> once admitted to the privileges of such a refined and cordial home, there was no possibility of giving them up. Nowhere else could we find such fresh literature, or such intelligent interest in vital questions of the day. . . . That house was our gateway into the widest realms of thought and the richest fields of duty. The family were the teachers to whom we owe the best part of our education. . . . Such hospitality is seldom witnessed. There was seldom an empty bed, or a vacant seat at the table. Famous and friendless guests often sat together there, and colors and creeds were alike forgotten.[33]

Structurally, the M'Clintock-Hunt-Pryors, Post-Hallowells, and Wright-Motts represented an older, rural pattern of family life, dominant in colonial America but declining in the early nineteenth century. In such families, homes were centers of both production and reproduction, the basis of both private and public life, part of interlocking networks of parents, siblings, and spouses. They were not havens from the world. Instead, they were the very basis of community life. Although we know less about the families of other signers, we do know that these Quaker family patterns were not unlike Stanton's own.[34]

Culturally, these Quaker homes also explicitly reflected a belief that women and men expressed the Inner Light, so they defined husband-wife relationships in terms of equality and mutual respect. According to one who knew them well, Thomas and Mary Ann M'Clintock were "equal heads of the family." Women and men shared both status and decision-making power, reflecting Lucretia Mott's favorite wedding advice, "In the true marriage relationship the independence of the husband and wife is equal, their dependence mutual, and their obligations reciprocal."[35]

Quaker marriage ceremonies reflected this vision. A Quaker man and woman married each other, without the external authority of priest or minister. The marriage of Thomas M'Clintock and Mary Ann Wilson in Burlington, New Jersey, on January 13, 1820, was typical. Thomas M'Clintock, "taking the said Mary Ann Wilson by the hand, did, on this solemn occasion, openly declare, that he took the said Mary Ann Wilson to be his Wife, promising with Divine assistance to be unto her a loving and faithful Husband until Death should separate them; and then, in the same assembly, the said Mary Ann Wilson, did, in like manner declare, that she took him the said Thomas M'Clintock to be her Husband, promising with Divine assistance to be unto him a loving and faithful Wife until Death should separate them."[36] Like most Quaker brides and grooms, Thomas and Mary Ann then signed a marriage certificate, describing what they had said. Everyone who attended the wedding also signed the certificate, as witnesses. These names appeared in no particular order. Sometimes (but not always) parents of the newly married couple appeared toward the top, but the lists were not usually separated by gender, age, or other relationship.

Naming patterns also indicated relative gender equality in Quaker families. While women generally took their husbands' names when they married, they did so not to indicate submersion in their husbands' identities but to follow, as marriage certificates generally recorded, "the custom of Marriage." Sometimes, wives were buried under their maiden names rather than their married names. Rachel Dell Bonnel, for example, was listed on her gravestone under her maiden name.[37]

Such an emphasis on equality between husbands and wives did not lead to constant bickering, as critics feared. Quaker marriages seemed relatively happy, some of them even extraordinarily so. "What a noble and truthful tribute does *Amy* pay to *Isaac* Post," wrote William C. Nell to Amy, "in saying '*I wish every woman was as happily yoked as I am!*'" Martha and David Wright differed on many issues, including woman's rights. She was much more reform-oriented than he was, and she never hesitated to say so. Perhaps because she was able to disagree with him so frankly, however, she also openly expressed her affection. From her sister's house in Philadelphia, she wrote to David in 1839 that "I enjoy my visits more, it seems to me, than I ever did before, but my thoughts revert to you, my love, with warmest affection."[38]

* * *

These Quaker families were linked by a worldview that differed in significant ways not only from the dominant culture around them but also from other Quaker groups. Quakerism was not a monolith, and these Friends were at the edge of many established Quaker meetings. Their commitment to equality forced them to test the boundaries (and eventually to go beyond the boundaries) of the tradition that had shaped them.

Although Richard P. Hunt's name does not appear on the extant membership lists of the Junius Monthly Meeting, he was born into a Quaker family, and Elizabeth Cady Stanton remembered him as one of a "trio of good men" (including Thomas M'Clintock and Henry Bonnell) who, with their families, "were the life" of the annual meetings of Friends of Human Progress. His son, William, recalled him as a Quaker "who believed that 'faith without works is dead' and who practiced his spirituality in the world rather than in the meeting house."[39]

Like Hunt, Martha Wright was not officially a member of any Quaker meeting after her disownment in 1825. Nevertheless, she continued to identify herself as a Friend. "My parents," she later told a student from Auburn Seminary, "were Quakers, and I am one." Like the Hunts, the Wright family did not join any Quaker meeting (Auburn itself had none), nor did the family attend services at any other church. Some of their neighbors found this upsetting. When fourteen-year-old Eliza Wright visited neighbor Sarah Bostwick, "Mrs B. asked her," reported Martha, "if she never went to meeting—'no'—nor didn't any of us? 'no' 'rather heathenish' sd. Mrs. B.—which Eliza thought rather impolite (which is worse than heathenish). She might have told," reflected Martha, "that her parents held meetings at home, and as for sermons the children hear them every day and lectures too."[40]

Unlike the Hunts and the Wrights, the Posts, M'Clintocks, and Pryors were solidly a part of organized Quaker life. Quaker born and bred, they continued to play an active role in monthly, quarterly, and yearly meetings until the mid-1840s. Thomas M'Clintock was a prominent Quaker scholar and minister, deeply rooted in Quaker literature and history, and one of the leaders among Friends, both in Philadelphia and in western New York. By 1835, Lucretia Mott called him "a biblical scholar of some renown." Isaac and Amy Post staunchly maintained their Quaker connections, even when they were divided from their local meeting by their abolitionist convictions.[41]

By 1845, however, the M'Clintocks and the Posts, too, found themselves pushed to the periphery of the Quaker establishment. The Posts withdrew from Rochester Monthly Meeting in 1845. The M'Clintocks left Junius Monthly Meeting in 1848. Even when they finally chose to leave, however, they did not choose to worship alone. So attached were they to corporate worship that the Posts attended "free meetings" in Rochester in the mid-1840s. And when the M'Clintocks withdrew from Genesee Yearly Meeting in 1848, they organized a new Quaker meeting, the Congregational Friends. Amy and Isaac Post were among its staunchest members.

Whether Quakers by birth or by continuing commitment, the M'Clintocks and Hunts, Martha Wright, Lucretia Mott, and the Posts belonged to a group that, even more than Baptists, reflected an emphasis on individual conscience and on a personal relationship with God. The Bible was not the only source of religious truth, these Quakers believed. Through the Inner Light, shining in every person, God's own Spirit still spoke in human hearts. George Fox, seventeenth-century mystic and founder of Quakerism, described the insight that led to his own path out of spiritual chaos in 1647: "There is one, even Christ Jesus," he recorded, "that can speak to thy condition." "What had any to do with the Scriptures," Fox asked crowds all over England, "but as they came to the Spirit that gave them forth. You will say, Christ saith this, and the apostles say this; but what canst thou say? Art thou a child of Light and hast walked in the Light, and what thou speakest is it inwardly from God?" Quakers gave many names to the Spirit. They called it the Light, the Royal Seed, the Bread of Life, the Wisdom, the Truth's Voice, and that of God in every one. Whatever its name, they knew that it must be experienced personally (or "experimentally," as they often said).[42]

Howard Brinton, author of the classic *Friends for Three Hundred Years,* placed Quakers firmly in the mystical tradition. What saved Quakers from anarchy, argued Brinton, was their parallel emphasis on a corporate identity. Individuals were certainly led by God. The Truth of personal leadings, however, would be tested within local meetings. Quakers reflected, reaffirmed, and sought to resolve this tension between individualism and community every time they met together for worship or business.[43]

Quakers not only insisted that the Inner Light must be experienced personally and corporately, but they also believed that the Light was universal, inherent in every human being. The Light, they often said, was the inner gospel, "preached to every creature under heaven." All could possess the "Light and Spirit of God." Such Quaker universalism was the basis for Friends' testimony against war. As George Fox said, he lived "in the virtue of that life and power that took away the occasion of all wars." It also led to respect for other living creatures, to a sense of "unity with the creation." And it led to an inclusiveness that puzzled and alarmed more traditional Christians. From a Quaker perspective, "all such may be honored as stand in the life of the truth." So Quakers preached to Native Americans and African Americans as well as to Europeans and Turks, to poor as well as rich, to women as well as men.[44]

Concern for "that of God in everyone" led Quakers to express early opposition to slavery. While George Fox himself never advocated abolitionism, he did preach to African Americans as well as European Americans in the New World. Much of the credit for Quaker abolitionism belonged to John Woolman, a New Jersey tailor, whose travels as a Quaker minister in the 1740s and 1750s brought him to see slavery's effects first-hand and to plead eloquently for its abolition.[45]

Ideals of equality also led Quakers to welcome women as well as men. As early as 1656, George Fox wrote a pamphlet defending the right of women to prophesy. A second one followed, *Concerning Sons and Daughters, and Prophetesses speaking and Prophesying in the Law and the Gospel.* In 1666, Margaret Fell, one of George Fox's early converts, wrote a pathbreaking book, *Women's Speaking Justified,* while serving a four-year prison sentence. Three years later, Margaret Fell, then a fifty-five-year-old widow with eight children, married George Fox, ten years her junior. Their marriage became a model egalitarian relationship for Quakers.[46]

Schisms plagued Quakers in the nineteenth century, shattering Friends into several different factions. In the process, however, Quaker energies were released into the larger world, and Quakers became some of the most influential leaders in major reform movements, including abolitionism and, most particularly, woman's rights. Historians of Quakerism have generally viewed these years of schism as a tragedy, "the darkest and saddest in the history of Quakerism." Yet for Quaker women, Nancy Hewitt argued, these splits may have been "a historical moment when the disruption and decline of male authority was accompanied by the nurturance and expansion of woman's power." Such splits shattered a Quaker power structure that had crystallized around male-dominated meetings of ministers and elders. In so doing, they opened opportunities for some Quaker women to express themselves more fully not only within the Society of Friends but also outside of it.[47]

In the 1820s, Friends throughout the United States struggled with differences over theology and structure that split the Society apart. In 1827–28, two major groups—Hicksites and Orthodox—claimed to be the true heirs of seventeenth-century Quaker founders. Each side agreed that "there is one, even Christ Jesus, that can speak to thy condition." The Orthodox, however, identified Jesus as divine, the only Son of God. They emphasized the Bible as the only revealed word of God. And they believed that Christ's death was an atonement for inherent human sin. The Hicksites, on the other hand, equated Christ with the Indwelling Spirit. The Bible itself could be understood only by those who listened to the Inner Light, the "Christ Within," and who accepted the fact that God continued to speak to each person, every day. Ongoing revelation and personal experience, not Bible reading and Christ's death on the Cross, were the essentials of such Quakerism. Influenced strongly by Elias Hicks, a Long Island Quaker, such Friends came to be known as Hicksites.[48]

Thomas M'Clintock was a major Hicksite leader, "the most resourceful and talented of all the Philadelphia reformers," "an exact, thoughtful, and tolerant man of balance and insight, always careful about speaking the truth." In 1826, M'Clintock edited the first volume of Elias Hicks's *Sermons,* and in 1831, he worked on an eight-volume publication of the *Works* of George Fox.[49] In 1837, M'Clintock summarized his own basic beliefs. The "evidence of the spirit" was "the only true authority of the scriptures to every individual mind," he argued, and "the testimony of the spirit in the heart is to be *the rule.*"[50]

The M'Clintocks were one of the last families in a lengthy Quaker migration from eastern New York, southeastern Pennsylvania, and New Jersey. In 1815, these immigrants formed Junius Monthly Meeting. Of the 199 members of this meeting, 168 became Hicksites who helped organize Genesee Yearly Meeting in 1834.[51]

These Quakers retained traditional values. In 1840, people still referred to Thomas M'Clintock as an "old Quaker," although he was only forty-eight years old, because his dress and long flowing hair reminded them of George Fox. Henry Bonnel refused to pay war taxes and consequently "suffered much from fines and imprisonment, and distraint of his goods." Amy Post continued to use "thee" and "thou." So did Elizabeth M'Clintock. The M'Clintocks kept the older spelling of their name even when contemporaries began to change it to "McClintock."[52]

In their commitment to equality, Quaker reform families—including the Hunts-M'Clintocks-Pryors, Post-Hallowells, and Wright-Motts—reflected a holistic worldview. They believed that change could not be piecemeal but must be integrated into all of life. Distinctions between public and private, male and female, old and young, African American, European American, or Native American, rich and poor, love and work, family and community, home and the world, and eventually even life and death were blurred or nonexistent. So they pursued all reforms at once, inside their families as well as in the larger world.

As centers of community life, homes also became centers of reform. Parents often passed their radical views on to their children. Benjamin and Sarah Fish's family, all members of Rochester Monthly Meeting, offered one model. Their daughter Catharine, born in 1824, early became a reformer. At twelve years old, she was collecting signatures on antislavery petitions. When she was fifteen, her family banished all wine from the household. Catharine and her sister also kept an anti-tobacco pledge on the parlor table, which they asked their young male friends to sign. The Fish family lived for a brief period at a utopian community in Sodus Bay, northwest of Rochester. There Catharine met and married antislavery agent Giles B. Stebbins. When they went to Niagara Falls on their honeymoon in August 1846, they invited the whole Post-Hallowell family to go with them, including Amy and Isaac Post; Amy's sister Sarah Hallowell; and Amy's stepdaughter Mary, along with Mary's husband, William Hallowell. In July 1848, all the women of this honeymoon party—Amy Post, Sarah Hallowell, Mary Hallowell, and Catharine Fish Stebbins—signed the Seneca Falls Declaration of Sentiments.[53]

Other Quaker families followed similar patterns. Martha Wright's brother-in-law "was amused to find M.A. [Marianna, Martha's oldest child] and the other children such strong abolitionists." Like Gerrit Smith, Martha Wright had slave-owning relatives. When William Pelham, her Kentucky-born, slave-owning brother-in-law (her first husband's brother), came to visit, he talked freely about his own eight slaves, four adults and four children. He meant to free them, he said, when he died. "David tried to get him to take a [reform] paper," Martha commented, "but he didn't choose any."[54]

Reflecting a concern with immediate and complete change, change that incorporated families, many of these Quakers supported communitarian experiments, especially those based on the work of eighteenth-century philosopher Charles Fourier. All of these intentional communities consciously defined family, gender roles, and property rights differently than did the mainstream culture around them. Nuclear families became less important; the community itself became a family. While women often continued to perform "women's work" in housewifery and child care, they also often found new opportunities in farm or factory work. Individual ownership of property became less important than communal ownership.

Fourier advocated social harmony, based on the creative expression of each person's individual gifts and the communal ownership of property. Albert Brisbane, who promoted Fourierism through the pages of the *New York Tribune,* spoke in August 1843 to "a large and highly respectable audience" in Seneca Falls.[55]

Perhaps Thomas M'Clintock was among them, for when abolitionist John A. Collins set up a Fourieristic community near Skaneateles, New York, Thomas M'Clintock was impressed enough to sign a public letter of support and to consider moving there himself. George and Margaret Pryor did just that, attracted by the allure of working "not for the benefit of any particular class, but for the entire race," to battle not merely against the effects of evil but against its causes. "Society is based upon antagonisms," argued the communitarians. "Men cannot practically obey the great precept of our Savior—'Love thy neighbor as thyself.' . . . The equality of the race is no where recognized. Men must first place themselves in love relations."[56]

Martha Wright was curious but considerably more skeptical. "I was amused," she noted, "at an intimation from some of the communities, mentioned in the [National Anti-Slavery] Standard, that what they wanted now was *working bees,* they had enough of *drones*—After all I opine human *nature* is pretty much the same, in & out of communities—My taste is decidedly to hire others to do the laborious part of living, while I rest—if I can—When money is as scarce as provisions are in the Skats. community—let one's inclination be as it may, the only way is to grub & work, & sweep & dust, & wash & dress children, make gingerbread, and patch & darn." Of the interest shown by the Pryors and M'Clintocks, she remarked bemusedly that "I should have thought that Mrs. Pryor would long ago have done as Mary Ann McClintock proposed doing—keep their own house in readiness, & stay there, ready to receive her husband when he was tired. I should think all the rest would go forthwith to the asylum."[57]

Three reforms—woman's rights, Indian affairs, and antislavery—highlighted most visibly the egalitarian, holistic world-view of these Quaker families. Each concern emerged from Quaker activities. Each would lead Quakers to work with the "world's people." In so doing, each would lead them one step further out of the tradition that had given them birth. When forced to choose between membership in the Society of Friends and their own egalitarian vision, they would chose to follow their vision. The turning point came in 1842, when Genesee Yearly Meeting incorporated equality between women's and men's meetings, Seneca Indians lost their lands at Tonawanda, and the American Anti-Slavery Society initiated a new and aggressive campaign.

The first change reflected a vision of equality between women and men. Historically, separate Quaker women's meetings had provided the basis for women's growth. In 1831, *The Friend; or, Advocate of Truth* noted that Quaker women had "intelligence, sound sense, considerateness, discretion . . . that is not found in any other class of women, as a class," and attributed these qualities to "an extensive and a separate share" that women played within Quaker meetings.[58] Working with other women, Lucretia Mott, Abby Kelley, Amy Post, the M'Clintocks, Margaret Pryor, and Martha Wright learned whatever they knew about self-respect, letting their lives speak, and public organizing.

Although women Friends conducted their business separately from men, men's meetings had veto power. "Women's monthly meetings are not to receive nor disown members without the concurrence of men's monthly meetings," read the discipline of New York Yearly Meeting.[59] In June 1838, Genesee Yearly Meeting decided to do something about this inequity. Acting on a proposal initiated by Junius Monthly Meeting, Genesee Yearly Meeting agreed to revise the Discipline to reflect absolute equality between men's and women's meetings, so "that men and women shall stand on the same footing in all matters in which they are equally concerned." When Genesee Yearly Meeting reprinted the *Discipline* in 1842, they noted that "male and female are one in Christ Jesus," and "men's and women's meetings stand on the equal footing of common interest and common right."[60]

As Quaker women began to speak in public, their ideas of gender equality influenced people in the wider world. Although the earliest female lecturers—English woman Fanny Wright and African American Maria W. Stewart—were not Quakers, Quaker women dominated the small group of women speakers who emerged from the abolitionist movement of the mid-1830s. Sarah and Angelina Grimké had become "convinced Friends" in the 1820s. Abby Kelley's mother was a Quaker and had raised her children as Quakers. Lucretia Mott was thoroughly rooted in Quakerism. William Lloyd Garrison allied himself with Quaker women and publicized their work through the *Liberator.*

Their interest in woman's rights also led them to read and absorb other woman's rights literature. Isaac Post's sister recommended the *Liberator* to him, for example, because it supported antislavery, peace, and woman's rights. Sarah Grimké's *Letters on the Equality of the Sexes and the Condition of Woman* also met with their approval. Sarah Hallowell wrote to sister Amy Post in 1838 that "cousin Henry" had a copy of "Sarah Grimke's letters on woman's rights."[61] Jacob Ferris, an antislavery lecturer and a member of Galen Preparative Meeting of Junius Monthly Meeting, echoed Sarah Grimke's language when he described the attitude of both women and men in the Galen Anti-Slavery Society. "Women's duty and accountability to God are the same as those of man," wrote Ferris. "Therefore, they are both equal in religious rights. In the sight of God there is 'neither male nor female.'"[62]

Some of them, at least, read and agreed with British writer Mary Wollstonecraft's 1795 *Vindication of the Rights of Woman,* the first full-length feminist book in English. Lucretia Mott discovered Wollstonecraft by the 1820s. Martha Wright mischievously used Wollstonecraft to startle conservative visitors. "When I am expecting anybody that will be shocked," she wrote to her sister, Lucretia, "I hunt up Mary Wollstoncraft's Right of woman . . . or something of that sort of Electrical Machine to display on the table."[63]

In their personal lives, Quakers tried to carry out their ideals of woman's rights. In 1846, Martha and David Wright discussed why they paid Thomas, their gardener, more than they paid Miss Soule, their seamstress. "I don't see why a woman should not have the chances of laying up something against the age of rheumatisms and poor sight, as a man," Martha argued. David disagreed: "Why, a man had a family to support." But, Martha retorted, "half the laboring men's wives support the family and their husbands beside—by taking in washing, &c." "David went off," concluded Martha, "to hoe his corn or cut asparagus and wouldn't hear any more such nonsense."[64]

Martha and David Wright thought of sending their daughter Eliza to study medicine at the proposed new homeopathic college in Auburn. "How nice it would be," thought David, "for Eliza to study medicine." Martha thought so, too, as long as they had special classes for ladies. "I don't see why there might not be women physicians," Martha wrote to Lucretia Mott in 1846, "though in difficult cases I think I should *rayther* prefer a real bona fide doctor." In 1848, Elizabeth Blackwell graduated from the Geneva Medical College (along with Peter Wilson, a Seneca Indian) to become the first "real bona fide" woman doctor (as opposed to a homeopathic doctor) in the United States.[65]

Since the Bible was such an important source of ideas for Americans in the 1840s, these women became very adept at finding biblical support for their egalitarian ideas. Auburn was home to the Auburn Theological Seminary, a training school for Presbyterian ministers, and Martha Wright delighted in what she saw as their theological backwardness. She gleefully reported an anecdote about a male student in confrontation with the wife of a local doctor, who thought "that women were capable of managing matters much better than men were willing to admit." The young man brought a Bible and inquired "if that book didn't say that Man should be the head of the family." "'Yes,'" replied Mrs. Dr. Smith, "'and doesn't the same book say that woman is a *crown* to her husband?'" "David thought," confided Martha, "that if he was the head and she the crown to the head, she was certainly 'top of the heap.'"[66]

The second major issue dealt with Native Americans. When Native Americans lost most of their land to European Americans after the American Revolution, they faced economic realities that strained existing gender roles. In New York, traditional Haudenosaunee culture was organized around female-headed clans. Each clan included all of the clan mother's daughters and grandchildren. As heads of families, women controlled the land, not in the European American sense of holding title to it but in the Indian sense of using it. Political power reflected the importance of Iroquois women in both production and reproduction. Motherhood became the basis for status and respect. Clan mothers chose the chiefs, and women were one of the three major interest groups, along with the chiefs and the warriors. When the Haudenosaunee lost most of their lands after the American Revolution, men spent less time hunting and more in farming, and women were encouraged to turn from farming to housewifery.[67]

When Congress passed the Indian Removal Act of 1830, most Native Americans east of the Mississippi were forced to leave their homelands for new territory in the West. With the help of sympathetic whites, led by Quakers, some Senecas successfully resisted this pressure. In the 1830s, when Senecas faced the loss of the Tonawanda reservation west of Rochester, Quakers actively supported them. Sympathizing wholeheartedly with their "Indian brothers," who were "likely to be robbed of their *property,* by a powerful and unprincipled company of Speculators," Friends invited Seneca chiefs and warriors into their meetinghouses and circulated petitions on their behalf, both among Friends and among "the world's people," obtaining signatures "from *all kinds* of religious and political parties, civil and *military officers.*" One petition went to Congress in February 1841 from Rush, a township near Rochester. Six more went from Cayuga County. As one Friend noted in 1842, "We pulled the wires, and these '*worlds people*' danced to them."[68]

Seneca women, too, actively defended their land. In March 14, 1842, eight Seneca women, representing 207 women at the Tonawanda Reservation, signed a petition (perhaps written with the help of Amy Post) to President John Tyler. Minerva BlackSmith, Widow Little Beard, Susan BlackSmith, Jo-no-que-no, Gar-near-no-wih, O-no-do, De-wa-does, and Gar-e-was-ha-dus declared, "We are astonished to hear that the Tonawanda Reservation, we have to give up. All our women of the other reservations, of the Seneca Nation, are of the same mind, all are in trouble." "We the women of the Tonawanda," they continued, "have exerted our influence, in trying to have our Chiefs to be united in their mind in their councils & they have done so,—not one of our Chiefs here, have signed the Treaty. . . . You may be astonished to hear this from us," the women acknowledged, "as we have never done so [sent a petition] before. We think much, and are attached to these places, which the Great Spirit has given to his Red children of the Country." In spite of such a heartfelt appeal, the Senecas lost both the Tonawanda and Buffalo Creek homelands. With Quaker help, however, they renegotiated the 1838 Treaty of Buffalo Creek and managed to regain the Cattaraugus and Allegany Reservations.[69]

Abolitionism was the third major reform. In 1827, when a few Pennsylvania Quakers began to boycott all goods made with slave labor, Thomas M'Clintock became the first secretary of the Free Produce Society. After the M'Clintocks moved to Waterloo, they continued to promote goods "free from the labor of slaves." They wore linen or wool instead of cotton and used maple sugar or honey instead of cane sugar. When Sarah M'Clintock Hunt died in 1842, she explicitly requested that her body not be wrapped in slave-grown cotton but in "tow cloth," that is, linen.[70]

Waterloo was among the earliest of upstate villages to respond to antislavery organizing. As early as December 1836, the same month that Thomas M'Clintock bought Samuel Lundy's drugstore, twenty Waterloo residents formed their own antislavery society. Twenty-five people in nearby Macedon, probably also members of Junius Monthly Meeting, formed an antislavery society in April 1837. They faced considerable opposition. As late as 1846, neither the courthouse nor any of the churches were open to antislavery lecturers. Only one "upper chamber" in Waterloo (quite possibly the room above Thomas M'Clintock's drugstore) was available for abolitionist gatherings. But abolitionists persisted; they signed petitions, hosted lecturers, sold literature, organized fairs, and offered a haven to people escaping from slavery. In February 1839, Waterloo abolitionists sent several representatives to the Antislavery Convention of Western New York, held in Penn Yan. Richard P. Hunt and Sarah Hunt both attended. So did George and Margaret Pryor.[71]

In Rochester, beginning in 1835, abolitionists organized three separate societies: a Rochester City Anti-Slavery Society (whose contact person was George A. Avery, Henry B. Stanton's brother-in-law), a Rochester Female Anti-Slavery Society, and a Rochester Female Colored Anti-Slavery Society. By 1837, noted the *Liberator,* the men's society in Rochester had seven hundred members and was the second largest in the country. The four-hundred-member female society (probably by now including both whites and blacks) was the largest women's antislavery organization in the United States.[72]

Local antislavery societies found an immediate focus in the antislavery petition campaign. Seneca County was no exception. In March 1838, Thomas M'Clintock and his son, Charles, supported a petition to remove the "foul blot" of slavery by the prohibition of "this inhuman traffic between the states." Among the sixty male signers were several other Quakers, including Azaliah Schooley, William S. Dell, Richard Dell, and Richard P. Hunt. A year later, in February 1839, local petitioning reached its pinnacle when Waterloo citizens sent twelve separate petitions to Congress. For the first time, women participated. Six petitions carried women's names only. Four had only men's names. Two more included the names of men and women together.

The petition campaign joined people from several different religious traditions into one national effort. In Waterloo, Mary Ann Gridley, Presbyterian, gathered signatures from several Episcopalians. Heading two more petitions were the names of Mary Ann M'Clintock and Elizabeth W. M'Clintock. Farther down the list, Mary Ann and Sarah M'Clintock signed, noting their ages (sixteen and fourteen).[73]

Year after year for more than a decade (in 1838–39, in 1844, in 1849, and again in 1850), abolitionists from Seneca County, centered in Waterloo, gathered at least 1,315 signatures on at least eighteen antislavery petitions. Because most people signed two or three or even more petitions, the total number of people who participated in this campaign was probably about four hundred. Men alone signed nine of these petitions; women alone signed seven. Two petitions carried signatures of both women and men.[74]

In Rochester as in Waterloo, Quakers participated in the petition movement. Benjamin and Sarah Fish signed the large 1836 petition. So did Mary Post. In the fall of 1837, Amy Post signed a large petition from the women of western New York. In December 1838, Isaac Post joined 156 other male citizens of Rochester in requesting Congress to reconsider a resolution to table all antislavery petitions, believing that this "virtually denies to Americans the sacred & constitutional *right of Petition,* a right, in the opinion of your memorialists, quite as important to *northern* freemen, as the '*patriarchal*' or any other '*peculiar institution*' possibly can be to *southern* citizens."[75]

With startling swiftness, ordinary Quakers moved directly into the national abolitionist movement, transcending purely Quaker concerns. In September 1839, Thomas M'Clintock made his own position public, as he transmitted to the *Liberator* a letter written by abolitionist agent James C. Jackson to "two women of this vicinity" (perhaps those in the M'Clintock household). The rights of women were the prime concern, and William Lloyd Garrison was the hero. "The great point in the cause of human rights, to be settled *now,*" Jackson argued, "is, whether woman is henceforth to be regarded as the equal coadjutor of man, in *man and woman's redemption;* and the antislavery cause will not progress one whit till we settle this point. . . . Who shall rally if woman does not?" asked Jackson, echoed by Thomas M'Clintock.[76]

The following spring, Thomas M'Clintock and Richard P. Hunt sent Garrison a practical gift, four yards of "super olive mixed" woolen cloth, made in the Waterloo Woolen Mills, "free from the taint of slavery." Garrison planned to wear his new "*free suit*" on his forthcoming trip to the World Anti-Slavery Convention in London, and he praised M'Clintock lavishly:

> You have a soul capable of embracing the largest idea of humanity. . . . I regard you as one of those whose countrymen are all the rational creatures of God, whether they are found on "Greenland's icy mountains," or on "India's coral strand"—whether their complexion be white, red, or any other color—whether they are civilized or savage, christians or heathens, elevated in point of intelligence and power, or sunken in degradation and helplessness. When this spirit shall universally prevail among men, there will be no more wars, no more slavery, no more injustice. Then will be held the jubilee of the human race; and every thing that hath breath shall praise the name of the Lord.[77]

A year later, in an article in the *National Anti-Slavery Standard,* M'Clintock explained his own vision. "Religion," he argued, "has been emphatically embodied, not in speculative theories, but in practical righteousness, in active virtues, in reverence to God, in benevolence to man—the latter being the only sure test of the former." "Where much is given," he advised, "much is required. We

Thomas M'Clintock and his family were key players in the new organization of Congregational Friends (Friends of Human Progress) and in the Seneca Falls woman's rights convention. The Declaration of Sentiments was written in the parlor of their home in Waterloo, and daughters Elizabeth and Mary Ann M'Clintock were major organizers of the convention. From John Becker, *History of Waterloo* (Waterloo, New York: Waterloo Library and Historical Society, 1949). Reprinted by permission of Waterloo Library and Historical Society.

are all stewards of the grace of God. We must use our talents for "the renovation of the world."[78] And use his talents he did. In the 1840s, M'Clintock threw himself wholeheartedly into antislavery activity. He became an agent for the *Liberator,* sold antislavery almanacs, lectured on abolitionism, wrote abolitionist articles, organized local antislavery meetings, and became an officer in the American Anti-Slavery Society.[79]

Abolitionist activities entailed an economic cost. His business suffered, and a one-time opponent noted that "he was really an object of dread to us," and that "an insulting effigy was once attached to his sign." Townspeople objected to M'Clintock's theological views, noted fellow reformer Giles B. Stebbins, as well as to his antislavery activity. "We come to you as friends," they told M'Clintock, "to warn you that your bold preaching and your open association with these heretics and fanatics will greatly hurt your business. We have no objection to your having what opinions you please, but your course is very distasteful to many people, and will injure you." M'Clintock thanked them for coming but noted, "I was trained up to obey the monitions of the spirit, and be true to my best light. . . . I must speak the truth, and abide the consequences."[80]

Isaac T. Hopper, New York City bookseller and printer, was the most famous example of what could happen to Quakers who promoted radical abolitionism. When he supported publication of an article critical of conservative Quakers, New York Yearly Meeting charged him with exciting "discord and disunity among friends" and disowned him.[81] This act served as a catalyst for liberal Friends in Genesee Yearly Meeting. James C. Jackson addressed an open letter to M'Clintock and Griffith M. Cooper in the *National Anti-Slavery Standard* on April 8, 1841. Jackson recognized the historic importance of Quakers as abolitionists. But, he asked, "What then is the actual condition of the Society of Friends, as respects their testimony upon slavery at the present day? Have they the spirit of their fathers, or are they wearing their off-cast robe?" "*No* society can preserve its unity," he emphasized, "who will not bow itself to the slave's redemption." Which way would Genesee Yearly Meeting go? What would Thomas M'Clintock and Griffith Cooper do? In Rochester, people were asking Amy and Isaac Post the same questions. "What will be the course of *your* Yearly Meeting?" Oliver Johnson queried in June 1842.

Isaac and Amy Post feared that they, like Isaac Hopper, would be forced to leave the Society of Friends. They asked advice from John Ketcham, who belonged to the Friends' antislavery association in New York City. Ketcham responded, "I am . . . not far from thy sentiment that our light (if we have any) would be more likely to shine where it would do good by uniting with all without distinction of Sect or creed." There is "warfare going on at the East," he told them, "between Antislavery and the Church. . . . *Church* is *Church,* wherever it be, and . . . it would be dificult to find one that is right unless it be our friend Lucretia's church, 'Thy sect is the righteous of Earth.'"[82]

Abolitionist radicalism precipitated dissension not only among Friends but within the American Anti-Slavery Society. When supporters of William Lloyd Garrison and woman's rights packed the May 1840 meeting in New York City, Abby Kelley stood at the center of this storm. Her election to the Executive Committee of the American Anti-Slavery Society in May 1840 was the final blow to maintaining a cohesive organization. Kelley herself felt an increasing conflict between her commitment to abolitionism and her membership in the Society of Friends, and in 1841, she resigned from her Uxbridge, Massachusetts, meeting. "The fundamental principles of the Society have . . . taken deep root in my heart," she assured the Uxbridge Monthly Meeting, and she was "filled with surprise, and bowed down with grief, in view of the fact that the New England Yearly Meeting, of which we were a part, took ground in direct opposition to its own professed principles on the question of slavery." Without waiting to be disowned, Abby Kelley took the initiative: "I hereby disown all connection or fellowship with the Society of Friends," she wrote, "feeling it a duty to 'come out and be separate, and have no communion with the unfruitful works of darkness.'"[83]

In upstate New York, political abolitionism drew much support away from the American Anti-Slavery Society. In May 1842, the American Anti-Slavery

Society decided to fight back. Delegates agreed to raise fifty thousand dollars and to organize (and reorganize) local antislavery societies in every northern state. They would send twenty agents into the field. Eight of these would go to upstate New York to deliver "upwards of *six hundred lectures,*" announced John Collins, their general agent. They would hold a series of county conventions, beginning in Buffalo in August and working their way east to Oneida County by the end of October. Two of their best speakers, Abby Kelley and Frederick Douglass, once enslaved in Maryland, would be present at every meeting.[84]

Sallying forth in the middle of July, Kelley invaded the very heart of political abolitionism: the Liberty Party convention held at Cazenovia, New York, just a few miles from Gerrit Smith's home in Peterboro. What she said enraged many of the two thousand people in her audience. Gerrit Smith and others accused her of asserting "that all political action is 'dirty'—but that the Liberty Party is 'dirty, dirtier, dirtiest.'"[85]

In August, Kelley met Douglass and other agents (including Jacob Ferris, Thomas M'Clintock, and George and Margaret Pryor, all members of Junius Monthly Meeting) to carry this message across the state of New York. Several agents spoke at every stop, but it was Abby Kelley whom people came to hear. Her looks were appealing; her dress modest. She was, according to one observer, "a very intelligent looking person; [with] a clear blue eye, a delicate complexion, fair hair, and a lady-like hand. Her voice is very musical, her smile expressive, and her manner modeled upon the best pattern for a public speaker." She dressed simply, in Quaker garb. "A snowy kerchief crossed upon her breast" was her only decoration.[86]

But wherever she went, she inspired riots. Not only was she a woman speaking in public and a radical abolitionist, but she also traveled with men, including Frederick Douglass. Although Margaret Pryor accompanied her, people hissed with "the forked tongue of slander": "Tis enough to know of her that she accompanies a pack of men about the country." "Even Aunt Margaret Prior's Quaker bonnet and honest, almost angel face was not sufficient to shield us," noted Kelley. "We were sometimes called a 'traveling seraglio.'" Many Americans agreed with the *Washington Globe* when it advised Kelley to "go spin; attend to your household; get married, if you can" and "mind your own business."[87]

Mostly, however, Kelley upset her audiences because of what she said. "Of one thing rest assured," she confided to a friend, "I never make compromises." Any institution that permitted slavery to exist, anywhere, was wrong. Churches were proslavery. The federal government was proslavery. Anyone who supported them was a sinner. The Constitution was a proslavery document—a covenant with death and an agreement with hell, William Lloyd Garrison said—and people should withdraw from the Union rather than support it. They should also withdraw from churches that allowed slave-owners as members.[88]

On the first of August, the anniversary of British West Indian emancipation,

Kelley lectured in Rochester with "great earnestness and ability." In September, "unflagging in her speech and . . . enthusiastic in her zeal," she addressed a large crowd of both men and women in Waterloo. Although she impressed even her critics with "her eloquence, her good looks, her full mellow voice, and her evident sincerity," she met the same criticism in Waterloo that she encountered everywhere else. Why could not "a lady with such advantages of person and talent . . . have found a more appropriate sphere of action—one better befitting her sex?" wondered one newspaper reporter.[89]

At the end of the tour, Kelley reported good news. "Such frankness, such readiness to receive the truth, and to follow it, is rarely found," she wrote to the *Liberator* in September. "Third partyism is not at all to be considered. It will trouble no one, who fights with truthful weapons. In the language of T. D. Weld, 'it will beat its own brains out.'" By the spring of 1843, she was even more enthusiastic. "There are but few, I ween, who now regard us as a 'woman's rights, no-government society, under the antislavery mantle,' though many thought this a year ago. . . . Whereas, a few months since, Abby Kelley was regarded as 'half witch and half devil,' . . . this horrible monster in human shape is transformed into a very common-place woman, and receives innumerable invitations to lecture in places where, three months since, all doors were closely barred against each and every agent, or volunteer, of the American Society."[90]

To crown their "glorious anti slavery effort," the American Anti-Slavery Society sent William Lloyd Garrison himself to central and western New York in the fall of 1842. "There has been a special curiosity to see and hear me," Garrison reported. In November, he attended regional antislavery meetings in Rochester, Syracuse, and Utica. Mobs attacked them in Syracuse and Utica, but in Rochester he received a calmer welcome.[91]

For the first time, "old organizationists," that is, members of the American Anti-Slavery Society, from the whole Genesee region met together in coordinated action. The M'Clintocks (Thomas, Mary Ann, and daughter Mary Ann) arrived from Waterloo with Abby Kelley. The conference endorsed moral suasionist goals: abolish slavery immediately; work for complete social, political, and religious equality for free people of color; and withdraw from every church, political party, or government that supported slavery in any form. "Recognizing the inspired declaration that God 'hath made of one blood all nations of men, for to dwell on all the face of the earth,' and in obedience to our Saviour's golden rule, 'All things whatsoever ye would that men should do to you, do ye even so to them,'" they urged the citizens of New York to use all their "moral influence" to send petitions to Congress, hold antislavery fairs, circulate antislavery books and newspapers (including the *Liberator*), support traveling agents, refrain from voting, and form a new society, the Western New York American Anti-Slavery Society. The convention elected Samuel D. Porter, from Bethel Church, as president, but Quakers dominated the list of officers. At least twenty of the thirty-four vice presidents and members of the Executive Committee were Quakers. Isaac Post and Sarah Hallowell were among them, as well as Waterloo Friends Margaret Pryor, Richard P. Hunt, and Thomas M'Clintock.[92]

After the Rochester convention, Garrison spoke to crowds in the Orthodox Quaker meetinghouse at Farmington. "Very few Quakers were present," noted Garrison, "owing to a strong prejudice against us." From there, he went to Waterloo, where he stayed overnight with the M'Clintock family and spoke twice on Sunday and again on Monday evening in the courthouse, in company with John Collins, Abby Kelley, and Jacob Ferris, "I occupying the greater part of the time," he noted, "in blowing up the priesthood, church, worship, Sabbath, &c." And so Waterloo had its first exposure to Garrison himself.[93]

The Western New York Anti-Slavery Society was the crucible that heated the fires not only for radical abolitionism but also for the woman's rights movement. From the very beginning, women were major leaders. Nine of the original officers were women. In November 1842, five Quaker women—Amy Post and Sarah A. Burtis from Rochester; Abby Kelley from Lynn, Massachusetts; Phoebe Hathaway from Farmington; and Mary Ann M'Clintock from Waterloo—organized the first abolitionist event after the convention, an antislavery fair.[94]

The women felt overwhelmed. They were few in number, "entirely unacquainted with the detail of Fairs," rushed for time, and in need of materials, "calicoes silks &c &c . . . as this is the hardest place to get one cents worth given for the cause." But they did their best. In Rochester, they organized an antislavery sewing circle to create items to sell at the fair. The sewing circle's twenty members included only one member of a "professed Church," Sarah Burtis reported to Kelley. The presence of black women created "a division in our ranks" and led to the loss of several of the most active white organizers, "but I assure thee," Burtis added, "we do not sacrifice principles for numbers."[95]

Time was short, and problems seemed almost insurmountable. Rochester women wanted to hold the fair on February 22, "the birth day of the great, good, pious, immortal, slaveholding, Washington!" On January 16, they met with the M'Clintocks and Margaret Pryor in Waterloo to assess their progress. The fair would be very limited, wrote Sarah Burtis to Abby Kelley the following week, "owing to opposition on *almost* every hand and discouragements in regard to *friends*." But they had winter clothes and food to sell, and even a small effort would be a beginning. Could Kelley persuade women in Boston and Utica to send them articles for sale?[96]

On February 2, 1843, the *National Anti-Slavery Standard* finally published a notice, probably written by Kelley, with a request for donations for the fair. "Our friends will choose for themselves what they shall furnish, remembering that everything saleable in our market, will be gratefully accepted. All the various kinds of clothing for children; caps; bags; aprons; children's toys; bedding, gentlemen's furnishing, &c. &c. Everything that people wish to buy." Farm produce, too, was welcome, "grain, cheese, butter, pork, beef, potatoes, or other vegetables, wood, &c."[97]

The Rochester Fair exceeded everyone's expectations. Boxes of goods came from Waterloo, Utica, and Boston. The Boston box contained articles worth about $130, including contributions from England and Ireland. "Considering the shortness of the time to prepare in, and the dreadful dull and 'hard times' it was quite a magnificent a*ffair*," wrote John C. Hathaway from Farmington. "We had much genuine mirth and real good humor," wrote Elizabeth Neall, a M'Clintock cousin who was visiting from Philadelphia. Not incidentally, they raised three hundred dollars.[98]

This fair and the ones that followed were remarkably effective in raising money and gaining recruits. In organizing them, women abolitionists created a niche that only they could fill. Making and selling household items appealed directly to women, as both producers and consumers. Asking women to contribute handmade items for the fair "enlists the sympathy of the heart," they noted. "A kindly feeling is kindled up in the community, and many, before indifferent or cold-hearted, are found ready to lend a helping hand." By tapping into the increasing middle-class urban market, women raised considerable sums of money for the cause. They also spread the abolitionist message to purchasers, who confronted everywhere the motto, "Remember the poor slave."[99]

Work in antislavery sewing circles represented a natural step for women. Accustomed both to sewing and to working with other women in Quaker meetings for business, these women found it easy to combine the two activities. Yet organizing antislavery fairs represented a drastic departure from their own cultural norms. Like the petition movement, fairs brought Quaker women directly into contact with the larger world, and working with the world's people opened them to criticism from Friends in their own meetings. From this very traditional female activity, sewing, grew an untraditional but very effective network of women reformers, whose work sustained Frederick Douglass's *North Star* and led directly into the new movement for woman's rights.

These fairs also increased tension between reform Quakers and their local meetings. Conservatives did not endorse the argument that a fair was simply "a *store,* open a *few days* instead of *the whole year.*" Rochester Monthly Meeting appointed a committee to "reason with" Amy Post, especially "in regard to her duty towards her family." Nathaniel Potter—a prophet-like preacher who traveled from town to town, calling people to justice and to God—affirmed Post's resolve with spirit messages. "The language of the Spirit now is," he reported in October 1843, "—Dear Sister be faithful. . . . Open thy mouth in the cause of the dumb, and those appointed to destruction.—'Endure the cross and despise the shame.'—for some will be ready to say, 'it is a shame for a woman to act the part which the Lord will require at thy hands.' . . . 'Male & female are one in Christ Jesus,' our head.—Now do not begin to make excuses, for I feel there is danger of it."[100]

Amy Post never made excuses. Instead, she took up the challenge. She copied letters from the monthly meeting to the preparative meetings on abolitionist stationery, carrying the famous drawing of a shackled man with the motto, "Am I Not a Man and a Brother?" "I expect they will have a fresh charge against me soon," she noted, ". . . and I have but little doubt but that imploring immage will disturb their quiet, at least I hope it will."[101]

The core group of women who sponsored the first fair continued to hold fairs regularly for many years. In October 1843, Elizabeth M'Clintock and Rhoda Bement, from Seneca Falls, organized a fair in the Temperance Hall in Seneca Falls on October 4–5. They advertised "a most beautiful variety of useful and fancy articles, many of which have been contributed from Rochester, Syracuse, Utica, Albany, Boston and many other places." Admittance was half a shilling (about six and a quarter cents). In the evening, speeches, vocal music, and a concert by the Geneva Band afford a rare "feast of reason and flow of soul." This was the first recorded example of women from Waterloo and Seneca Falls working together.[102]

By 1847, fairs in Waterloo had made a positive impact. Twenty-three women sponsored the fair, and they found broad support among Rochester citizens. Mary Ann M'Clintock reported to Amy Post that "we feel very much elated with our success thus far. We have taken book and pencil in hand and called upon many of our worthy citizens to obtain their donation for the refreshment table—and marvelous to tell have not met with a solitary denial. Either Anti-Slavery is becoming very popular or they are held in some inexplicable spell." William Henry Seward, ex-governor of New York, sent cordial regrets that he could not attend.[103]

Organizing these fairs kept abolitionist women in touch with each other not only locally but also nationally and internationally. The 1843 fair had included articles from England, sent through Boston. Without English goods to sell in 1844 or 1845, Rochester women failed to reach their 1843 standard. By 1846, however, in part because Frederick Douglass was then in England, Amy Post felt confident enough to appeal to Elizabeth Pease, an English abolitionist Friend, for help. "It is not great things that we ask for," she wrote, "but small things from you, will do great things for us, we are now, what the Boston friends were in days that are past, few in number, and circumscribed in means, while our concern for the poor slave is lightly esteemed and evilly spoken of."[104]

The money they earned gave them considerable clout within the American Anti-Slavery Society, since the women themselves could choose how to spend their assets. Rochester abolitionists preferred the *Liberator* to the *National Anti-Slavery Standard,* for example, and refused to support the *Standard* with proceeds from the fair in 1846. Instead, they invited Frederick Douglass to come to Rochester as an abolitionist agent. "No man has ever been amongst us," Amy Post reported, "who in our opinion is better qualified for usefulness in the antislavery field." Encouraged by these women, Frederick Douglass moved to Rochester in 1848 to begin publication of the *North Star.*[105]

Moving back and forth from town to town, Kelley stitched together a patchwork of abolitionists—women and men, African American and European American—dominated by Quakers. In so doing, she rejuvenated Garrisonian abolitionism in upstate New York and put into place key players in the woman's rights movement. They were a small group, and they often felt overwhelmed. Amy Post wrote to Abby Kelley in December, 1843, that "I feel almost discouraged to think how little life there is amongst us, scarcely knowing what they are doing in the next town to us, and even Seneca Falls friends have to depend upon Abby Kelley to inform us what they have done or wish to do." In 1847, they continued to lament that "the active friends of the cause are few." But their ability to organize meetings, raise money, and recruit support made them powerful out of all proportion to their numbers.[106]

Their work drew them into national antislavery activities. In May 1843, flushed with success from the Rochester Fair, the M'Clintocks attended the annual anniversary meeting of the American Anti-Slavery Society in New York City. Quaker women, with their "quaint neat dresses" and "gentle faces," came out in large numbers. What they heard energized them. The prospects of the American Anti-Slavery Society were brighter now that at any time since the society's foundation, asserted the annual report. They had held ten thousand meetings in the last year, attended by at least two hundred thousand people. In a mark of his increasing commitment, Thomas M'Clintock joined the Board of Managers of the American Anti-Slavery Society, a position he retained for five years; in 1848, he became a vice president.[107]

Letting their whole lives speak, these egalitarian Quakers also opened their homes to people escaping from slavery. In Rochester, the Post family worked with Frederick and Anna Douglass. Amy Post estimated that 180 people passed through her house one year in the 1850s. Among them was Harriet Jacobs, who, with Amy Post's encouragement, wrote a remarkable account of her life in slavery in North Carolina.[108]

Waterloo residents, both African American and European American, also participated in Underground Railroad activities. In 1850, six of the sixty-three African Americans in Waterloo may have been formerly enslaved, based on census listing of their birthplaces as Maryland, Virginia, or unknown. Almost one-third of Waterloo's African Americans were directly connected with these possible fugitives. With stable family structures and access to both jobs and education, the African American community in Waterloo, although marginal economically, established itself as an identifiable and accepted presence in the village. In Thomas M'Clintock's view, "there were some smart men here."[109]

European American Quakers in Waterloo had close ties to some of these African Americans. According to the 1850 U.S. census, two Quaker households contained black children or teenagers. The M'Clintock household included eight-year-old S. L. Freeman and seventeen-year-old Mary Jackson. George and Margaret Pryor counted seventeen-year-old Matilda Rany as a member of their household.

Some Waterloo Quakers used their homes as stations on the Freedom Trail. Family legend suggests that Richard P. and Jane Hunt used a large room over the carriage house attached to the rear of the main building as a haven for freedom seekers. One visitor to the M'Clintock house recalled that Jermain Loguen—who had fled slavery himself to become an AME Zion minister and a key Underground Railroad supporter in Syracuse, New York—stayed with the M'Clintocks on his way to Canada in 1851. Loguen, reported the visitor, "was a man of noble countenance and gigantic stature, well armed, and determined to die rather than be re-enslaved. He was apprehensive and wakeful, walking in his room during most of the night, and if his pursuers had come, the house of a man of peace would have been the scene of a deadly struggle."[110]

Martha and David Wright also harbored fugitives in Auburn. In January 1843, an African American man appeared in the Wright kitchen, with a note recommending him to the care of James C. Fuller (a Skaneateles Quaker) and others of the "spiritually minded." In return for food, a night's lodging (on the settee in the kitchen), and fifty cents for a ride, he filled the furnace with wood. Although daughter Eliza was "as afraid as could be of him," son Tallman was curious. When Tallman went down to the kitchen early "to have some interesting conversation with him about the land of chains," he was "much disappointed" to find the fugitive already gone. Unfortunately, so was Tallman's tippet, or hat.[111]

Underground Railroad activity was a natural extension of the network that linked these households together into havens for antislavery lecturers. The M'Clintocks offered their home as a regular stop for traveling Quaker ministers, as well as for such antislavery agents as Abby Kelley, Frederick Douglass, C. C. Burleigh, William C. Nell, and William Lloyd Garrison.[112] The Posts became particularly famous for their hospitality to abolitionists and gave a special welcome to black abolitionists. J. B. Sanderson thanked the Posts in April 1845 "for the letter full of kindness from 'Home,' my Rochester *Home,* Anti-Slavery's Home. How can I forget those who made it such a Home to me?" For Frederick Douglass, the high point of his first lecture tour through upstate New York was a visit with the Posts. Amy and Isaac Post, thought Douglass, were "two people of all-abounding benevolence, the truest and best of Long Island and Elias Hicks Quakers. They were not more amiable than brave, for they never seemed to ask, What will the world say? But walked straight forward in what seemed to them the line of duty, please or offend whomsoever it might." Black abolitionist William C. Nell called Amy Post "the Presiding Genius of 36 Sophia St."[113]

Many black abolitionists fully shared the Posts' concern for woman's rights. Reporting on the American Anti-Slavery Society's annual meeting in New York City in 1845, J. B. Sanderson wrote to Amy Post that "a few years ago men in this city hissed at the mere idea of Women's speaking in public in promiscuous assemblies; now men come to antislavery conventions, attracted by the announcement that women are to take part in the deliberations and they are often more desirous of hearing women, than men—The world is becoming habituated to it. . . . Woman is rising up, becoming free. . . . *Man* cannot be *free,* while the developer of his heart, soul, moral character, or the maker of man, in the highest sense, *Woman,* is enslaved to conventionalism." William C. Nell offered his consistent support. "You have my Godspeed in every effort where *Woman's* influence can be *fully* and *Freely exercised,*" he assured the Posts. Frederick Douglass, too, whole-heartedly espoused the rights of women. The *North Star* bore the masthead, "Right is of no Sex—Truth is of no Color—God is the Father of us all, and we are all Brethren."[114]

In spite of such support from non-Quakers, egalitarian Quakers within Genesee Yearly Meeting faced considerable opposition within their own meetings. When Jacob Ferris tried to speak in Rochester Monthly Meeting, he was interrupted by one member, defended by others, and finally allowed to speak. "I am astonished," Ferris said. "Is this the Society of Friends that attempts to put down a *member,* because he speaks against the sin of slavery?"[115]

Many Quaker meetings also excluded abolitionist lecturers who were not Quakers. In August 1843, Frederick Douglass and fellow black abolitionist Charles Lenox Remond traveled to Mendon, New York, just outside of Rochester, with "a small party of friends." There they spoke "to many in front of the Friends' meetinghouse, which was closed against us," reported Remond, before addressing "one of the most crowded audiences I ever saw" in a neighboring church.[116]

Abolitionists defended themselves by citing their support for Seneca people as a precedent. "Why this great difference between a *red* man, and a *black* man?" they asked. "Why is it a *crime* to admit those into our houses, who are pleading the cause of the slave, while we admit those who plead for the Indian?" When Friends invited Seneca chiefs and warriors to speak in their meetinghouses, they "were not then told to '*keep in the quiet*'—to '*keep out of the world by mixtures.*' . . . Now, Friends, what *was* all this for? Why, for the very thing abolitionists are now pleading for, namely—*universal right to all men.*"[117]

Neither logic nor confrontation eased tensions. By 1844, Amy Post found it a "trial" to go to meeting. From Long Island, Amy's mother, Mary Kirby, sympathized, but she was not optimistic. "Lamentable inded is the state of society. I pity you. . . . Thou said thou should take no hasty steps. If I have any right to say I desire you not to hope you will overcome their evil with good." She advised them nevertheless to hold on. "Dear Children," she concluded, ". . . stand and wait patiently it seams to me they will be overcome by your good and consistant lives."[118]

Phoebe Post Willis, Isaac's sister, sent them the same message. "Do not I prey thee gratify them so much as to think of resigning thy right of membership . . . to think of one member of society wishing another member to withdraw that has an equal right with himself how preposterous. Tell Amy 'to stick to the old ship' and hope for better days." It was too late, however. By April, both Amy and Isaac had withdrawn from the Society of Friends.[119]

By 1845, Rochester Quakers were holding "free meetings," open to anyone, male or female, Quaker-born or not. These gatherings echoed the free church movement supported by many abolitionists and became the prototype for a new model of Friends' meetings that would emerge at key points across the Northeast in 1848.[120]

As they recognized the futility of carrying all of Quakerism along the abolitionist road, reform Quakers within Genesee Yearly Meeting shifted to a new but related theme, the distribution of power within the Society of Friends itself. They focused their attack on separate meetings of ministers and elders. In theory, all power came from God, and all living creatures embodied the Inner Light. In practice, however, Quakers recognized that some people had special gifts, either in public preaching or in pastoral care, and they acknowledged such talent by recognizing such people as ministers or elders. Lucretia Mott was an acknowledged minister. So was Thomas M'Clintock. While these Friends met with everyone else for worship and business, they also met separately, as committees of oversight for the meeting. Sometimes, their attempts to guide the meeting led to what others thought were unwarranted attempts to control it. Therein lay the problem. When elders tried to suppress the spiritual leadings of reformers within the meeting (as, for example, when they denied abolitionists the right to speak), their opponents protested. Unable to convince key Friends in powerful positions to endorse their cause, reformers decided to attack the power structure itself.

It was no coincidence that these questions of power emerged in 1843, the same year the M'Clintocks withdrew from active participation in Genesee Yearly Meeting and just a month after Thomas M'Clintock returned from the annual meeting of the American Anti-Slavery Society. Although the M'Clintocks remained Hicksite Friends for another five years, they ultimately could not reconcile their own radical egalitarianism with continued membership in Genesee Yearly Meeting.

In letting their lives speak, these Quakers broke down distinctions between talk and action, between personal and public lives, between ideals and life. They viewed their lives as a whole, and everywhere, in every way, they tried to live and act in ways that respected that of God in themselves and each other. As they worked for woman's rights, Indian rights, and abolitionism, they distilled their ideals of equality, continuing revelation, and the inner Light into practical work in the larger world. With Daniel Anthony, father of Susan B. Anthony, most of them could truly say, "I am a member of that Society which has for its Teretory no less sphere than all creation & for its members every rational creature under Heaven."[121]

In the meantime, in 1843, Abby Kelley, whose lectures the year before had set upstate New York on fire, had work to do in Seneca Falls. Seneca Falls (and the world) would never be the same.[122]

CHAPTER 5

Seneca Falls: Abolitionist Ferment

Looking back on her girlhood in Seneca Falls, Mary Bascom Bull remembered vividly the village's "spirit of reform," its "reaching out for perfection." Her own family was at the center of the storm. Her mother, Eliza Bascom, was by nature a retiring woman, but she did her part. For a whole year, she put her family on the vegetarian Grahamite diet, preparing graham crackers, graham gems (a muffin), and graham bread to serve with fruit, nuts, and cold water. She sewed flags for temperance parades and made fancy goods for antislavery fairs, but when it came to public speeches, she let her husband do the honors. He was more than willing to oblige.[1]

Ansel Bascom, Mary's father, was the most enthusiastic reformer in town. An erstwhile lawyer, politician, and land developer, his real passion was reform—especially legal reform, temperance, and antislavery—and he loved a good fight. People had to agree that Ansel Bascom was public spirited. He was "a good talker," "a fine leader," and "enterprising." Hadn't he served as the first president of the village of Seneca Falls? Hadn't he developed most of the waterpower and the building lots on the south side of the river? (He sold the lots cheaply, too, intending to develop the village rather than to make a lot of money. Getting rich was not Bascom's style. Anybody, he said, could get rich if they were mean enough.) Some of Bascom's neighbors thought that he was too "anxious to dig up the hatchet," "a mercurial citizen," "rather a poor follower," "peculiar," even "obnoxious." But they had to admit that he liked a good argument.[2]

In 1843, Ansel Bascom was a natural choice to set up meetings for Abby Kelley when she came to town. Kelley needed a large building, like a church. But her reputation had preceded her, and none of the churches would have her. She certainly attracted large audiences. Too large, some people thought, and most ministers boycotted her meetings. That was why she found herself, at 5 o'clock one Sunday afternoon in August 1843, speaking to a crowd gathered in the orchard around Ansel Bascom's house. The meeting opened with a reading from the book of Isaiah. Jabez Matthews, a member of the Presbyterian Church, led an antislavery hymn. Abby Kelley rose and asked for "a season of silence." Then she began. This nation is guilty of slavery, she charged. It is a sin. Your churches are connected with slavery, and they are guilty of that sin. They are not Christians if they are slaveholders, if they steal and sell men, women, and children, if they rob cradles. Northern churches were as guilty, in fact, as southern slaveholders, since northerners had the majority population and could make things right. That includes your Presbyterian Church, she went on. I happen to know something of your Mr. Bogue, the pastor of that church. Where is your Bogue today? Is he not connected with the South? Is he not in full fellowship with proslavery churchmen? These proslavery persecutions today follow the same spirit of persecution that existed in former ages. Mr. Bogue would see me burn at the stake, if he had it in his power, or murdered as abolitionists had been in the South.[3] Afterwards, Jonathan Metcalf admitted that "she bore pretty hard & severe on the northern churches."[4]

Just as 1842 marked the rejuvenation of moral suasionist abolitionism in upstate New York, 1843 was a turning point in Seneca Falls, and Abby Kelley's lectures were the pivot. At issue was a definition of community. In a time of rapid economic change, people of many different ethnic and social backgrounds had migrated to Seneca Falls. There they created the physical structure of a village: houses, stores, factories, schools, and churches. Around this skeleton, they draped, loosely, a formal political framework. And on that framework they worked hard to pin common cultural values, those ways of thinking and behaving that would allow them to continue to live and work together on common economic and political tasks. They agreed, for example, to share the cost of fixing the streets and the work of fighting fires. Every person in Seneca Falls was a member of this geographic, political, and cultural community.

Within this world, however, people created other social and cultural networks. Partly, they defined themselves by families. Who begat whom was not simply a conventional phrase from Old Testament stories but a real way for villagers to identify themselves and each other. Families consisted of extended kin groups and expanded households. Members were responsible for each other and in theory, at least, took care of each other.

Gender, too, became a way to assert common values. In theory, all women were mothers—or they had been or would be or ought to be. Mothers were caretakers of their children, husbands, neighbors, and communities. While men struggled to survive physically, financially, and morally in the rapidly changing world outside the home, women took care of the family and household, providing economically and even graciously for feeding, clothing, and sheltering people, asserting moral values untainted by outside temptations, motivated not by money but by love.

Community organizations also provided a way for people to express values that transcended the physical survival of themselves and their children. To some extent, these value-oriented institutions contributed to the stability of village life. For a people in motion, churches, political parties, and voluntary societies provided one source of cohesion and stability, one way of asserting some control over their often chaotic lives.

When someone like Abby Kelley came to town, however, these value-oriented institutions became not sources of stability but battlegrounds. People quickly recognized the limits of consensus. At least some of the citizens of Seneca Falls began to challenge the boundaries of behavior they had so carefully constructed. Even as they recognized their differences, however, most people managed to keep their conflicts within reasonable limits. Reverend Bogue, after all, did not actually burn Abby Kelley at the stake. But people realized that they trod a very narrow line between the need to live together and the need not only to defend but to promote their own moral and cultural values. Value-oriented institutions—churches, political parties, and reform organizations—both controlled and facilitated cultural conflict.

In the process of defining their worlds, people focused on the relationship between individuals and community. This conflict worked itself out in a debate about appropriate social structures: should social relationships emphasize equality or should they emphasize hierarchy? In an older world, people had clear ideas—based on race and ethnicity, class, age, and gender—of what others expected them to be. Roles fit a hierarchy: wealthy people had more authority than poor ones, whites more than blacks or Indians, old more than young, men more than women. By the late eighteenth century, inspired by the Declaration of Independence and by ideas of personal religious salvation, many Americans questioned the value of such hierarchies. To the extent that women and men defined themselves as moral beings, accountable to God, they also asserted their right to act according to their own consciences. In so doing, they demanded a new definition of social roles, one that respected individual rights as well as delineated responsibilities. Debates over roles were continuing and heated in Seneca Falls in the 1840s.

In Seneca Falls in 1843, conflicts over abolitionism exploded in a community already divided over religion and temperance. Carrying the antislavery banner, Kelley strode unflinchingly into the middle of negotiations over the delicate balance between equality and hierarchy, individuals and community. In the process, she fertilized the seeds of an emerging movement for woman's rights and left a legacy that would change Seneca Falls—and the world—forever.

Reformers in upstate New York developed movements in an environment different from that in other parts of the country. Part of New York's peculiarities came from rapid in-migration, as people followed economic opportunities. Just as rubbing dry sticks together creates physical fire, so the constant motion of people in upstate New York led to spiritual friction and spiritual fires. As people with different value systems and different world views confronted each other, over and over again, they generated sparks. These sparks ignited one community after another with the fires of revivalism and reform, until the whole region became known as the burned-over district.[5]

In terms of religious revivalism and temperance, Seneca Falls contributed to the general conflagration. But unlike Quakers in Waterloo, its citizens did not immediately embrace abolitionism. When the American Anti-Slavery Society sent its agents to organize local societies in the mid-1830s, Seneca Falls was not one of their successes. Nor did the town support the early petition campaign. Not until 1850 did people in Seneca Falls send an extant antislavery petition to Congress. Finally, residents were not active promoters of the Underground Railroad.[6]

Lack of interest in abolitionism was perhaps related to the small size of the African American population. By 1850, only sixteen African American women and eight African American men lived in Seneca Falls.[7] Although few in number, they were highly visible and not without status. They had jobs, owned property, and enjoyed the respect of their neighbors. When travelers arrived in Seneca Falls by train, they would see Solomon Butler waiting at the station. He was so well known that residents named a street after him. Joshua Wright, was a "Fashionable Barber and Hair Dresser" who offered shaves "on the true philosophical principles." "Instead of horrible associations and frightful contortions of visage," Wright asserted in an 1844 advertisement, "shaving, by the light of science, has been rendered an agreeable pastime."[8]

Such work brought modest financial rewards. An ordinary frame house, common to working-class families in Seneca Falls, might be worth six to eight hundred dollars in 1850. At least some black families owned such a house. In 1851, the village assessment record listed four black people who owned real estate; only one independent black household owned no property.[9]

One of these African American families most likely harbored fugitives from slavery. In 1850, Thomas James refused to tell the census taker where he had been born, and James's thirteen-year-old daughter, Martha, listed her birthplace as Canada. It seems likely that Thomas James and his wife, Sarah, had moved to Canada sometime before Martha's birth and had returned to the United States during the late 1830s or 1840s. Thomas James owned more than twice as much property as any other black family in the village, was a trustee of the Wesleyan Church, and signed an antislavery petition. He was also the person most likely to have been self-emancipated from slavery.[10]

Certainly, even relatively uninformed people in Seneca Falls could not avoid the problem of slavery by the late 1830s. The *Seneca County Courier* covered its whole front page in September 1839 with the story of the schooner *Amistad*, which was captured by Africans who were its main cargo. In the same issue, local readers could find "Anti-Slavery Earthenware, a new pattern, well-adapted to remind freemen of their own enjoyments and natural rights" advertised for sale in New York City "for country merchants."[11]

Seneca Falls abolitionists began to organize in the late 1830s, but they focused their work on political antislavery rather than espousing more radical Garrisonian views. A countywide antislavery society had been established sometime in 1838, for in October 1839, the *Democrat* published a brief notice of "the next Annual Meeting of the Seneca County Anti-Slavery Society." Although it was held in the Methodist chapel of Waterloo, Daniel W. Forman, a Seneca Falls Presbyterian, was the secretary.[12]

By 1840, antislavery had become a national political issue, affecting the course of national politics. President Martin Van Buren, a Democrat from Kinderhook, New York, ran for a second term against Whig William Henry Harrison of Ohio. Harrison's qualifications included his birth in a log cabin and his reputation as a fighter of Indians. The Democrats thought that he had been nominated "not because of his principles or talents;—but because of the *want* of them." His real strength lay, they argued, in his refusal to answer questions about his political views. John Tyler, a Virginia slaveholder, ran as Harrison's vice president. The Whigs touted Harrison's humble birth and paraded log cabins and liberty balls down the streets of Seneca Falls, shouting their slogan, "Tippecanoe and Tyler, Too." For president, the new Liberty Party nominated James G. Birney, a former Alabama slaveholder turned abolitionist, just returned from traveling with the Stantons to the World Anti-Slavery Convention.[13]

Local abolitionists enthusiastically entered the political fray. They denounced as robbers and "pillar[s] of hell" all those citizens and Christians who refused to endorse the immediate abolition of slavery. Such rhetoric did not prevent Jonathan Metcalf, president of the local antislavery society, from accepting the Whig nomination for justice of the peace.[14] Local Whigs also nominated Ansel Bascom for town supervisor and member of the New York Assembly. The *Democrat* was delighted. Bascom had unsuccessfully courted the Democratic nomination to the state assembly the year before, and his sudden conversion to the Whig party offered opponents a target too tempting to resist. The year before, chortled the *Democrat,* Whigs had called Bascom "an ally of the enemy—a retailer of falsehoods—a man who conceived nothing but evil—a demagogue." So why did Bascom deserve anyone's vote now?[15]

Bascom lost the election, but by only three votes out of almost eight hundred. Seneca Falls returned narrow Democratic majorities for all major offices. William Henry Harrison may have lost Seneca Falls, but he carried Waterloo (by 12 votes out of 542), New York state, and the nation. Harrison lost Seneca County by only fifteen votes. The Liberty Party made its presence felt, but barely. It received only six votes for president, four votes for governor, three votes for lieutenant governor, and five votes for senator in Seneca Falls. In Waterloo, only two men cast their votes for Liberty Party candidates in each of these offices.[16]

Local abolitionists continued to promote antislavery candidates in the early 1840s. In September 1841, Daniel W. Forman, Jabez Matthews, and Abram Failing joined twenty others in a call for a countywide convention of abolitionist electors to meet at the Seneca House in Seneca Falls. "We war not with Whig or

Democrat," they vowed, "but only against that *Aristocracy* which in denying to the poor laborer the enjoyment of his 'inalienable rights,' *subverts* the fundamental principles of Freedom." They called themselves the Liberty Party, they argued, "because we are for *that* liberty which knows no distinction in the blessings it confers between a sable or a light complexion, but recognizes in the sooty African a brother. . . . We are Whigs, we are Democrats; but neither the one or the other, if as such we must blot out from the charter of our liberties the self-evident truth, 'that all men are created free and equal.'" In 1842 and 1843, local Liberty Party members seized their momentum, such as it was, to promote "a thorough organization of the Liberty Party in the county." In spite of the third-party threat, Seneca Falls continued to return Democratic majorities in the early 1840s. Waterloo wavered, sometimes going Whig, sometimes Democratic.[17]

The *Seneca Falls Democrat* professed to be an antislavery paper, but its abolitionist views were moderate. In the strongest terms, it condemned any ideas of breaking up the Union, using violence, or supporting the British as a way to attack slavery. When Mexico invaded Texas (then the independent Lone Star Republic) in 1842, the *Democrat* viewed the invasion as an antislavery plot, in which African Americans, abolitionists, and the British all joined to set slaves in Texas free. Among other shocking actions, reported the *Democrat,* some abolitionists condemned "all churches which fellowship with others than Abolitionists" as "sinks of iniquity and gateways of hell." All such ideas were "startling, immoral, and treasonable," decided the *Democrat.* "In saying this, we mean no offence to the honest, old-fashioned, uniform, antislavery men: These we revere. With them, we believe Slavery to be the greatest of evils,—and with them, we should rejoice in its entire and speedy abolition." But "the intemperate conduct of modern Abolitionists" had done more than anything else to prevent the abolition of slavery. Only slaveholders, acting voluntarily, could free slaves.[18]

With sentiments such as these, the *Democrat* could not be expected to welcome radical abolitionists to Seneca Falls. And it did not. When Abby Kelley gave her first lectures there in August, 1842, the *Democrat* reported her comments under the headline of "Treason! Treason!!!" William Lloyd Garrison himself spoke at the Court House in Waterloo in November 1842. He advocated, said the *Democrat,* "all his unpopular and obnoxious doctrines . . . such as non-resistance, the woman-question, anti-church and anti-clergy views." By promoting such ideas, the *Democrat* argued, Garrison "is not only insulting the good sense of every true abolitionist, but . . . he is materially retarding the abolition of slavery."[19]

Kelley thought otherwise, and in August 1843, she set out to convert Seneca Falls residents from their moderate views to an abolitionism that encompassed disunion, come-outerism, and woman's rights. She was largely successful. "There is not—or I had better say there *was* not," reported Kelley, "when I came to the Falls . . . one person really worthy [of] the name abolitionist. There are several now, who I think will soon leave their churches."[20]

Kelley held six meetings in Seneca Falls that week. Three convened outdoors before the Baptists finally invited her into their meetinghouse, which she packed to overflowing. "Tis a stubborn place," she thought, but people told her that "there was never such a general awakening on any subject in the place." Opponents tried to break up the crowds; someone threw a rotten egg. Seneca Falls was a temperance town, however, and without liquor to fuel their rage, the rowdies quickly lost their enthusiasm. Women in Seneca Falls, with Kelley's help, organized an antislavery fair and made "a handsome sum of money" to support more abolitionist lecturers.[21]

Passionate debate over Kelley's speech was symptomatic of larger turmoil in Seneca Falls. In 1843, the whole village was embroiled in a churning sea of moral questioning, most clearly reflected in local churches, which began to unravel that year. All of the splits had their roots in religious enthusiasm. They took, however, two main forms. One was the Millerite movement. The second was abolitionism itself.

Millerism swept up hundreds of people in Seneca Falls in 1843. All of them expected the world to end, literally and almost immediately. William Miller, veteran of the War of 1812 and grassroots biblical scholar from Washington County, New York, read his Bible carefully. Based on calculations from the Book of Daniel and the Book of Revelation, he concluded that the Second Coming of Christ would occur in 1843, probably in October.[22]

When Miller himself arrived in Seneca Falls, most people were skeptical. A local doctor, O. R. Fassett, confessed that he attended Miller's first lectures only out of curiosity, believing that Miller "was one of the worst men that ever lived." Fassett was impressed, however, with Miller's respectable appearance and his consistent references to the Bible, so he decided to attend the rest of his talks. "I thus reasoned if you speak I must hear," Fassett later wrote to Miller, "if it be truth it is of the utmost importance that I as an individual know it, if it be error there was no need of embracing it." Intrigued, he began to study Miller's ideas carefully, to compare them with other commentaries on the Bible, and to discuss them with friends. "I broke up the fallow ground of my heart," he reported, "I studied, prayed, wept and confessed my sin—and light broke more and more into my soul." So powerful was Fassett's conversion that he ended up as a travelling Millerite lecturer.[23]

Although Millerites appealed to people of many religious backgrounds, Baptists in Seneca Falls found themselves at the center of the swirling storm. Throughout 1843, E. R. Pinney, minister of the local Baptist Church, preached earnestly and desperately every Sunday (and often during the week, too) on the imminent arrival of the last judgment. Elon Galusha, eloquent Baptist minister and Millerite from Lockport, New York, lent urgency to Pinney's message when he spoke in Seneca Falls. "Fly to Jesus," urged Galusha, "*swiftly fly;* your sins confess; for mercy plea, while He is on the mercy seat." For soon, "the song of revelry . . . will cease; the voice of mirth be heard no more forever; the chilling horror will suddenly seize upon you—the sheltering rocks will not protect you; the falling mountains will not hide you; the fiery stream will not spare you; the wail of anguish will not relieve you—Nor gushing tears; nor mercy's name; nor bleeding Lamb will then avail you!" At his own expense, Pinney distributed 2,000 copies of a pamphlet he named the *Trump of Jubilee.* Local people responded with alacrity. Membership in the Baptist Church doubled in 1843, as 125 converts received baptism. The Methodist Episcopal Church lost several of its members to the Millerites.[24]

No Second Coming occurred in October 1843. Believers moved the date to March 1844, but E. R. Pinney could wait no longer. On February 24, 1844, he ascended the Baptist pulpit for the last time. He denounced the Baptist Church as Babylon and preached from Revelations 18:4, the classic come-outer text: "And I heard another voice from heaven saying, Come out of her my people, that ye be not partakers of her sins, and that ye receive not of her plagues." Then he grabbed his hat and walked out. Fifty-three members left their pews and walked out right behind him. Altogether, the Baptists lost about eighty members, a third of their membership, to the Millerites.[25]

Millerism split the Baptist Church. Abby Kelley and her brand of radical abolitionism splintered most of the rest. Attacking churches and government as proslavery, Kelley created an antislavery revival. Seneca Falls "is stirred to its deepest foundations and henceforth we shall have a permanent foothold here," Kelley wrote on August 13.[26]

At issue was the locus of power, the same issue that consumed the Quakers. Everyone agreed that God was the ultimate authority. But did God's voice come through church officials? Or did God speak directly to each person? As they answered these questions, Christian churches fell along a rough spectrum. Some emphasized doctrine and institutional hierarchy: truth flowed from God to Jesus and then through priests or ministers to the people. Others highlighted personal experience and ongoing revelation: everyone should obey the dictates of personal conscience, the voice of God within. Roughly, this spectrum ranged from Catholics (the most hierarchical) through Episcopalians, Methodists, Presbyterians, Congregationalists, Baptists, and, finally, Quakers. Whether, and how, churches would be affected by abolitionism depended in large part on where they stood along this spectrum. On the hierarchical end, antislavery agitation appealed almost not at all to Catholics or High Church Episcopalians. At the egalitarian end, all Quakers opposed slavery. Abolitionism had the most direct impact on those churches in the middle of the spectrum, where antislavery beliefs heightened, often unbearably, the tension between individual conscience and institutional responsibility.

Abolitionists asked Americans to compare the existence of slavery with the ideals of both the Declaration of Independence and the Bible. Was slavery compatible with the belief that "all men are created equal"? Could slavery be reconciled with the mandate to "love your neighbor as yourself"? Could Christians support slavery and still believe that "there is neither Jew nor Greek, bond nor free, male nor female, for ye are all one in Christ Jesus"?[27] Obviously not, replied abolitionists. As they began to act on their egalitarian ideas, they eroded hierarchical relationships, not only between slaves and masters but also between themselves and organized religious groups.

In Seneca Falls, the impact of abolitionism on middle-spectrum churches was profound, ranging from Baptists (the most receptive) to Presbyterians (who kept their organization together but at the price of losing antislavery members) to Methodists (whose membership split in two). Baptists were closest to Quakers in their emphasis on the primacy of individual conscience. Even before Kelley came to town, they declared themselves unwilling to worship with supporters of slavery. In July 1842, they passed a resolution refusing to let slaveholders or their sympathizers use their pulpit or take communion with them. In 1843, they were the only church in Seneca Falls to open their doors to Kelley.[28]

Methodists tried to equivocate. The local congregation was clearly antislavery, but they belonged to a nationwide church that included slaveholders. How could they balance their commitment to abolition with their commitment to Methodism? In early 1840, they appealed to their own Genesee Conference "to adopt some prudent antislavery resolutions for consideration at the next General Conference." One proposal pleaded earnestly for compromise. "We love and revere the Methodist ministry," they affirmed, "and to confirm our profession we here give our humble assurance, that though you may be opposed to abolition measures, that if you will support the doctrine of our discipline in regard to slavery, and do your utmost—to exterminate this great evil from the Church, we will, God being our helper, pray for your success, and support your laudable endeavors till the termination of our lives." The general conference voted this down.[29]

Antislavery Methodists had nowhere to go but out. In 1843, they formally organized a new church, the Wesleyan Methodist Church, "with a hierarchy neither of power nor of color." Delegates meeting in Utica, New York, represented six to eight thousand dissident Methodists, most of them from upstate New York.[30] They opposed war, secret societies, the use of tobacco and alcohol, sexual promiscuity, and, most of all, slavery. American slavery, they said, was "the most flagrant wholesale robbery that was ever practiced under the sun," and "to remain connected with the pro-slavery churches . . . is to disobey the command of God, which require us to have no fellowship with the unfruitful works of darkness, and not to be partakers of other men's sins, but to come out from among them."[31]

At the heart of this new organization was a different form of church government. The Methodist Episcopal Church had been organized from the top down. Wesleyans embraced a congregational form. Essential authority remained within the local church. Both ministers and laity represented their own congregations at regional and national conferences. God spoke to individual Wesleyans directly, and no bishop or itinerant preacher could prevent local ministers and churches from carrying out what they believed to be God's will.

In March 1843, two months before the first national Wesleyan convention, Seneca Falls Methodists formed their own Wesleyan Church. Joseph Metcalf, a sixty-year-old Methodist farmer, initiated debate. Amazed to learn of the complicity of his own beloved church in the sin of slavery, Metcalf ordered ten subscriptions of *Zion's Watchman,* a Methodist antislavery newspaper, to be sent to church members. "The struggle between church attachment and obvious duty was severe," reported George Pegler, the first Wesleyan Methodist minister in Seneca Falls. "But the command of God was paramount to every other consideration." Much to the surprise of the regular Methodist minister, more than sixty Methodists withdrew to form the "First Wesleyan Methodist Society of Seneca Falls."[32]

In the summer of 1843, Seneca Falls Wesleyans built a meetinghouse, a brick building forty feet wide by sixty feet long, in a "very plain style." It was the first Wesleyan chapel in western New York and the largest religious building in the village. Heading the subscription list, with five hundred dollars, was Joseph Metcalf. Richard P. Hunt gave one hundred dollars. Ordinary people, such as Joel Bunker, a lock-tender, donated five or ten dollars, some of it in brick, produce, tailoring, blacksmithing, or team work.[33]

True to their abolitionist origins, Wesleyans opened their meeting house to antislavery and reform lecturers. It was, they said, "a free discussion house." Politicians could not use their church, but anyone else was welcome. The building became a haven for abolitionists, a place they could use when every other place was closed to them. Two Garrisonian abolitionists (J. C. Hathaway, a white Quaker abolitionist from Farmington, and Charles Remond, a black abolitionist from Boston) spoke there in 1846. Local abolitionists, even those who were not of Methodist background, gravitated toward the Wesleyans. Thomas James joined the Wesleyans and became a trustee in 1850. And in July 1848, the Wesleyan Chapel would be the obvious place—in fact the only available place—to hold the woman's rights convention.[34]

Presbyterians put up the most dramatic and successful resistance to radical abolitionism in Seneca Falls. They held their church together by driving away their most committed abolitionists. In 1837, conflicts over abolitionism and theology had split the national Presbyterian organization. "Old School" Presbyterians ousted "New School" churches, including almost all Presbyterian congregations in upstate New York. Abolitionists attacked the General Assembly as "a cage of unclean birds," controlled absolutely by the "slaveholding demon." Every time Old School Presbyterians met, avowed Charles Grandison Finney, "there was a jubilee in hell."[35]

Presbyterians in Seneca Falls disavowed the proslavery Old School. They thought of themselves as moderate and responsible abolitionists. Meeting in October 1843, church members adopted a resolution against slavery and distributed three hundred copies of it. Their minister, Horace P. Bogue, claimed antislavery leanings. He had in fact been an agent for the American Colonization Society. Founded in the 1817, this society early attracted the support of white southerners, whose opposition to slavery was coupled with fear of living with free African Americans. To resolve their dilemma, colonizationists established the country of Liberia as a haven for free people of color.[36]

To the American Anti-Slavery Society, however, colonizationists were apologists for race prejudice, part of the problem of slavery rather than part of the solution. In the 1830s, abolitionist agents engaged colonizationists in dramatic confrontations. In 1842, the new Western New York Anti-Slavery Society attacked the American Colonization Society in its very first resolution. "Resolved," they wrote, "that he cannot be opposed to slavery, who is not avowedly an abolitionist . . . who is for colonizing any portion of the American people to a distant land because of an unwillingness to give them equal religious, political and social rights and immunities."[37]

It was no wonder, then, that Abby Kelley had no respect for "your Mr. Bogue." And it was no wonder, in turn, that the Reverend Mr. Bogue should be less than sympathetic to radical abolitionists in his own congregation. Immediately after Kelley's lectures, the church conducted perfunctory inquiries about Presbyterians who had attended. They were "satisfied with any kind of apology," reported Ansel Bascom, "& put no body upon trial."[38]

The conflict, however, could not be contained. It came into the open in the vestibule of the new Presbyterian church on the first Sabbath of October 1843. There, Presbyterian Rhoda Bement confronted (privately, she avowed) Bogue with a grievance. He had, she said, ignored antislavery notices that she had laid on his desk that morning (and the week before, too). What began as a conversation ended in a shouting match, overheard by everyone. According to Bement, Bogue denied that he had seen any notices and accused Bement of being "very unchristian, very impolite and very much out of your place to pounce upon me in this manner." "I told him I thought differently," Bement responded. "I thought I had a right to put the notices on the desk & to ask him why he didn't read them."

"You seem to doubt my veracity, the truthfulness of what I say," Bogue replied.

"Mr. Bogue I'll tell you why I doubt it," said Bement. "You told me you was an abolitionist & I supposed if you was an abolitionist you would read abolition notices that were bro't here. I bro't one last Sabbath and it wasn't read."[39]

According to Bogue, Bement "had done wrong & should be punished." True to his word, Bogue convinced Seneca Falls Presbyterians to put Rhoda Bement on trial. Other charges against Bement suddenly surfaced. Not only had she acted in an unchristian manner toward Reverend Bogue in the vestibule. She had also refused to attend communion or other meetings when Reverend Bogue officiated. Nor, it seemed, had she taken communion wine (although she had eaten communion bread) for many months. And finally, she had, "in a conspicuous manner" attended the "exhibition made by Abby Kelley on the first Sabbath of Aug. last . . . while the church to which Mrs. Bement belongs were attending upon divine service."[40]

Bement's trial brought dozens of people to the witness stand and kept the whole village in turmoil for two full months. Manuscript minutes of the proceedings filled sixty pages in the church record book. Seneca Falls riveted its attention on temperance, abolitionism, and woman's rights. Some of the testimony must have made Bogue's supporters regret that they had ever raised these issues.

As to the wine, Bement argued in her defense that it was not pure "juice of the grape"; it seemed contaminated by "alcohol or some kind of drug," and it was too strong for a person with temperance principles. Others in the church supported her view. Delia Matthews testified that "the last time I partook of the wine it was very offensive; it was very strong alcoholic wine. I have been absent the last two communions and at the two previous communions I refused to partake of it." Jonathan Metcalf, the same man who helped organize the Wesleyan Church, reported that the Methodists saw no need to serve wine as their communion drink. For the past year, they had successfully used unfermented grape juice, boiled and diluted.[41]

Most of Bement's trial focused on Kelley's abolitionism, and Bement reserved her strongest defense for the abolitionist firebrand: "Exhibitions made by Abby Kelly!" she exclaimed. "Is it right? Is it honest? So to misname a christian discourse, a gospel lecture . . . showing christians their duty to carry the glad tidings of liberty & salvation to 2½ millions of human beings held in worse than Egyptian bondage, & that we of the north are the slaveholders."[42]

Opponents viewed Kelley's speech differently. They were particularly outraged by a pledge that Kelley had urged her hearers to sign. This pledge was probably a version of the "Tea Total Pledge" that she had used throughout upstate New York. Intended to be provocative, it accurately summarized the radical abolitionist position. In it, signers agreed that slavery was "a heinous sin and crime, a curse to the master and a grievous wrong to the slave." "We will never vote for any candidate for civil office, nor countenance any man as a christian minister, nor hold connexion with any organization as a christian church," signers agreed, unless political parties and churches refused to support "any provision of the Constitution of the United States in favor of slavery," publicly pledged themselves to "immediate and unconditional emancipation," disavowed all fellowship with those who claimed slaves (abolitionists would not agree that anyone could actually own another person) or with those who voted for "slaveclaimants or their abettors." Finally, signers of the pledge agreed not to support those who might attempt to put down forcible slave resistance.[43]

Abby Kelley thought this pledge to be "the greatest aid of any measure I have ever adopted, in producing agitation. It throws corrupt politicians and sectarians into most delightful spasms." She defended herself from critics who thought the pledge too severe. It "merely asserts a withdrawal of support from all that supports slavery, politically and ecclesistically," she affirmed. "What's the difference between writing one's principles on paper, and by the life also, and writing them out by the life only?"[44]

The pledge, and the trial testimony about it, certainly made Bogue's supporters squirm. When Fanny Sackett was asked why she did not sign the pledge, she confessed that "I thought I would be bound to withdraw from the church & did not like to do so." Ansel Bascom, one of Bement's supporters, heard her make an even stronger statement: "I considered that it required those who signed it to come out of all pro-slavery churches, and *I considered this a pro-slavery church.*" Bascom reported that one of the members of the session remarked that "*the poison has gone deeper than the surface.*" For Cornelia Perry, Kelley's talk was the first abolitionist discussion she had ever heard. She had never considered the question much before, she confessed. "Our ministers had never told us anything about it & I had supposed there was no very great sin in it." Bascom wrote gleefully to Kelley afterward that "this was supposed by some to be a severer rebuke than any given by Abby Kelley herself."[45]

Woman's rights were also at issue in this trial. In her challenge to male religious authority, Bement provided a powerful role model; ten women followed her to the witness stand. Men as well as women focused on gender issues. Authorities asked Jabez Matthews whether he considered it proper and "clearly established in the Bible," "for a female to call a promiscuous meeting for the purpose of addressing them on Moral & Religious subjects?" even when it was "contrary to the established sentiment of the church to which they belong." Matthews replied, "I believe it is."[46]

On January 30, 1844, the session found Bement guilty of "disorderly and unchristian conduct." Bement refused to apologize. "I have but one thing to say," she told her judges: "For if I be an offender or have committed any thing worthy of death I refuse not to die; but if there be none of these things whereof these accuse me, no man may deliver me unto them—I appeal not unto Caeser but unto God." Actually, she did appeal unto Caesar, too, when she took her case to the regional committee of ministers and elders that met at Waterloo a week later. "A good audience attended at Waterloo," reported Bascom to Abby Kelley, "and more good was probably done by the spirit of *the devil exhibited* by the clerical members of that body than they have ever done by their preaching. . . . Your name has become a terror to the Presbytery."[47]

Presbyterians in Seneca Falls sustained Reverend Bogue's good name, but they paid a price. They lost not only the Bements but also other abolitionist members. Jeremy and Rhoda Bement left Seneca Falls for Buffalo, where Jeremy died of cholera in 1849. Daniel W. Forman, abolitionist elder, found a more congenial spiritual home among the Wesleyan Methodists. Sally Freeland Pitcher and Harriet Freeland Lindsley joined him.[48]

Abolitionist tensions were magnified so intensely in the Seneca Falls Presbyterian Church because, although officially Presbyterian, it was in fact "presbygational." Many members were Congregationalists by tradition and choice. Emphasizing local control and individual conscience, they were receptive to abolitionism in a way that the dominant Presbyterian hierarchy was not.[49] The odyssey of Jabez and Delia Matthews illustrates this pattern. Jabez Matthews supported Kelley's right to speak publicly, as a woman and an abolitionist, in Seneca Falls in 1843. He and his wife, Delia, left Seneca Falls in 1846 to become Presbyterians in Prattsburg, New York, and then in Waterloo. When they finally returned to Seneca Falls, however, they joined the reorganized Congregationalists. Ultimately, the Matthews family remained faithful to the Congregational tradition.[50]

Thanks to Abby Kelley, people in central and western New York had a clear chance, five years before the woman's rights convention, to think about just how far woman's rights ought to go. Some of them were ready to say, with Sarah Grimke, "[m]en and women were created equal; they are both moral and accountable beings, and whatever is right for a man to do, is right for a woman." Such thoughts made more orthodox thinkers nervous and even angry. What would these impractical reformers think of next?

Mobilization of both political and nonpolitical abolitionist networks would bring dozens of supporters to the Seneca Falls woman's rights convention in July 1848. As early as 1843, however, the stage for the Seneca Falls convention had been set, the supporting cast picked, and the first tentative rehearsals had begun.

CHAPTER 6

Women and Legal Reform in New York State

Martha Wright, ever the chronicler, entertained her sister Lucretia Mott with vignettes from Auburn's social life. In 1843, the topic of the hour was a proposed act to grant married women the right to own property. Parlor conversations echoed legislative debates. Frances Seward and her husband, Governor William Henry Seward, owned a home in Auburn, where Mrs. Seward (raised a Quaker herself) often invited David and Martha Wright to tea.

In some ways, Seward was more reform minded than her husband. She used their home as a haven for fugitives from slavery. She also supported the married woman's property act. She owned a copy of a pamphlet edition of the Ogdensburgh Lyceum lecture, *On the Political Rights of Women,* and judging by her marginal notes, she had read it carefully. She lobbied for the married woman's property bill at Albany social affairs, and she continued her efforts at home in Auburn. The Wrights, neighbors and friends, attended one such party. "The conversation at tea," Martha reported to Lucretia, "was on women having the property that their parents had accumulated for them, secured to them before marriage. A measure which Mrs. Satterlee and Mrs. Governor Seward advocated and David and Mrs. Worden [Frances Seward's sister] opposed. I agreed with the former. . . . David thought a wife shared in her husband's good fortune, and should be willing to share his reverses, and *in nine cases out of ten when a man failed in business it was traceable to a wife's extravagance.* Now," concluded Martha, "I think its a great shame for David to make so ungallant a speech as that, even if it was the truth which it is not."[1]

The issue that fueled disagreements at the tea party divided the whole population of New York. Between 1843 and 1848, New Yorkers were embroiled in questions not only about abolitionism but also about the nature of citizenship—

for people without property, African Americans, and women. Who should be allowed to vote? Who should be allowed to own property?

Voting rights for women emerged as part of a long debate about the meaning of the Declaration of Independence. When Americans signed the Treaty of Paris in 1783, the shooting war was over, but the political revolution was by no means complete. What did the Declaration of Independence, with its vision that "all men are created equal," really mean? If "life, liberty, and the pursuit of happiness" were natural and "unalienable rights," then they must belong to everyone, rich and poor; black, red, and white; young as well as old; female as well as male. If government derived its "just powers from the consent of the governed," did poor men have as much power as rich? Black or Indian as much as white? Women, of whatever race or color, as men? Children as much as adults? Immigrants as much as native-born? Obviously not, but where would Americans draw the line?[2]

One basic response emerged in the early nineteenth century. In state after state, Americans drew boundaries of legal equality, political power, and citizenship rights along lines of gender and race. Increasingly, they granted legal and political equality to all adult white males, regardless of wealth or place of birth. At the same time, they maintained property qualifications for free African Americans and excluded all slaves and women (along with infants, children, idiots, and felons) from full citizenship. As class became less important in defining formal legal and political power, race and sex became more so.

Advocates of equal suffrage for African Americans and women based their arguments primarily on the natural rights philosophy embodied in the Declaration of Independence. Many Americans, however, modified their commitment to natural rights. They agreed with seventeenth-century philosopher John Locke's original definition of rights. In a state of nature, Locke proposed, everyone had a right to "life, liberty, and property." For two reasons, liberty depended on independent property ownership. First, without property, one's political views (and votes) could always be purchased by those who held the purse strings. People without property, economically dependent, could never be politically independent. Second, without property, one did not pay taxes. Only those who paid taxes or served in the military contributed to maintaining the state. Males without property could argue that they still contributed militia service. Women without property had no such alternative. And if they gave nothing to support the government, why should they have a voice in its policy?

Under English common law, the basis of New York's law, no married woman could own property. When a woman married, she submerged her legal identity with that of her husband. In the words of William Blackstone, whose codification of English common law strongly influenced American codes, "By marriage, the husband and wife are one person in law: that is, the very being or existence of the woman is suspended during the marriage." Since a married woman had no legal existence, the argument ran, she could not own property.

Since she could not own property, she did not pay taxes. Since she did not pay taxes, she could not make independent political decisions.[3]

Obviously, if women controlled their own property, such an objection would disappear. To allow married women to own property was to remove the last logical obstacle to a woman's right to vote. The movement for a married woman's property act, then, became a dress rehearsal for woman's suffrage.

In practice, women's roles were not as circumscribed as laws alone would suggest, and the idealism of the American Revolution brought protofeminist challenges to gender inequities. Some of them were private, as in the famous exchange between Abigail and John Adams in 1776, when Abigail suggested that women might foment their own "Rebelion" if patriot leaders did not "remember the Ladies."[4] Abigail Adams was not alone in her views. In 1775, Thomas Paine wrote that women were "constrained in their desires in the disposal of their goods, robbed of freedom and will by the laws, the slaves of opinion." Massachusetts author Judith Sarget Murray published an essay, "On the Equality of the Sexes," in 1790, in which she argued that existing inequalities between women and men were not natural attributes but were based on education. British radical Mary Wollstonecraft voiced similar opinions that same year in her *Vindication of the Rights of Woman,* which went through several American editions.[5]

Most Americans, however, devised a kind of compromise position for women, an identity that Linda Kerber has called republican motherhood. This ideal, Kerber argued, allowed women to play both public and private roles. Women as mothers carried on traditional roles within the home. But in the new republic, motherhood assumed added significance. As moral preceptors, mothers sacrificed their own personal interests for the good of their children. By so doing, they became models of civic virtue, profoundly influencing their sons and daughters, future citizens all. A republican mother had her limits, however. As Kerber noted, "She was not to tell her male relatives for whom to vote. She was a citizen but not really a constituent."[6]

Meanwhile, the new federal government shunted the question of woman's citizenship rights aside. The U.S. Constitution, although ostensibly ordained and established by "we the people of the United States," never mentioned women. No one questioned that women were part of "the people." Women were citizens, and they were counted both as free persons and as slaves as the basis for apportioning representatives to the new Congress. But the founding fathers never anticipated more. For them, the politically active citizen was always male. Every gender-specific pronoun in the Constitution, for example, referred to males.

At least a few Americans noticed this exclusion of women. In *Alcuin,* a fictional dialogue written in the 1790s, Charles Brockden Brown presented a conversation in which a young man asked Mrs. Carter if she were a federalist. Anticipating later woman's rights arguments, Carter replied with heavy irony. "What have I, as a woman, to do with politics? Even the government of our country, which is said to be the freest in the world, passes over women as if they were not. We are excluded from all political rights without the least ceremony. Lawmakers thought as little of comprehending us in their code of liberty, as if we were pigs, or sheep. . . . No, I am no federalist. . . . The maxims of constitution-makers sound well," she agreed. "All power is derived from the people. Liberty is everyone's birthright. . . . Plausible and specious maxims! but fallacious." She imagined a line of potential voters. One was turned away because he was less than twenty-one years old. The second failed because he had not lived in the state long enough. The third was not eligible because he did not pay taxes. The fourth was dismissed because he was African American. Her turn approached. "'I am not a minor,' say I to myself. 'I was born in the state, and cannot, therefore, be stigmatized as a foreigner. I pay taxes, for I have no father or husband to pay them for me. Luckily my complexion is white. Surely my vote will be received. But, no, I am a woman.'" Her conclusion? "I cannot celebrate the equity of that scheme of government which classes me with dogs and swine."[7]

As Mrs. Carter recognized, voting was a central attribute of full citizenship. Since the Constitution left requirements for voting in the hands of the states, it was at the state level that challenges to the exclusion of women from the formal political process first reached the level of debate. During the Revolution itself, most state governments failed to deal with the issue. For its new state constitution in 1777, for example, New York adopted its colonial constitution virtually intact, granting the franchise only to propertied males.

New Jersey was an exception. There, the 1776 constitution gave voting rights to "all inhabitants of this Colony, of full age, who are worth fifty pounds Proclamation money, clear estate" and who had lived in the same county for twelve months prior to the election. "All inhabitants" included women, both African American and European American. Legislative acts in 1790 and 1797 referred to voters as "he or she," and women voted regularly in local, state, and national elections. In 1807, however, the legislature used the occasion of widespread fraud in one local election to exclude women from voting. At the same time, they virtually eliminated property qualifications for adult white males.[8]

By substituting gender and race instead of property as qualifications for suffrage, New Jersey set a pattern that New York followed in 1821, when it called a convention to establish a new constitution. In 1777, those who framed the first New York constitution gave equal voting rights to adult males, without regard to color. Both European American and African American men could vote for members of the General Assembly if they were twenty-one years old; had lived in one of the counties of the state for six months before the election; and either owned a freehold worth twenty pounds, rented property of forty shillings, or were listed as a freeman in the cities of Albany or New York. Voting requirements for senators were stricter, limited to those who owned freeholds clear of debt worth at least one hundred pounds.[9]

In 1821, New Yorkers created a new state constitution, and they made a distinction between European American and African American men. White men had only to be at least twenty-one years old, to have lived six months in the state, and to have paid road taxes or served in the militia during the last year. No free black male could vote, however, unless he had lived in the state at least three years and owned property worth $250 or more.[10]

Neither the extension of white male suffrage nor the restriction of black male suffrage came easily in 1821. Both issues absorbed days of debate. Speakers repeated "the same arguments, and the same language too, . . . three or four times over," until at least one member found the whole discussion "tedious and sickening."[11] Such repetition suggested the pervasiveness of republican ideals, but these ideals took different forms, depending on race. Tension between liberty and property dominated the discussion of white suffrage. Equality emerged as the main theme in the discussion of black suffrage.

The arguments at this convention presaged every major theme that would emerge in the fight for woman's suffrage a generation later. These were serious debates, rooted in conflict about the basic functions of government and about the meaning of the Declaration of Independence itself. Decisions to exclude any citizen from voting were based, as proponents and opponents alike quickly pointed out, on expediency rather than on natural rights, on fear, prejudice, or social factors rather than on logical applications of ideals of liberty and equality.

Advocates of property qualifications for white voters took their main stand on requirements for electing senators. On September 22, 1821, Chief Justice Ambrose Spencer moved that "every free male" (presumably including African Americans) who had lived in the state for a year and who had an interest "in law or equity, in his own or in his wife's right, in any lands or tenements in this state, of the value of 250 pounds over and above all debts charged thereon" should be entitled to vote for senators. "The senate was intended as the guardians of our property generally," Spencer asserted, and property qualifications for senatorial electors would help maintain that position. Chancellor James Kent concurred. Farmers helped promote "moderation, frugality, order, honesty, and a due sense of independence, liberty, and justice," Kent argued, and the senate should protect these landed interests.[12]

The battle was on. Both sides debated in republican terms, but they used very different assumptions. For Spencer, Kent, and their supporters, government existed not to protect the inalienable rights of "life, liberty, and the pursuit of happiness" but to protect "Lives, Liberties, and Estates, which I call by the general name, *Property.*" Life, liberty, and property, suggested Judge William Van Ness of Columbia County, "are the three great objects for which all governments are instituted, and to which all minor considerations should bend."[13]

As a corollary to this fundamental belief, advocates of property qualifications shared a profound suspicion of people who had no real estate. Without property, they had "of course no interest in the government," asserted Van Ness. They could never make independent political decisions. Universal suffrage would give the vote to single men, transients, factory workers, and laborers, all employed by other, wealthier men. And "that man," asserted Mr. S. [Sanford?], "who holds in his hands the subsistence of another, will always be able to control his will. Such a person will forever be the creature of the one who feeds, shelters, clothes, and protects him."[14]

Conservatives feared that rapid changes in the state's economy would actually increase the number of such propertyless men. Canals, cities, and factories would undermine the strength of farmers, destroy widespread education, and corrode the civic virtue of New York's citizens. The freehold qualification was, said Ezekiel Bacon, delegate from Oneida County, "a sort of moral and independent test of character." Whereas farmers promoted "good morals, and the general diffusion of education and intelligence," as J. Sutherland argued, western New York would soon become "the workshop . . . of a very considerable portion of this union," and New York City would be "the London of this western world." Such economic growth would lead to a geometrical increase in "a class of citizens, who, destitute alike of property, of character, and of intelligence, neither contribute to the support of its institutions, nor can be safely trusted with the choice of its rulers." Already New York City had, as General [Stephen or Jacob R.] Van Rensellaer asserted, a "vast mass of combustible matter." Faced with so dire a prospect, conservatives could only conclude with Jonas Platt that voting was "neither a right nor a franchise, but was, more properly speaking, an office . . . a public trust."[15]

To support their contention, conservatives offered precedents. No person dependent upon another had ever voted, they asserted, nor had anyone argued that they should. Elisha Williams, delegate from Daniel Cady's boyhood home in Columbia County and the same man who had invested so heavily in Waterloo real estate, made a powerful case. Take women, for example. "By the universal consent of mankind," noted Williams, "one half, and truth no less than politeness compels me to add, the better half of the whole human family, is at once and utterly excluded from any participation of sovereignty." Of the male population, no infants, foreigners, paupers, or felons could vote. In fact, only one-tenth of the total population were "the actual, legitimate sovereigns of the state." If all people were born equal in political rights, if self-government were indeed a natural and unalienable right, such unequal distribution of political power would be "usurpation; it would be tyranny." In fact, concluded Williams, the United States was "an elective republic." "Most surely, it does not follow that all who are protected by government . . . are also entitled to a voice in the designation of the men who administer that government. All have lives to be protected; but all living are not, therefore, entitled to become electors. All are entitled to civil and religious liberty—the minor as extensively as the adult—the female as extensively as the male—yet they have not all a voice in choosing their rulers; many a female, as well as many a legal infant, is in possession of large estates, but they cannot vote." And so he rested his case.[16]

Advocates of universal white male suffrage challenged Williams's argument. Referring explicitly to the Declaration of Independence, they attacked the idea that property ownership automatically produced civic virtue or political independence. Daniel D. Tompkins, president of the convention, argued heatedly that "property, sir, when compared with our other essential rights, is insignificant and trifling. 'Life, liberty, and the pursuit of happiness'—not of property—are set forth in the declaration of independence. Property is not even named." John Cramer argued that even poor men had honesty and integrity. Governmental stability rested not on property ownership but on "the virtue and intelligence of the people." And David Buel echoed this belief. "Property, as such," he contended, "is not the basis of representation. Our community is an association of persons—of human beings—not a partnership founded on property."[17]

In spite of such arguments, the convention was not yet ready to grant unrestricted voting rights to all adult males. Delegates were, however, ready to compromise. They agreed that militia service or payment of taxes to build and maintain roads was sufficient contribution to the community to qualify white men, but not African American men, for suffrage.

Opponents of black suffrage produced a variety of convoluted arguments. Some argued that since African Americans owned little property and were not allowed to serve in the militia, "they are seldom, if ever, required to share in the common burthens or defence of the state." Others suggested that whites would control black votes or that black voters would enhance the power of New York City. The whole state, suggested one delegate, would "be controlled by a few hundred of this species of population in the city of New-York." Underlying this was a partisan political issue: the Democratic-controlled constitutional convention feared that black voters would flock to the Federalists.[18]

All of these arguments rested on openly avowed racist assumptions. Blacks, asserted Mr. Ross, chair of the committee on suffrage, "are a peculiar people, incapable . . . of exercising that privilege [of voting] with any sort of discretion, prudence, or independence. They have no just conceptions of civil liberty." The right of suffrage would not elevate blacks to a just idea of their responsibilities any more than it would elevate "a monkey or a baboon." With only slightly more tact, Samuel Young declared: "This distinction of colour is well understood. It is unnecessary to disguise it, and we ought to shape our constitution so as to meet the public sentiment. If that sentiment should alter—if the time should ever arrive when the African shall be raised to the level of the white man . . .—when the colours shall intermarry—when negroes shall be invited to your tables—to sit in your pew, or ride in your coach, it may then be proper to institute a new Convention, and remodel the constitution so as to conform to that state of Society."[19]

Ross, Young, and other opponents of black suffrage argued that voting rights were a matter of expediency, not a natural right. "That all men are free and equal," suggested Ross, "applies to them only in a state of nature, and not after the institution of civil government; for then many rights, flowing from a natural equality, are necessarily abridged. . . . The truth is, this exclusion invades no inherent rights. . . . It must therefore necessarily rest on the ground of expediency." Samuel Young took the argument further. "Is the right of voting a natural right?" he asked. "If so, our laws are oppressive and unjust. A natural right is one that is born with us. No man is born twenty-one years old. . . . It is a question of expediency."[20]

To support their position, opponents of black suffrage made the analogy with Native Americans, women, children, and aliens. If these groups could be disfranchised, and who argued otherwise, why could blacks not be excluded as well? "Even the better part of creation [women]," noted Ross, "are not permitted to participate in this right. No sympathies seem to be awakened in their behalf, nor in behalf of the aborigines, the original and only rightful proprietors of our soil." Colonel Young took up the cry. "If you admit the negroes, why exclude the aborigines? They have never been enslaved. They were born free as the air they breathe." "If there is that natural, inherent right to vote, which some gentlemen have urged," he continued, "it ought to be further extended. In New-Jersey, females were formerly allowed to vote; and on that principle, you must admit *negresses* as well as *negroes* to participate in the right of suffrage. Minors, too, and aliens must no longer be excluded, but the 'era of good feelings' must be commenced in earnest."[21]

Supporters of black suffrage asserted that voting was a natural right. To deny suffrage to African Americans would be "repugnant to all the principles and notions of liberty . . . and to our declaration of independence," said R. Clarke. In addition, it would be unconstitutional. The Constitution based both representation and taxation on the number of free inhabitants of each state. "All colours and complexions are here included," Clarke noted. "It is not free 'white' persons. No, sir, our venerable fathers entertained too strong a sense of justice to countenance such an odious distinction."[22] As to African Americans not serving in the militia, "Sir, whose fault is this?" suggested Clarke. It was the fault of whites, who refused to serve with blacks in time of peace. Wartime, however, posed a different problem, and blacks had served with distinction in both army and navy during the War of 1812. Black sailors were responsible for American victories on Lake Erie and Lake Champlain.[23] It was true that African Americans were numerous enough to affect the outcome of elections in New York City. But there, as James Tallmadge from Dutchess County pointed out, only 163 blacks had voted in the previous election.[24]

This brought advocates of black suffrage to the heart of the matter—racial prejudice. As Abraham Van Vechten of Albany queried, "Do our prejudices against their colour destroy their rights as citizens?" Federalist Peter Jay, son of John Jay who had authored the 1777 state constitution, continued the defense. All the arguments against black voting, he pointed out, can be summed up in one, "that we are accustomed to look upon black men with contempt—that we will not eat with them—that we will not sit with them—that we will not serve with them in the militia, or on juries, nor in any manner associate with them—and then it is concluded, that they ought not to vote with us—how, sir, can that argument be answered by reason, which does not profess to be founded on reason?" Let us not contradict our profusely expressed beliefs in the equality of all men, he argued, "merely to gratify odious, and I hope, temporary prejudices." After all, "what crime have they committed for which they are to be punished? Why are they, who were born as free as ourselves, natives of the same country, and deriving from nature and our political institutions, the same rights and privileges which we have, now to be deprived of all those rights and doomed to remain forever as aliens among us?"[25]

Those in favor of suffrage for African American men ultimately rested their arguments on assertions of equality. Peter Jay pleaded in religious rhetoric that "we are all the offspring of one common Father, and redeemed by one common Saviour—the gates of paradise are open alike to the bond and the free." Jonas Platt, delegate from Oneida County, passionately summed up the whole argument in republican terms. "The obligations of justice are eternal and indispensable," he asserted. "Our republican text is, that all men are born equal, in civil and political rights." What if the constitution excluded all people of German, Low Dutch, or Irish ancestry? "Would not every man be shocked at the horrid injustice of the principle?"[26]

Platt attacked the speech of the chair of the suffrage committee who "exultingly told us, that ours is the only happy country where freemen acknowledge no distinction of ranks—where real native genius and merit can emerge from the humblest conditions of life, and rise to honours and distinction. It sounded charmingly in our republican ears. . . . [U]nfortunately for our patriotic pride, it is not true." He then pointed to the chair's resolution that would degrade thirty-seven thousand free black citizens "below the common rank of freeman" by denying them the right to vote. "As a republican statesman," Platt concluded, and "as a man and a father, who expects justice for himself and his children, in this world; and as a Christian, who hopes for mercy in the world to come; I can not, I dare not, consent to this unjust proscription."[27]

Nothing, however, could sway the majority of convention members. Fear, prejudice, and expediency overcame all appeals to justice, morality, or natural rights. In its final form, the suffrage amendment included the provision that men of color must have been citizens for three years and have a freehold of at least $250. It passed overwhelmingly, 72 to 32. As for the whole constitution, only eight delegates voted against it. Twenty-four, however, abstained, primarily because they objected to extending the vote for white adult males. Among them were the four delegates from the young Elizabeth Cady's home county of Montgomery.[28]

Excluding women, children, and Indians from voting—nine-tenths of the population, according to Elisha Williams—provided a powerful precedent for limiting African American suffrage. Yet as the link between liberty and property came under continued attack, some citizens wondered why African Americans and women, too, should not vote. William Ray, a poet from Auburn, New York, raised the question in his *Poems, on Various Subjects, Religious, Moral, Sentimental, and Humorous* in 1821. Among them, perhaps in the humorous category, he included a "Petition to the Convention in Behalf of the Ladies." In it, he suggested,

That ev'ry one must have a vote,
Who does not wear a petticoat,
    Is generally admitted;
But why should women be denied,
    And have their tongues completely tied,
For party broils well fitted.
. . . .
But you, immortal statesmen, you,
Keeping the lovely sex in view
    At your august convention,
Will frame the constitution so
    That ladies can t'election go,
Without the least detention;

For, should you otherwise decree,
The direful consequence may be
    Diminish'd population;
And this I'm authoris'd to say,
If women's rights are flung away,
    Is their determination.[29]

By the 1830s, advocates of woman's political rights came from many different backgrounds. Pure republican logic motivated some. Among them was Abraham Lincoln. Running as Whig candidate for the Illinois state legislature in 1836, he stated his position clearly in the *Sangamo Journal.* "I go for all sharing the privileges of the government," he wrote, "who assist in bearing its burthens . . . admitting all whites to the right of suffrage, who pay taxes or bear arms (by no means excluding females)."[30]

Most of the singers in this political chorus, however, were trained in one of two schools, abolitionism or the legal reform movement. Not surprisingly, abolitionists were especially sensitive to the rights of women. Parallels between the powerlessness of slaves and that of women, black or white, were inescapable. Angelina Grimké, for example, came right to the point. "Are we aliens because we are women?" she asked. "Are we bereft of citizenship because we are the mothers, wives, and daughters of a mighty people? Have women no country—no interest staked in public weal—no liabilities in common-peril—no partnership in a nation's guilt and shame?" For an abolitionist, it was a logical query, and it stirred many to a thoughtful response.[31]

Harriet Martineau, English author and personal friend of many American abolitionists, included a discussion of the political nonexistence of American women in her widely read 1837 *Society in America.* "One of the fundamental principles announced in the Declaration of Independence is," she wrote, "that governments derive their just powers from the consent of the governed. How can the political condition of women be reconciled with this?"[32] John Greenleaf Whittier, one of Henry Stanton's abolitionist coworkers, raised a similar question with Lucretia Mott a year or two later. "*Give women the right to vote,*" Whittier declared, "and you end all these persecutions by reform and church organizations."[33]

Unlike abolitionists, most legal reformers in the 1830s approached woman's rights indirectly. They focused on the right of married women to own property, often to protect family assets from business losses or profligate sons-in-law. Such a goal seemed reasonable to propertied families. In 1836, only one legislator opposed forming a select committee to study married woman's property rights. Yet the New York legislature debated the issue for twelve years. Why? Because everyone recognized that allowing married women to own and control their own property would open the door to other rights for women. For those who held a republican vision of the world, property rights and political rights were inextricably bound together. As George Geddes, assemblyman from Onondaga County, realized, married woman's property rights raised "the whole question of woman's proper place in society, in the family and everywhere."[34]

Between 1815 and 1828, the question of married woman's property rights had been at least temporarily resolved, as equity courts, left over from colonial New York, allowed wealthy families to protect woman's property rights through prenuptial agreements and legal trusts. These trusts were clearly defined under the leadership of James Kent, chancellor of New York from 1814 to 1823, whose ideas about equity and legal protection for married women influenced generations of Americans. His four-volume *Commentaries on American Law,* written between 1826 and 1830, was the most influential work on law since Blackstone. It went through eleven editions by 1867.[35]

Many New Yorkers, however, viewed equity courts as fortresses of privilege for the wealthy. In their enthusiasm for democratic ideals (at least for white males) in the 1820s, Americans attacked equity courts as too far removed from the will of the people. Influenced in part by the English Utilitarian Jeremy Bentham, Americans began to try to simplify their laws, purging them of inequities left over from English common law. In December 1828, the New York state legislature passed the *Revised Statutes of the State of New York,* which limited the power of equity courts and threw into confusion the question of married woman's property rights. Premarital agreements, certain kinds of trusts, and the ability of married women to will property to others were all threatened. After 1828, no married woman could be legally secure in her control of property.[36]

The *Revised Statutes* generated opposition far beyond the Cady law office. Into the middle of this legal quagmire came Fanny Wright, controversial reformer and author of *Views of Society and Manners in America* (1821). As a radical proponent of equal rights for working people, African Americans, and women, Wright edited, with Robert Dale Owen, the *Free Enquirer* and helped organize New York's working-class political movement. Wright left New York City in 1830, after only a year of residence, but she had done much to raise questions about the rights of women to education, property ownership, divorce, and birth control.[37]

Neither Wright nor her compatriots were able to translate their radical egalitarian vision into effective legal action. That role fell to a sympathizer of Wright, Thomas Herttell. Herttell was a New York City lawyer and member of the New York State Assembly. Solomon Southwick, one of Herttell's friends and critics, noted that Herttell had once belonged to "that old and pure Republican School." By the late 1820s, however, Herttell was pursuing a "wild career," embracing a variety of reforms associated with Fanny Wright. These he tried to implement in the New York state legislature. He worked to abolish imprisonment for debt, establish a system of universal education, and prevent the appointment of official chaplains for the state legislature.[38]

He also worked for legal rights for married women, specifically for the right of married women to own property. In 1836, he introduced a resolution to appoint a select committee on married woman's property. This bill attracted the attention of Ernestine Potoski Rose. Rose was born of Jewish parents in Pyeterkow, Poland. In 1834, she formed a group in England called "The Association of all Classes of all Nations, without distinction of sect, sex, party condition, or color." After her marriage to William Rose in 1836, she moved to New York City and began to lecture extensively throughout the state.[39]

In the course of Rose's travels, she circulated a petition among women to support Herttell's bill for married woman's property rights. It was with "a good deal of trouble," she remembered, that she convinced five women to sign this petition. "Women at that time had not learned to know that she had any rights except those that man in his generosity allowed her," Rose explained. Rose's petition marked the first time that any woman except Fanny Wright had taken public action for legal reform in New York. She continued to generate petitions until the legislature finally passed a married woman's property act in 1848.[40]

With the assistance of John Savage, former chief justice of the New York State Supreme Court, and John C. Spencer, a highly respected lawyer and legislator, Herttell rewrote his proposal and introduced it again in 1837. His new bill was thorough and clear. "Its primary *principle,*" he wrote, "is to preserve to *married women* the title, possession, and control of their estate, both real and personal *after* as *before* marriage;—and that no part of it shall innure to their husbands, solely by virtue of their *marriage.*" This bill would protect the property of married women from "injury and waste by means of the unprovident, prodigal, intemperate, and dissolute habits and practices of their husbands" and would "save it from loss through the husband's misfortunes and crimes." In short, he wrote, this bill would make both husband and wife "exclusively answerable for his or her own misconduct."[41]

Herttell argued that married women's legal disabilities originated in the common law of England, which was incompatible with New York's constitution. He phrased his argument in republican terms: "That 'all men are born free and with equal rights,' is an admitted maxim in the moral and political creed of all advocates and friends of free government. That this truth is meant to apply exclusively to the *male* sex, will not be urged by any who have a due regard for their reputation for common sense." Citing the Declaration of Independence, he argued that the Constitution was intended to secure equal rights for all citizens "and hence to preserve the rights of private property *equally to all*— . . . *female*, equally with *male citizens*, and the *married* equally with the *un*married, of *one sex* equally with the *other*."[42]

Herttell could not have made a clearer, stronger argument for equal rights, and it applied just as well to political as to property rights. Yet, perhaps for pragmatic reasons, he stopped short of directly advocating women's right to vote. Instead, he expounded on the virtues of women as republican mothers. "Mothers are the natural, and most immediate guardians and *primary teachers* of their infant offspring," he argued. Yet how can they bring moral, intellectual, or political benefit to the community when they are "deprived of their rights, despoiled of their property, slandered in their character, neglected in their right education, and thus degraded in their condition" by remnants of the common law?[43]

Herttell's bill did not pass, and he himself left the assembly after 1840.[44] Others, however, boldly continued the argument that Herttell had begun. Conservatives feared what radical reformers hoped for. The connection between married woman's property rights and the right of women to vote was so strong that it delayed revisions in the property law that almost everyone desired. Assemblyman John O'Sullivan submitted a bill in 1841, which never reached a vote. In 1842, as chair of the Judiciary Committee, he again reported favorably on such a bill. The committee, he noted, expressed "their unanimous opinion in favor of a more liberal extension of the rights of married women." Nevertheless, the committee concluded, "in a change so important and delicate, in what may be regarded as the very fundamental institution of society . . . no degree of caution can be too great." The press of business was too heavy, committee members decided, to give this question the attention it deserved.[45]

A comprehensive bill finally emerged in 1846. Stating that the "rights of married women, at common law, are among the remnants of feudal law that linger among us," the committee proposed a bill that gave married women the right to own property, to will it to whomever they chose, and to sue and be sued in matters relating to their separate estate. In response to a petition from Thomas Herttell, the bill also declared that habitual drunkenness was a legitimate cause for divorce.[46]

None of these bills became law. Yet extensive delays only encouraged further debate and broadened public consciousness. By the 1840s, Elizabeth Cady Stanton remembered, married woman's property had become "the topic of general interest around many fashionable dinner-tables, and at many humble firesides. In this way all phases of the question were touched upon, involving the relations of the sexes, and gradually widening to all human interests—political, religious, civil and social."[47]

Extensive debates converted large numbers of women to the cause. As Stanton remembered, "the press and the pulpit became suddenly vigilant in marking out woman's sphere, while woman herself seemed equally vigilant in her efforts to step outside the prescribed limits." Paulina Wright (Davis) of Utica and Elizabeth Cady Stanton joined Ernestine Rose in speaking to legislative committees. Stanton talked with many legislators, she remembered, "both of the Senate and Assembly, in society, as well as in committee rooms."[48]

In the early 1840s, support for woman's suffrage emerged alongside property rights. In 1843, the *Seneca Falls Democrat* noted that its rival paper, the *Seneca Observer,* "suggests that the right of voting should be extended to females in common with males, and thinks it is a violation of the great doctrine of equal rights that such is not the case." Perhaps the editor of the *Observer* had been inspired by a series of lectures given at the Broadway Tabernacle in New York City. Published in the *New York Herald* under the pseudonym of Brother Jonathan, these discussions advocated not only legal rights but also voting rights for women.[49]

Discussion of woman's property rights and political rights reached a crescendo in 1846, when New York called a new constitutional convention. Debate centered on two related questions: Should married women be allowed to own property? And who should be allowed to vote in New York? Voters elected convention delegates in April 1846. Seneca County sent Ansel Bascom, the irascible Seneca Falls reformer. In Waterloo, a meeting of citizens "without distinction of party" unanimously endorsed Bascom as a person "who has, by his past course, given evidence of a hearty desire to accomplish a radical change in the organic law of the State." His credentials included publication of a legal-reform journal called the *Memorialist.* At the convention, Bascom became a leader in the battle for married woman's property provisions and the fight for black suffrage.[50]

When the convention finally began to debate the married woman's property provision on October 2, delegates generally favored it. Bascom proposed an amendment to protect the rights of men as well as women. Neither husband nor wife, he argued, should be liable for the debts of the other. Bascom's amendment was defeated, but the original motion passed by a substantial margin, 58 to 44.[51]

Three days later, however, at the request of Charles O'Conor of New York City, the convention reconsidered their endorsement. The provision for married woman's property, asserted O'Conor, was "more important than any which had been adopted—perhaps than all the rest of the constitution. If there was any thing in our institutions that ought not to be touched by the stern hand of the *reformer*, it was the sacred ordinance of marriage." O'Conor was unmarried, forty-two years old, and born of Irish parents. Articulate and forceful in debate, he was one of the few public figures willing to argue outright that English common law appropriately defined the position of women. He lauded the common law because it "recognized the husband as the head of the household, merged in him the legal being of the wife so thoroughly, that in contemplation of law she could scarcely be said to exist." The common law "was based upon the gospel precept, 'they twain shall be one flesh,'" and it was "pure as its origin." O'Conor's arguments convinced the convention to reverse the married woman's property provision, 59 to 50.[52]

Reformers also lost the battle for black suffrage. African Americans, with the support of white abolitionists, promoted equal suffrage at their annual state conventions, and they argued for it in republican terms. "We merely put forth our appeal for a republican birth-right," they pleaded. "We fully believe in the fundamental doctrines set forth in the Declaration of Independence. We acquiesce in the sentiment that 'governments derive their just power from the consent of the governed.' And we say it is injustice of the most aggrieved character, . . . to deprive us of a just and legitimate participation in the rights of the state."[53]

Many European American citizens agreed. Among them was Horace Greeley, influential editor of the *New York Tribune.* "So far as we have any partialities," he concluded, "we are of course against the African blood and hue. But reared in and devoted to Republican principles, how *can* we say that they should not enjoy the sacred right of Self Government the same as other men?"[54]

The June 30 report of the Committee on the Rights and Privileges of Citizens raised the issue of suffrage in the language of equal rights, asserting that "men are by nature free and independent, and in their social relations entitled to equal rights," and that "all political powers is inherent in the people."[55] On July 28, Ansel Bascom moved to amend the committee's first point to read: "Men are by nature free and independent, and in their social *and political* relations entitled to equal rights." By including political rights, Bascom wanted to endorse voting rights for African American men. Perhaps he was aware that he also laid the groundwork for debates about woman's suffrage.[56]

When delegates at last took up this report on August 6, they plunged into heated exchanges about the very nature of democracy. Bascom's amendment had "promoted much sensation." He defended it, however, arguing that "we derived our right to sit here, we derived all our political rights from their fearless publication by the Declaration of Independence. If the time has come when such a body of men as this feared to say that the political rights of men were equal, for one he desired to know it." He found out. The convention defeated his motion, 42 to 33.[57]

Bascom's supporters refused to give up. George A. S. Crooker, a lawyer from

Cattaraugus County, immediately proposed to include the whole first clause of the Declaration of Independence in place of Bascom's resolution. A voice from the audience shouted out, "Why not move to insert the whole Declaration of Independence?" Levi S. Chatfield, a lawyer of Scottish background from Otsego County, wanted to add the words "without regard to color," to make the point perfectly clear. It would then read, "All men are created equal and are endowed by their Creator with certain inalienable rights, *without regard to color,* among them are life, liberty, and the pursuit of happiness."[58]

This was too much for the opposition. Charles O'Conor, the same man who so successfully opposed the married woman's property clause, resorted to ridicule. "Will the gentleman accept an amendment to that or an addition," he asked, "viz: the words 'age *or sex*!'" The convention laughed, but Chatfield never missed a beat. "Oh, certainly," he replied.[59]

Crooker, waving the Declaration of Independence, defended his motion. Blacks were "born and bred upon our soil," he pleaded. "And here in the house of their birth we dare to deny them the sacred right of suffrage on account of the shade or color of the skin. . . . It is might and power alone that gives right. It is the robber's right. But I confess I was not prepared to hear it declared in this hall, that the principles of the declaration of independence are mere abstractions. If we have indeed come to this . . . we have very far departed from the 'faith once delivered to the saints.' We have lost sight of the principle of equal rights, and our government is indeed a despotism." The Bascom-Crooker-Chatfield amendment lost, 42 to 19.[60]

Charles O'Conor had raised the question of equal rights for women in jest, to discredit black suffrage rights in the eyes of the majority of the convention. Some New York citizens took the matter seriously. Residents from at least three counties (Albany, Jefferson, and Wyoming Counties) sent petitions to the convention asking for woman's suffrage. They couched their request in true republican language. Six women from Depauville, Jefferson County, for example (Eleanor Vincent, Lydia A. Williams, Lydia Osborn, Susan Ormsby, Amy Ormsby, and Anna Bishop) argued that "that all governments must derive their just powers from the consent of the governed." "The present government of this state," they asserted, "has widely departed from the true democratic principles upon which all just governments must be based by denying to the female portion of the community the right of suffrage . . . and by imposing upon them burdens of taxation . . . without admitting them the right of representation. . . . Your Memorialists therefore ask your honorable body . . . to extend to women equal . . . civil and political rights with men." Woman's rights, they noted, were not new. They belonged by inheritance to women as citizens of the state of New York.[61]

No taxation without representation seemed a powerful argument. So did the idea that suffrage was a natural right. Most delegates, however, twisted these republican arguments into a caricature. Women became pawns in the political fight against black suffrage, just as they had been in 1821. Excluding women citizens from voting, opponents of black voting rights argued, proved that voting was not a natural right but a privilege. Since women could be denied suffrage, so could black men. If we concede, said John A. Kennedy, a Baltimore-born paint dealer from New York City, that voting is a natural right, "to whom would it belong? . . . Not male citizens of natural age and diverse colors only. No, sir; natural rights recognized no more distinctions in age or sex, than in color or condition. Nor did they stop with our women and children: but fairly and honestly carried out, would extend the exercise to every human being who might happen to be on our soil on an election day." "Civilized society throughout the world," on the other hand, "limited political privilege, to mature age and the male sex," about one-fifth of the population. If this was too small a proportion of voters, Kennedy suggested, "females of mature age, of our own race" should be given the vote before "a people who were foreigners in our midst."[62]

Friends of black suffrage countered with arguments of their own. One delegate challenged Kennedy's analogy between blacks and women. Women, said David S. Waterbury of Delaware County, "are protected in their rights and privileges by husbands and brothers. Where do you find any one to stand up for the colored man? Not one."[63] Most advocates of black suffrage, however, argued in republican terms. Feelings ran high. Benjamin F. Bruce, a farmer from Madison County, made "an impassioned appeal in behalf of equal rights." Federal Dana, a farmer from Madison County and one of Gerrit Smith's former clerks, created "considerable excitement and much confusion" with his defense of black suffrage. A. W. Young, an author from Wyoming County, quoted from the Declaration of Independence to argue that "if Thomas Jefferson could only witness their conduct and hear their language, he would disown all such democrats."[64]

Some Americans were both black and female. For them, these debates had special relevance. At least one black woman articulated her own awareness of race, sex, and class. "The colored woman who would elevate herself," wrote M. E. Mills from Albany, "must contend not only with prejudice against poverty [and] prejudice against color but prejudice against her sex. Which of these is the most cruel I am not prepared to say. But that all three combined are enough to crush a Lion I am prepared to testify."[65]

Reformers outside the convention quickly rallied. One of the most outspoken was Samuel J. May. Radical abolitionist and peace advocate, May had recently been called as minister to the Unitarian Church in Syracuse, New York.[66] In November 1846, he gave an uncompromising sermon in favor of woman's suffrage. Women had been prevented from voting on a temperance referendum in the spring of 1846, he noted, at the same time that "the *men* of our nation presumed to plunge us into the multiform calamities, crimes, and expenditures" of a war against Mexico. Nor had women ever been asked to give an opinion on the new constitution. To look at the constitution, he suggested, one would never suspect that "there were any women in the body politic." It was, he argued, "all unequal, all unrighteous—this utter annihilation, politically considered, of more than one half of the whole community. . . . This entire disfranchisement of females is as unjust as the disfranchisement of the males would be." "I fain would hope," he concluded, "that, when next the people frame a constitution for this state, the stupendous fact will not be overlooked *that more than one-half of our population are females, to whom equal rights and equal privileges ought to be accorded.*"[67]

Elisha P. Hurlbut, a New York City lawyer, reflected the same arguments in his *Essays on Human Rights, and Their Political Guaranties.* "Woman's rights are as sacred to the law as man's," he asserted, and "her concern with government is as great and important as his own." "There seems to be no escape from the claims of woman to the full rights of citizenship," he concluded. If her nature is the same as man's (and Hurlbut believed that it was), then "she can claim to exercise the elective franchise of common right." If her nature was different, then men "cannot properly represent her. . . . This would entitle women not only to vote, but by their votes to elect a separate branch of the Legislature."[68]

Nowhere did republican ideology emerge more clearly as a basis for both property rights and citizenship rights for women than in a speech given before the lyceum in Ogdensburgh, New York. The lecture was probably given by John Fine, a Democratic lawyer and congressman from St. Lawrence County, in 1847, when Fine unsuccessfully ran against Daniel Cady for Supreme Court justice.[69] Judge Fine argued strenuously for married woman's property rights as well as for the right of women to vote and to hold office. "THAT ALL ARE CREATED FREE AND EQUAL; THAT THEY ARE ENDOWED BY THEIR CREATOR WITH CERTAIN UNALIENABLE RIGHTS; THAT AMONG THESE ARE LIFE, LIBERTY, AND THE PURSUIT OF HAPPINESS—is acknowledged to be the fundamental doctrine upon which this Republic is founded," Fine asserted. This idea "is freedom's golden rule. . . . None should ever be allowed to restrict its universality. Women, as well as men, are entitled to the full enjoyment of its practical blessings."[70]

Life, liberty, and the consent of the governed were the bywords of these reformers. For radical suffrage advocates, voting rights were natural rights. Property ownership was not relevant. But for those who believed that voters should have some personal obligation to the government, the idea that married women could own property opened up a Pandora's box full of possibilities. If women paid taxes, what could, logically, keep them from voting? Conservatives would have to fight a hard battle, just as they had successfully done with black men, to keep women property owners, whether black or white, from voting. And they would have to make their arguments on the basis of expediency, not natural rights.

Twelve years of debate about married woman's property culminated in April 1848, when the state legislature finally took action. John Fine introduced a bill in the Senate in January for a married woman's property act. Judge Fine had personal reasons for introducing such a bill. His wife had brought property of her own to their marriage, and he had experienced great difficulty in trying to keep it separate from his own.[71] George Geddes, one of Fine's supporters, also had a special interest in this bill. He had a young daughter, and he feared that he might die in middle age, leaving her without financial protection. On February 23, 1848, he submitted a petition from three hundred voters in Syracuse, supporting the bill.

Senators lined up on both sides of the issue. "The measure was so radical, so extreme," noted Geddes, "that even its friends had doubts; but the moment any important amendment was offered, up rose the whole question of woman's proper place in society, in the family, and everywhere." Gender relationships, as defined in New York state law, seemed too big a question to tackle piecemeal, but Geddes and others saw no alternative. "We meant to strike a hard blow," he confessed, "and if possible shake the old system of laws to their foundations, and leave it to other times and wiser councils to perfect a new system." The bill finally passed the Senate on March 29, 1848, 23 to 1.[72]

In April 1848, the New York state assembly addressed the problem. Again, they were prodded by petitions from citizens. One in particular revealed the importance of revolutionary rhetoric and grassroots commitment in sustaining support for woman's rights. In March 1848, forty-four ladies (married, as they were careful to assert) petitioned the legislature from the towns of Darien and Covington in Genesee and Wyoming Counties. With potent sarcasm, they argued,

> That your Declaration of Independence declares, that governments derive their just powers from the consent of the governed. And as women have never consented to, been represented in, or recognized by this government, it is evident that in justice no allegiance can be claimed from them.
>
> Your laws after depriving us of property, of the means of acquiring it, and even of individuality, require the same obedience from us as from free citizens.
>
> We therefore think, common justice and humanity would dictate, that when you class us and our privileges with those of idiots, and lunatics, you should do the same with regard to our responsibilities; and as our husbands assume responsibility for our debts and trespasses, they should also for our misdemeanors and crimes; for justice can never hold lunatics, idiots, infants, or married women, (as the law now is,) accountable for their conduct.
>
> When women are allowed the privilege of rational and accountable beings, it will be soon enough to expect from them the duties of such.
>
> Our numerous and yearly petitions for this most desirable object having been disregarded, we now ask your august body, to abolish all laws which hold married women more accountable for their acts than infants, idiots, and lunatics.

Perhaps inspired (or shamed) by such rhetoric, the New York state legislature did pass its first Married Woman's Property Act, in April 1848.[73] The *His-*

tory of Woman Suffrage called this bill "the death-blow to the old Blackstone code for married women in this country." And so it has seemed to historians. At the time, however, its immediate impact was muted. Stanton herself minimized its specific provisions, for she cited the lack of married woman's property rights as one of her main points at the Seneca Falls convention, perhaps realizing that most other states did not yet have such legislation.[74]

Legislative discussion of the legal rights of married women, phrased in republican terms, set the stage for further steps by women themselves. As Stanton noted, the Married Woman's Property Act "encouraged action on the part of women," since "if the men who make the laws were ready for some onward step, surely the women themselves should express interest in legislation." In April 1848, no one could guess what that action might be. Stanton herself would translate, within the short space of three months, the sense of energy and possibility that emerged from the agitation for the Married Woman's Property Act into an organized political effort for the rights of women in every area of life, including the right to vote.[75]

PART 3

The Event: Converging Paths

CHAPTER 7

Adversity and Transcendence, June 1847–June 1848

June 1847 to June 1848 was a year of transition for Elizabeth Cady Stanton. After 1840, it was the most significant year of her adult life. Personal turmoil forced Stanton to turn outward, to forge for herself a public persona that balanced her private stress and affirmed her sense of control over her life. She emerged with a renewed zest for living and with a sense of purpose that would sustain her for the rest of her life.

Just before she moved from Boston to Seneca Falls, Stanton wrote to her cousin, Elizabeth Smith Miller, that Henry "dreads the change from Boston to Seneca," and she worried that he "will long for the strong excitement of a city life." For herself, she had no fears, for "the country and that climate is very delightful." Besides, she was well acquainted with the village and its people.[1]

Ironically, it was Elizabeth who would suffer most in Seneca Falls. Henry spent much of his time elsewhere, first as editor of the *Emancipator* and then on legal business and political campaigns. Elizabeth's first year in Seneca Falls was marked by isolation, overwork, stress, and change. She faced special challenges as a single parent. Henry did not officially move from Boston to Seneca Falls until February 1848, ten months after Elizabeth. Without dependable household help or parents and siblings close by, Elizabeth found her three young boys difficult to manage. Health problems added to her burdens—malaria for her family, a possible miscarriage for herself. The death of an infant nephew in her own home underscored life's fragility and her own lack of control.

Personal and familial problems helped keep her on the sidelines of three major public events—the passage of the Married Woman's Property Act in New York; the formation of the Liberty League and the Free Soil Party; and the organization of a new Quaker group, the Congregational Friends. Nonetheless, she was energized by passage of the Married Woman's Property Act and revitalized by debates over political abolitionism with Gerrit Smith and her husband, Henry. In addition, she reconnected with Quaker abolitionists through Lucretia Mott. These developments helped Stanton distill the swirling and inchoate currents of grassroots support for woman's rights into a plan of action, just as personal ties of affection and friendship helped her reweave the web that supported her life. The Seneca Falls woman's rights convention was the first fruit of her renewed sense of purpose.[2]

After the World Anti-Slavery Convention in June 1840, the Stantons returned home to live with Elizabeth's parents. Henry studied law "most vigorously" with Daniel Cady while Elizabeth spent two "pleasant and profitable years reading law, history, and political economy, with occasional interruptions to take part in some temperance or anti-slavery excitement." Elizabeth Cady Stanton taught a Sunday school for African American children in Johnstown. She also visited her sister and brother-in-law Tryphena and Edward Bayard in Seneca Falls in 1841, where she renewed her interest in homeopathic medicine. "I have seen wonders in Homeopathy and Animal Magnetism at Seneca," Stanton reported to her cousin Elizabeth Smith Miller, and "I intend to commence life on Homeopathic principles."[3]

In Seneca Falls, Stanton also gave her very first public lecture, a temperance speech, to a group of one hundred women. "I was so eloquent in my appeals as to affect not only my audience but myself to tears," she reported to Elizabeth Neall. "[I] infused into [my] speech a homeopathic dose of womans [*sic*] rights" and intended, she said, to "keep before the people."[4]

Among antislavery friends, Stanton found herself poised between Garrisonians and political abolitionists. Although Henry was a core leader of the "new organization," Elizabeth found herself sympathizing with the Garrisonians. Here, as in so many other ways, she found strength from Lucretia Mott. Mott thoroughly embraced Elizabeth. "I love her now as one belonging to us," she wrote to Richard and Hannah Webb in Ireland. "I never could regard her Henry quite as a New-Organizationist," she confessed. "Remind Henry, she wrote Elizabeth, that he "must not let the study of law be all-absorbing—forget not that he early dedicated himself to the slave's cause."[5]

Henry would never forget abolitionism, but he continued to espouse political action. He reported in the summer of 1841 that "the temperance & abolition folks continue to get 2 or 3, & sometimes 4 or 5, long speeches a week out of me." He spoke about twenty times in July and August 1841 and threw himself into organizing a temperance and antislavery party whose motto was *"No Slavery! No Alcohol!"*[6]

Caught in the middle of debates between Garrisonians and political abolitionists, Elizabeth Cady Stanton made her own bridge between them. She made no secret of her Garrisonian sympathies. She was unalterably committed to woman's rights, and she found her most congenial friends among Garrisonians.

At the same time, she recognized the strategic value of political action. "Are you among those who rejoice at the success of the 'liberty party'?" she asked Elizabeth Neall; Stanton answered her own question: "I do very much." "Slavery is a political question created & sustained by law, & must be put down by law."[7]

In February 1842, she clarified her position in a letter to British abolitionist Elizabeth Pease. American abolitionists had formed two major parties, she explained, but "there is in fact a third party, which is a sort of connecting link between the two grand divisions composed of those who have strong sympathies with both. . . . I am one of this party." On the one hand, Garrison "is a great reformer, an honest, upright man, ever ready to sacrifice present interest to stern principle, & having no fear of man. I have full confidence in him." I am, however, "not yet fully converted to the doctrine of no human government," she asserted.

> I am in favour, therefore, of political action, the organization of a third party as the most efficient way of calling forth & directing action. So long as we are to be governed by human laws, I shall be unwilling to have the making & administering of those laws left entirely to the selfish & unprincipled part of the community, which would be the case should all our honest men refuse to mingle in political affairs.[8]

Sorting her own way skillfully through the web of abolitionist intrigue, Stanton never wavered in her commitment to woman's rights. Abolitionist women were not sure of her allegiance, however; when she attended antislavery meetings with Henry in New York City, probably in May 1841, no one told her of separate meetings for women. Elizabeth Neall confessed later that they feared Stanton would not want to attend. Stanton reassured her. "Nothing would have pleased me more," she declared,

> than to have been present at a womans business meeting, where I might have seen the faces & heard the voices of Abbey Kelly [*sic*] & Lydia M. Child. How could I know of the existence of such meetings [when] no one told me. Had I known of them why should I have been disinclined to go? because Henry might not have wished me to do?—You do not know the extent to which I carry my rights. I do in truth think & act for myself knowing that I alone am responsible for the sayings & doings of E.C.S.[9]

She would maintain this position for the rest of her life. Henry would control neither her thoughts nor her actions.

She took it upon herself to promote woman's rights everywhere. "The more I think on the present condition of woman, the more am I oppressed with the reality of her degradation," she wrote to Mott. "The laws of our country, how unjust are they! our customs, how vicious! What God has made sinful, both in man and woman, custom has made sinful in woman alone." She found two copies of Sarah Grimké's *Letters on the Equality of the Sexes and the Condition of Woman,* then out of print, and circulated one in Johnstown and one in Seneca Falls. She begged Elizabeth Neall to send her whatever writings she could find on woman's rights. She read the *National Anti-Slavery Standard,* and she subscribed in her own name to the *Liberator,* "and that is the only woman's rights food I have for myself and disciples." Sarah Grimké herself responded to Stanton's plea for more copies of the *Letters,* lending Stanton several copies.[10]

By the end of 1841, Stanton's political ruminations were intertwined with another, very personal, concern: she was expecting her first child. "The puzzling questions of theology and poverty that had occupied so much of my thoughts," she recalled, "now gave place to the practical one, 'what to do with a baby.'" She announced the impending birth in terms of woman's rights. Perhaps just as revealing, she used the analogy of a book. "I am looking learned . . . these days, as if I had conceived some great idea," she wrote to Elizabeth Neall. "*If my domestic cares are not too great* I shall come out with my first production in March. If the true sentiments of an author appear in his works then will my work ever breath[e] love & justice, equality for woman." Daniel Cady Stanton (whom the family called Neil) was born at Johnstown on March 2, 1842.[11]

Elizabeth proved to be a strong-willed and intelligent mother, while Henry was a charming, irrepressible, and loving husband and father. Separated from Elizabeth for the first time after Neil's birth, Henry wrote to his wife with love and longing and barely veiled sexual allusions:

> I long to be with you again, to enjoy your smiles & kisses. I suppose you hardly think of me for a week together. You have the sweet little Kiddy to play with & embrace & so you forget all about "the peppy." But, reflect: where would the kiddy have been but for me?! . . . Kiss the dear Kiddy, & tell his mother that I long to kiss him & her (especially the latter) for myself & not by proxy.[12]

As Elizabeth solidified her commitment to woman's rights, Henry solidified his to political abolitionism. Lucretia Mott was not happy. "You will see H. B. Stanton's name among the 3rd [*sic*] party speakers in Boston," she wrote to Richard and Hannah Webb in Ireland on February 25, 1842. "How sorry I am that he has thus sold himself!"[13]

Quite likely, Henry's political ambitions played a part in his decision in the spring of 1842 to set up his law practice in Boston, where the fight between old and new organizationists was thickest. By the beginning of 1843, Elizabeth herself was in Boston. "I am enjoying myself more than I ever did in any city," she confessed. "I attend all sorts & sizes of meetings & lectures. I consider myself in a kind of moral museum & I find that this Boston affords as many civilities in her way, as does the British museum in its."[14]

The list of people that Elizabeth Cady Stanton knew in Boston that winter reads like a who's who of New England reformers. She took tea with William Lloyd Garrison and his family, attended antislavery fairs organized by Maria W.

Chapman and other Boston women, and went to mass meetings in Faneuil Hall. Though the hall was "a large, dreary place," whose only ornament was an American eagle with the gilt worn off its beak, "giving it the appearance . . . of having a bad cold in the head," she "never grew weary of the conventions" and enjoyed not only the speakers but also the songs of the Hutchinson family. She persisted in her attendance at philosophical conversations with Elizabeth Peabody and Bronson Alcott, though she confessed to Oliver Johnson that "I did not know what they were talking about." ("Neither do I" was Johnson's prompt response.) Among those she visited often were Joseph and Thankful Southwick, whose home was a haven for both white and black abolitionists.[15]

In the Southwick home about 1841, Stanton first met Frederick Douglass. She was most impressed. "He stood there like an African Prince," she wrote, "conscious of his dignity and power, grand in his physical proportions, majestic in his wrath, as with keen wit, satire, and indignation he portrayed the bitterness of slavery." Afterward, true to her reputation, Stanton gave him a personal lecture on woman's rights. She "did me the honor to sit by my side," he remembered, "and by that logic of which she is master, successfully endeavored to convince me of the wisdom & truth of the then new gospel of woman's rights."[16]

In Boston, she again saw Lucretia Mott, probably for the first time since the London meeting. Once more, they talked about a woman's rights convention. "Remember," Mott reminded Stanton later, "the first convention originated with thee. When we were walking the streets of Boston together in 1841, to find Elizabeth Moore's daughter, thou asked if we could not have a convention for Woman's Rights."[17]

For Henry Stanton, politics often took precedence over business. In 1844, he ran for Congress as a "martyr" on the Liberty Party ticket in Essex County. It was a hard-fought race. Henry gave a speech almost every night for eight weeks. "I have worn myself down with incessant labors," he reported. When "the long agony" was over, 11,000 men had voted for the Liberty Party (up from 8,750 the year before), but the Whigs had taken the state by a small majority.[18]

Such stresses, combined with the Boston climate, threatened Henry's health. In November, seeking healthier air, the Stantons moved to Chelsea, a Boston suburb. Their new house had an "upper piazza" and "a fine view over land and water," Elizabeth noted contentedly to her mother.[19]

For the first time, Elizabeth was mistress of her own home, and she was delighted. With two servants, she ran her household with "that same feeling of pride and satisfaction that a young minister must have in taking charge of his first congregation." She was a perfectionist, and the smallest tasks inspired her to excellence. "I studied up everything pertaining to housekeeping," she remembered, "and enjoyed it all."

> Even washing day—that day so many people dread—had its charms for me. The clean clothes on the lines and on the grass looked so white, and smelled so sweet, that it was a pretty sight to contemplate. I inspired my laundress with

> an ambition to have her clothes look white and to get them out earlier than our neighbors, and to have them ironed and put away sooner.[20]

Cooking, too, inspired her. "I had all the most approved cook books, and spent half my time preserving, pickling, and experimenting in new dishes." Even cleaning brought out her "love of order and cleanliness." She gave a man "an extra shilling to pile the logs of firewood with their smooth ends outward, though I did not have them scoured white, as did our Dutch grandmothers."[21]

She thought of herself as an artist, creating not a painting but a "clean, orderly, beautiful" home, furnished with the best three-ply carpet and with images of their reform-minded friends, including James G. Birney, Myron Holley, and Gerrit Smith. "We are serious about this," Henry reported to Gerrit Smith, as if Smith might find a request for his bust hard to believe. They had a round dining table, "always covered with a clean cloth of a pretty pattern and a centerpiece of flowers in their season, pretty dishes, clean silver, and set with neatness and care." "I put my soul into everything," Stanton remembered.[22]

Henry had been well recognized as an antislavery lecturer before he arrived in Boston. Now he was also an established lawyer and a seasoned congressional candidate, if not yet a congressman. With their own new house, the Stantons began to define themselves and their marriage, family, and work on their own terms. They entered a circle of committed, middle-income abolitionists not as admiring outsiders but as equals.

Elizabeth spent long weeks of each winter in Albany, "the family rallying point," with her parents. By March 1844, she had returned to Albany for the birth of her second son, Henry. Her husband was not present for the birth, but his affectionate concern continued unabated. "I long to see you, my lovely Lee," he wrote, "I am lonesome, cheerless, & homeless without you."[23] The Stantons' third son was born in Chelsea on September 18, 1845. Gerrit and Ann Smith were then visiting, and the Stantons named their new boy Gerrit Smith Stanton (and called him Kit or Gat). "If the prospects are that he will not make a great man," reported Henry to Gerrit, "we shall change his name."[24]

Through all these geographic and social moves, Elizabeth Cady Stanton deepened her commitment to woman's rights. Privately, she shared her thoughts with friends, often in the form of funny stories. John Greenleaf Whittier inspired her to quote poet Thomas Moore's "Proposals for a Gynaecocracy," which suggested that

> As Whig Reform has had its range,
> And none of us are yet content,
> Suppose, my friends, by way of change,
> We try a Female Parliament;
> And since, of late, with *he* M.P.'s,
> We've fared so badly, take to she's.

She also noted for Whittier's edification that according to "an old Scotch philosopher," "idea is the feminine of idiot."[25]

Through all of these changes, Stanton continued to struggle with the conflict between traditional Calvinist teachings and more optimistic religious ideas. Ever uncomfortable with the strict Presbyterianism of her childhood, she had nevertheless joined the Johnstown Presbyterian Church in 1839, the year before her marriage. In the 1840s, she faced the same issues that many thoughtful people confronted: Was the Bible the only word of God, or did God continue to speak to humans every day? Were all human beings sinners, requiring salvation through Christ's death on the cross, or were human beings essentially good, containing something of God in each person?

Lucretia Mott was one of Stanton's most important mentors. "What is the result of all the enquiries of thy open, generous, confiding spirit?" Mott wrote to Stanton in March 1841. "Art thou settled on the sure foundation of the revealed word of God to the inner sense? Or is thy mind still perplexed with the schemes of salvation, and plans of redemption which are taught in the schools of Theology?" Mott went on to describe her own religious views. "It is lamentable that the simple & benign religion of Jesus should be so encumbered with the creeds & dogmas of sects—Its primitive beauty obscured by these gloomy appendages of man." Mott continued, "I long to see obedience to manifested duty—leading to practical righteousness, as the christian's standard—the test of discipleship—the fruit of faith." As for "forms of worship and abstract theories," she advocated "large liberty-unbounded toleration."[26]

In Boston, Theodore Parker became Stanton's most important spiritual guide. When he delivered his famous sermon "The Permanent and Transient in Religion," he found himself ostracized by almost all established religious groups. Stanton, however, was enthralled. That first winter in Boston, she found his lectures so "soul-satisfying" that she sat through the whole series twice. When the sermons moved to Chelsea, she took the ferry to the city and then walked two miles to hear Parker preach. One very warm Sunday, she was so tired that she slept through the whole sermon. Her Baptist friends "made all manner of fun ever afterward of the soothing nature of Mr. Parker's theology."[27]

Deeply impressed by these reformers and religious optimists, Stanton's own worldview crystallized in the mid-1840s and formed the basis of her actions for the rest of her life. One document, the first speech she had given after her 1841 lecture on temperance in Seneca Falls, illustrated her spiritual growth. Quite possibly she gave this speech at the Peterboro Free Church about 1846 or 1847. She entitled it "Fear," and in it, she summarized her own transition from religious fear to optimism. Rejecting Calvinist ideas about the depravity of man, she affirmed her new confidence in the goodness of God and human nature.[28]

The original state of nature, Stanton argued, created fear in "man." And "our whole system of education combines with external nature to make us still more the slaves of fear." For little children (and here we must infer especially for one little child, Elizabeth Cady herself),

> nursery rhymes, ghost stories, & a gloomy theology, of a powerful devil, & a great God who loves not wicked children is poured upon the innocent mind until the most thoughtful & sensitive come to live in constant dread of some undefined terrors here & a fearful looking for of judgement to come hereafter. Everywhere is the childs [*sic*] fears played upon, at home, at school, in the sanctuary. Parent, Teacher, Priest, all join in this first work! . . . Is there one man or woman in this house that does not plead guilty to this charge? And still more, violence is regarded as a religious duty & defended as a law of *Heaven.*[29]

The result of this emphasis on fear, she concluded, was "man everywhere crushed by institutions." Chief among these institutions was slavery. "Behold the most christian nation in the globe with its slavery, its standing army, used now chiefly to keep four millions of Africans in bondage, its church pledged to both."[30]

For Stanton, as for Mott, Parker, and Ralph Waldo Emerson, the answer to fear was the use of human reason.

> Man is a being of reason. It is chance, accident, mystery, the unknown, the unfathomable that appalls the soul. The healthy normal condition of mind & body is repose. A sound mind in a sound body is the birthright of man. . . . All that remains for us to do then is to bring ourselves into harmony with these fixed immutable laws that govern the great universe of matter [and] mind believing that "all seeming evil is universal good / all discord, harmony not understood."[31]

Ultimately, the task that faced all people was to deliver themselves from the last fear—fear of criticism. "Let us have more faith in one another. Let us trust each soul to seek out its full development believing that its native soil is truth towards which it will as surely gravitate as the needle to the pole."[32]

In this speech, thoughtful and mature, Stanton synthesized the intellectual integrity that she had achieved by the mid-1840s. She needed this sense of trust in her own truth-seeking soul, for she was about to enter a year of tension greater than any she had experienced since the religious turmoil of her youth. Her emotional and intellectual upheaval began with a physical move in the spring of 1847, to the small city of Seneca Falls, New York.

The Stantons had hardly been in Boston a year when they began to think about moving. As early as 1844, Henry had written to Gerrit Smith, outlining his fears of the "Massachusetts 'East winds,' so famous in the annals of consumption." For the past year, he noted, "I have been subject to colds on my lungs, attended with protracted inflammation & a slight cough." Henry had good reason to fear. His mother had died of consumption. And Henry, his daughter remembered, was "a chilly mortal, always feeling drafts, always putting on extra clothing," who "always had a delicate throat and chest."[33]

Henry outlined three requirements: "(1) A healthy location. (2) A good situation for business. (3) A free atmosphere on the subject of abolition." He had considered Albany but knew that Daniel Cady, who was then living in the capital, "would be distressed always if I ever said a word in favor of any unpopular subject." He had thought of Cincinnati, but it was "too far away, & I don't like the character of its inhabitants." He was most attracted, he wrote, to central New York, "because I am considerable acquainted with its local laws & the practice of its Courts, & my profession would sit naturally upon me there."[34]

In 1847, the Stantons decided to move to Seneca Falls. In that year, Daniel Cady was elected to the New York Supreme Court. The new Judge Cady needed a place to stay when he served circuit courts in central New York. Cady also had business investments, including a farm and a plaster mill, in Seneca Falls. If the Stantons moved to Seneca Falls, they could offer a haven for Elizabeth's father, supervise his business interests, and provide a better climate for Henry's health. Almost certainly, they were also motivated by Henry's own political ambitions. Seneca Falls would offer a good place for Henry to run for office.

When Elizabeth Cady Stanton moved to Seneca Falls in 1847, however, she moved without Henry, who stayed behind to edit the antislavery newspaper the *Emancipator*. Elizabeth began a year of life as a single parent, a year of emotional and physical stresses more severe than she had ever known, testing both her religious values and her reform commitments. The result would be a renewed sense of personal integrity for Stanton and a new movement—the woman's rights movement—for the world.

In May 1847, Stanton left her parents' home in Johnstown and moved west to Seneca Falls. Unencumbered by children, she was armed only with a check from her father to fix up a house that Daniel Cady had agreed would be hers. Her new home and the two acres on which it sat illustrated in microcosm the whole transition of land in North America, from Native Americans to European Americans, from hunting to farming to industrial development. Originally in the homeland of Cayuga Indians, the Stanton lot was part of a large tract purchased by the Bayard Company in 1798. In 1807, this company built its first mill, the lower Red Mill, at the foot of the Stanton hill. By 1832, William Bayard and his brother, Samuel—land speculators, farmers, and millers—had acquired seventy-three acres along the south side of the Seneca River. Samuel and his wife, Jane Dashiel Bayard, had a farm there, complete with pine trees and front walks. While Samuel Bayard farmed, William Bayard operated the mill. Sometime between April 1835 and November 1836, William married Romainea Dashiel, sister of Samuel's wife.[35]

About the time of his marriage, William Bayard built a new house for his bride. Within a year, severe economic depression dashed the hopes of both Bayard families. In 1838, they were forced to mortgage, for $15,000, all of their seventy-three acres except the house and lot at the corner of Washington and Seneca Streets.[36]

Although William and Romainea Bayard continued to live in the house, probably up until 1843, the Bayard brothers recognized that their days as landowners in Seneca Falls were almost over. On December 10, 1842, all of their property was sold at public auction. The Bayards had a year to redeem their property; if they failed, they would lose it entirely. Samuel planned to go to Buffalo to resume newspaper writing. In January 1843, he wrote candidly to Thurlow Weed, offering to contribute columns to Weed's newspaper: "I am utterly and irrevocably bankrupt," he confessed. "I am in actual want." By 1845, both Samuel and Jane had moved to the town of Fairfield in the territory of Iowa. It is probable that William and Romainea, too, left Seneca Falls.[37]

Disaster for the Bayards was economic opportunity for Daniel Cady, who acquired the property through his agent and former law student, Elisha Foote. Within a decade of its construction, William and Romainea Bayard's house had become Stanton's own.[38] But when Stanton arrived in the village in the spring of 1847, she saw only a neglected building surrounded by weeds. It had stood empty for some time and was badly in need of repairs. Undaunted, she threw herself into remodeling her new home. Her father had told her, "with a smile": "You believe in woman's capacity to do and dare; now go ahead and put your place in order."[39]

Stanton felt happy with her new responsibilities. She took a careful survey of the property, consulted with "one or two sons of Adam"; bought "brick, timber, and paint"; "set the carpenters, painters, paperhangers, and gardeners at work, built a new kitchen and wood house, and in one month took possession." Stanton's daughter Margaret later recalled that Stanton had also added "several porches."[40] Inside, Stanton filled the house with cool, clear colors: blue or green patterned paper, green chaise lounge, white dishes with blue patterns, and blue and white coverlets. A piano and guitar reflected her love of music.[41]

In form, the Stanton house reflected the newly popular Greek Revival style. Standing on a two-acre corner lot, the house faced west, toward the village. It had a two-story center gable, flanked by one-and-a-half-story wings on each side; at least one rear wing; at least one front porch, which the family called a piazza; and one back porch. This gable-and-wing plan was intended to imitate a Greek temple and to reflect the kinship between the new American democracy and the democracy of fifth-century Athens. Between 1830 and 1870, people in upstate New York built thousands of buildings of similar plan, most of them painted white to imitate the marble of Greek temples and to suggest a contrast between civilization and wilderness.[42]

When she finished, Stanton had a long and rambling house. Her son Gerrit would later remember it as a "mansion," "surrounded by lawns, trees and several acres of grounds." The curved staircase, the sidelights around the front door, the wood-grained woodwork in the front parlor, the old-fashioned fireplace, and the many porches added touches of elegance to an otherwise simple dwelling.[43]

In truth, Elizabeth's new house was large compared with most of those in Seneca Falls. In 1860, it ranked in the top 7 percent of assessed valuation for houses in its neighborhood. It was, however, far from a grand dwelling. It did not compare with Charles Hoskins's large brick house across the river, with Gary V. Sackett's cut stone abode with its huge Federal doorway on the south side, or even with Oren Tyler's farm house in the Stantons' own neighborhood. It was large, but it was built in several sections, each part modest in size and relatively plain in detail.[44]

In front of the house, a circular drive surrounded a mound and ended in two front gates, with a flagpole and a hand pump nearby. A clothesline was strung out in back, near the vegetable garden. A smokehouse, certainly an outhouse, two large cherry trees, and a grape arbor stood in the yard. By 1856, a hedge in front and a board fence on the east and south bordered the property. The yard played a major part in both the family's food supply and their recreational life. As for Henry, "Never a day passed in summer," Elizabeth recalled, "that he did not go the round of the garden." Henry once won a bet with a neighbor that he could raise the largest watermelon. Elizabeth traded flower seeds. Neighborhood children were invited to help themselves to grapes and pure water. Guests sat "under the shady trees of the Stanton estate, while waiting for the dinner bell to ring," remembered one of the Stanton sons.[45]

People sometimes called this place Locust Hill, because of all the locust trees. Stanton called it Grassmere, perhaps a reference to the poet William Wordsworth's home in the lake country of England, which she had visited on her honeymoon.[46]

The Stanton house stood right beside the most important east-west travel corridor in the northeastern United States. The old Genesee Road, converted into the Seneca Turnpike, passed along the north side of the Stanton lot. Just beyond it, the Seneca and Cayuga Canal and the Seneca River connected local residents with the longer and more famous Erie Canal. Across the river, the railroad provided fast, up-to-date passenger transportation. Road, canal, and railroad connected Seneca Falls with major cities to the east and west. For many visitors, the Stanton corner was their first introduction to the village of Seneca Falls. Drivers of the big red Concord stages tooted their horns at the Stanton corner to announce their arrival. Canal boat captains directed their bands to play as they rounded the Stanton hill.[47]

Like Stanton herself, this house stood at the fulcrum point of change. Physically, it anchored outlying farms to the village of Seneca Falls, linking a land-based economy with a new order based on revolutions in transportation and manufacturing. Like her, this house represented a bridge between old wealth based on land and new wealth based on money, between a republican corporate worldview and a liberal competitive one.

* * *

In June 1847, Daniel Cady himself inspected his daughter's work. He must have been pleased with what he saw. Surprisingly, given the confusing state of the law relating to married women's property, Daniel Cady decided to give this house directly to Elizabeth. On June 22, 1847, he deeded the entire house and lot to "Elizabeth Stanton, the wife of Henry B. Stanton of the City of Boston," "in consideration," he wrote, "of the love and affection which I have for my daughter." It would be almost a year before New York passed the Married Woman's Property Act. Both Elizabeth and her father were all too aware of this. Yet such was Daniel Cady's distrust of his son-in-law that he tried to protect Elizabeth as much as he could from Henry's financial instability. Perhaps Daniel simply decided to take a chance that Henry would not usurp Elizabeth's property. Or perhaps he arranged a trust that he believed would protect Elizabeth's ownership. After Daniel Cady's death in 1859, Elizabeth also owned her father's farm in Seneca Falls, which she probably had supervised all along.[48]

Although local map makers and tax assessors identified the property as Henry's, Elizabeth remained the sole owner. It was a pattern that she later recommended to others, and it certainly affected the dynamics of their marriage. While most wives were dependent on their husbands for financial support, Elizabeth Cady Stanton always securely controlled her own house and land. If anything, Henry was more dependent on Elizabeth's financial assets than she was on his. Elizabeth's independent property ownership as well as her continuing reliance—financial and emotional—upon her parents gave her a sense of identity that was clearly separate from Henry.[49]

In 1847, as she settled into a routine with her children, Stanton viewed this house as a symbol not only of her independence but also of her isolation, confinement, and overwork. She quickly realized that Seneca Falls, whatever its attractions, was not Boston. Engrossed in her duties as a housewife and mother, she found herself demoted from household manager to household drudge, doing much of the work herself. What helpers she had seem to have been young girls, daughters of neighboring families, who needed constant supervision and training. Her pleasure in housekeeping disappeared. For this prolific letter writer, it is a measure of her stress that only one letter (and that of doubtful date) exists from Elizabeth Cady Stanton from May 1847 to July 1848.[50]

In those first months in her new home, Stanton recalled fifty years later, "my life was comparatively solitary, and the change from Boston was somewhat depressing."

> To keep a house and grounds in good order, purchase every article for daily use, keep the wardrobes of half a dozen human beings in proper trim, take the children to dentists, shoemakers, and different schools, or find teachers at home, altogether made sufficient work to keep one brain busy, as well as all the hands I could impress into the service. Then, too, the novelty of house-

keeping had passed away, and much that was once attractive in domestic life was now irksome. I had so many cares that the company I needed for intellectual stimulus was a trial rather than a pleasure. . . . I suffered with mental hunger, which, like an empty stomach, is very depressing.[51]

Added to this were health problems. Seneca Falls, like much of the Genesee region, was wetter than it would be after the forest had been cleared. Swamps bred mosquitoes, which carried malaria. All of Stanton's children, as well as her servants, came down with chills and fever. Treating them homeopathically took three months. "Cleanliness, order, the love of the beautiful and artistic, all faded away in the struggle to accomplish what was absolutely necessary from hour to hour. Now I understood," Stanton remembered, "as I never had before, how women could sit down and rest in the midst of general disorder." As she always did in times of stress, Stanton took her children and went back to her parents' house in Johnstown. Johnstown, rather than Seneca Falls, remained "that harbor of safety, home."[52]

Contributing to her exhaustion and stress, Stanton may have suffered a miscarriage sometime during this year. Evidence for this is circumstantial but compelling. Without using some form of birth control or suffering a physical disability, the Stantons, like most couples, could be expected to have a child every two years. In fact, their two oldest children, Daniel Cady Stanton and Henry Brewster Stanton, had been born almost exactly two years apart (on March 2, 1842, and March 15, 1844). Only a year and a half separated Henry from his younger brother Gerrit Smith Stanton. Yet Elizabeth and Henry would not have another living child until the birth of Theodore on February 10, 1851, five years and five months after Gerrit's birth.[53]

Were the Stantons practicing birth control methods in the late 1840s? As Kathryn Kish Sklar has argued, family limitation was a possibility. Abstinence, withdrawal, douches, and the rhythm method were options. We know, however, that Elizabeth longed for a girl, and a few clues suggest that she had not planned the gap between Gerrit's birth in 1845 and Theodore's in 1851.[54]

Two weeks before Theodore's birth, when Abby Kelley Foster wanted to give another antislavery lecture in Seneca Falls, Stanton wrote to her regretting that "I can neither meet you at the depot nor attend your meeting in consequence of a kind of biennial clumsiness to which I have been subject many years." About the same time, she reported to Martha Wright that she was "incapacitated by one of her *biennial attacks.*" Had Stanton been regularly pregnant every other year for a long time? We know that she had one miscarriage in the spring of 1849, when Martha Wright reported that "there was a reason for despatching that jar of pickles so quick. She has miscarried at 5 mo. with a little girl—a great disappointment." If Stanton had indeed experienced a state of "biennial clumsiness" for "many years," she may also have had a miscarriage in 1847 or early 1848.[55]

One more tragedy touched her in this year before the convention. In June, Henry's younger sister, Frances Stanton Avery, visited the Stantons in Seneca Falls. Quite likely her husband, George, came with her. The Averys had been married seventeen years. They had watched three of their seven children die in infancy or early childhood, including three-and-a-half-year-old Delia, who had just died on June 12, 1848. Tragedy struck them again in Seneca Falls. On June 27, only fifteen days after Delia's death, their youngest child, George, died of whooping cough on his first birthday, at the Stanton home.[56]

Perhaps these tragedies reminded Stanton of the fragility of life, for sometime during this year, she captured a permanent image of herself and her children in daguerreotypes. In this picture, Stanton sat, unsmiling and grim, clutching squirming children, Daniel and Henry, on either side. She gripped her boys so tightly that the veins stood out on the backs of her hands. As the children continued to wiggle, they blurred the picture. Dressed in a dark dress with a white kerchief tucked in at her neck, she may have consciously been re-creating her mother's image from a portrait done many years earlier, but the photograph, unlike her mother's painting, could not hide the evidence of stress. She was a woman besieged.[57]

Stanton's life was not, however, all drudgery. Quite likely, she went in March to hear John S. Jacobs, a "self-emancipated slave" from North Carolina, brother of Harriet Jacobs, and Jonathan Walker, from Florida, tell of their adventures. Almost certainly, she went to the Wesleyan Chapel in early May to hear her friend, Frederick Douglass.[58]

Perhaps too, Stanton took advantage of lighter entertainment. It would have been hard to imagine, for example, how she could have kept her boys away from Sands, Lent, and Company's Hippoferaean Arena, which came to town in June 1848. Their huge parade included a pair of trained elephants (named Jenny Lind and Romeo) and ten Egyptian camels drawing the Sacred Egyptian Dragon Chariot of Isis and Osiris, on which sat a full brass band. They were followed by such people as Rosalthe Madigan, "the Fairy Amazonian Princess of the Aracua," and Sig Peroz, "the unrivalled Contortionist," and "the beautiful FAIRY CARRIAGE drawn by 20 LILIPUTIAN PONIES!" And that was only a prelude to the performance in the company's "pavilion," lit by "solar gas."[59]

While Elizabeth tended home and children, Henry plunged with his usual enthusiasm into work and reform politics. He sent her long letters from Washington. He continued to edit the *Emancipator,* and he began to publish regular installments in the *National Era* of what would become, in 1849, his first book, *Reforms and Reformers in Great Britain.* Henry relished being close to power. So did Elizabeth, and Henry's relative freedom only exacerbated her sense of confinement.[60]

In 1848, however, three developments opened opportunities for Stanton to assume a creative public role. In April 1848, New York finally passed the Married Woman's Property Act. In June, two new political parties, the Free Soil Party

Elizabeth Cady Stanton and sons Daniel and Henry, about 1848. Courtesy of Coline Jenkins-Sahlin.

and the Liberty League, emerged from the remnants of the old Liberty Party. And finally, also in June, Quakers in Rochester and Waterloo, supported by Lucretia Mott, organized a new group called the Congregational Friends. Mott and the Congregational Friends validated Stanton's own sense of identity and precipitated the Seneca Falls woman's rights convention itself.

For Stanton, these political movements were profoundly personal. Her own intimate relationships gave her a ringside seat from which to view what were, for reformers, seismic organizational shifts. When Stanton finally found her public voice, people paid attention to her, not only because she was a powerful speaker but also because her personal relationships legitimized her leadership role. People were predisposed to listen to the daughter of Judge Cady, the niece of Gerrit Smith, the wife of Henry B. Stanton, the friend of Lucretia Mott. Stanton's own remarkable talents lay at the core of her success, but her family and friends provided a springboard for her public career.

The Married Woman's Property Act had special relevance for Stanton. Not only had she lobbied for it for many years but she also now had a deed to her own home. But what did home ownership mean to a married woman? As a woman, wife, and resident of New York, Stanton personally faced legal disabilities, and she fought back at every level. Ansel Bascom, the controversial lawyer and reformer, used to walk down to inspect Stanton's progress on the house. The two of them "had long talks, sitting on boxes in the midst of tools and shavings, on the status of women." Stanton confronted him with the contrast between his endorsement of "the political equality of women" and his refusal to pursue women's equality at the convention. "He had not the courage," Stanton recalled, "to make himself the laughing-stock of the convention. Whenever I cornered him on this point, manlike he turned the conversation to the painters and carpenters."[61]

In Stanton's mind, debates about the Married Woman's Property Act were an essential factor in creating a climate for a woman's rights convention. Because of public discussion on this issue, she argued, demands made in the Seneca Falls convention "were not entirely new to the reading and thinking public of New York." Supported by conservatives as well as liberals, the Married Women's Property Act had generated widespread controversy over all aspects of gender relations in New York. The *History of Woman Suffrage* made the connection even more explicit. "Discussions in the constitutional convention and the Legislature, heralded by the press to every school district," it noted, "culminated at last in a woman's rights convention." Among nonabolitionists, it was the single most important factor in creating a climate of support for woman's rights.[62]

At the same time, national political developments created a new context for antislavery action. In May 1848, the end of the war between Mexico and the United States left traditional political allegiances unstable and opened new opportunities for antislavery politicians. The United States had forcibly acquired vast new lands, including all of Texas, the territory of New Mexico, and California. Would these territories be slave or free? In 1846, David Wilmot, a young congressman from Pennsylvania, had proposed that Congress forever exclude slavery from all these territories. Abolitionists quickly rallied around the Wilmot Proviso. Charles Sumner, a leading antislavery Senator, predicted that "the Mexican War and slavery will derange all party calculations. . . . The Abolitionists have at last got their lever upon a *fulcrum* where it can operate."[63]

The year 1848 was a presidential election year, and antislavery politicians prepared to use this fulcrum fully. They had three basic options. Some wanted to maintain the old Liberty Party as a separate organization. Others advocated a separate antislavery party with a platform that also embraced other issues. Still others wanted to merge the old Liberty Party with Whig and Democratic dissidents to form a new and broader coalition.

These shifting sands strained old alliances, and the Stanton household was right at the center of the tension. Henry B. Stanton shifted loudly and enthusiastically from one end of the spectrum to the other. Gerrit Smith, just as obdurate if not as loud, stood firmly on the middle ground. Henry Stanton initially worked to maintain a separate, single-issue Liberty Party. When that failed, he threw his energies toward creating a new coalition, the Free Soil Party, that drew broadly from the ranks of former Liberty Party members as well as upon disaffected elements in the Whig and Democratic parties. Gerrit Smith supported the Liberty League, which condemned slavery as unconstitutional and also dealt with a wide variety of other issues. Debates between her husband and her cousin offered Elizabeth Cady Stanton a new incentive for acting in her own way in the public world.

On June 8–10, 1847, the Liberty League met at Macedon Lock, New York, just north of Seneca Falls. Labeling the Liberty Party a "one idea" party, the Liberty League advocated total reform and protection of the rights of "ALL MEN," both black and white. They espoused only one central concept, that of a just government pursuing "stedfastly and undeviatingly, wherever they are revealed to us, the TRUE and the RIGHT" and "THE PROTECTION OF HUMAN RIGHTS." Any action that violated natural rights should be opposed. According to William Goodell, this included monopoly of land and restraints on free trade. Gerrit Smith expanded this position, calling for an immediate end to the Mexican War, a dismantling of the entire U.S. military system, the end of all restraints on free trade, direct taxation of the American people, federal investment in harbors and streams, use of federal force to put down insurrections by oppressors, use of the Constitution for the "widest, sternest, deadliest war against slavery," free settlement of public lands, suffrage for immigrants, the end of property and race restrictions on voting, and the exclusion from office of both slaveholders and anyone who advocated selling liquor. The Liberty Party, Smith argued, saw itself as a temporary group, whereas he wanted to establish a permanent organization, with a commitment to promoting the "equal rights of all men—equal justice to all men."[64]

Beyond the issue of "one-ideaism," a second difference separated Liberty Leaguers from other political abolitionists: they insisted that the U.S. Constitution was an antislavery document. Such a policy meant that the federal government could attack slavery anywhere it existed. It could prohibit slavery in the District of Columbia, as well as within any state or territory. The Constitution, Smith noted in a letter to Salmon P. Chase, one of his leading opponents, was established "to secure the blessing of liberty." It guaranteed "the right of the people to be secure in their persons," that "no person shall be deprived of life, liberty, or property, without due process of law," and that "the United States shall guaranty to every State in this Union a republican form of government." What could be a clearer statement of the right to "abolish every part of American slavery?"[65]

Liberty Leaguers were to political abolitionists what Garrison and the nonresistants had been to the antislavery movement in the late 1830s. They embraced all reforms at once, equally and uncompromisingly. What separated Liberty Leaguers from Garrisonians was their definition of the Constitution as an antislavery document and their subsequent willingness to use political power. And unlike Garrison or egalitarian Quakers, they still spoke of human rights as male rights.

Henry B. Stanton, more pragmatic than either Smith or Garrison, cared less for moral purity than for political power. A platform that tackled all problems at once was not likely to get anyone into office. Stanton was willing to work with whatever candidate he thought most likely to win. In 1847, Stanton vigorously promoted the candidacy of John P. Hale, an antislavery senator from New Hampshire. "The aim of the Liberty party is not only to maintain a principle," he asserted, "but to accomplish an object. It goes for SUCCESS, and if one candidate can carry us more rapidly, and as safely forward towards victory than another, is he not *the* man for our party and our cause?" If the Liberty Party refused to nominate Hale, Stanton claimed, he himself would turn to whichever Democratic or Whig candidate endorsed the Wilmot Proviso.[66]

Conflict between Hale's supporters and the Liberty Leaguers came to a head on October 20–21, 1847, when the Liberty Party held its national convention in Buffalo. Gerrit Smith opened the debate with a resolution that "slavery, whether in the District of Columbia, or in any other part of the Nation, is clearly and utterly unconstitutional." The resolution was defeated, 195 to 137. The second day, Smith tried again. This time, trying tactfully to promote the multiplank platform of the Liberty League, he asked that the Liberty Party consider what its duties would be if it won the election. Again he lost, 103 to 26.[67]

Henry B. Stanton left the convention victorious. Lobbying with Joshua Leavitt and Lewis Tappan, Stanton helped convince the convention to nominate John P. Hale for president. Gerrit Smith did retain considerable support. In an informal poll, he received 44 votes for president, while Hale received 103. Officially, however, delegates gave their unanimous endorsement to Hale.[68]

Sitting in the gallery at the New York State Democratic Convention in Syracuse in September 1847, Stanton was an eyewitness as radical Democrats (nicknamed Barnburners) stalked out of the convention over Democratic refusal to oppose the extension of slavery. Barnburners made clear their own "unqualified aversion and disgust for slavery." They were dedicated instead to "Free Trade, Free Labor, Free Soil, Free Speech and Free Men."[69]

Where others saw disaster, Stanton saw glorious possibilities. His optimistic personality gave him an energy, a vitality, and a charm that made him an extraordinarily effective coalition builder. In March 1848, he assured Hale that Barnburners and ordinary Democrats, too, were even more radical on the slavery issue than their public statements indicated. In May, the national Democratic convention refused to accept New York's Barnburner delegates, so they organized their own convention in Utica on June 22. Meanwhile, Whigs in Philadelphia alienated antislavery men within their own party by nominating Zachary Taylor, Mexican War general and Alabama slaveholder, for president. Suddenly, the possibility of a great national antislavery party, drawing on dissident Whigs and Democrats as well as former Liberty Party members, seemed very real.[70]

Henry Stanton seized the moment. In Seneca Falls in June, he helped organize local support for a new third party opposing the extension of slavery. On June 13, 1848, the *Seneca County Courier* published an invitation "to the freemen of Seneca Falls," signed by 196 men, about one-quarter of all potential voters in the village, Stanton among them. They invited all "Electors of Seneca Falls, irrespective of Party" to meet in the Wesleyan Chapel to consider "the Baltimore and Philadelphia nominations [i.e., for the Democratic and Whig parties], and the course of action which existing circumstances require of Northern freemen." Chaired by Jacob P. Chamberlain, operator of the lower Red Mills and neighbor to the Stantons, the meeting agreed that old party issues were now unimportant. The real goal was to find candidates for president and vice president who would restrict slavery, "the chiefest curse and foulest disgrace that attaches to our institutions." The author of these stern resolutions? None other than Ansel Bascom, who was about to run for Congress himself.[71]

Downplaying old party issues and old party antagonisms suited voters in Seneca Falls, who in past elections had split almost evenly between Whigs and Democrats, with only a handful of staunch antislavery men daring to vote for the Liberty Party ticket. Merging political parties was also exactly what Henry Stanton had in mind. By now, he was an ardent fusionist. So what if the basis for a new organization was not the abolition of slavery everywhere but merely its confinement? Keep slavery out of the territories, thought Stanton, and the whole system would die. "Confine it to its own limits, restrict it to its own means, and it soon must perish," argued the *Emancipator* in February 1847.[72]

Not everyone agreed, least of all Gerrit Smith. Quite likely, Smith brought the battle between fusionists and purists directly into the Stanton household. Officially nominated for president at a Liberty League meeting in Rochester on June 2, Smith may have stayed at the Stanton house before he went to Buffalo to deliver the major address at what would become known as the National Liberty Convention.[73]

One can imagine the discussions between Smith and the Stantons around the dining room table. Almost certainly, Gerrit Smith's radical, inclusive politics awakened Elizabeth Cady Stanton's own keen sense of justice. Almost certainly, too, Stanton challenged Gerrit Smith to think not only about issues of race and class but also about gender. As a woman, Stanton may have argued, she was excluded from positions of power not only in the larger world but also within the political antislavery movement. Political parties, no matter how radical, were limited to voters. By definition, all voters were male and most of those were white. We can imagine Stanton arguing, with passion, that if Gerrit Smith really wanted to include *all* Americans, to protect the rights of *all* people, he needed to think about women as well as about men. Whoever first raised the idea of voting rights for women, it seems reasonable to assume that, once more, Gerrit Smith and Elizabeth Cady Stanton would build on their mutual respect and on their love of a good argument to reach beyond themselves, to carry their egalitarian commitments to conclusions that neither of them may have envisioned before.[74]

Smith went first. In his Buffalo speech the following week, Smith included, for the first time, a demand for "universal suffrage in its broadest sense, females as well as males being entitled to vote." Throughout the meeting, speakers recognized support from women as well as men. When Smith was asked if he would serve as president of the United States, Smith replied, "What man is there before me, or woman, either," who would not take such an opportunity to resist oppression? The convention gave Lucretia Mott five votes for vice president (out of eighty-four), the first time in U.S. history that a woman had been proposed for federal executive office. Finally, in *The Liberty Party of the United States, to the People of the United States,* an address probably written by Gerrit Smith, delegates accepted a lengthy paragraph about suffrage for women. "Neither here, nor in any other part of the world," they argued, "is the right of suffrage allowed to extend beyond one of the sexes. This universal exclusion of woman . . . argues, conclusively, that, not as yet, is there one nation so far emerged from barbarism, and so far practically Christian, as to permit woman to rise up to the one level of the human family." Elizabeth Cady Stanton could not have said it more clearly herself.[75]

African Americans were usually absent from white-dominated political gatherings, but they were well represented at this National Liberty Convention. Henry Highland Garnet, a minister from Troy, was one of the convention's vice presidents. Samuel R. Ward, abolitionist editor, received twelve votes as candidate for vice president of the United States. The convention also produced the *Address of the Liberty Party to the Colored People of the Northern States.* Finally, among the speakers was Frederick Douglass, Elizabeth Cady Stanton's friend from Boston days, now an abolitionist lecturer and editor of the *North Star* in Rochester.[76]

As Smith met with the Liberty Leaguers at Buffalo, Henry Stanton attended the Barnburner state convention at Utica on June 22. Barnburners nominated Martin Van Buren for president and endorsed strong opposition to any extension of slavery into the territories. Slavery, they proclaimed, was "a great moral, social and political evil—a relic of barbarism which must necessarily be swept away in the progress of Christian civilization." Meanwhile, Ohio opponents of slavery's extension called for a national meeting in Buffalo, New York, on August 9–10. Such a meeting would include Liberty Party men, dissident Democrats, and antislavery Whigs (often called Conscience Whigs), as well. Henry B. Stanton's highest hopes were coming true.[77]

Some Liberty Party men had trouble contemplating support for Martin Van Buren. After all, he had no real track record as an antislavery man. On the contrary, he had opposed the delivery of abolitionist mail in the South; he had supported the return to Spanish slave traders of people who had sought asylum in the United States from the *Amistad;* and he objected to the abolition of slavery in the District of Columbia. Henry Stanton, however, had no qualms about Van Buren. Van Buren might not support Liberty Party positions on all points, Henry conceded to John Greenleaf Whittier, but "the truth is we Liberty men have got some *isms* that are too refined for use." The key issue, he reiterated, was opposition to the extension of slavery, and Van Buren stood firm on that.[78]

Henry Stanton leaped into the fight with characteristic gusto. Along with Ansel Bascom, he devoted the weeks before the national convention to frenzied campaigning across the state. On July 12, reported the *New York Tribune,* the Honorable H. B. Stanton gave a speech of "great power and eloquence" in Warsaw, New York. Two thousand people attended, and sixty of them were delegated to go to the Free Soil convention to be held in Buffalo in August. A few days later, Stanton spoke in Canandaigua. On August 3, he and Ansel Bascom addressed a capacity crowd in Seneca Falls. With Charles Hoskins as secretary, the meeting elected 102 delegates, including Stanton, Bascom, Milliken, Chamberlain, and Hoskins, to the Buffalo convention. The next week, Henry Stanton spoke to full houses in towns all along the Hudson Valley.[79]

Henry was sure that Elizabeth would understand. After all, this might be Henry's great chance to combine his antislavery principles with his political ambitions. He was a brilliant public speaker, and there was no doubt that his voice was needed in the field. Henry felt alive!

Not so Elizabeth. She may have understood Henry's needs, but she did not feel any better about her own situation. Henry's travels all over the northeast, his influence within the abolitionist movement, his reports of exciting meetings only exacerbated Elizabeth's own sense of stagnation. And whatever she thought, she was not one to endure grievances in silence. Elizabeth did not realize it then, but a dramatic deliverance from her frustration was about to come.

The M'Clintock family was at the center of these momentous changes. In June, they and other reform-minded Friends were shaken to their core by a cataclysmic split within the Genesee Yearly Meeting of Friends, a split that in turn reconnected Stanton with Garrisonian abolitionism and the network of egalitarian Friends in central New York.

In the mid-1840s, disagreements among Friends continued to be acrimonious and fundamental. Partly they centered, as they had for a decade, on abolitionism. Although the Posts had followed Isaac Hopper, Eliab W. Capron, Benjamin Fish, and others out of Quaker meetings, the M'Clintocks, the Pryors, and other egalitarian Friends continued to affirm their commitment both to the American Anti-Slavery Society and the Society of Friends. And conservative Quakers continued to protest, objecting especially to using Quaker meetinghouses for abolitionist lectures. On a cold December day in 1847, three black abolitionists, Frederick Douglass, Charles Remond, and Martin Delany, found themselves holding a meeting in a schoolhouse in Mendon, New York, because "Friends meeting house [was] closed against us on the ground that our views differed from theirs." Such rejection was intolerable to Douglass's Quaker allies.[80]

Egalitarian Quakers continued to believe that practical work to abolish slavery was imperative, even if it led them to work with non-Quakers. Daniel Anthony, a Rochester Quaker, reflected this tension in a letter to his daughter Susan on June 4. "O what use is preching & all this pretended or blind devotion, . . . so long as this horable business of traffic in the bodies of men, women & children is sanctioned & actually carried on by those making the highest pretentions to goodness." Anthony noted that "if a member be attentive active in proclaiming the evils of Slavery he is disowned at once as a disturber of the quetude of their religious proceedings." Anthony had already given up his own commitment to established Friends.[81] Quakers such as Anthony felt they could no longer allow their commitment to social reform to be constrained by their commitment to Quaker meetings.

Quaker abolitionist feelings ran high. They were intertwined with ideas about power and about who had the right to make decisions in meetings. If all Friends were equally children of the Light, why should ministers or elders have a right to impose their own views on others? Many Friends thought they did not. The result would be what the *Pennsylvania Freeman* called a "moral earthquake" in meetings all over the northeastern United States.

The split began in June 1848, when two hundred Friends left the regular Genesee Yearly Meeting and expressed their views in *An Address to Friends of Genesee Yearly Meeting, and Elsewhere.* They emphasized two points: practical reform and the right to follow their own spiritual leadings. For many years, they explained, "we have failed to realize that unity, the existence of which was indispensable to enable us, as a body, to advance the great principles of righteousness embraced in some of the most needful reforms of this age . . . such as the mighty sins of War, Slavery, Intemperance, &c., which are afflicting the human family, cursing the Divine principles of man's nature, alienating man from his God and from his brother." Furthermore, Friends have struggled with the "growth among us of a spirit of proscription and intolerance. A spirit which has been unwilling to concede to every equal brother and sister those rights which it claimed for itself—the rights of conscience, and action in conformity to apprehended immediate Divine requiring."[82]

For five years, ever since the issue had first been introduced by Michigan Quarterly Meeting in 1843, Genesee Yearly Meeting had struggled with the question of individual versus institutional authority. In 1846, it had appointed a committee to visit Michigan Friends. In 1847, after a two-day debate, both men's and women's meetings endorsed the committee's proposal. Unless Michigan Quarterly Meeting resumed the Meeting of Ministers and Elders, the committee concluded, "to relax the discipline and abandon the institution that time and change have left us" would not be "in accordance with the Gospel of truth," and that "way does not open to release them from the duties and obligations required of *other* Quarterly meetings." If they "continue to disregard the injunctions of the discipline and the authority of the church, this meeting can no longer continue to receive their representatives or their reports." Dissenters from this action, according to their own account, appealed to "justice and honor, and the principles of the society which were being violated. But in vain. The measure was taken, the purpose inflexible. Party predilection had an unalterable ascendency over justice and truth. In this state of confusion, disorder, and dissatisfaction, the meeting ended."[83]

In June 1848, the issue erupted again, finally uncontainable. Genesee Yearly Meeting, held at Farmington in Ontario County, opened calmly enough. On the warm and pleasant Sunday morning of June 11, Friends filled the meetinghouse to overflowing. Many people had to stand outside. Several male speakers, "not very talented," commented Benjamin Gue, who sat in the audience, made people restive before Lucretia Mott rose and delivered "one of the best sermons I ever listened to."[84]

The next day, reported Gue, "commenced the great struggle which ended in the separation of the society." John Searing and Margaret Brown made a brief report "To Genesee Yearly Meeting of Men & Women Friends" from "a part of the Committee" which transmitted to Michigan Quarterly Meeting "the report *and conclusion* of last year." The committee deeply deplored "the feeling that appears to prevail in the minds of some friends in Michigan either to separate themselves from society or compel the latter to yield its order, its discipline, its long established institutions! When we reflect upon the disaster and desolation, that always attend efforts to control or distract religious society, that operate so powerfully upon the great cause of pure and vital Christianity, we feel that the efforts now making to relax the discipline, and abandon the institutions that time and change have left us, are not in accordance with truth." The battle was on.[85]

Angry accusations left over from the year before quickly destroyed any possibility of harmony. The clerk of the men's meeting refused to accept a report from Michigan Quarterly Meeting. His opponents refused in turn to support him as clerk. Neither party was willing to compromise. Dissidents argued that the clerk had violated "a fundamental, recognized principle of Friends" and had invaded "the sacred rights of conscience, rights of inestimable value, not only to the Society, but to the world at large."[86]

Debate continued into the third day. Finally, the clerk spoke. "It was evident," he declared, "there were two parties in the Meeting, whose views were irreconcilable. He was willing to grant equal honesty to both. He had made a minute recording himself clerk, he explained, and if that part of the Meeting who united with him, was prepared that he should read it with the understanding that he was recording a minute of separation, he would proceed. He was then vociferously urged to proceed 'ON THAT PRINCIPLE.'" He read the minute. Friends who disappoved remained "entirely still" and declined to participate further in the meeting.[87]

The women's meeting experienced a similar break. "Great confusion and much painful feeling" left over from the year before was reinforced by the "silent indifference" of the clerk, who refused to read the report from Michigan Quarterly Meeting. "Very many friends" requested that last year's minute, excluding Michigan Quarterly Meeting, be read. When the clerk showed "no disposition to comply," someone remarked that "'she saw no harm in reading that minute;' whereupon the assistant clerk immediately read the minute." Michigan Quarterly Meeting, it noted, should have been informed of the action taken against them. Without such official notification, Michigan Friends had decided to send representatives to Yearly Meeting anyway. A proposal by "a dear friend from another Yearly Meeting" (perhaps Lucretia Mott) to alter the discipline "relative to Meetings of Ministers and Elders" (probably to acquiesce in Michigan Quarterly Meeting's request to abolish such meetings) was "united with by many friends, but was contumeliously rejected by the party having their subservient clerk." No further discussion seemed possible. The official minutes noted only that "it has been a time of deep trials and suffering to many."[88]

In both the men's and women's meetings, sympathizers of Michigan Quarterly Meeting spread the word that "Friends who loved *true* order and could not unite with the arbitrary measures which had been adopted" would meet the afternoon of the next day. "A large body of men and women friends," probably about two hundred of them, met on Wednesday, Thursday, and Friday for "deeply interesting and feeling" conferences. Significantly, they seem to have met not as separate men's and women's meetings but together.[89]

Among the dissidents were many Quakers from Waterloo and Rochester. Deanna Dell Bonnel, assistant clerk of the women's meeting, was probably there. So were Amy and Isaac Post and Daniel Anthony, from Rochester. So was Lucretia Mott. And so were Thomas and Mary Ann M'Clintock. Thomas, in fact, was one of the clerks of the meeting. (The other clerk was Rhoda DeGarmo.) And Thomas was the author of *An Address to Friends of Genesee Yearly Meeting, and Elsewhere.* Lucretia Mott's sympathies were all with the reformers, "The high handed measure of those in power," she wrote later, "must eventually open the eyes of the people to the impropriety and danger of conferring such power on our fellow mortals."[90]

Generally, the dissidents seemed to take the split philosophically and to be relieved rather than distraught. Daniel Anthony, ever passionate, ever thoughtful, reported to Susan B. Anthony, still teaching in Canajoharie, New York, that "Farmington Yearly meeting at thier last getting together divided—That portion of its members who take the liberty of holding up to view the wickedness of War—Slavery Intemperance—Hanging &c . . . That portion of the society who are not exactly satisfied to confine their operations for ameliorating the conditions of man within the compass of an old shriveled up nutshell and who are of opinion that each individual should have a right to even think as well as act for himself & in his own way to assist in rooling on the wheel of reform has left the more orthodox—wise and self righteous part of the society to attend to nothing but matters of pure & undefiled religion." Lucretia Mott put it more succinctly. "Three yearly mgs. will be formed this autumn on radical principles," she reported to English Friend Richard D. Webb, "—doing away with select mgs. & ordaing. ministers, men and women on perfect equality. . . . What a wonderful breaking up there is among sects."[91]

In October, this group met again. They called themselves the Congregational Friends, and they adopted a statement, *The Basis of Religious Association,* describing their new congregational form of government. Each local meeting would make its own decisions. Men and women would meet together, not separately. No person was to be subordinate to another. There were to be no ministers and no hierarchy of meetings. Members need not agree on any points of doctrine, nor were they to be tied to creeds or rituals. Instead, they would focus on practical philanthropy. "The true basis of religious fellowship," they agreed, "is not identity of theological belief, but unity of heart and oneness of purpose in respect to the great practical duties of life." The author of *The Basis of Religious Association*? None other than Thomas McClintock.[92]

Just as the Free Soilers of Seneca Falls had broken out of traditional political parties, so had the Waterloo Quakers broken away from their traditional religious affiliation. Both had split away over issues of equality. Both did so in dramatic and emotionally wrenching ways.

There were differences between the two groups. Some were obvious. One group was from Seneca Falls; the other from Waterloo and west. One group focused on politics; the other on religion. Some differences were more subtle. Take the question of equality, for instance. For the Free Soilers, equality was intertwined with freedom: freedom from bondage for enslaved people, freedom to move west without competition from a slave system. The most radical Free Soilers, such as Henry Stanton, hoped their action would destroy slavery; more conservative ones simply wanted to keep the West open for white settlers like themselves. Quaker concern for equality was of a different order. While they, too, linked equality with freedom, they did not stop there. Their ultimate goal was not freedom from human authority but obedience to God's authority. Equality between one person and another in human terms was necessary but not sufficient. Each person owed allegiance to a higher order.

There was another difference, too. For most Free Soilers, equality and freedom had to do with political, legal, and moral issues outside the family. Political equality meant male equality only. Legal and moral equality referred primarily to the abolition of slavery. Freedom to move west into nonslave territory meant freedom to move west as a family. Nothing in the rhetoric of Free Soilers suggested that freedom and equality might apply to women as well as men—not so for the Quakers. For them, equality in human relationships meant obedience to the dictates of the Inner Light. And the Inner Light was the birthright of every person, white or black, adult or child, man or woman. In essential questions, no human hierarchy of any kind must be allowed to interfere with God's ongoing revelation to each person, daily, outside the family or within it. While their June 1848 *Address to Friends* would speak of "man's nature," they would address themselves to "every equal brother and sister" and to "beloved brethren and sisters."[93]

William Lloyd Garrison had absorbed this notion of total equality, too, and of the inclusion of all people. Agents of the American Anti-Slavery Society had spread it across the country. As one of these agents, Abby Kelley had done her work well. Her agitation in Seneca Falls had not been for nothing. Some Free Soilers in Seneca Falls, Ansel Bascom, for example, and Henry B. Stanton, too, had absorbed this legacy. They were open to more inclusive, Quakerly, ideas of equality than was the national Free Soil Party.

After their wrenching meeting in June, Friends went home, not quite sure what they had done, not quite sure who they were or what to do next. They needed, they felt, another meeting. Seneca Falls Free Soilers, too, went home after their June 15 meeting. They were all fired up, ready to do something. But what? Henry Stanton and Ansel Bascom used their energy for public speaking. Everybody devoured the *New York Tribune* for the latest news. But local Free Soil men needed more. What would this new party do for them? Where did they stand? What should they do next? Like the Quakers of Waterloo, they were ready for a good public discussion. Little could either group have imagined what form that discussion would take.

CHAPTER 8

Declaring Woman's Rights, July 1848

In July 1848, revolution was in the air. As Americans confronted dramatic economic and social change, they had to redefine old values to meet the demands of a new world. Talk of revolution was not new in 1848. People had debated the idea for years. But in the spring of 1848, *revolution* became a household word. Through detailed newspaper reports, Americans followed the latest revolution in France. American reformers responded sympathetically. In Boston, a meeting of working men congratulated "our brothers" of France on their "glorious Revolution." In Rochester, Frederick Douglass asserted that the French revolution reverberated around the globe. "Thanks to steam navigation and electric wires . . ." Douglass argued, "a revolution now cannot be confined to the place or the people where it may commence, but flashes with lightening speed from heart to heart, from land to land, till it has traversed the globe, compelling all members of our common brotherhood at once, to pass judgment upon its merits. The revolution of France, like a bolt of living thunder, has aroused the world from its stupor."[1]

In 1848, as in every year, the Fourth of July also reminded Americans of another revolution—their own. On that day, for seventy-two years, as long as most people alive could remember, orators in every village across the United States had repeated the words of the Declaration of Independence. July 4, 1848, was no exception. After parading up one side of the river and down the other, people in Seneca Falls gathered for a celebration in Ansel Bascom's orchard. Dexter Bloomer recited with passion the familiar litany. "We hold these truths to be self-evident, that all men are created equal, that they are endowed by their Creator with certain inalienable rights, that among these are life, liberty, and the pursuit of happiness."[2] The Declaration of Independence became both a connection to the past and an avenue to the future. It helped bridge the chasm from a world in which individuals fit themselves into institutions—of family, church, and government—to a world in which institutions were likely to change to meet the needs of individuals.

Abolitionists, however, questioned the meaning of the Declaration and its celebration. Frederick Douglass called it "this anniversary of American hypocrisy." With heavy irony, he recorded its celebration in Rochester:

> If the ringing of bells, waving of banners, irregular discharge of fire-arms, . . . and the uproarious shouts of an apparently purposeless multitude, [he asserted], be an evidence of a love of the great principles of human freedom, as set forth in the American Declaration of Independence, then are the people of Rochester and vicinity the most devoted of all the lovers of liberty. But out of all the thousands that congregated here, probably not more than one hundred desire to see those principles triumphant in this country.

"Their's," he concluded, "is a white liberty."[3]

Most people in Seneca Falls and Waterloo took the idea of revolution less seriously. In an emerging market economy, advertising captured the word itself and transformed its meaning. Throughout the spring, for example, Tyler and Underhill, Seneca Falls dry goods merchants, reminded local residents of "Another Revolution!! Great Excitement at Seneca Falls!! Tyler & Underhill have just received their stock of Spring Goods by Rail Road. . . . READY MADE CLOTHING of all kinds and qualities . . . Also Sugar, Tea, Coffee, Molasses &c. &c." In even bigger letters, J. S. Clark, M.D., and C. W. Mattison, Druggist, announced in the *Union Advertiser,* a free advertising flyer published on July 11, 1848, "REVOLUTION. Drugs and Medicines, paints, oils & dye stuffs, Paper Hangings . . . Stationery, Miscellaneous and School BOOKS. Lamps and window glass. SARSAPARILLA."[4]

But in Seneca Falls and Waterloo, another kind of revolution was about to begin. On July 11, the same day these advertisements appeared, the *Seneca County Courier* carried a notice for a woman's rights convention, to be convened eight days later at the Wesleyan Chapel in Seneca Falls. Stanton would call it "the greatest movement for human liberty recorded on the pages of history—a demand for freedom to one-half the entire race." It proclaimed to all the world, in a new version of the Declaration of Independence, "that all men *and women* are created equal."[5]

* * *

The authors of this notice were a group of Quaker women, joined by Elizabeth Cady Stanton. After Genesee Yearly Meeting, radical Quakers went home. They had agreed to meet again in October. But what would they do in the meantime?

James and Lucretia Mott spent a long visit with Lucretia's sister, Martha

Wright, in Auburn. They also carried out an extensive reform agenda. They went to "Gennessee Yearly & all the radical quarters this year," Lucretia reported. They visited prisoners at Auburn prison. They made "trips of a few hundred or a thousand miles or so, to the Indians & Negroes in Canada." The character of Mott's message was consistent, reported the *New York Tribune.* She "fearlessly opposes Slavery of all kinds, and advocates thorough Education for all, Peace and Land Reform. She . . . insisted that Practical Christianity was the only thing important-creeds and forms being of little account." Everywhere Lucretia and James went, they distributed antislavery pamphlets.[6]

High on their list of priorities were travels to communities of self-emancipated slaves in both the United States and Canada. They visited African American families in Buffalo, Detroit, Chatham, Dawn, London, and Toronto. They were impressed by the "kindness and hospitality" of African Americans in Canada, as well as their interest in education and the "generous aid" they gave to new arrivals.[7]

They also visited "the few hundreds left of the Seneca Nation." What the Motts saw at Cattaraugus were a people in conflict. The Senecas were deeply divided over both political and religious issues. In politics, one group advocated a change from the traditional clan-based system of choosing leaders to an elective system. The Senecas, remarked Lucretia Mott, were "imitating the movements of France and all Europe, in seeking larger liberty—more independence." They officially become the Seneca Nation in 1848.[8]

For the Seneca, as for their European American neighbors, religious disagreements were intertwined with political debates. Two white missionaries encouraged converts to Christianity. Adherents of the traditional religion (probably incorporating the teachings of the early nineteenth-century prophet Handsome Lake) carried out the "sacred festivals of their fathers," noted Mott, "and are not disposed to exchange them for the 'bread and wine' &c., of the Christian party."

The Motts took no sides. "We might be found equally discountenancing each form, and recommending our Quaker non-conformity," Lucretia Mott explained. Instead, "we commended them to the 'Great Spirit,' believing that those who danced religiously, might be as nearly perfect, as were those who communed in some other chosen form—neither of these being the test of acceptance." They witnessed the strawberry dance. "Grotesque though the figures were," Mott reported,

> fantastic their appearance, and rude their measured steps, and unharmonious their music, yet, in observing the profound veneration of the hundreds present, some twenty of whom were performers, and the respectful attention paid to the speeches of their chiefs, *women as well as men,* it was far from me to say, that our silent, voiceless worship was better adapted to their condition, or that even the Missionary, Baptism, and Sabbath, and organ are so much higher evidence of a civilized, spiritual and Christian state.[9]

What the Motts described had major implications for the roles of women and men within Seneca society. Whether political change would bring "larger liberty—more independence," as the Motts contended, was debatable. Certainly, the change did not enhance the power of Seneca women. By adopting yearly election of chiefs, the Senecas eroded the traditional right of clan mothers to select chiefs for life (and to depose them if necessary). Emulating a European American model, they limited voting to males. Land sales, however, would have to be approved by a vote among the women themselves.

It is not clear that James and Lucretia Mott recognized the significance, in gender terms, of what they were seeing. It is, however, intriguing to realize that, just before they attended the Seneca Falls woman's rights convention, they had been close observers of a traditional culture in which woman's roles were highly valued, and they had witnessed part of a debate over the importance of voting rights and an elective system.[10]

The Motts had planned to visit prisoners, African Americans, and Senecas. They had not, however, counted on attending another convention, this one devoted to woman's rights. For Lucretia Mott, the first inkling that something new might be emerging came some time on or before the weekend of July 8–9. Perhaps after Quaker meeting on Sunday, July 9, Mott found herself at what she supposed would be a simple tea party in Jane and Richard Hunt's home in Waterloo. With her were "several members of different families of Friends, earnest, thoughtful women." Mott's sister, Martha Wright, had accompanied her, probably on the train from Auburn that morning. Most likely, Mary Ann M'Clintock and perhaps also her two oldest daughters, Elizabeth and Mary Ann were there. Jane Hunt hosted the meeting, and Richard P. Hunt probably joined them for part of the afternoon.[11]

What began as a tea party, focusing on the upsetting events of last month's Meeting, turned into something quite different. For Jane Hunt, perhaps at Lucretia Mott's request, invited Elizabeth Cady Stanton to tea. Her presence transformed this meeting from a small gathering of Friends into a revolutionary planning session.

Stanton likely approached the Hunt house with some excitement. She carried with her the memories of her first year in Seneca Falls, the stress of physical illness and of Henry's long absence, the excitement of Henry's recent political triumphs and of Gerrit Smith's new Liberty League, the death of Henry's small nephew. Here, at last, she would find women she could really talk to, women who might understand, as Henry did not, the difficulties of managing children and household virtually alone.

As Stanton stepped into the main hall of the Hunt house, she surely noticed the furnishings, simple but comfortable, reflecting the family's concern for intellectual as well as physical health: an oil cloth on the floor, a stair carpet held down by rods, a hall table, and, along one wall, a large map of the United States.

Jane Hunt, c. 1860s. Jane Hunt hosted the tea party where Elizabeth Cady Stanton and others wrote the call for the first woman's rights convention. Reprinted by permission of Friends Historical Library, Swarthmore College.

Entering the parlor, she noted a large carpet (about nine by ten feet), a square center table with a marble top, a red velvet sofa, two rocking chairs, and six parlor chairs, probably now drawn up from their usual places along the wall to surround the tea table, where Jane Hunt's tea pot and her best cups and saucers might now be arrayed. The windows had no curtains but instead were covered, when desired, with window shades, probably painted in the fashion of the day. A work stand, tray, umbrella, two candle sticks, and a mirror completed the room.[12]

Jane Clothier Master Hunt had come from Philadelphia in the winter of 1845–46 to become Richard P. Hunt's fourth wife. Only thirty-six years old in 1848, she had a year-old son, William, and had just given birth two weeks before to a daughter, Jane. Richard's three older children completed their family. Probably they also had three live-in servants to help with household and garden work. Because she was nursing her new baby, Jane Hunt may have retired early from the tea party to rest. Quite likely, one of the household help served the tea and cleared the teapot and cups afterwards.[13]

As she stepped into Jane Hunt's parlor that afternoon, Stanton might have felt, at first, like an outsider. Everyone else had known each other for many years, and each was related to at least one other woman in the room. All, like their hostess, were originally from the Philadelphia area. All of them were part of the egalitarian Quaker group that had walked out of Genesee Yearly Meeting. Quite likely, they expected to discuss Quaker concerns and to make plans for the future. If so, they had not reckoned with the power and the passion that their new visitor brought.

Stanton was delighted to see Lucretia Mott again. Immediately, they picked up the topic they had begun in London in 1840 and had continued in Boston in 1842, "the propriety of holding a woman's convention." Such a convention seemed more important to Stanton now than ever. Responding to a sympathetic audience, Stanton released her pent-up anger and frustration. She "poured out," as she remembered, "the torrent of my long-accumulating discontent, with such vehemence and indignation that I stirred myself, as well as the rest of the party, to do and dare anything." "The general discontent I felt with woman's portion as wife, mother, housekeeper, physician, and spiritual guide," Stanton remembered later,

> the chaotic conditions into which everything fell without her constant supervision, and the wearied, anxious look of the majority of women impressed me with a strong feeling that some active measures should be taken to remedy the wrongs of society in general, and of women in particular. My experience at the World's Anti-slavery Convention, all I had read of the legal status of women, and the oppression I saw everywhere, together swept across my soul, intensified now by many personal experiences. It seemed as if all the elements had conspired to impel me to some onward step.[14]

Hunt family tradition suggests that Richard P. Hunt joined the tea party during this discussion. Hearing the women discuss their rights with such passion and believing that "faith without works is dead," he asked, "Why don't you do something about it?" Certainly, it was the sense of the meeting, as Quakers would say, that something should be done.[15]

The only thing they could think of, in fact, was to call "a public meeting for protest and discussion." "We decided to hold a convention at once," Stanton remembered, "while Mr. and Mrs. Mott were with us, in central New York." As the only experienced speaker among them, Lucretia Mott was essential. With her reputation and talent, she would attract crowds. Not since Abby Kelley's visit five years ago had people in Seneca Falls had a chance to hear a woman lecture in public. But if Stanton and the Friends were to take advantage of Mott's brief stay, they must act at once. They would hold the meeting as soon as possible, in the only place open to reformers, the Wesleyan Church in Seneca Falls.

And so, "before the twilight deepened into night," the women wrote a brief notice:

> WOMAN'S RIGHTS CONVENTION.—A Convention to discuss the social, civil, and religious condition and rights of woman, will be held in the Wesleyan Chapel, at Seneca Falls, N.Y., on Wednesday and Thursday, the 19th and 20th of July, current; commencing at 10 o'clock A.M. During the first day the meeting will be exclusively for women, who are earnestly invited to attend. The public generally are invited to be present on the second day, when Lucretia Mott, of Philadelphia, and other ladies and gentlemen, will address the convention.[16]

Deliberately, the women left the notice unsigned. The *Minutes* of the convention reported that "the Women of Seneca County, N.Y." called the convention, and that is how these women wanted to be recognized: not for themselves as individuals but as representatives of local citizens. Stanton herself probably called on Saron Phillips, minister of the Wesleyan congregation, to be sure that the chapel would be available, before she added the details about place and time.[17]

Someone took the message to the office of the *Seneca County Courier,* on Cayuga Street, just around the corner from Hoskins's store. Nathan Milliken, the editor, published it on Tuesday, July 11. Other papers, such as the *Ovid (N.Y.) Bee,* probably picked the notice up from the *Courier* and carried it beginning on Friday, July 14. Lucretia Mott sent a copy to the *North Star,* which also printed it on Friday, July 14.[18]

These women (and perhaps Richard P. Hunt, too) did a remarkable thing. They recognized that their personal situation was not their problem alone. Stanton realized that the real source of her frustration was not Henry, whatever successes or failures he might have. It was not her own isolation, the tedium and stress of parenting a household alone, or her limited opportunity to enjoy friends or read books. It was not even the tragedy of death in her family.

It was instead a problem that she, as a woman, shared with every other woman. It was a problem of cultural values, which assumed that every woman, no matter what her talents, would be defined by her sex. It was also a problem of social structure, since it was social institutions—family, work, community, the law—that kept women and men so neatly apart, so boxed into assigned places. And ultimately, it was a political problem, because without a different distribution of power, there could be no changes.

Stanton spoke that day with such intensity because her whole life had brought her to this point. And the women who listened found her arguments compelling. Not only did they recognize the justice of her case but they also knew that another way was possible. They themselves had explored that other way; they had followed the Inner Light, and it led toward dignity, mutual respect, and equality, for women as well as men.

With a mere eight days between the publication of the call and the meeting itself, what were these women to do? None of them had organized a whole convention before, but among themselves, they had considerable public experience. Lucretia Mott was well known as a public lecturer, and Stanton had given at least two speeches. The M'Clintocks had organized Quaker meetings, antislavery conventions, and antislavery fairs. They all recognized that speakers and resolutions would draw crowds and generate debate.

Stanton got right to work. She began to outline ideas for her own "great speech," as Mott called it, probably a proposed declaration for the convention as a whole. Conscious of its importance as the convention's major statement, she asked the M'Clintocks for advice. On Friday, July 14, she scrawled a note to Elizabeth M'Clintock. "Dear Lizzie," she began. "Rain or shine I intend to spend Sunday with you that we may all together concoct a declaration. I have drawn up one but you may suggest any alterations & improvements for I know it is not as perfect a declaration as should go forth from the first woman's rights convention that has ever assembled. I shall take the ten o'clock train in the morning & return at five in the evening, provided we can accomplish *all our business* in that time." Elizabeth M'Clintock's energy and vision made her a key player in organizing the convention. Besides being "attractive in manners and appearance," Stanton noted later, she "had rare executive ability, was capable of intense enthusiasm and earnest in her convictions of truth."[19]

Stanton continued to work on her draft, and Lucretia Mott encouraged her efforts. "I was right glad to hear of thy resolve," she wrote from Auburn the Sunday before the meeting, "& hope thou wilt not give out." James Mott wanted Stanton to "reserve it [her main presentation] for the second day, so that he & others may be able to hear it."[20]

Finally, Stanton, Lucretia Mott, and Elizabeth M'Clintock began to publicize the meeting. The M'Clintocks made sure that the Congregational Friends were aware of the proposed gathering, while Stanton herself talked to people in Seneca Falls. One can imagine her stopping to see Charles Hoskins in his dry goods store, for example, urging him to attend for the sake of his three daughters. Certainly she must have spoken to her neighbor Jacob Chamberlain, mill owner, who had presided at the Free Soil meeting in June, and father of four girls himself. Men such as these most likely passed the word to customers and friends who passed through their store and mill during the few days before the convention. Stanton and M'Clintock also wrote to reformers outside the local area. On Friday, July 14, Stanton reported to M'Clintock that "I have written to Lydia Maria Child, Maria Chapman & Sarah Grimke, as we hope for some good letters to read in the Convention." These women apparently did not respond, but Elizabeth M'Clintock had more success with Frederick Douglass. "To be sure I will do myself the pleasure of accepting your kind invitation to attend the proposed woman's convention at Seneca Falls," he wrote to M'Clintock on Friday. "I think that one or two more of the Post family will be present also." "Your notice," he added, "did not reach me in time for this paper—but happily I received one from our mutual Friend Lucretia Mott." Douglass may have come to the convention in part to recruit readers for his newspaper. If so, he did well, for several people in Seneca Falls became subscribers.[21]

To Lucretia Mott in Auburn, Stanton wrote a "kind letter of information and invitation." Mott sent a verbal reply by Mary Ann M'Clintock, who had stopped at the Wright home in Auburn on her way home from a meeting in Deruyter, New York. "I requested her to tell thee," wrote Mott on Sunday, July 16, "how poorly my husband was, and that it was not likely I should be able to go to Seneca Falls, before the morning of the convention." Mott expected to be at the Wednesday planning session, for women only. Martha Wright would come with them. "James continues quite unwell," Lucretia reported. "I hope however that he will be able to be present the 2nd day." Don't expect her daughter Martha, however, Mott warned, who "thinks she is not quite enough of a reformer to attend such a convention." "The true reason," thought Mott, was that "she is more interested just now, with her cousins here & her time being short she dont incline to leave them."[22]

On Sunday morning, July 16, Stanton again traveled to Waterloo, this time to visit the M'Clintocks. Boarding the cars at 10:00 A.M., she would have reached the M'Clintock house at midmorning. As Stanton entered the parlor, just off the hallway to the left, she sat down once more at a tea table, a small round mahogany tilt-top table with a center pedestal and unusual, C-shaped feet. This time, only the M'Clintock family sat with her. Surely Mary Ann M'Clintock was there, along with her two oldest daughters, Elizabeth, twenty-seven years old, and Mary Ann, twenty-six. Perhaps Thomas M'Clintock joined them for dinner and stayed to talk afterwards. Twenty-five-year-old sister Sarah was also there, although she seems not to have taken a major part in the discussions. Brother Charles poked his head in the door at least once. Probably the youngest M'Clintock daughter, Julia, who had celebrated her seventeenth birthday a month before, was also in the house. Their task was to revise Stanton's draft of a declaration, to write appropriate resolutions, and "to consider subjects for speeches."[23]

They were in good humor, even though all of them felt rushed. They had only three days to present a workable agenda. They knew their task would not be easy, although "having no experience in the *modus operandi* of getting up conventions . . . they were innocent of the herculean labors they proposed. On the first attempt to frame a resolution; to crowd a complete thought, clearly and concisely, into three lines; they felt as helpless and hopeless as if they had been suddenly asked to construct a steam engine," Stanton remembered.[24]

Most important would be the declaration itself. For ideas, they "resigned themselves to a faithful perusal of various masculine productions," including the reports of "Peace, Temperance, and Antislavery conventions." But none of these reports captured the fervor they all felt about woman's rights. "All alike," Stanton declared, "seemed too tame and pacific for the inauguration of a rebellion such as the world had never before seen." So, "after much delay, one of the circle took up the Declaration of 1776, and read it aloud with much spirit and emphasis, and it was at once decided to adopt the historic document, with some slight changes such as substituting 'all men' for 'King George.'" Everyone, recalled Stanton, pronounced it to be "just the thing." Again, in Quakerly style, the group had forged an idea that transcended any individual contribution.[25]

They had found their voice. They would call their manifesto a "Declaration of Sentiments," after the founding document of the American Anti-Slavery Society in 1833. But this declaration was to be, in reality, a second Declaration of Independence. The new document captured their imaginations. It also captured the spirit of a generation. It would be the single most important factor in spreading news of the woman's rights movement around the country in 1848 and into the future.

Carrying out this idea, however, proved harder than it first had seemed. To adapt the preamble was easy enough. But the original declaration had listed eighteen grievances of the colonists against King George. Where could these women, themselves "fortunately organized and conditioned," find eighteen grievances to match them? "We all knew that women must have more grievances than men, in the nature of things," Stanton recollected, "but what they were was the question." As the *History of Woman Suffrage* later noted, these women "had not in their own experience endured the coarser forms of tyranny resulting from unjust laws, or association with immoral and unscrupulous men, but they had souls large enough to feel the wrongs of others, without being scarified in their own flesh."[26] So they carried out "a protracted search . . . through statute books, church usages, and the customs of society." "After hours of diligent searching, of creeds, codes, customs and constitutions," Stanton recalled, "we were rejoiced to find that we could make out as good a bill of impeachment against our sires and sons as they had against old King George."[27]

"Several well-disposed men," Stanton noted, helped them collect their complaints. Henry Stanton himself helped with several "extracts from laws bearing unjustly against woman's property interests." Not all of the helpers did so without noting, as had the women themselves, the irony of the situation. When Charles M'Clintock overheard the women laughing in the parlor, he put his head in the door and remarked, "maliciously," as Stanton teased, "'Your grievances must be very grievous indeed, if it takes you so long to find them.'"[28]

Whatever difficulties they had, they overcame them. They would be ready with a declaration, and a strong one, too, on July 19. And they had at least a handful of resolutions to help them focus the discussion.

Stanton alone was responsible for one main point. The word *political* had not appeared in the call to the convention. But Stanton, thinking about this at home, decided "that woman's political rights should be brought prominently before the meeting." Most especially, she decided, women must have a right to vote. So she added several points to the Declaration of Sentiments and resolutions. In its final form, the declaration charged that man had never permitted woman "to exercise her inalienable right to the elective franchise." Resolution number nine echoed this idea: "Resolved, that it is the duty of the women of this country to secure to themselves their sacred right to the elective franchise."[29]

Stanton had learned her lessons well. She had not forgotten the long debates over married women's property. Nor had she forgotten abolitionist discussions over women's position and voting. Then she had been a newcomer to reform, a young person, and a woman. Now she would take matters into her own hands, and she would organize other women to do the same.

Elizabeth Cady Stanton's commitment to voting rights for women was, in part, a logical extension of the position she had outlined much earlier. Valuing Garrison and the nonresistants for their purity and integrity, she had nevertheless recognized, even then, the usefulness of voting to promote antislavery principles. Both her insight and her courage became sharper, deeper, and more compelling after her discussions with Gerrit Smith just a few days before the woman's rights convention. Smith had just made a demand for woman's suffrage at the Liberty League convention in Buffalo. Stanton could do no less in Seneca Falls.

Such a context strengthened her resolve. It also fueled opposition, both from Henry Stanton, whose political abolitionism was of a different mold, and from the Quakers, whose Garrisonian commitments (as well as their Quaker tradition) precluded as a matter of principle any involvement with secular politics, including voting. Henry was "thunderstruck," "amazed at her daring," when she confidentially showed him her proposed suffrage resolution. He was so disgusted with her obstinance, in fact, that he would not attend the convention. "You will turn the proceedings," he declared, "into a farce." "I must declare the truth as I believe it to be," she insisted. And so Henry was off again, to lecture once more for free soil. Stanton recruited emotional and physical support from her sister Harriet Eaton, who came with her son, Daniel Cady Eaton, to visit during the convention. Still, with hasty preparations and with opposition from those she loved best, it was no wonder that Stanton faced the convention itself with some fear.[30]

Meanwhile, subscribers to the *Seneca County Courier,* the *North Star,* the *Ovid Bee,* and perhaps a few other local and regional papers had already read the call to the convention. At least some of them responded with excitement. When Charlotte Woodward, nineteen years old and probably living in the township of Waterloo, received the paper, she "ran from one house to another in her neighborhood, and found other women reading it, some with amusement and incredulity, others with absorbed interest." With a half dozen friends to lend moral support, Woodward felt brave enough to go to the convention, at least on the first day, when only women would be there. But would any women really appear? The call had mentioned Lucretia Mott, so they could count on her, at least. The day before the meeting, Nathan Milliken, editor of the *Courier,* had been good enough to add a special endorsement of his own for Lucretia Mott. "Mrs. Mott has a world-wide reputation as a philanthropist and public speaker," he noted. "We expect to derive much pleasure and profit from her remarks." Charlotte Woodward also felt sure that Elizabeth Cady Stanton was behind this meeting.[31]

Feeling anxious that they might be alone in the audience, and ready to return home at nightfall, these young women started off early on the bright clear morning of Wednesday, July 19, driving a horsedrawn democrat wagon. As they headed toward the Wesleyan Chapel in Seneca Falls, they noticed an unusual number of other wagons and carriages going in the same direction. Men drove some of these vehicles, although most of the occupants were women. When they reached Seneca Falls, they were surprised to find a crowd in front of the chapel, waiting for the door to open. Someone, it seems, had forgotten the key. Finally, young Daniel Cady Eaton, Stanton's nephew, climbed through a window and opened the door from the inside. The crowd found its way slowly into the church. Perhaps Elizabeth and Mary Ann M'Clintock, ushers, greeted young Woodward and her friends before they helped them find seats. Woodward asked for a seat way in the back, for she certainly had no intention of actually speaking.[32]

Charlotte Woodward may have been nervous about attending this convention, but Elizabeth Cady Stanton was terrified. As she stood at the front of the chapel at eleven o'clock, an hour after they had planned to begin, with all her law books and papers spread out in front of her, she may have comforted herself with the thought that today was a day for women only. Henry had his constituents, all male. These women would be hers. If this reform were ever to begin, it would have to begin with women themselves. She only hoped that others felt the same way.

A fair number of people had already gathered. Most of them were women, but at least a few children accompanied them. Daniel Cady Eaton, for example, attended with his mother. But men took no part in the first day's proceedings. On this day, they would be listeners only, not speakers, perhaps even remaining outside the building. Ironically, however, the presence of so many "uncommonly liberal men" on the first day of the convention gave Charlotte Woodward the "courage to stay over for the second day's sessions."[33]

As its first order of business, the convention appointed the young Mary Ann M'Clintock as secretary. She took clear notes throughout the whole two days. Then it was Stanton's turn. Taking a deep breath, she stated the object of the meeting—probably referring to the "Call" itself—to discuss the "social, civil, and religious condition and rights of woman." Lucretia Mott encouraged the women to speak freely in the meeting and not to be bound by the "trammels of education."

Then Stanton, probably with considerable trepidation, introduced the main business of the convention, the Declaration of Sentiments. Quite likely it was here, shortly before noon on this first morning, that most of the audience first confronted the idea of voting rights for women. They had come, after all, to debate social, civil, and religious rights for women. But woman's right to vote? That was another thing entirely. Lucretia Mott, who probably first heard about the idea of women voting when she arrived at the convention, was startled enough to retort, "Lizzie, thou wilt make the convention ridiculous." She and other Quakers were, however, willing to think about the issue. Someone asked to have the Declaration reread, paragraph by paragraph. "After much consideration, some changes were suggested and adopted." This was the document they would present tomorrow, when "the public generally," men as well as women, were invited.[34]

The group also agreed upon eleven resolutions. These were probably the ones that Stanton, the M'Clintocks, and perhaps Lucretia Mott had prepared in advance. All of them flowed from one basic premise, based on a philosophy of natural law and stated in their first resolution: "The great precept of nature," they began, "is conceded to be; 'that man shall pursue his own true and substantial happiness.'" This natural law, they argued, quoting "Blackstone, in his Commentaries," is "coeval with mankind, and dictated by God himself. . . . It is binding over all the globe, in all countries, and at all times; no human laws are of any validity if contrary to this. . . ." Resolved, therefore, "That such laws as conflict, in any way, with the true and substantial happiness of woman, are contrary to the great precept of nature, and of no validity." "Woman is man's equal," read one resolution, "—was intended to be so by the Creator, and the highest good of the race demands that she should be recognized as such." And the women did not forget Stanton's demand for the right to vote. In the ninth resolution, they suggested "That it is the duty of the women of this country to secure to themselves their sacred right to the elective franchise."[35]

On that first morning, the women also debated, "in an animated manner," "the propriety of obtaining the signatures of men to the Declaration." Yes, they voted, men should be asked to sign. They would defer the final decision, however, until the next day, when men themselves would be present to speak. And so the meeting adjourned to 2:30 P.M.[36]

In the afternoon, when, as Mary Bascom recalled, the "mercury [was] at 90 degrees," it must have been blazing hot under the Wesleyan church roof. But that did not deter the women from continuing their debates. They read the declaration once more, "an addition having been inserted since the morning session." The women voted to accept the amendment, and "papers [were] circulated," probably by Elizabeth and Mary Ann M'Clintock, "to obtain signatures."[37]

They finished the afternoon on a lighter note. Lucretia Mott read "a humorous article from a newspaper," probably "Hints for Wives," written by her sister Martha Wright. Martha herself, remembered Mary Bascom, "took little part in the proceedings, [even though] probably not a woman present was more capable of doing so." Martha would later apologize for her reticence. Her pregnancy depressed her, she wrote to her sister in October. "I plead guilty to being very stupid & dispirited at Seneca Falls," she noted, "the prospect of having more Wrights than I wanted tending materially to subdue the ardor & energy that wd. doubtless have characterized me at another time but I was glad of the privilege of looking on and shrinking as far as *shrinking* was practicable, into the insignif[ig]ance that under the circumstances was appropriate for me." Elizabeth M'Clintock ended the day with an address of her own, apparently her first public speech.[38]

By the end of the afternoon, Stanton must have felt relieved and exhilarated. She had met her first test. She had found her voice, and "greatly to her surprise," she realized that she could defend her arguments with ease.[39] Nor did she have to worry about a silent audience. The women had proved remarkably lively. And finally, this group had debated the Declaration of Sentiments seriously and intelligently. They had not laughed at it or ridiculed it. She had good reason, then, to expect the same response for the rest of the convention.

That evening, the women participants were joined by a large audience of area residents at the Wesleyan Chapel for a special attraction. Lucretia Mott, "so well known as a pleasing and eloquent orator," spoke by candle light, reported the *Seneca County Courier,* with "eloquence and power" on the progress of reforms. In a "neat and impressive style," Mott gave an "eminently beautiful and instructive" outline of "the gradual advancement of the causes of Temperance, Anti-slavery, Peace, &c." She then alluded briefly to the "rights and wrongs of women" and expressed the hope that this movement "would soon assume a grandeur and dignity worthy of its importance." Mott had wondered earlier if Stanton planned "to have any reform or other Meeting during the sittings of the Convention," and she had hoped that this convention would be "followed in due time by one of a more general character." This evening's talk was her effort to put woman's rights into the larger context of reform in general. Turnout was large. Some were attracted by curiosity, but they were "intelligent and respectful." Eliab W. Capron, who signed the Declaration of Sentiments the next day, described Mott's speech as "one of the most eloquent, logical and philosophical discourses we ever listened to."[40]

Mott ended with an invitation to the gentlemen "to let their voices be heard on the great subject" of woman's rights. Frederick Douglass made the only response. As the only other nationally recognized reformer at the convention, he had already taken an outspoken stand. On every issue of his paper, the masthead read, "Right is of no Sex—Truth is of no Color—God is the Father of us all, and we are all Brethren." To Mott's request for comments, Douglass responded with a "brief and humorous apology," brief perhaps because he had just had his tonsils removed three weeks before.[41]

Word was out: there was excitement at the Wesleyan Chapel. The next morning at 10 A.M., when the convention officially reconvened, people thronged in. Whether drawn by commitment or curiosity, both men and women made their way to the meeting, on foot, by horseback, in wagons, and in carriages. Several observers testified as to the crowds. Stanton herself reported that "the house was crowded at every session." Rhoda Palmer, who drove with her father, Asa, from north of Geneva, remembered that the convention was "largely attended." Young Mary Bascom, thirteen-year-old daughter of Ansel and Eliza Bascom, confessed that she "did not remember a crowd, but we all differ as to terms." For at least the evening sessions, people filled the first floor and overflowed to the upstairs gallery. Amelia Bloomer, soon to be editor of the temperance journal the *Lily*, returned to Seneca Falls from an out-of-town visit and arrived late the second day. The crowd was so "immense," she remembered, that she had to take a seat in the upstairs gallery.[42]

As the meeting began on Thursday, July 20, Elizabeth Cady Stanton stood at the front of the Wesleyan Chapel. She was so frightened, she remembered, that she felt like "suddenly abandoning all her principles and running away."[43] With effort, she calmed herself. As she looked around, she recognized many people. Some were neighbors from Seneca Falls—Free Soilers and abolitionists for the most part. Others were Quakers from Waterloo, Rochester, or Macedon, a small town north of Waterloo. Frederick Douglass, already famous as an abolitionist orator and now embarking on a new career as editor of the *North Star*, had come with Quaker women from Rochester.

Stanton took special courage from two of these Quaker families. Elizabeth and Mary Ann M'Clintock impressed people as "beautiful women, with dignified and self-possessed manners not often seen in women brought up as they were in a country town." They were dependable, efficient, and enthusiastic allies, and Stanton knew that she could count on them to manage the convention's details. Most heartening of all, Lucretia Mott was here. She and her sister Martha Wright had taken the train (the cars, as they called them) from Auburn the day before, on Fourth Day (Wednesday) morning. Lucretia Mott and Martha Wright had probably accepted Stanton's "kind invite" to stay overnight at the Stanton house. James Mott, although he had been sick, was also present on this second day. Not too much could go wrong when the M'Clintock sisters and the Motts were here.[44]

In 1880, Mary Bascom recalled what she had seen as a young girl sitting in the audience: "The whole scene comes before me as vividly as if it were yesterday," she recalled, "the old chapel with its dusty windows, the gallery on three sides, the wooden benches or pews, and the platform with the desk and communion-table, and the group gathered there; Mrs. Stanton, stout, short, with her merry eye and expression of great good humor; Lucretia Mott, whose presence then as now commanded respect wherever she might be; Mary Ann McClintoc, a dignified Quaker matron with four daughters around her, two of whom took an active part in the proceedings."[45]

Overwhelmed by the large audience of both women and men, the women held a quick consultation. Then they invited James Mott, experienced in such matters, to take the chair. Tall and dignified, Mott moved to the front of the room. The crowd fell silent. Latecomers hurriedly took their seats, assisted once more by the M'Clintock sisters. This day was to be the real test for woman's rights. The women had agreed among themselves about what they wanted to say. Would the larger world accept these ideas, too?[46]

Stanton began to read, slowly and clearly, the convention's Declaration of Sentiments. The audience must have been surprised and at first puzzled to recognize words of the Declaration of Independence, as comforting to their ears as the most common verse from the King James version of the Bible.[47]

> When, in the course of human events, it becomes necessary for one portion of the family of man to assume among the people of the earth a position different from that which they have hitherto occupied, but one to which the laws of nature and of nature's God entitle them, a decent respect to the opinions of mankind requires that they should declare the causes that impel them to such a course.
>
> We hold these truths to be self-evident; that all men and women are created equal; that they are endowed by their Creator with certain inalienable rights; that among these are life, liberty, and the pursuit of happiness; that to secure these rights governments are instituted, deriving their just powers from the consent of the governed.

This preamble contained only one major change from the Declaration of Independence. The new declaration asserted not that "all men are created equal" but that "all men *and women* are created equal." Two small words only, nestled in the old comfortable phrases, made all the difference. They transformed the awareness and jostled the consciousness of every person who heard them. And so people were inclined to listen with considerable interest. But where would such an idea lead? It took them, as they well knew, to revolution. This was not a revolution of the colonists against King George. It was a revolution of women against patriarchal institutions: the law, the family, religion, work, education, and, most startling of all, of politics.

> The history of mankind is a history of repeated injuries and usurpations on the part of man toward women, having in direct object the establishment of an absolute tyranny over her. To prove this, let facts be submitted to a candid world.
>
> He has never permitted her to exercise her inalienable right to the elective franchise.
>
> He has compelled her to submit to laws, in the formation of which she had no voice.

The facts that Stanton and the M'Clintocks had gathered to support their assertions fell into several main categories. First were those charges, four of them, dealing with civil and political rights. These reflected Stanton's personal contributions. Essentially, they were all variations on one theme, stated outright in the first grievance: "He [man] has never permitted her [woman] to exercise her inalienable right to the elective franchise."[48]

The second major category dealt with legal discrimination, especially for married women. Stanton found it easy to list examples here. She had been especially concerned with woman's legal rights since the years she had spent as a girl in her father's law office. She came up with six legal grievances, more than those in any other section. If married, she charged vehemently, stung by how ridiculous a notion this was, a woman was "civilly dead." She was without property rights, "even to the wages she earns." Morally, she was "an irresponsible being," who could "commit many crimes with impunity, provided they be done in the presence of her husband." She was compelled to recognize her husband as her master, and he, in turn, had "power to deprive her of her liberty, and to administer chastisement," that is, to punish her, physically or otherwise. Divorce laws presupposed the "supremacy of man," gave "all power into his hands," and were "wholly regardless of the happiness of women" in determining child custody. Finally, "after depriving her of all rights as a married woman," men did not deal any more justly with single women. Single women who owned property found themselves taxed "to support a government which recognizes her only when her property can be made profitable to it." Undoubtedly, many in the audience translated this in their heads, as they were meant to do, into the clarion call of the earlier revolution, "no taxation without representation."[49]

Having dealt with political rights and legal rights especially, Stanton turned to the rights of women in work, education, and the church. Man had "monopolized nearly all the profitable employments, and from those she is permitted to follow, she receives but a scanty remuneration," she charged. He had closed to woman "all avenues to wealth and distinction," including theology, medicine, and law. He had denied woman a college education. He had kept her subordinate in the churches, "claiming Apostolic authority for her exclusion from the ministry, and, with some exceptions, from any public participation in the affairs of the Church." (Since Jesus was a man, argued most church men, he had called only men, beginning with the twelve apostles, to become ministers. When the women mentioned "exceptions," they were thinking, perhaps, of Quakers.)

The last category of grievances highlighted the values that supported the whole system of oppression. First among them was the double standard of morality. Man, they charged, "has created a false public sentiment, by giving to the world a different code of morals for men and women, by which moral delinquencies which exclude women from society, are not only tolerated but deemed of little account in man."

Second was man's usurpation of the "prerogative of Jehovah himself," when he claimed it "as his right to assign for her a sphere of action, when that belongs to her conscience and her God." If one grievance contained the key to all the others, this was it. Here was not a complaint about exclusion from a specific area or about the specific treatment of women by men. Here was a question of power, authority, and autonomy. This was not a matter of fact, as the other grievances had been, but of belief. As such, it separated those who advocated woman's rights from those who upheld the institutions of a male-defined world.

Finally, Stanton and her cohorts recognized the personal cost, for women, of the constant repression of female power. Man "has endeavored," they wrote, "in every way that he could to destroy her confidence in her own powers, to lessen her self-respect, and to make her willing to lead a dependant and abject life." Such a cry comes from the heart. Was this Stanton's own contribution, or did it perhaps reflect the passion of Elizabeth M'Clintock? The ultimate effect of this pattern of discrimination was to destroy the self-confidence and self-respect of individual women, to make women "dependant" and "abject." Yet if all men and women were truly created equal, entitled to those inalienable rights of life, liberty, and the pursuit of happiness, then human institutions were clearly out of tune with the right order of Nature and of God. Human institutions, not natural law, must be changed.

The women then declared that "in view of this entire disfranchisement of one-half the people of this country, their social and religious degradation,—in view of the unjust laws above mentioned, and because women do feel themselves aggrieved, oppressed, and fraudulently deprived of their most sacred rights, we insist that they have immediate admission to all the rights and privileges which belong to them as citizens of these United States."

Although they anticipated "no small amount of misconception, mis-representation, and ridicule," they agreed to use "every instrumentality within our power" to reach their goal. That included all the organizational methods they had already learned from abolitionist and temperance movements: employing agents, printing tracts, petitioning state legislatures and Congress, trying to get support from "the pulpit and the press," and, finally, organizing more conventions.

This document is remarkable for what it excludes as well as for what it includes. Just as many male abolitionists had tried to sidestep the question of woman's rights, so these woman's rights advocates did not mention the question of race. Did they mean that all women, not only native-born white women but also black women, Native American women, and immigrant women, should be citizens of the United States? The Declaration of Sentiments certainly suggests so. But could this goal be realized without raising other questions, as well? Perhaps Lucretia Mott's speech on the progress of reforms the evening before had put woman's rights reform into this larger perspective. Perhaps those who discussed the declaration in the convention itself drew such parallels. Or perhaps they decided to focus officially on woman's rights alone, to avoid dealing with contemporary controversies that so embroiled the antislavery movement.

When Stanton finished reading the declaration, several people responded. Lucretia Mott led them off. Ansel Bascom "spoke at length on the property bill for married women, just passed the Legislature, and the discussion on woman's rights in that [1846] Convention." S. E. Woodworth, a young (and bankrupt) dry goods merchant, who attended the convention with his fiancé, Mary Gilbert, a local milliner, added his comments. Four Quakers, including Thomas and Mary Ann M'Clintock and two Rochester Friends, Amy Post and Catharine F. Stebbins, also spoke. Frederick Douglass added his support, and Stanton, too, made a speech.[50]

There was never, however, any doubt about the outcome. Eliab W. Capron, editor of the *Auburn National Reformer,* reported that the convention adopted these resolutions "nearly as they were originally drawn up" by the women alone the day before. Not even those lawyers who opposed the equal rights of women dissented, commented Capron. What could be, as Stanton wrote later, more "timely, rational, and sacred" than this, to extend to women "all the rights and privileges which belong to them as citizens of these United States," and to do so by peaceful means? The convention agreed. Unanimously, they adopted the Declaration of Sentiments on late Thursday morning.[51]

Elizabeth and Mary Ann M'Clintock once more offered the declaration for signatures. Signing probably continued through the noon hour, into the afternoon, and perhaps through the evening, too. One hundred people responded. Sixty-eight women signed the document itself. "Firmly relying upon the final triumph of the Right and the True," they agreed, "we do this day affix our signatures to this declaration." Thirty-two men signed separately. Allowing men to sign a separate list "in favor of the movement," while women signed the document itself was a deft compromise between those (including Stanton) who wanted women to make their own demands and those who believed men also should have a voice.[52]

While Mary Bascom was "certain that every man, woman, and child present signed the declaration," we know that cannot be true. She herself, for example, was not a signer, nor was her father, who had been one of the first speakers. Amelia Bloomer, who attended the evening meeting, did not sign, nor did Asa Palmer, Rhoda Palmer's father. Neither did the three youngest M'Clintocks, Charles, Sarah, and Julia. If as many as three hundred people attended the meeting at any one time, then the signers probably represented only about one-third of those actually present. We do not know why as many as two-thirds of the attenders did not sign. Had they come to the meeting simply out of curiosity? Were they shy? Did they disagree with the whole effort? Did they disagree with the emphasis on political rights? Some male Quakers did not believe in participating in the supposedly corrupt political world themselves, so why would they promote it for women? Or did many men abstain out of respect for those who wanted women alone to present the declaration to the world?[53]

At midday, the meeting adjourned for dinner. Those who had come from a distance, and perhaps some of the local people, too, gathered their children around them and walked to their wagons, where they had brought food for themselves and their horses. Henry C. Wright, abolitionist agent, described a similar scene at an antislavery convention in Salem, Ohio, a few months later: "[T]he wagons are standing all around in the woods, the horses detached from them and tied to trees, eating oats and hay, and brushing away the flies with weapons furnished them by nature. The men, women, and children, gathered into those wagons to eat their apples, peaches, pears; peach, apple, and every pie, bread and butter, cake, and cold chicken." "Thus have I spent the intermissions," he concluded, "taking my dinner here in the grove in some wagon, or sitting on a log, or on the roots of some large tree." Those who attended the Seneca Falls convention probably spent their intermissions in much the same way.[54]

On both days, dinner offered a chance for the adults to continue their debates, for children to play, and for young people to socialize. Mary Bascom probably took some such opportunity to flirt with Charles M'Clintock, five years her senior. Charles was "a fellow-lover of mischief without much reverence for elders and betters," recalled Mary, and he enjoyed telling her about his "audacious talk," teasing Stanton and his mother and sisters when they had such difficulty finding eighteen grievances for the Declaration of Sentiments.[55]

When the convention reconvened at 2 P.M., the women, well pleased with the morning, introduced the series of resolutions they had first presented the day before. Nathan Milliken, editor of the *Seneca County Courier,* attended part of the afternoon's meeting. The resolutions, he wrote, were "spirited and spicy." After some discussion by Mott, Stanton, Thomas M'Clintock, Frederick Douglass, and George Pryor, the convention passed them all, as it had passed the Declaration of Sentiments itself, "no one expressing dissent." "To all persons who approved of the doctrines of the resolutions," Milliken noted, "repeated opportunities for reply were offered but no one responded to them." And finally, Stanton herself read "an extract from a letter of Wm. Howitt's, written soon after the exclusion of the female delegates from the World's Convention of 1840."[56]

The *Minutes* of the meeting, however, suggest some controversy. Certain resolutions, noted the official account, "from their self-evident truth, elicited but little remark; others, after some criticism, much debate, and some slight alterations, were finally passed by a large majority."[57]

Stanton recalled that all resolutions passed unanimously, with one exception, the ninth, drafted by herself, "urging the women of the country to secure to themselves the elective franchise." Opposed by her husband, by Lucretia Mott, and by many others, Stanton nevertheless was determined to present her resolution to the convention and the world. She wanted "to demand the right of suffrage, then and there," she recalled, "because I saw that was the fundamental right out of which all others should necessarily flow." "How to put two sentences together I did not know," Stanton remembered. So she enlisted a powerful ally, Frederick Douglass. Douglass recognized the logic of her position, that "the power to choose rulers and make laws, was the right by which all others could be secured." Douglass gave a "brilliant defense" of the resolution. But, Stanton recalled, "he did not speak quite fast enough for me, nor say all I wanted said, and the first thing I knew I was on my feet defending the resolution, and in due time Douglass and I carried the whole convention."[58]

With the declaration adopted and signed and the resolutions endorsed, the main business of the convention was done. Yet spirits were high, the public excited. So the convention reconvened at 7:30 P.M. In spite of the heat and of the haying to be done early the next day, the church was almost full, with people in the balconies as well as on the main floor.

This time, Thomas M'Clintock, with long flowing hair, presided as chair. The meeting began, once more, with a reading of the minutes. This was becoming easy. So far, there had been no real opposition. They asked again for people to express objections to this new movement. No one spoke. So Stanton, buoyed up by the success of the meeting, "volunteered" a speech, "in defence of the many severe accusations brought against the much-abused 'Lords of Creation.'" Thomas M'Clintock contributed several extracts about women's legal disabilities from Blackstone's code.[59]

Lucretia Mott offered one final resolution: "That the speedy success of our cause depends upon the zealous and untiring efforts of both men and women, for the overthrow of the monopoly of the pulpit, and for the securing to woman an equal participation with men in the various trades, professions and commerce." Significantly, she emphasized here the efforts of "both men and women," and she mentioned only religion and work, not politics, as areas of concern. Was this perhaps an attempt to soothe over the two major disputes in the convention?[60]

Mary Ann M'Clintock Jr., not to be outdone, gave "a short, but impressive address, calling upon woman to arouse from her lethargy and be true to herself and her God." Frederick Douglass spoke once more, "in an excellent and appropriate speech," and the meeting ended with Lucretia Mott, who gave one of her "most beautiful and spiritual appeals." She "commanded the earnest attention," the minutes noted, "of that large audience for nearly an hour."[61]

And finally, as its last act, the convention appointed five women—Mary Ann M'Clintock, Eunice Newton Foote, Amy Post, Elizabeth M'Clintock, and Stanton herself—"to prepare the proceedings of the Convention for publication." Elizabeth and Mary Ann M'Clintock passed around a contribution box, and the committee made arrangements with Frederick Douglass to have the *North Star* print the minutes.[62]

So ended the first woman's rights convention. They had met for two full days, continuing far into the night. And in spite of the startling nature of the declaration, not one person spoke against it. There had been only two areas of contention: First, should men as well as women sign the declaration? And, second, should the convention demand the right of women to vote? These two issues provoked genuine disagreement and reflected a split not only within the convention as a whole but, more particularly, between Stanton and Mott. While Stanton believed thoroughly in equality of rights for women and men, she several times recorded her belief that women themselves should undertake this work. On the other hand, Mott advocated "the zealous and untiring efforts of both men and women." In terms of the second issue, voting, Quakers who did not participate in secular government themselves could hardly be expected to focus on suffrage as the main issue. No one, however, had argued with the main idea, that "all men and women are created equal."[63]

Stanton was elated and somewhat surprised by the "grand success" of the meeting. "The deepest interest was manifested to its close." "The house was crowded at every session, the speaking good, and a religious earnestness dignified all the proceedings," Stanton remembered. Frederick Douglass confirmed this impression. "Their whole proceedings were characterized by marked ability and dignity," he noted. "No one present . . . will fail to give them credit for brilliant talent and excellent dispositions. . . . There were frequent differences of opinion and animated discussion; but in no case was there the slightest absence of good feeling and decorum."[64]

No one has ever found Mary Ann M'Clintock's manuscript minutes from the Seneca Falls convention. Presumably they went with Frederick Douglass to Rochester to be printed by John Dick at the *North Star* office as a small (3" x 5"), twelve-page booklet, with a light blue cover.

The printed *Report* contained the names of the sixty-eight women who had signed the Declaration of Sentiments and the thirty-two men who had supported it. Forty years later, Frederick Douglass, himself one of the signers, would reflect on the composition of this group. "Then who were we," he asked, "for I count myself in, who did this thing? We were few in numbers, moderate in resources, and very little known in the world. The most that we had to commend us, was a firm conviction that we were in the right, and a firm faith that the right must ultimately prevail."[65]

Of these signers, only four—Douglass, Lucretia Mott, Martha Wright, and Stanton herself—would achieve national recognition. The others remained virtually unknown. Most of them came from either Seneca Falls or Waterloo, with a few more from Rochester or from small villages near Syracuse. (So many lived in Waterloo, in fact, that the *Buffalo Morning Express* referred to the meeting as the Waterloo Female Convention.) Most were mature adults in their thirties or forties, more likely than their neighbors to have come from families who migrated from New England. Only one signer, Susan Quinn, can be definitely linked to an Irish background. Her father, Patrick Quinn, was an illiterate gardener with $2,000 worth of property, a considerable accumulation in 1850. Coincidentally, Susan, at fourteen years old, was also the youngest signer. The oldest was probably Catherine Shaw, age eighty-one.[66]

Except for Frederick Douglass, no identifiable African Americans signed the Seneca Falls Declaration. By the 1850s, however, several African Americans, including Sojourner Truth, Mary Ann Shadd Cary, Sarah Remond, and William C. Nell, became vocal suffrage supporters. Twelve signers, all women, remain unidentified. These are the unknown soldiers of the early woman's rights movement.[67]

Family patterns reflected a difference between signers and nonsigners. Signers settled in close proximity to parents and siblings, and they often incorporated unrelated persons into their households. For the signers, families were not an escape from the world but the very basis of community life. Many women who signed the Declaration of Sentiments had strong identities as sisters as well as wives. They were used to relationships of respect, relative equality, and community responsibility. A few of the signers' families were headed by women.

Reflecting the importance of extended family networks, almost 70 percent of known signers came to the convention with one or more family members: parents came with adult children, husbands with wives, brothers with sisters. Stanton came with her sister Harriet Eaton and her nephew Daniel Cady Eaton. Four M'Clintocks signed the declaration, both parents and two adult daughters. Elisha and Eunice Newton Foote, husband and wife, signed together. Lucretia Mott and Martha Wright signed as sisters. And so the list continued.

All of these families came to the Seneca River villages to make a living and raise their families. Thus, the story of the woman's rights convention is rooted in the story of economic and social development in the villages of Seneca Falls and Waterloo. In terms of work and wealth, most signers came from families that bridged the old land-based economy and the new industrializing, market-oriented world. Their main income came from the law, milling, manufacturing, commercial farming, or retail sales. In property ownership, they ranged from Richard P. and Jane Hunt, the richest family in Seneca County, to George and Margaret Pryor, who were downright poor. Statistical analysis of property assessments (based on census and assessment records) suggests no relationship between property ownership and signing the Declaration of Sentiments.[68]

Although economic status was not a good indicator of who would support the woman's rights convention, signers were certainly influenced by debates over the Married Woman's Property Act. Signers were more likely than were nonsigners, for example, to have daughters in the household or to be female heads of households.[69]

Religious affiliation also played an important role in attracting people to the convention. Quakers from Waterloo, Rochester, and probably Cayuga and western Onondaga Counties, too, formed the single largest religious group. At least one-quarter of the total signers were Quakers. Those who came from Seneca Falls and the immediate area were almost all Methodist, Wesleyan Methodist, or Episcopalian. Methodists sent at least four members to the convention, including Jacob P. Chamberlain, Catharine Paine, Isaac Van Tassell, and Betsey Tewksbury. Two more signers were affiliated with the Methodist Church, although they did not join it. Robert Smallbridge was married there in 1841, and in 1847–48, Henry L. Hatley was a probationer.[70]

At least seven members of the Wesleyan congregation, three of them former Methodists, signed the Declaration of Sentiments, including Joel Bunker; Sally Pitcher; Henry Seymour; Samuel and Sophronia Taylor; Sarah Whitney; and Saron Phillips, minister of the church. Three other signers had family members associated with the Wesleyans, including Eliza Martin, whose husband, Joshua, was a Wesleyan, and Elizabeth and Mary Conklin, whose father, William, belonged to the church.[71]

Seneca Falls Catholics, Presbyterians, and Baptists showed little enthusiasm for woman's rights. Catholics avoided the convention entirely. Only one participant, fourteen-year-old Susan Quinn, had even an indirect Catholic connection. Her father, Patrick Quinn, had been a founder of the Catholic Church in Seneca Falls but joined the Episcopalians in 1842. Only one former Presbyterian, Delia Matthews, wife of Jabez Matthews (who had supported Abby Kelley's right as an abolitionist and a woman to speak in public in 1843) signed the Declaration of Sentiments. Only one Baptist endorsed it, and his motive may have been as much personal as political. S. E. Woodworth was engaged to marry Mary Gilbert, a local milliner. With her sisters Ann and Ruth, Mary Gilbert made most of the ladies' hats in town. Woodworth and Gilbert attended the woman's rights convention together, and both signed the Declaration of Sentiments.

Surprisingly, several Episcopalians supported the woman's rights convention, including the energetic Ansel Bascom; Malvina Beebe Seymour and her husband, Henry W. Seymour; Hannah J. Latham (whose daughter Lavinia was also a signer); Experience Porter Gibbs; Susan Quinn; and Rebecca Race. Charles Hoskins, another signer, had joined Trinity Episcopal Church in December 1833 but later dropped his membership.[72]

These Episcopalians came to the convention partly because key members of the church urged them to go. Certainly Charles Hoskins's opinions carried weight with his neighbors. So, undoubtedly, did those of Elizabeth Cady Stanton herself, who attended (but never joined) Trinity Episcopal Church. It was easy for her to walk to the simple wooden building on Bayard Street, a few blocks from her own house. Mostly, she said she attended Episcopal services because her boys liked the minister dressed in a skirt and because, she said, it gave her one hour a week of peace and quiet.[73]

Most importantly, however, the majority of signers can be linked directly to one of two egalitarian networks: either the Free Soil Party in Seneca Falls or the Congregational Friends of Waterloo and Rochester. In June 1848, both groups had broken traditional ties, the Free Soilers with traditional political parties and the Congregational Friends with established Quaker meetings. Both groups came to the woman's rights convention to explore the meaning of their newly articulated commitment to equality, not only in terms of race or religion but also in terms of gender. Stanton, with ties to leaders among both Free Soilers in Seneca Falls and Congregational Friends in Waterloo, acted as what network theorists would call a broker, bringing the two groups together to form an entirely new movement.[74]

Congregational Friends were all abolitionists and woman's rights advocates. They were centered in Junius Monthly Meeting. Rhoda Palmer recalled that "every member" of this meeting attended the convention. Members or former members from Rochester Monthly Meeting and Scipio Monthly Meeting also attended.[75]

The Hunt-M'Clintock-Pryor family of Waterloo were the key to organizing the Seneca Falls convention itself. While Lucretia Mott was the most famous Quaker present at the Seneca Falls convention, the M'Clintocks were Stanton's most important local allies. Mott herself recognized this. "I have never liked being called 'the moving spirit of the convention,'" she wrote to Stanton in 1855, "when to thyself and the M'Clintocks belong the honor." Six members of the extended M'Clintock family (including Thomas and Mary Ann M'Clintock; their daughters Elizabeth and Mary Ann; the elder Mary Ann's half sister, Margaret Pryor; and her husband, George Pryor) signed the Declaration of Sentiments. Five members of the extended Hunt family (including Richard and Jane Hunt; two of Richard's adult sisters, Hannah Plant and Lydia Mount; and one of his nieces, Mary E. Vail) also signed. Together, they formed the largest family network at the convention.

In Rochester (forty miles west of Seneca Falls), Amy and Isaac Post anchored the other major Quaker woman's rights network. At least four of the Post family, including Amy; her sister Sarah L. Hallowell; her stepdaughter, Mary Hallowell; and at least one other local Quaker, Catharine Fish Stebbins, signed the Declaration of Sentiments, along with Frederick Douglass, who worked closely with the Posts. This group supported the woman's rights convention so enthusiastically that they organized a second meeting, two weeks after Seneca Falls, in Rochester itself.[76]

Outside of Waterloo and Rochester, other Quakers rallied to the woman's rights call. Six people (including Eliab W. Capron; Elias J. Doty and Susan R. Doty; their niece Caroline Barker and her husband, William G. Barker; and Maria W. Wilbur) came from the towns of Williamson, Galen, or Macedon in Wayne County, just north of Seneca Falls. They belonged to Farmington, Rochester, or Junius Monthly Meetings.[77]

In Seneca Falls, support for woman's rights was based in the emerging network of Free Soil advocates. Of the signers of the Declaration of Sentiments from Seneca Falls, 69.2 percent of them lived in a household affiliated with the Free Soil movement. Only 21.2 percent of nonsigners' households included someone involved with Free Soil. Free Soil supporters whose households included at least one signer of the Declaration of Sentiments represented a variety of commercial, industrial, and service occupations. Jacob P. Chamberlain, miller, shared Free Soil views with William Conklin, gardener; A. C. Gibbs, grocery store owner; Charles Hoskins, merchant; Oliver S. Latham, builder; Joshua Martin, boat builder; Nathan J. Milliken, editor of the *Seneca County Courier;* Whiting Race, lumberman (and president of the village in 1848); Henry Seymour, pump maker; Robert Smallbridge, cooper; S. D. Tillman, lawyer; Isaac Van Tassell, cooper; S. E. Woodworth, dry goods merchant; and Henry B. Stanton himself.[78]

In the *Seneca County Courier,* Nathan Milliken, editor and himself one of the signers of the Declaration of Sentiments, summed up local response to the woman's rights convention. The meeting was "novel in its character," he explained to his readers, "and the doctrines broached in it are startling to those who are wedded to the present usages and laws of society. The resolutions are of the kind called radical." Like Douglass, Milliken emphasized that in spite of the radicalism, "some of the speeches were very able—all the exercises were marked by great order and decorum." As for the Declaration of Sentiments and resolutions themselves, Milliken predicted that "they will provoke much remark," ranging from curiosity to respect to "disapprobation and contempt."[79]

Little did anyone realize just how accurate his predictions really were. Local in its origins, the Seneca Falls convention would touch off an immediate and far-reaching public debate about the role of women in a democratic republic.[80] Like a magnet, the Declaration of Sentiments drew the attention of Americans everywhere to the issue of woman's rights. Its accusations, rooted in ideas of natural rights and captured in the familiar rhetoric of the Declaration of Independence, challenged conventional ideas about women and men, citizenship and power, and touched the core of American identity. From 1848 on, Americans would be confronted with what Elizabeth Cady Stanton, never modest about the woman's rights movement, would call "a rebellion such as the world had never before seen."

CHAPTER 9

The Road from Seneca Falls, 1848–1982

When the convention was over, participants congratulated themselves on how smoothly, how earnestly, and with what self-assurance they had debated such controversial issues. Imagine their surprise, then, when newspapers around the country made fun of their efforts. "No words could express our astonishment," recalled Elizabeth Cady Stanton, "on finding, a few days afterward, that what seemed to us so timely, so rational, and so sacred, should be a subject for sarcasm and ridicule."[1]

Certainly, she had evidence enough of contemptuous responses. While the *Rochester Advertiser* simply dismissed the convention as "extremely dull and uninteresting," other newspapers were downright vituperative, calling those who attended the convention "erratic, addle-pated comeouters," while the convention itself was "a most insane and ludicrous farce."[2]

Many editors feared the effect that equal rights for women would have on men's roles. The *Mechanic's Advocate,* in Albany, New York, recognized that woman's rights advocates wanted "to divide with the male sex the labors and responsibilities of active life in every branch of art, science, trades, and professions." "This is all wrong," protested the *Advocate.* And if men performed "an equal share of the domestic duties," this would "set the world by the ears . . . and prove a monstrous injury to all mankind." In Massachusetts, the *Lowell Courier* complained that the ideas expressed at Seneca Falls would lead to a reversal in gender roles: "The lords" must "wash dishes, scour up, be put to the tub, handle the broom, darn stockings, patch breeches, scold the servants, dress in the latest fashion, wear trinkets, look beautiful, and be as fascinating as those blessed morsels of humanity whom God gave to preserve that rough animal man, in something like a reasonable civilization."[3]

The *Philadelphia Public Ledger and Daily Transcript* argued that "a woman is nobody. A wife is everything. A pretty girl is equal to ten thousand men, and a mother is, next to God, all powerful. . . . The ladies of Philadelphia, therefore, . . . are resolved to maintain their rights as Wives, Belles, Virgins, and Mothers, and not as Women."[4]

A few editors reacted positively to the convention's goals. The *Herkimer Freeman,* in upstate New York, was particularly enthusiastic. "Success to the cause in which they have enlisted! A railroad speed to the end they would accomplish! . . . I look forward to woman's emancipation with the most intense anxiety; I hail it as a great jubilee of the nation." Antislavery newspapers echoed this excitement. W. C. N. (probably the African American abolitionist and woman's rights advocate, William C. Nell) wrote to the *Liberator* that "proof was abundantly submitted at these Conventions of woman's equality with man, exploding the absurd dogma of her incapacity to take care of herself." The *Daily Centre-State American* in Nashville, Tennessee, cautiously noted that "a respectable audience" attended the convention, and "the most perfect order was preserved throughout." The *St. Louis Daily Reveille* took a stronger stance: "The flag of independence has been hoisted for the second time on this side of the Atlantic, and a solemn league and covenant has just been entered into by a convention of women at Seneca Falls, New York."[5]

Other editors kept an open mind. They had no enthusiasm for woman's rights, but they did not reject the idea outright. Horace Greeley, editor of the *New York Tribune,* gave a full and fair report of the convention and then added his reluctant support, reminiscent of his stance toward African American suffrage. If Americans really believed in the idea that "all men are created equal," he argued, they must endorse even the right of women to vote: "When a sincere republican is asked to say in sober earnest what adequate reason he can give, for refusing the demand of women to an equal participation with men in political rights, he must answer, None at all. . . . However unwise and mistaken the demand, it is but the assertion of a natural right, and such must be conceded."[6]

In fact, in contrast to Stanton's recollections, the majority of newspapers throughout the country provided either positive support or relatively neutral reactions to the Seneca Falls convention. When Timothy Terpstra, a historian, surveyed editorials in seventy-one newspapers across the country, he found fifty-eight newspaper articles dealing with Seneca Falls. Forty-two percent of them opposed the convention; 28 percent gave a neutral report; and 29 percent responded favorably.[7]

Locally, however, many signers, especially women, were intimidated by such vehement debate. "So pronounced was the popular voice against us, in the parlor, press, and pulpit," wrote Stanton in her autobiography, "that most of the ladies who had attended the convention and signed the declaration, one by one, withdrew their names and influence and joined our persecutors. Our friends gave us the cold shoulder and felt themselves disgraced by the whole proceeding." Stanton gave no clue about which particular women changed their minds. Perhaps most of them were women from Seneca Falls whose prior reform experience had been limited to temperance work. It seems unlikely that Quakers would have responded to this pressure.[8]

Forty years later, Stanton remembered that her own father "took the night train and rushed up to Seneca Falls to see if I was insane." Stanton's sister, Harriet Cady Eaton, who had also signed the declaration, was "in great consternation" about what to say to their father, but Stanton had no fears. They talked until midnight, and Stanton confidently asserted that she had the best of the argument.[9]

Elizabeth Cady Stanton felt invigorated. The Seneca Falls convention brought her out of her feelings of depression and unease and gave her a renewed sense of purpose. In the following decade, Stanton immersed herself in woman's rights, temperance, and dress reform while maintaining an ever-growing household of children. At the same time, she remained, at least to observers, calm, cheerful, energetic, and witty. From 1848 to the end of her life, she never wavered from her commitment to woman's rights and liberal religion.

One key to Stanton's effectiveness after 1848 was her ability to enlist allies, starting with Elizabeth M'Clintock, her "intimate friend for many years." Attacks on woman's rights brought out the fighting spirit in both of them, and the two Elizabeths began a close personal and political friendship, prefiguring the productive and long-lasting friendship that Stanton would later develop with Susan B. Anthony.[10]

On August 2, Stanton and Elizabeth M'Clintock carried their energy to Rochester, where Amy Post and the circle of abolitionist Friends in Rochester had organized a sequel to the Seneca Falls convention. Several people who had attended the Seneca Falls convention played key parts in the Rochester meeting, including Amy Post, who convened the meeting, Lucretia Mott, Elizabeth and Mary Ann M'Clintock, Sarah L. Hallowell, Mary H. Hallowell, Catharine A. F. Stebbins, Frederick Douglass, and Stanton herself. Three of the five officers of the convention, the two Hallowells plus Catharine Stebbins, had signed the Seneca Falls Declaration of Sentiments.[11]

Both Elizabeth Cady Stanton and Elizabeth M'Clintock found the limits of their woman's rights activism challenged when the meeting elected a woman, Abigail Bush, as president. "To our great surprise," reported the minutes of this convention, "two or three other women—glorious reformers, well deserving the name—coming from a distance to attend the meeting, at first refused to take their seats upon the platform, or otherwise co-operate with the Convention, for the same cause." One of those opponents was Elizabeth Cady Stanton. Another was Elizabeth M'Clintock. So fearful was M'Clintock about the ability of a female chair that she refused her own nomination as secretary. Both Stanton and M'Clintock quickly recovered from their initial shock, however, as they realized that the "gentle but heroic President" was fully capable of conducting a well-ordered meeting. Stanton apologized to Amy Post in a letter written shortly after the convention. "I have so often regretted my foolish conduct in regard to the President of the Convention at R. The result proved that your judgement was good & Mrs. Bush discharged her duties so well that I was really quite delighted that we were able through her to do up our business so well without depending on any man. My only excuse is that woman has been so little accustomed to act in a public capacity that she does not always know what is due to those around her."[12]

There were other differences between the conventions at Rochester and Seneca Falls. The Rochester convention made no apologies for focusing on the political and industrial rights of women, including a discussion of wages and working conditions for seamstresses and domestic workers. Participants also felt freer to criticize the ideas of the declaration. And Frederick Douglass was not the only black person to speak in favor of woman's rights. William C. Nell, a black abolitionist then working with the *Liberator,* also gave a major speech. The Rochester convention easily adopted the Seneca Falls Declaration of Sentiments in its entirety, including its demands for woman's suffrage, with 107 signatures. When the president asked for comments, one man remarked that his only objection was "that there was too much truth in it!"[13]

Stanton wrote to Amy Post that "our conventions both went off so well that we have great encouragement to go on. What are we next to do? We have declared our right to vote. The question now is how shall we get possession of what rightfully belongs to us?" Stanton answered her own question. She and other woman's rights advocates would write, speak, generate petitions, hire agents, and organize more conventions.[14]

Not all of Amy Post's correspondents were so enthusiastic. When Post's brother, John Willis, received an account of the Rochester meeting, he decidedly disapproved. He thought that he should write to Isaac (Amy's husband) "and request him to persuade his wife to try to have a little more stability, and to act more like a sensable woman." "In your Declaration," he noted, "you say that the history of mankind is a history of repeated injuries and usurpations on the part of man towards woman having in direct object the establishment of an absolute tyranny over her. If thee means Isaac when thee says all that thee might as well leave him and come to L. Iland [Long Island] and live." Warming to his subject, he continued, with a touch of humor, to describe "a society in Boston that I think would suit thee and Sarah and some of rochester women exceedingly well theire whole business as I understand it is, to take charge of other people['s] concerns. . . . [T]his would keep you in plenty of business,—without runing all over with your petitions to get signers in order to send to the legeslator for them to pass a law giving you the privilage of voting which I presume they never will do." The only way that women might have everything they wanted, he suggested, was to "get up an instrument of writing in verry strong language and let every unmarried woman pledg her self that she will not marry any man untill the laws are so altered as to place woman on an equality with man in every respect even to wearing of pants if she wished to do so[,] and if the unmarried women will all sign it and stick to it for a few years[,] say about 20[,] I am persuaded you will bring them to any turrms you may wish."[15]

Stanton had other, more practical, ideas. Elated by the success of the Seneca Falls and Rochester conventions, she and M'Clintock set right to work. First, they began to write. On the Sunday after the Seneca Falls convention, Reverend Horace P. Bogue, the Presbyterian pastor in Seneca Falls, preached a sermon opposing woman's rights. Stanton and M'Clintock sat in the pews and took notes. At the Rochester meeting, they presented a joint report, M'Clintock reading their notes and Stanton responding with their own biblical arguments for woman's rights. They turned their convention remarks into a letter to the editor of the *Seneca County Courier,* arguing that "the Bible is the great Charter of human rights, when it is taken in its true spiritual meaning," and that those who followed Christ must obey his commandments, including the injunction that there is "neither Jew nor Greek, male nor female, bound nor free, but all are one in Christ Jesus."[16]

In her own characteristically vigorous, vivid prose, Stanton followed up their letter to the *Courier* with another to George Cooper, editor of the *National Reformer* in Rochester. "If God has assigned a sphere to man and one to woman," she argued, "we claim the right to judge ourselves of his design in reference to *us.* . . . We think a man has quite enough in this life to find out his own individual calling, without being taxed to decide where every woman belongs. . . . There is no such thing as a sphere for a sex."[17]

So pleased were Stanton and M'Clintock with their letters to editors that they considered writing a book about woman's rights. Lucretia Mott thought that was "just what is needed," but she herself declined to write a chapter, saying, "It is not in my line." They could, she suggested, borrow historical sections from Sarah Grimké and use some excellent ideas from Mary Wollstonecraft. Stanton would rejuvenate the idea of a book on woman's rights in 1856 but not until the publication of *History of Woman Suffrage* in 1881, spurred on by Susan B. Anthony and Matilda Joslyn Gage, would such a history actually materialize.[18]

She and Elizabeth M'Clintock did not intend to carry the burden alone, however. Sometime in the late summer or fall of 1848, they received copies from the *North Star* press of the printed minutes of the Seneca Falls convention. Stanton inscribed hers with "Read and circulate" and sent them to other woman's rights advocates. Martha Wright received about a dozen of them in Auburn, with a note from Stanton asking her to keep her pen busy and "not let a day pass without writing something." Although Wright laughed at "the idea of *my* pen," she did distribute almost all of the reports, and the rest she sent to Lucretia Mott to give away in Philadelphia. Mott had already sent one of hers to Richard and Hannah Webb in England.[19]

In September, Stanton gave her first major speech on woman's rights at the

Quaker meetinghouse in Waterloo. She wore the latest fashion, "a kind of turban & bows," which struck some of her listeners as "rather Theatrical." In spite of her attire, she had a respectful audience. Whether they agreed with her or not, they could hardly fail to miss her points. According to natural rights, God's law, women were equal to men. Women therefore had a right to vote. And woman's rise would benefit men as well. She argued with allusions to personal experience, religion, the American democratic tradition, natural rights philosophy, and the ultimate harmony of the spheres.[20]

Stanton reminded her audience that, at the Seneca Falls and Rochester conventions, "we did assemble to protest against a form of government existing without the consent of the governed & to declare our right to be free as man is free. . . . And, strange as it may seem to many, we then & there declared our right to vote according to the Declaration of the government under which we live." Nowhere, Stanton stated with conviction, "not even under what is thought to be the full blaze of the sun of civilization," is woman's position "what God designed it to be." There was one way to change that: give women the right to vote. "This right is ours," she proclaimed. "Have it we must. Use it we will. . . . The great truth, that no just government can be formed without the consent of the governed, we shall echo and re-echo in the ears of the unjust judge." Perhaps in deference to her audience, perhaps reflecting her own growing attachment to Congregational Friends, she used Quaker phrases—"thou," "Friends," "Spirit within"—liberally.[21]

When her speech was finished, she invited discussion. Quaker-style, the audience remained silent for a long time. Finally, an older man rose, wearing a traditional broad-brimmed Quaker hat (not as fancy, apparently, as Stanton's turban). He was Henry Bonnell, wealthy farmer and uncle of Rachel Dell Bonnell, one of the signers of the Declaration of Sentiments. In a sing-song voice, he gave his judgment: "All I have to say is, if a hen can crow, let her crow," emitting the word *crow* Stanton recalled, "with an upward inflection on several notes of the gamut." The meeting quickly broke up, "with mingled feelings of surprise and merriment." Stanton felt "somewhat chagrined at having my unanswerable arguments so summarily disposed of." But Bonnell reassured her after the meeting: "I am thoroughly with thee on this question! I did not intend to raise the laugh on thee, but on our opponents who deny woman's right to speak in public."[22]

So important was this speech to Stanton that, years later, she tied the manuscript with a ribbon of pale blue (her favorite color). In the margin, she wrote a note to her daughters: "Dear Maggie and Hattie,—This is my first lecture. It was delivered several times immediately after the first woman's rights convention. It contains all I knew at that time. I did not speak again for several years. . . . I give this manuscript to my precious daughters, in the hope that they will finish the work which I have begun."[23]

On October 6–7, 1848, Stanton may have attended (and perhaps even spoken at) the first annual meeting of the Congregational Friends at Farmington, New York. There they adopted the *Basis of Religious Association,* authored by Thomas M'Clintock. This group was one of three yearly meetings (including Michigan and Green Plains, Ohio) to be formed that fall on what Lucretia Mott called "radical principles," that is, "the promotion of righteousness," noted the *Basis,* "of practical goodness—love to God and man," "in harmony with the principles of Divine government." They abolished all separate meetings of ministers and elders, joined men's and women's meetings together in perfect equality ("which is not now the case, 'by a jug full,'" Mott noted), and even admitted "such of their sober neighbors as incline to sit with them." The Congregational Friends changed their name to the Progressive Friends in 1854 and later to the Friends of Human Progress. Their meetings focused on abolition, woman's rights, and peace, trying to reach Mott's ideal balance between the "'Light within' & righteousness *without.*" From 1849 to 1871, nineteen signers of the Declaration of Sentiments, including Stanton, participated regularly in these annual conferences.[24]

Stanton found these Friends so congenial that, by 1852, she called herself a Congregational Friend. When Martha Wright heard a rumor that Stanton had joined the Episcopal Church, Stanton replied indignantly that "I am a member of Junius meeting and not of the Episcopal Church. I have heard that infamous report and feel about it very much as if I had been accused of petty larceny. . . . If my theology could not keep me out of any church my deep and abiding reverence for the dignity of womanhood would be all sufficient." Among Congregational Friends she found a congenial network of support for both her woman's rights ideas and her liberal religious values, and she continued to meet with the Friends for several years.[25]

Stanton, the M'Clintocks, and others followed their writing, speaking, and conventions with several more projects to promote woman's rights. Stanton suggested hiring an agent, for example, and an invitation actually went out to Lucy Stone. Stanton also organized a petition campaign for woman's right to vote. After her first speech at the Congregational Friends Meeting, she collected signatures on a petition to the New York state legislature. When she tried to press her friends into service, however, not all of them were pleased. Martha Wright confessed to her sister that "I must answer a letter from Mrs. Stanton which I received a few days since, requesting me to *take charge* of this District and procure signers to a petition for the right of Suffrage for Women. What on earth shall I tell her? I should smile to see myself trotting round this benighted region, where there are not three women who would consider it safe to touch such a petition unfumigated."[26]

Many others besides Stanton, however, felt a new sense of energy and joy after the Seneca Falls convention. Whether they heard about it from friends or read about it in newspapers, small groups of people in towns across the northeastern United States responded with excitement to the Declaration of Sentiments.

Emily Collins, from South Bristol ("one of the most secluded spots in western New York"), had been a rebel from girlhood against customs and laws that "crushed my aspirations and debarred me from the pursuit of almost every object worthy of an intelligent, rational mind." She had long "pined for that freedom of thought and action that was then denied to all womankind," she remembered. She had even written an admiring letter to Elizabeth Blackwell, who in 1848 became the first woman in the United States to graduate from medical college. "But not until that meeting at Seneca Falls in 1848," she recalled, "did I take action." By October, she had organized a Woman's Equal Rights Union, whose fifteen or twenty members met twice a month, and they began to work immediately. "Living in the country," she reported to a Rochester sympathizer, "where the population is sparse, we are consequently few; but hope to make up in zeal and energy for our lack of numbers." Collins had certainly read the Declaration of Sentiments, for she concurred in all of its proposed actions. "A press entirely devoted to our cause seems indispensable," she noted. "A lecturer in the field would be most desirable; but how to raise funds to sustain one is the question." Most significantly, she agreed that "the elective franchise is now the one object for which we must labor." The Woman's Equal Rights Union quickly sent a petition to the legislature, signed by sixty-two supporters, men as well as women. For many years, the union continued to argue for woman's suffrage, both locally (through debating clubs) and statewide (through legislative petitions). For the rest of her life, Emily Collins would continue her work for woman's suffrage, first in Rochester and then in Louisiana.[27]

South Bristol represented in microcosm the impact of Seneca Falls on woman's rights organizing throughout the Northeast. Within the next few years, woman's rights advocates organized a series of local conventions in small towns in Pennsylvania, Ohio, and New York. Many of these were organized by Congregational Friends.

In all her extant correspondence in the summer and fall of 1848, Stanton gave not a hint of Henry Stanton's vigorous activity on behalf of the Free Soil Party. He campaigned across upstate New York and reported to Elizabeth that "I am quite a free soil lion!!!"[28] In the second week of August, Henry played a major role at the huge Buffalo Free Soil convention, persuading Liberty Party men to shift their allegiance from John P. Hale to Martin Van Buren as the Free Soil presidential candidate. While the new party took a stand on tariffs, internal improvements, and homestead lands, it said nothing about civil rights for African Americans. Many Liberty men felt betrayed. But the vast majority of political abolitionists voted with the Free Soil Party as the best of their limited choices.[29]

Gerrit Smith and a small group of former Liberty Leaguers absolutely refused to join the Free Soil Party. Late in September 1848, they met at Canastota, New York, taking over the Liberty Party's name while adopting the platform of the Liberty League. Meanwhile, as a spokesman for the National Liberty Party, Gerrit Smith continued to promote equal rights for all people, including women. "Resolved," he proposed at the convention in Syracuse in 1852, "that the Liberty Party cannot consent to fall below, nor, in any degree, to qualify, its great central principle, that all persons—black and white, male and female—have equal political rights, and are equally entitled to the protection and advantages of Civil Government." Elected to Congress that year, Smith incorporated in his political creed the belief "that political rights are not conventional, but natural—inhering in all persons, the black as well as the white, the female as well as the male."[30]

Election results in 1848 were disappointing to Free Soil and Liberty Party members alike. In the November elections, Whig candidate Zachary Taylor became president of the United States, defeating both Lewis Cass, the Democratic nominee, and Martin Van Buren. In fact, not one single electoral vote went to Van Buren. He did, however, finish second in three states, including New York. In Seneca Falls, the Free Soilers had done their work well. Van Buren won by a margin of 300 votes, and Ansel Bascom took the town (but not the rest of the congressional district) with a majority of 340. Henry B. Stanton reaped his own reward a year later, when he was elected to the New York state legislature on the Democratic ticket.[31]

In the midst of Henry's campaign for the legislature in the fall of 1849, Elizabeth was engaged in a campaign of her own. When Elizabeth M'Clintock, then a clerk in her father's drugstore, tried to get a job with Lucretia Mott's son-in-law Edward M. Davis as a silk merchant in Philadelphia, Stanton became her advocate. "I have hung out my sign as the pilot to guide and direct all young maidens who wish to launch their bark on an untried sea," she wrote to Lucretia Mott in September 1849, and now Elizabeth M'Clintock and Anna Southwick "have decided to be famous silk merchants in Philadelphia. . . . Ah! me, those woman's rights conventions have spoiled our lovely maidens. Now instead of remaining satisfied with the needle and the schoolroom they would substitute the compass and the exchange."[32]

"The fact of a serious application flew like wild-fire," both in Philadelphia and New York, Mott reported a month later. Davis had solicited the opinions of his clerks in both cities, and Mott enclosed a summary of their discussions. The New York clerks affirmed that "we are heart, soul and body in favor of advancing woman, at least to a stand of self dependence." Philadelphia clerks were not so sure. In theory, women should have equal opportunities. But in practice, did these women have the experience, the capital, and the commitment to succeed? Begin in a retail store, Davis advised, where women had a record of success, and Mott invited M'Clintock and Southwick to stay with her while they investigated job possibilities for themselves. Mott also sent two other documents: a series of caricatures, drawn by clerks in both Philadelphia and New York, representing women doing all kinds of men's work, and a dramatized version of the whole issue written by Maria Mott Davis, Mott's daughter and Edward M. Davis's wife.[33]

In forwarding this material to Elizabeth M'Clintock, Stanton ignored Mott's invitation and focused on the caricatures. "Good Heavens!! what fools these Quakers are!" she wrote to M'Clintock. "I cannot tell you how indignant I feel after looking through this bundle of nonsense." Characteristically (and perhaps mindful of M'Clintock's feelings), she also proposed action. "I intend to write an epistle to these helpful sons of Adam," she wrote. "My letter [to Mott] it seems has taken the grand rounds. I hope the next one I send will receive the same attention. . . . I shall expect you on Sunday to tea now do not promise anyone to return before dark."[34]

Their tea party proved to be a productive one, for M'Clintock and Stanton produced a drama in verse, together with some caricatures of their own. The play was "of some intellectual vigor," thought Stanton, "which I backed up with a little of my irony, just enough to show our incapacity, to use that *manly* weapon *ridicule*." "You must write us what you think of the drama, & caricatures & if they equal those sent by the 'Lords of Creation,'" she wrote to Mott, "and if the individuals served up preserve their good nature & equanimity under this western flagellation. . . . Fear not that we shall be discouraged, no, we have full faith in 'the good time coming.' Truth is mighty & I know woman will yet stand on an even pedestal with man."[35]

Elizabeth M'Clintock was not only angry but hurt. "We had no thought that we would so publicly become subjects for caricature & ridicule," she wrote reproachfully to Mott. "Thee speaks in thy letter of 'reasons of some weight.' I regret, dear Lucretia, that the paper containing them must have been forgotten. I have looked for it in the package but could not find it. . . . We send you drama for drama, caricature for caricature.—Not that we should have chosen this mode of combat but in all equal warfare you are compelled to use such weapons as your adversary chooses."[36]

Lucretia Mott was astonished. In a letter to "my two Elizabeths," she began, "I would not for the world have thus 'slain a [wo]man to my wounding, and a young [wo]man to my hurt.' Why, I had not the slightest idea, that you would receive the answer to your application, and the childish & playful documents accompanying it, as you did. It was very far from Edward M. Davis' feelings, or those of his '*House*,' whom he consulted, to treat the matter with the contempt or ridicule, which those caricatures would seem to indicate." Mott thought "the fact of its eliciting discussion up & down Market St. was certainly encouraging. I was delighted with *that* & thought when mentiong. it, you would be pleased too. In short, so far from being hurt, or at all daunted, by what has occurred, growing out of this application, I think you or *we* have great reason to be encouraged."[37]

Whether or not she was mollified by this explanation, Elizabeth M'Clintock decided not to go to Philadelphia. In 1850, she was still working in her father's pharmacy. She was very serious about working outside her home. Although U.S. census takers in 1850 did not normally list occupations for women, Elizabeth M'Clintock insisted that she be identified as a "clerk." And so she was.

In their search for wholeness, the M'Clintocks and several other Congregational Friends went beyond worldly concerns. In the new spiritualist movement, they explored the permeability of boundaries between life and death. As early as 1841, they had experimented with "animal magnetism," a kind of clairvoyance which transported them to other places within this world. Now, impressed by the spirit rappings heard by the Fox sisters outside Rochester, New York, they began to hold regular séances in their home. Other woman's rights supporters, especially among the Quakers, also joined this movement. Isaac Post, Amy Post's husband, collected testimonials from people who had attended the Fox sisters' séances and concluded that, indeed, the rappings they heard came from the spirit world. By 1851, Isaac Post himself had become a medium. A year later, he published *Voices from the Spirit World, being Communications from Many Spirits, by the hand of Isaac Post, Medium.* Even Elizabeth Cady Stanton thought she heard spirit rappings, though she remained skeptical.[38]

Stanton blossomed in other ways. Paramount among her concerns was her family. Stanton kept trying to have a daughter, and, apparently, she was not shy about letting the whole village know it. Local tradition suggested that Stanton would run a red flag up a pole for a boy and a white flag for a girl. When her fourth child, a son, was born in 1851, Stanton received "compliments and a hearty welcome for Theodore Weld Stanton" from Lillian Mynderse, who lived across the river and who wrote in the name of her three-year-old daughter, Lillias. Although Lillian/Lillias was "quite surprised that Theodore was allowed to live long enough to send greeting to his friends," she sent Stanton "a bottle of temperance wine" so that she could "drink to better luck next time." Given Daniel and Margaret Cady's desperate desire for a living son, it must have seemed ironic to all the family that Elizabeth and Henry's first four living children were all boys.[39]

Finally, Elizabeth Cady Stanton had a daughter. Margaret Livingston Stanton, named after her maternal grandmother, was born on October 20, 1852. "Rejoice with me all Womankind, for lo! a champion of thy cause is born," she wrote to Lucretia Mott. By the time her daughter Harriot was born on January 20, 1856, Stanton was less enthusiastic. "Not as another baby, then, was I welcome, but as a girl their hearts rejoiced over me," Harriot recorded in her autobiography. Their last child, Robert Livingston Stanton, was born three years later on March 14, 1859. Stanton's children remembered her as "a most devoted mother; she sang and played for us on both piano and guitar, and told us wonderful stories." She loved dancing and games, including chess, and she always played to win.[40]

Stanton did not reserve one standard for home and another for the world. Like her Quaker comrades, she used her home as the basis for creating a new world order. She carried out her political values in her home life, and she used her home as a basis for her public activity. She made changes in the physical structure of her house that symbolized these connections between home and world. Every time Henry went away, joked a neighbor, Elizabeth would cut a new door or window in the house. By the late 1850s, the Stantons had ten doors to lock every night, and Henry complained that his epitaph would read "died of fresh air."[41]

Consistent with her respect for individual rights, Stanton rarely, and perhaps never, punished her children physically. Sometimes her alternative strategies worked well; sometimes they did not. When son Henry, a budding inventor at nine years old, tried out his design for a life preserver by floating his baby brother Theodore down the Seneca River, Stanton punished him by sending him to his room and forbidding him to take the baby out of the yard. Shortly afterward, coming home from church with a friend, she saw Theodore seated "in the chimney top, with the inventor standing beside him." Henry defended himself by saying, "Mother, you told me not to take the baby out of our grounds, now that chimney is in our yard."[42]

A young music teacher, trying to give piano lessons to a recalcitrant Theodore, found no help from Elizabeth, who merely said, "Theodore, be a reasonable being." Forced to bribe her reluctant pupil, the music teacher promised that if Theodore would stay for his lesson, she would sing one of his favorite silly songs, "Grasshopper sitting on a sweet potato vine," whose simple chorus was interspersed with inventive stories about Stanton family antics.[43]

In the midst of family life, Stanton continued her public work. She did this partly by making her home a neighborhood gathering place. She invited young people to dance and socialize at her house. To minimize entertainment chores, she would serve only simple refreshments, sometimes coffee and cake, sometimes inviting guests to help themselves to grapes from the arbor and water from the pump. She organized "conversationals" patterned after those developed in Boston by Margaret Fuller. Men and women of different social backgrounds met Saturday nights to discuss ten-minute essays on different topics each week. Everyone shared responsibility for presiding over the discussions before the evening ended in music and dancing. According to her daughter Margaret, she started a dancing school and a gymnasium, with swings and bars, and she put a billiard table in the barn.[44]

She also used her home and family to entertain reformers from out of town. She dressed her older boys in white suits and paid them to serve her guests. Just as her family helped her reform efforts, reformers sometimes found themselves drawn into her family life. Troubled by her sons' constant swearing, Stanton asked advice from Lucretia Mott, who, with Susan B. Anthony, was then staying with the Stantons. Mott came up with an idea: if everyone swore during dinner, the boys might be shamed out of their habit. "So when they gathered around the board," as Stanton's daughter Margaret told the story,

> Mrs. Mott in her trim white kerchief and cap, said, "Mrs. Stanton, May I give thee some of this damn chicken?" The boys looked up amazed, but as neither mother, Susan, nor Mrs. Mott cracked a smile, and as the oaths flew quick and fast, the children soon enjoyed the fun, and all joined in. This was kept up for

> three meals, but on the fourth some distinguished guests were present who had been let into the secret—still the oaths of the three notable ladies flew about the table. The boys were distressed, as they served the guests and noticed the looks of horror on their faces, and when they got their mother alone, they gathered about her and said with tears in their eyes, "Mother, what will Governor Seward and Wendall Phillips think of your swearing like that?" "Well," she said, "if you will all stop, I will also." And they did.[45]

Her neighbors did not always appreciate Stanton's radical woman's rights stand, and sometimes her children paid the price. "I remember running home with tears streaming down my face," Harriot recalled, "after escaping from a jeering circle of children yelling, 'Your mother believes in woman's rights! Your mother believes in woman's rights!' and, throwing myself into mother's arms, asking her, 'Muzzer, what is *'iman's 'ights*?'"[46]

Most importantly, Stanton was able to continue her woman's rights work because she found a new friend, Susan B. Anthony. On Tuesday afternoon, May 12, 1851, William Lloyd Garrison arrived in Seneca Falls with George Thompson, a famous British abolitionist, for an antislavery meeting, one of many stops on a tour of central New York villages. George Pryor, a signer of the Declaration of Sentiments, accompanied them. "We found the Methodist Church well filled," reported Pryor, "with a first-rate audience." In the audience was a thirty-one-year-old Quaker school teacher and reformer, Susan B. Anthony. On a street corner after the meeting, Amelia Bloomer introduced her to Elizabeth Cady Stanton. "There she stood," Stanton recalled, "with her good, earnest face and genial smile, dressed in gray delaine, hat and all the same color, relieved with pale blue ribbons, the perfection of neatness and sobriety. I liked her thoroughly, and why I did not at once invite her home with me to dinner, I do not know." Stanton had invited Garrison and Thompson to dinner, and she excused her neglect on the grounds that she must have been thinking about the speech she had just heard or the dinner she had to prepare or the antics of her three lively boys.[47]

Stanton more than made up for her initial lack of hospitality, however. In the heady days of the 1850s, when Stanton's continued childbearing kept her close to home, Anthony kept Stanton in touch with the rapidly growing woman's rights movement. "Whenever I saw that stately Quaker girl coming across my lawn, I knew that some happy convocation of the sons of Adam was to be set by the ears, by one of our appeals or resolutions," Stanton remembered. Stanton, in turn, supplied Anthony with ideas and speeches. "Night after night, by an old-fashioned fireplace," Stanton wrote, "we plotted and planned the coming agitation. I forged the thunderbolts and she fired them." Their friendship would last for fifty-four years, until Stanton's death.[48]

Stanton also wrote letters, articles, and speeches under her own name. Theodore and Harriot's earliest memory of their mother was of her writing at her desk. Beginning in 1849, she found a regular outlet for her writings in the

Lily, edited and published in Seneca Falls by Amelia Bloomer. Writing as "Sunflower," Stanton moved the *Lily* from its primary focus on temperance to a broader woman's rights orientation. When Stanton advocated the "short dress" in 1852, national readers named the new outfit "the bloomer costume," after Amelia Bloomer herself. Although Stanton abandoned dress reform in the mid-1850s, other people, such as Dr. Mary Walker, continued to promote pants as the most comfortable and proper women's attire. In the 1850s, Stanton also wrote articles for other papers, including the *New York Tribune.* She became president of the New York State Women's Temperance Association in 1851. She supported the new People's College, a coeducational college open to both African Americans and European Americans. And in 1854, she addressed the New York state legislature, the first woman ever to do so.[49]

By the 1850s, Stanton was productive, in charge of her life, and able to handle most situations with confidence and humor. Her wit, her charm, her high-spirited sense of fun, her "unfailing cheerfulness," and her ability to express herself were on their way to becoming legendary. She was absolutely clear about her belief in equality for women. Writing to James G. Birney's wife in 1849, for example, she declared that "on one subject I am as firm as the rock of ages, and that is the right of woman to complete equality everywhere on this planet and in every succeeding position she may hold anywhere in the universe of matter or of mind." In the decade after the 1848 convention, Stanton assumed with confidence the personal characteristics that would dominate the rest of her life.[50]

After the summer of 1848, most of the signers went back to their ordinary lives.[51] In Seneca Falls, local residents emphasized the signers' continuing sense of social responsibility. For male signers, this meant a commitment to politics and old-fashioned civic virtue. Jacob Chamberlain, the Stantons' neighbor, took his antislavery sentiments to the Whig Party when the Free Soil movement fizzled out. As a Republican, he was elected to the New York state legislature in 1859 and to Congress in 1861. He reorganized the old Seneca Woolen Mills in 1855 into the Phoenix Company, which became one of the main industries in Seneca Falls. In 1852, Dun and Bradstreet listed him as "a very safe man," worth $25,000. He maintained his lifelong commitment to the Methodist Episcopal Church and died in 1878, aged seventy-six.[52]

Charles Hoskins continued to run his store, using shillings and pence, until he passed it on to his son Lansing in 1880. His three oldest daughters, Frances, Laura, and Annette, became preceptresses at the Seneca Falls Academy, and another daughter, Helen, married one of the teachers. In his nineties, he still looked after his own business affairs, and local people said he "worked early and late, not alone for his own private interest, but for the material interest of the place. No man in Seneca County is better known and none more highly respected than Mr. Hoskins." He died in 1895, aged ninety-six.[53]

For female signers, social responsibility often meant continuing commitment to their roles as wives, mothers, and neighbors. When Experience Porter Gibbs died in 1899, the same year as her sister and fellow signer, Eliza J. Martin, her obituary emphasized not her individual characteristics but her success in filling various social roles. The community lamented the loss of "a good and true woman, a loving, thoughtful wife, and a tender and considerate mother. . . . She was a kind neighbor and a steadfast friend. In her home she exalted womanhood and motherhood. Her life was one of simplicity and devotion to duty. She lived for and loved those by whom she was surrounded."[54]

Catharine Paine was the daughter of Thomas Paine, who made candles by machine methods. In 1853, the twenty-three-year-old Catharine married a Methodist minister, David Blaine, and, wearing a Bloomer costume, traveled by steamer, mule, and canoe to become one of the founders of the Methodist Episcopal Church in the Pacific Northwest. She bore her first child alone, while Seattle was under siege by Native Americans in 1856. The Blaines returned to Seneca Falls about 1863 and lived in various villages in central New York and Pennsylvania until they retired to Seattle.[55]

Elisha and Eunice Newton Foote made names for themselves in two different fields. Elisha became a judge of the Court of Common Pleas in Seneca County. He specialized in patent law and patented several inventions himself, including a skate, a drying machine, and a reaping and binding machine. He became commissioner of the U.S. Patent Office from 1866 to 1869, wrote a work on calculus, and became a member of the National Association for the Advancement of Science. Eunice Newton Foote was also a scientist and an inventor. In 1856 and 1857, she read papers on physics before the American Association for the Advancement of Science, and in 1860, she received a patent for "filling for soles of boots and shoes." Their daughter Mary Newton married a U.S. senator from Missouri; became active in art and urban design in both St. Louis and Washington, D.C.; was elected president of the Missouri State Woman's Suffrage Association; and published three books on cooking and health. Elisha and Eunice's daughter Augusta also published three books, two cookbooks, and a scientific work on sea beaches.[56]

In other cases, womenfolk proved more successful than their male relatives. S. E. Woodworth, despite his reputation for honesty, failed three more times in business during the 1850s. His wife and fellow signer, Mary Gilbert, and his sister-in-law Ann Gilbert did much better with their millinery business. His niece Grace Woodworth became a photographer in Seneca Falls.[57]

Susan Quinn, who at fourteen was the youngest signer of the declaration, lost her mother in 1853. She married a local lawyer, William B. Clark, and in December 1855 bore twin children. One of these twins died three months later, and the other died at two years old. William and Susan Quinn Clark moved into her father's house on Garden Street, and Patrick Quinn lived with them before his death in Waterloo in 1884. For forty-four years, William Clark was a successful lawyer and justice of the peace.[58]

Most signers from Seneca Falls disappeared from local historical records. We may never know what happened to Joel Bunker; Elizabeth and Mary Conklin; Cynthia Fuller; Ann Porter, sister of signers Experience Gibbs and Eliza Martin; Henry Hatley; John Jones; Lucy Jones; Sarah Sisson; Robert Smallbridge; Sophronia Taylor; Isaac Van Tassel; Sarah Whitney; and Justin Williams.

Even more prominent citizens faded from the historical record, including Nathan Milliken, editor of the *Seneca County Courier;* Saron Phillips, minister of the Wesleyan Methodist Church; Rebecca Race, whose husband was president of the village of Seneca Falls in 1848; Malvina Seymour, bonnet maker; and her husband, Henry W. Seymour, pump maker.

Signers outside Seneca Falls, already widely scattered, became more so after 1848. Still, many carried their radical ideals with them through their lives. In Waterloo, the untimely death of Elizabeth M'Clintock Phillips's husband, Burroughs, in 1855 and of Richard P. Hunt in 1856 influenced the M'Clintock family to move to Easton, Pennsylvania. Still subscribers to the *Liberator,* the M'Clintocks changed their subscription to their new home in July 1856. Waterloo neighbors, "of all sects and parties," once so unhappy with Thomas M'Clintock's radical ideas, now "urged him to stay, and offered substantial aid to enlarge his business." When he left, it was "amidst regrets well-nigh universal."[59]

In Rochester, Amy Post continued her interest in abolitionism, Native American rights, spiritualism, woman's rights, and the Friends of Human Progress. With Frederick Douglass, they made their home a center of Underground Railroad activity. Amy Post did not slacken her work even after her husband, Isaac, died in 1872. In November 1872, she joined Susan B. Anthony in trying to vote in Rochester. She continued to attend meetings of the Friends of Human Progress until 1887. In 1888, the fortieth anniversary of the Seneca Falls convention, she attended the International Council of Woman's Suffrage in Washington, D.C. When she died on January 29, 1889, at age eighty-seven, she left behind an estate of $20,000 but a far richer legacy of her active involvement in reform. Friends remembered her as "a woman of strong character and pronounced opinions," combined with a "singularly equable temperament." Frederick Douglass noted that "few better than I know the excellence of her character, the kindness of her heart, the strength and firmness of her convictions, the serenity of her spirit, the evenness of her temper, and the breadth and fullness of her benevolence. Her love of God was manifest in her love of humanity, and she was never ashamed to include Indian or African in the bonds of human brotherhood and friendship."[60]

Martha Wright continued to support the woman's rights movement from her home in Auburn. Shy about public speaking but dignified in public appearance, she frequently presided over state and national woman's rights conventions. She became secretary of the 1852 woman's rights convention in Syracuse, vice president of the 1854 Philadelphia meeting, president of three conventions (in Cincinnati, Saratoga, and Albany) in 1855, president of the 1860 national convention in New York City, and president of the National Woman Suffrage Association in 1874.[61]

Perhaps Martha Wright's most important contribution came from her life itself. Like Stanton, Wright used egalitarian values to weave a web that integrated her home life and her woman's rights work into a coherent whole. Reformers, including Frederick Douglass and Susan B. Anthony (whom the Wright family referred to as "Banthony") frequently stayed with them. In a letter to Wright's daughter Eliza Wright Osborne, Anthony recalled the "many, many calls and visits at the dear old family home on Genesee St. Your Mother's most hearty greetings and how I always felt sure Mrs. Stanton's and my plannings were right when Mrs. Wright gave her sanction."[62]

In turn, Wright's home life reflected her political convictions. Her relationships with her children, for example, continued to mirror her woman's rights values. In September 1848, for example, she wrote to her sister Lucretia Mott about a small incident involving her four-year-old son, Frank. "Frank showed his estimate of *Woman* the other day," she noted wryly, "by using his fist to mash his next potato better than Ma did, adding 'men can mash potato better than women.'"[63]

Two of Martha Wright's daughters, Eliza Wright Osborne and Ellen Wright Garrison, became woman's rights activists themselves. Eliza remained in Auburn, voted in school elections, and tried two or three times to vote at regular elections, "to the intense embarrassment of the poll officials," her grandson wrote, "as she was rather an awesome old lady." Ellen married William Lloyd Garrison Jr.[64]

Frederick Douglass spent the rest of his life in pursuit of equal rights and justice for African Americans and for women, beginning with his attempt in the fall of 1848 to get his own children admitted to Rochester schools. He turned increasingly toward political abolitionism. He supported the Civil War as a war against slavery and sent two of his sons to fight in it.[65]

After the war, in opposition to Stanton and Anthony, he supported the Fifteenth Amendment, which gave the vote to black men but not to black women. He did, however, join the National Woman's Suffrage Association and regularly attended its conventions. At the 1888 meeting, he noted his continued commitment:

> There are few facts in my humble life to which I look back with more satisfaction [he noted], than to the one . . . that I was sufficiently enlightened at that early day, and when only a few years from slavery, to support Mrs. Stanton's resolution for woman suffrage. I have done very little in this world in which to glory, except this one act, and I certainly glory in that. When I ran away from slavery, it was for myself; when I advocated emancipation, it was for my people; but when I stood up for the rights of woman, self was out of the question, and I found a little nobility in the act.[66]

Douglass served as marshall to the District of Columbia under the Hayes administration, the first appointment of any African American to a post requiring Senate approval, and in 1889, he was appointed minister to the Republic of Haiti. He died in 1895, aged seventy-eight, after returning from his very last public appearance, at a national woman's rights meeting in Washington, D.C., where he sat on the stage next to Susan B. Anthony.[67]

In 1850, however, none of the signers knew what lay ahead. For those who had sustained their commitment through the initial storm of criticism, the mood was upbeat. "Ridicule is giving way to reason," wrote Stanton. "Our papers begin to see that this is no subject for mirth, but one for serious consideration." Woman's rights supporters held their first national woman's rights convention in Worcester, Massachusetts. Until the Civil War, they held annual conventions every year except 1857. Throughout the 1850s, woman's rights advocates used the Seneca Falls Declaration of Sentiments as a touchstone. In 1855, Stanton herself began to write a history of the woman's movement.[68]

Some of the best-known advocates of woman's rights, including Lucy Stone and her sister-in-law Antoinette Brown Blackwell, reached a new peak of activism in the 1850s. Most woman's rights speakers were European American, but African American women, including Sojourner Truth and Frances Ellen Watkins Harper, also began to fight for woman's rights as well as for African American rights.[69]

In the early 1860s, woman's rights conventions were suspended as the country fought a war over slavery and its own existence as a nation. In 1862, the Stantons left Seneca Falls for New York City. There, Stanton and Anthony formed the Women's National Loyal League, which collected more than four hundred thousand signatures to support the Civil War as a war to abolish slavery. As historian Faye Dudden argued, this work gave them "an advanced education in legislative maneuver and partisan politics."[70]

After the Civil War, they put their new knowledge to good use. With radical Republicans and other former abolitionists, they worked to gain freedom, citizenship, and political rights for people who had been enslaved as well as for women. In 1866, Stanton, Anthony, Mott, and others formed the American Equal Rights Association, to promote political rights for African Americans as well as for women. This coalition split apart over the Fourteenth Amendment, which for the first time inserted the word "male" into the Constitution.

Debates over the Fifteenth Amendment, which granted voting rights to formerly enslaved men but not to women, exacerbated differences. Frederick Douglass supported black suffrage first. "The right of woman to vote is as sacred in my judgment as that of man," he wrote,

> and I am quite willing at any time to hold up both hands in favor of this right. . . . [But] I am now devoting myself to a cause [if] not more sacred, cer-

> tainly more urgent, because it is one of life and death to the long enslaved people of this country, and this is: negro suffrage. While the negro is mobbed, beaten, shot, stabbed, hanged, burnt and is the target of all that is malignant in the North and all that is murderous in the South, his claims may be preferred by me without exposing in any wise myself to the imputation of narrowness or meanness towards the cause of woman.

Stanton's commitment was absolutely to universal suffrage. "Do you believe," she wrote to Wendell Phillips, "the African race is composed entirely of males?"[71]

Recognizing that their cause was "in deep water," Stanton and Anthony formed their own group, the National Woman's Suffrage Association (NWSA). Opponents of the Stanton-Anthony camp, including Lucy Stone and her husband, Henry Blackwell, formed the American Woman Suffrage Association (AWSA). The NWSA promoted their ideas in a newspaper, the *Revolution,* whose motto was "men their rights and nothing less; women, their rights and nothing more." In 1866, Stanton ran for Congress from the Eighth District of New York City, receiving twenty-four votes.[72]

Events surrounding the 1876 Centennial celebration focused new attention on the rights of women as citizens. Courageous and creative, Susan B. Anthony and five others, including Matilda Joslyn Gage, from Fayetteville, New York, pirated press passes to gain entry to the main events and to present a Declaration of Rights of Women. Dedicated to their "daughters of 1976" and signed by hundreds of women, both black and white, this declaration asserted that "now, at the close of a hundred years . . . we declare our faith in the principles of self-government; our full equality with man in natural rights. . . . We ask of our rulers, at this hour, no special favors, no special privileges, no special legislation. We ask justice, we ask equality, we ask that all the civil and political rights that belong to citizens of the United States, be guaranteed to us and our daughters forever."[73]

As the first generation of suffragists grew older, they began to incorporate a stronger awareness of their own history. The turning point came in 1878. That year, woman's rights activists affiliated with Stanton and Anthony met at the First Unitarian Church in Rochester to celebrate the thirtieth anniversary of the Seneca Falls convention. It was "a grand convention," Stanton reported. Sojourner Truth came. So did Frederick Douglass. At the convention's close, eighty-six-year-old Lucretia Mott bade the world a public farewell. Mott spoke twice, for half an hour each time. Then Frederick Douglass, "with tender eloquence . . . bade her 'good-bye' for the association, and, taking his arm, with her bonnet swinging in her hand, she passed slowly down the aisle, amid the sobbing of the audience, speaking still the words of good cheer as she went away from our earthly sight forever."[74]

Publication in 1881 of the first three volumes of the *History of Woman Suffrage,* edited by Stanton, Anthony, and Gage, highlighted the use of history to further the cause of woman's rights. So did Stanton's serialized version of her life, published by Clara Colby in the *Woman's Tribune*.

Stanton and Anthony and their supporters continued to use commemorations of Seneca Falls as a way of measuring their progress, both as women and as citizens. In 1888, suffragists organized an international woman's meeting to commemorate the fortieth anniversary of Seneca Falls. The tone was celebratory. Stanton contrasted the status of women in 1848 with the "marked change in public sentiment that this magnificent gathering of educated women from both hemispheres so triumphantly illustrates." But, she cautioned, "we do not intend to rest our case until all our rights are secured." Frederick Douglass labeled Seneca Falls as the beginning of a movement that had reached new strength in the United States. Now, suffragists looked forward to developing new links across national boundaries.[75]

The decade of the 1890s was a watershed for the woman's movement. The merging of the National Woman Suffrage Association and the American Woman Suffrage Association in 1890, with Elizabeth Cady Stanton as president, brought a new sense of national purpose. At the same time, it highlighted the tensions that had always divided woman's suffragists. Trying to meld strong personalities into a single cohesive army took considerable powers of persuasion, diplomacy, and organizational expertise. In this quest for organizational integrity, Susan B. Anthony tried to use Stanton and Seneca Falls as potent weapons.

On November 12, 1895, the National Council of Women held an extravagant celebration at the Metropolitan Opera House for Stanton's eightieth birthday. In a gesture symbolizing the national importance of Stanton's own local action in organizing the Seneca Falls convention, Stanton received two silver commemorative dishes. One recognized her as the founder of the National Woman's Suffrage Association in 1869 and as a leader of the national woman's movement ever since. The other, presented by "the Ladies of Seneca Falls," commemorated Stanton as the organizer of the 1848 Seneca Falls convention.[76]

In her own address to the meeting, Stanton retold the story of Seneca Falls in a version that was increasingly assuming mythical status. This origin myth was intended to unify all woman's rights advocates, whatever their contemporary disagreements, by affirming their farsightedness, courage in the face of adversity, and connection to one central event, the Seneca Falls convention. Not coincidentally, it also reiterated Stanton's own central role. Seneca Falls was "the first woman's rights convention ever held in the world," asserted Stanton, and she quoted Wendell Phillips's statement that it was "the inauguration of the most momentous reform yet launched upon the world, the first organized protest against the injustice that has brooded for ages over the character and destiny of one-half the human race." At the same time, the Seneca Falls convention had led to personal as well as political transformation. "I would say to one and all," Stanton reflected, "that in demanding justice and equality for all women, I have secured larger liberties for myself."[77]

Much to Anthony's chagrin, Stanton's radical ideas created further discord in the woman's suffrage movement. Stanton herself scorned Anthony's increasingly pragmatic emphasis and devoted her own energies toward provocative liberal ideas. The two friends split over Stanton's warm endorsement of Frederick Douglass's second marriage to a white woman. In 1895, Stanton edited and published *The Woman's Bible,* a compendium of biblical quotations about women, with comments. *The Woman's Bible* brought together the twin themes of religion and woman's rights to which Stanton had devoted her life. It so dismayed more conservative suffragists, however, that only with difficulty was Anthony able to prevent the National American Woman Suffrage Association (NAWSA) from passing a resolution of censure against Stanton in 1895.[78]

In 1898, the fiftieth anniversary of the Seneca Falls convention, Stanton published her autobiography, *Eighty Years and More.* At the same time, NAWSA, upset by Stanton's irrepressible radicalism, held only a perfunctory celebration of the fiftieth anniversary of Seneca Falls. Billed as a "religious service," which undoubtedly infuriated Stanton, it highlighted a sermon by Anna Howard Shaw and two hymns by John G. Whittier. Matilda Joslyn Gage prepared a speech for the occasion, read in abridged form in her absence. Gage credited the "heroic souls" at the Seneca Falls convention with initiating "the most unselfish reform ever launched upon the world." "From that moment," she argued, "justice took fresh significance; a new era of hope and progress dawned, the meaning of freedom broadened not in this country alone but to the world." More substance, and probably more enthusiasm, emerged in at least one local celebration. The Sherwood Equal Rights Association, located in a small town southeast of Seneca Falls, dominated by Quakers, including abolitionist and woman's rights advocate Emily Howland, held a special meeting to celebrate the fiftieth anniversary of Seneca Falls. Between forty and fifty people heard talks on women and the law, women in education, industry, the professions, nursing, and politics.[79]

On October 26, 1902, at the age of eighty-seven, Elizabeth Cady Stanton died. Her last public act was to write a letter to President Theodore Roosevelt, urging him to support woman's suffrage, with a second letter to Mrs. Roosevelt, dictated the day before Stanton's death. In spite of their increasing political differences, neither Stanton nor Anthony ever repudiated their friendship. Hanging over Stanton's flower-covered coffin was Susan B. Anthony's portrait. Susan B. Anthony herself died in her Rochester home in 1906, having asserted in her last speech that "failure is impossible."[80]

After her husband died, Harriot Stanton Blatch, Stanton's daughter, returned from England. She was appalled at the condition of the organized suffrage movement. It "bored its adherents and repelled its opponents," she thought. Determined to infuse new energy, she founded the Equality League of Self-Supporting Women and, in 1908, brought an influential group of reformers to Seneca Falls to celebrate the sixtieth anniversary of the first woman's rights convention. Among them was one signer of the declaration, Mary H. Hallowell, along with Antoinette Brown Blackwell, one of the earliest woman ministers, and Stanton's own cousin Elizabeth Smith Miller. Several children of early reformers, including Fanny Garrison Villard (daughter of William Lloyd Garrison), Eliza Wright Osborne (daughter of Martha Wright), and Harriot Stanton Blatch herself, gave speeches. So did well-known European American suffragists, including Maud Nathan and Anna Garlin Spencer, as well as African American leader Mary Church Terrell, who spoke about Frederick Douglass.[81]

In its report of the meeting, the *Seneca Falls Reveille* emphasized the hometown convention as the beginning of a movement that was now worldwide. Women worked for their rights not only in the United States, England, Germany, and France but also in Latin America, Turkey, India, China, and Japan. In Finland, New Zealand, and Australia, women even had the right to vote. Among the thousands who attended this sixtieth anniversary meeting, reported the *Reveille,* were several people from Europe as well as different parts of the United States.[82]

Commemorating the demand for woman's right to vote, the 1908 meeting put up a bronze plaque sculpted by Elizabeth St. John Mathews on the wall of the old Wesleyan Chapel: "On this spot stood the Wesleyan Chapel where the first Woman's Rights Convention in the world's history was held, July 19 and 20, 1848," it read. "At that meeting Elizabeth Cady Stanton moved the following resolution, which was seconded by Frederick Douglass: Resolved, That it is the duty of the women of this country to secure to themselves the sacred right to the elective franchise." For this group, suffrage was the most important remaining unresolved point of the Seneca Falls Declaration of Sentiments.[83]

Renewed organizing in the 1910s resulted in huge suffrage marches in New York City and Washington, D.C., thousands of names attached to suffrage petitions, and votes on two suffrage proposals in New York. The first was in 1915, when suffragists celebrated the one hundredth anniversary of Stanton's birth with ceremonies at the Hotel Astor in New York City, as well as in Seneca Falls. When a referendum on state woman's suffrage came to a vote in November 1915, however, voters in Seneca Falls and rural upstate New York in general voted against the proposal. The New York State Woman Suffrage Association reported that "the rural vote . . . defeated us worst." In Seneca County, suffrage lost by 1,207 votes.[84]

In 1917, New York finally passed a state woman's suffrage amendment, with strong support from urban working-class neighborhoods in New York City and from soldiers who turned in absentee ballots. In the Seventh Campaign District, however, "the home of Susan B. Anthony and the first Woman's Rights Convention," the press was "professedly neutral or openly antagonistic and wrought great damage to suffrage in public opinion. More than any other one influence it was probably the cause of our failure to secure a majority. Also, the capitalist class in the district generally worked against us." The result? "Every county lost." Although upstate New Yorkers had voted against the amendment, women in

Seneca Falls and the surrounding area took advantage of their new power to vote. In Seneca Falls itself, 913 women voted in 1918, and 263 more voted in 1919.[85]

In spite of its lack of enthusiasm for suffrage in the 1910s, Seneca Falls remained a symbol of woman's rights. In 1914, an unknown suffragist penned an updated version of the Seneca Falls Declaration of Sentiments, arguing that "the history of our government is a history of repeated injustices to women (as wives, mother, and wage-earners) and of repeated usurpations by men, many of them with the avowed object of protecting women. But the direct result has been the establishment of a Government which benefits by the knowledge and experience of only one-half of the people, and which cannot fully represent the interests and the needs of the other half of the people." In 1915, as part of New York's effort to pass a suffrage law, Harriot Stanton Blatch printed a brief sketch of her mother's life, and Margaret Stanton Lawrence, Stanton's other daughter, wrote an essay, perhaps intended for publication.[86]

In all of New York, however, only one signer of the 1848 Declaration of Sentiments remained to take her place at the polling booth. Rhoda Palmer was 102 years and five months old when she cast her first ballot in Geneva in November 1919. At age thirty-two, she had attended the Seneca Falls convention, and five years later, she had attended another in New York City. She still retained her eyesight and her keen sense of humor, entertaining guests and showing them collections of paintings she had created in her younger years. Rhoda Palmer died less than a year later, on August 9, 1919, at the home of her nephew, only two doors from the house where she had been born in 1816.[87]

In 1920, passage of the Nineteenth Amendment to the Constitution finally gave women all over the country the right to vote. The struggle had lasted seventy-two years from the Seneca Falls convention. It had included 480 campaigns directed toward state legislatures, 19 battles at the federal level, and a huge ratification campaign in 1919 and 1920. In February 1919, the Sixty-fifth Congress defeated the amendment by one vote, leaving proponents no choice but to introduce it again in the Sixty-sixth Congress in May 1919, where, with the election of new members, the woman's suffrage amendment finally passed on August 26.[88]

Now the struggle began for ratification by the states. President Woodrow Wilson supported the woman's suffrage amendment, but opponents put intense pressure on state legislators to defeat it. Suffrage activists were equally diligent. The key vote came from Tennessee, where twenty-four-year-old Harry Burn, youngest member of the House, took his mother's advice to "help Mrs. Catt put 'Rat' in Ratification," and voted yes. On August 26, 1920, the Nineteenth Amendment became part of the U.S. Constitution, enfranchising women, the majority of the U.S. population.[89]

When the Nineteenth Amendment finally passed, only one signer of the original Seneca Falls Declaration of Sentiments—Charlotte L. Woodward Pierce—still lived. In the spring of 1921, she was ninety-two years old, frail, rapidly going blind, but mentally very alert. She had lived in Philadelphia for sixty years. Although she had qualified to vote in the last election, she had not gone to the polls, she said, because she was ill on Election Day. "And now I do not go out any more. No, I'm too old—I'm afraid I'll never vote." And, as far as we know, she never did.[90]

With the passage of the Nineteenth Amendment, suffragists turned again to Seneca Falls, commemorating the end of the suffrage movement by reflecting once more upon its beginnings. This time they incorporated the local story firmly into the national heritage by placing a marble monument of Elizabeth Cady Stanton, Lucretia Mott, and Susan B. Anthony, carved by Adelaide Johnson, in the U.S. capitol building.[91]

At the same time, suffragists worked to create an exhibit at the Smithsonian Institution, centered around the work of Susan B. Anthony, Elizabeth Cady Stanton, Lucy Stone, and the NAWSA. The M'Clintock tea table, around which Stanton and the M'Clintocks had drafted the Seneca Falls Declaration of Sentiments, formed the centerpiece.[92]

NAWSA met for the last time in Washington, D.C., in April 1925. In the call for this meeting, President Carrie Chapman Catt placed NAWSA's work clearly in the tradition of Seneca Falls. Her tone remained celebratory. "The dreams of those brave souls, who in 1848, shocked the world by their challenge, have," she wrote, "been realized. That which was then pronounced the wild vagaries of unbalanced minds are today accepted as matters of fact, not only in our own country, but in half the nations of the world." The "tedious struggle . . . never paused nor hesitated until the aim of the women of 1848 was written in the constitution."[93]

As the organized woman's movement merged into the political mainstream in the 1920s and 1930s, the story of Seneca Falls remained crystallized in its earlier form. Its key elements were repeated again and again, with little attempt to add new information or to seek a larger historical context. The Seneca Falls convention reflected a delicate balance between an older emphasis on responsibility and a newer emphasis on rights. The same tension between rights and responsibilities continued to energize woman's movements in the post-1920 period. The meaning of the debate shifted, however.

But with the vote now won, woman's rights advocates used the Seneca Falls Declaration of Sentiments in contemporary ways. Those who believed that the goals of Seneca Falls had now been fulfilled emphasized women's responsibilities as mothers and as citizens. The League of Women Voters, for example, focused on woman's citizenship. So did the new Women's Committee of the Democratic Party. A younger and more militant group of former suffragists, however, emphasized not responsibilities but rights. Unlike the old NAWSA, which saw the Nineteenth Amendment as a fulfillment of the Seneca Falls agenda, the National Woman's Party, led by Alice Paul, argued that nothing *except* suffrage had yet been won for women. They dedicated themselves to eradicating the remaining restrictions against women. Alice Paul turned to the Seneca Falls Declaration of Sentiments to help set the future agenda. The Declaration of Sentiments, she believed, contained a "whole equality program . . . for women in all fields of life."[94]

The result was the announcement of a campaign for a new amendment to the Constitution, one that would guarantee equal rights for all Americans without regard to sex. It was no accident that Alice Paul chose to announce the Equal Rights Amendment (ERA) in Seneca Falls in 1923, at an extravagant celebration of the seventy-fifth anniversary of the original Seneca Falls convention. "The work of the Woman's Party is only a continuation of the fight for Equal Rights instituted in 1843 [*sic*]," she announced, "and it will go on until every trace of discrimination against women has vanished. . . . There shall be no inequalities between men and women within the United States or any place subject to its jurisdiction."[95]

On Friday evening, on the banks of Van Cleef Lake in Seneca Falls, with a background of trees and the moonlight river, young women dressed in Grecian costumes presented a dance pageant portraying women through time. The crowd represented every state in the Union. Mrs. O. H. P. Belmont, president of the National Woman's Party, reminded them why they had come. "We stand," she said, "on consecrated ground. The birth place of Woman's emancipation. . . . We shall come again to Seneca Falls;—come again in great triumph, to lay before this our shrine our final trophies of Victory, carrying high our banner." On Sunday, a cavalcade of more than one hundred cars carried delegates on a pilgrimage to Susan B. Anthony's house in Rochester.[96]

In spite of the efforts of the National Woman's Party to keep what they now called a feminist agenda at the forefront of public awareness, passage of the Nineteenth Amendment diluted the force of the woman's movement. Key pieces of legislation, such as the Sheppard-Towner Act, which funded clinics for early childhood and prenatal care, came and as quickly disappeared. Many women refused to support the ERA, believing that protective legislation for women workers was necessary. On the other hand, as women assumed active roles in politics, they had a powerful influence on both state and local issues. The New Deal, in particular, was in part an outgrowth of the earlier woman's movement. Molly Dewson, chair of the Women's Committee of Democratic Party, convinced President Franklin D. Roosevelt to appoint Frances Perkins as secretary of labor, the first woman ever to hold a cabinet position. Eleanor Roosevelt herself found personal and political support from key women.

Through these years, supporters of women's rights remembered Seneca Falls and Elizabeth Cady Stanton in a variety of public forums. In 1936, Governor Herbert Lehman declared Stanton's 126th birthday "Elizabeth Cady Stanton Day" throughout New York, while Eleanor Roosevelt sent a congratulatory telegram to the birthday celebration sponsored by the Business and Professional Women's group in Johnstown, New York. At the same time, a large coalition of former suffragists emphasized the demands of the 1848 convention as the inspiration for continued political work in the twentieth century. The National Woman's Party took the lead. In 1937, for example, it republished the Seneca Falls Declaration of Sentiments, pointing out that "all of these rights still remain to be won except the right to the franchise." They also continued to hold commemorative celebrations of Seneca Falls as a way to focus attention on contemporary feminist issues.[97]

In 1940, a larger group took up the same theme. About three hundred people met in the World's Centennial Congress in New York City. The connection with Seneca Falls was clear. Students from Vassar College enacted a skit listing the grievances of 1848; Eleanor Roosevelt chaired a roundtable discussion that included Pearl Buck and Margaret Mead; and speakers such as Judge Florence Allen and Rose Schneiderman from the National Women's Trade Union League contrasted women's situation in 1840 and 1940.[98]

Convention delegates met in an atmosphere dominated by the rise of totalitarian governments throughout the world, and they focused their Declaration of Purpose on efforts to spread democracy both at home and abroad. Chaired by eighty-one-year-old Carrie Chapman Catt, members of this congress dedicated themselves "to use our freedom to work for the progressive securing of freedom, social justice, and peace for all people. In progressing towards this goal, changes must be made in the social economic, and political life of this and other countries. The spirit of men and women must be transformed. . . . We rededicate ourselves to the democratic way of life; we pledge ourselves anew to support, defend, and preserve the Constitution of the United States."[99]

Time magazine viewed this as a sign that the women's movement was "no longer explicitly feminist." "Totalitarianism in destroying civil rights seldom discriminates between men and women." But could women in 1940 really be inspired to rally to this new version of the cause? "To make a good crusade," noted *Time,* "the crusaders have to be underdogs, preferably an abused minority." Carrie Chapman Catt herself conceded that "we have got our rights. Well, what are we going to do with them?" she asked. "We have got to re-establish rights for men."[100]

In 1948, the centennial of the Seneca Falls convention marked the high water point of commemorative celebrations of the 1848 convention. Organized by a committee of local women, the Seneca Falls celebration was a focal point of national attention. As many as two thousand people attended a series of meetings, highlighted by nationally known speakers. The U.S. Postal Service issued a new three-cent stamp honoring "100 Years of Woman's Progress." President Harry Truman sent a telegram. Local residents presented a pageant, "Woman Awakened," telling the story of the original Seneca Falls convention. Thomas Dewey, governor of New York, proclaimed July 19 "Equal Rights Day."[101] To be sure that people understood the connection with the original convention in 1848, the *Seneca County Press* published the traditional story of Seneca Falls, complete with pictures of Stanton and Mott, with a full version, including signatures, of the original Declaration of Sentiments. Other newspapers, including the *Christian Science Monitor,* retold the story.[102]

The mood at Seneca Falls was congratulatory, but speakers clearly had more than historical issues in mind. Seneca Falls was important because it spoke to contemporary needs. There was no consensus, however, about whether Americans in 1948 should emphasize past gains or continuing problems. The future of the feminist movement itself was debatable. Should women continue to work primarily for women's rights? Or had the time come to emphasize women's responsibilities as human beings and as citizens? In his telegram, President Truman emphasized the gains of the last one hundred years. American women "have justified the rights for which those women of vision launched the fight in 1848," he wrote. Robert E. Fellers, superintendent of the Division of Stamps in the U.S. Post Office, carried out the same theme. "Today," he noted, "one of the most potent precepts in our land is our belief in the essential rights and dignity of the human race—a belief that men and women shall have equal opportunity to enjoy the fruits of their labors; in the home, in the factory, in business, or whatever it may be."[103]

Subsequent speakers urged their audience to recognize not only how much women had gained but how much work they still had to do. Dorothy Kenyon (former municipal court judge of New York City and then U.S. delegate to the United Nations Commission on the Status of Women), keynote speaker at the mass meeting, balanced a recognition of past successes and continuing problems. "We have the vote," she acknowledged, "after a struggle that lasted 72 years. What we are doing with the vote is another matter." In terms of political representation, legal rights, and employment, women had gained much, but they still had more to do. Anna Lord Strauss, Lucretia Mott's great-granddaughter and president of the League of Women Voters, declared "that we as women will win more opportunities not in promoting a woman's block or proclaiming a new woman's movement but by taking full advantage of those opportunities now open to us. Let us think of ourselves as citizens first and our role as women second."[104]

At a mass meeting on July 20, 1948, a group of protesting women read a new declaration, the "Declaration of the Women of 1948 to the Women of 2048." In a world of material progress, why do people still live in fear, without adequate food or housing? they asked. "Because a pall of atomic fear blankets our land in 1948," they answered, "because death stalks our land in 1948. The potential for life, atomic energy, is not being used to expand life—but to shatter it with atom bombs of death." "We, the women of 1948, declare to you, the women of 2048," they pledged, that we "will win for ourselves and therefore for you, our freedom as women to bear and rear our children, to share equally with our brothers, our land's productive labor in the factory, on the farm, at the desk, and on the bench. We will win our freedom to share equally with our brothers the highest offices in all organs of the body politic. We will win for you a prosperous democracy at peace with the world." Thirty-four women listed their names on this declaration, including Susan B. Anthony II, Nora Stanton Barney (Stanton's granddaughter), Pearl Buck, Alice Hamilton, Margaret Sanger, and Mrs. Henry Wallace.[105]

The Woman's Bureau of the Department of Labor chose not to attend the Seneca Falls celebration, arguing that women workers needed protective labor legislation most of all. Frieda Miller, director of the Woman's Bureau, suggested that most discrimination against women in 1948 was not embedded in the legal system but in traditional customs. Women should work "to substitute fairness and understanding for bias and prejudice."[106]

Radio programs also highlighted the Seneca Falls centennial. The University of Michigan Broadcasting Service presented "The Declaration of Seneca Falls." And the Radio Division of the United Nations, through its Latin American Division, presented a radio adaptation in Spanish of the pageant at Seneca Falls.[107]

Other groups held celebrations elsewhere. The Congress of American Women held a service at Stanton's grave in Woodlawn Cemetery, New York City, at which Nora Stanton Barney, Stanton's granddaughter joined Haley G. Douglass, mayor of Highland Beach, Maryland, a grandson of Frederick Douglass, as speaker. The League of Women Voters sponsored a play, *One Hundred Years of Growing.*[108]

Major newspapers and magazines published editorials. The *Christian Science Monitor* argued that although the women and men of 1848 "were dubbed cranks and extremists by most of their contemporaries . . . [yet] today their ideals are commonplaces." "There is still, however," the *Monitor* noted, "much to be done. . . . There is still need for those fighters who are carrying on in the spirit of Seneca Falls and who now stand closer than ever before to the fulfillment of their dream of an equal rights amendment to the Constitution." The *Ladies' Home Journal* put it even more bluntly. "No one is so deceived," wrote the editor, "as to believe that women today enjoy complete equality with men. . . . [T]hey are still discriminated against because of sex only."[109]

Few women or men in the 1950s followed up on this challenge. Postwar suburban development and the baby boom kept many white women occupied with home and family, and attacks on liberal and reform groups in general discouraged organized women's rights activity.

Through most of the twentieth century, since Mary Church Terrell's 1908 speech at Seneca Falls, African American women had been conspicuously absent from Seneca Falls anniversary celebrations. Often excluded from white women's suffrage organizations, many black women found their activist roots in the post-Reconstruction South and in the urban North, where struggles for survival, education, and legal equality intertwined in a fight for their rights both as African Americans and women. Black women's club movements focused on self-help movements and the antilynching campaign, as well as political organizing. Although black women often argued for suffrage based on the natural rights tradition, they did not link their campaigns directly to Seneca Falls. European American women who celebrated Seneca Falls found themselves far removed from an awareness of the separate and often far more desperate struggle of African American women.[110]

By the mid-1960s, the women's movement had reinvented itself, almost divorced from personal connection with the earlier movement and even devoid of much knowledge of earlier activism. The National Organization for Women, organized in 1966, represented middle-class political and legal concerns. Women's liberationist groups sprouted up on college campuses. Groups as diverse as the National Black Feminists, the Women's Political Caucus, and the Coalition of Labor Union Women represented wide constituencies. All had been influenced by the civil rights movement of the 1950s and 1960s. All brought new grassroots support for women's issues. In 1972, overwhelming congressional approval for the ERA reflected changing national attitudes toward women.[111]

The second wave of the women's movement brought renewed interest in Seneca Falls itself. When U.S. women met in Houston, Texas, in 1977 to initiate the United Nations Decade of Women, relay runners carried a torch from Seneca Falls to Houston. Millicent Brady Moore, a Seneca Falls resident and descendent of Susan Quinn, the youngest signer of the 1848 Declaration of Sentiments, formally initiated the race by handing the lighted torch to the first runner. Twenty-six hundred miles and fourteen states later, the torch reached Houston. Following statements by Rosalynn Carter, Betty Ford, and Lady Bird Johnson, Billie Jean King accepted the torch and passed it to Susan B. Anthony, great-niece and namesake of Elizabeth Cady Stanton's lifelong friend, who quoted the first Susan B. Anthony's most memorable words: "Failure is impossible." Twenty thousand women, men, and children cheered as they welcomed this powerful symbol of the spirit of the connection to the Seneca Falls convention.[112]

Poet Maya Angelou greeted the runners with a new declaration, "To Form a More Perfect Union," signed by all the relay runners and by thousands along the torch relay route. Echoing themes from the Seneca Falls Declaration of Sentiments, Angelou, an African American, spoke for women all over the United States. "We American women view our history with equanimity," she stated. "We allow the positive achievement to inspire us and the negative omissions to teach us." "We promise," however, "to accept nothing less than justice for every woman."[113]

That afternoon, delegates heard the preamble to a proposed National Plan of Action.

"We are here," civil rights activist Coretta Scott King began, "to move history forward.

Actress Jean Stapleton continued, "We are women from every State and Territory in the Nation."

"We are women of different ages, beliefs, and lifestyles," said Lupe Anguiano, a founder of the National Women's Political Caucus.

Others read more:

"We are women of many economic, social, political, racial, ethnic, cultural, educational, and religious backgrounds.

"We are married, single, widowed and divorced.

"We are mothers and daughters.

"We are sisters.

"We speak in varied accents and languages but we share the common language and experience of American women who throughout our Nation's life have been denied the opportunities, rights, privileges and responsibilities accorded to men.

"We recognize the positive changes that have occurred in the lives of women since the founding of our nation. In more than a century of struggle from Seneca Falls 1848 to Houston 1977, we have progressed from being non-persons and slaves whose work and achievements were unrecognized, whose needs were ignored, and whose rights were suppressed to being citizens with freedoms and aspirations of which our ancestors could only dream.

"But despite some gains made in the past 200 years, our dream of equality is still withheld from us and millions of women still face a daily reality of discrimination, limited opportunities and economic hardship. . . . We do not seek special privileges, but we demand as a human right a full voice and role for women in determining the destiny of our world, our nation, our families and our individual lives. . . . We are part of a worldwide movement of women who believe that only by bringing women into full partnership with men and respecting our rights as half the human race can we hope to achieve a world in which the whole human race—men, women and children—can live in peace and security."[114]

The Houston convention was "a life-changing and history-changing event," noted the official report. "Neither individual women nor the country would ever be quite the same again." In 1980, propelled by renewed public appreciation for women's struggle for equality, Congress authorized a Women's Rights National Historical Park in Seneca Falls. Enabling legislation declared that "the Women's Rights Convention held at the Wesleyan Methodist Chapel in Seneca Falls, New York, in 1848 is an event of major importance in the history of the United States because it marks the formal beginning of the struggle of women for their equal rights." Furthermore, the Declaration of Sentiments "is a document of enduring relevance, which expresses the goal that equality and justice should be extended to all people without regard to sex."[115]

In July 1982, Americans celebrated the grand opening of Women's Rights National Historical Park. Five thousand people thronged the streets to affirm that, indeed, "all men and women are created equal." The country remained undecided, however, about what equality really meant. That same year, in spite of consistent majority support from 1970 to 1982, the ERA was finally defeated.[116]

Like the first wave of the woman's movement in the mid-nineteenth century, the reemergence of feminism in the middle to late twentieth century reflected dramatic underlying economic, social, and cultural changes. In the 1840s, those changes moved the United States from an agricultural to an industrial economy.

In the 1960s, they revealed seismic shifts in the world, from an industrial to a postindustrial economy, as U.S. workers turned gradually but inexorably from manufacturing to service and professional jobs.

In the late twentieth century, just as they had in the mid-nineteenth century, such deep economic changes created unstable social structures and cultural values. Women and men were confronted with not only the opportunity but the necessity of making new choices about their lives. Every issue raised at the Seneca Falls woman's rights convention except one—woman's suffrage—once again became a matter for heated public discussion. Americans debated, passionately, woman's rights in politics, the law, family, work, education, religion, morals, and personal respect.

Some debates assumed vastly different forms. Technological developments relating to birth control, abortion, and childbirth brought these issues to the forefront of public policy and made attitudes toward the Supreme Court's passage of *Roe v. Wade* in 1972 a political litmus test. Conflicts over increasingly sexually explicit popular culture divided feminists as well as nonfeminists. Whereas in the nineteenth century, gay and lesbian issues went virtually unnoticed in debates among the general public, in the twentieth century, Americans became increasingly vocal about gay and lesbian rights.

One major difference separated feminists of the late twentieth century from those of the nineteenth century: federal and state governments took over much of the woman's rights agenda. Beginning with the Civil Rights Act of 1964, which (almost by accident) included the word *sex* as well as *race,* federal and state governments enacted legislation for equal pay, for equal education, against discrimination in credit, against domestic violence, for early childhood education, for day care, and for a variety of other issues promoted by woman's rights advocates. Although the Equal Rights Amendment failed ratification in 1982, individual legislation, state by state, eroded many of the laws that once upheld the scaffold of legal discrimination against women.[116]

With their nineteenth-century brothers and sisters, Americans in the twenty-first century shared both the challenges and the opportunities that came with living in a country whose founding fathers declared that "all men are created equal." In Seneca Falls in 1848, one hundred women and men had changed that sentiment slightly:

> We hold these truths to be self-evident; that all men and women are created equal; that they are endowed by their Creator with certain inalienable rights; that among these are life, liberty, and the pursuit of happiness; that to secure these rights governments are instituted, deriving their just powers from the consent of the governed.

In the twenty-first century, Americans continued to struggle, individually and as a people, with the meaning of equality, inalienable rights, liberty, and the consent of the governed. What rights did all people have—whatever their sex, race, class, culture, age, physical abilities, or sexual preference—as citizens of the United States and the world? What responsibilities did they have, as individuals and as members of families and communities? These were not easy questions, and they never had easy answers.

Perhaps the best tribute that we in the present can pay to those in the past is to continue to ask the questions and continue our struggle to define the answers. Most of all, we can recognize that no matter how dramatically the world changes, the ideal that all people are created equal remains an anchor that defines us as Americans. Elizabeth Cady Stanton would have us do no less.

Notes

Throughout the notes, Elizabeth Cady Stanton is referred to as ECS, Susan B. Anthony as SBA, Henry Brewster Stanton as HBS, and Lucretia Coffin Mott as LCM. Quotations contain original spellings, without "*sic.*" Most citations refer to original documents housed in various archives, but since research for this book was completed, two essential collections of these documents have appeared in print: *The Selected Papers of Elizabeth Cady Stanton and Susan B. Anthony*, vol. 1, *In the School of Anti-Slavery, 1840 to 1866*, vol. 2, *Against an Aristocracy of Sex, 1866 to 1873*, ed. Ann D. Gordon (New Brunswick, N.J.: Rutgers University Press, 1997); and *Selected Letters of Lucretia Coffin Mott*, ed. Beverly Wilson Palmer (Urbana: University of Illinois Press, 2002).

Abbreviations for Repositories

AAS	American Antiquarian Society, Worcester, Mass.
BPL	Boston Public Library, Boston, Mass.
Columbia	Columbia University, New York, N.Y.
Cornell	Cornell University, Ithaca, N.Y.
FHL	Friends Historical Library, Swarthmore College, Swarthmore, Pa.
Harvard	Harvard University, Cambridge, Mass.
LC	Library of Congress, Washington, D.C.
Rutgers	Rutgers University, New Brunswick, N.J.
Schlesinger	Schlesinger Library, Radcliffe, Cambridge, Mass.
SFHS	Seneca Falls Historical Society, Seneca Falls, N.Y.
Smith	Smith College, Northampton, Mass.
SyU	Syracuse University, Syracuse, N.Y.
UR	University of Rochester, Rochester, N.Y.
Vassar	Vassar College, Poughkeepsie, N.Y.
WRNHP	Women's Rights National Historical Park, Seneca Falls, N.Y.

Prologue

1. Original daguerreotypes and photographs of the factories along the river and of the main street of Seneca Falls are located in the Seneca Falls Historical Society. Some have been reprinted in *As We Were: The Life and Times of the 19th Century in Seneca Falls, New York*, 2 vols. (Seneca Falls: Seneca Falls Historical Society, 1977).

2. Information about the weather comes from Mary A. Bull, "Woman's Rights and Other 'Re-

forms' in Seneca Falls," *Seneca Falls Reveille,* July 9, 1880, reprinted with an introduction by Robert Reigel, ed., *New York History* 46 (January 1965): 41–59; Jefferson Palmer, "Diary," July 1848, Montezuma, SFHS.

3. "East View of Seneca Falls Village," in John W. Barber and Henry Howe, *Historical Collections of the State of New York* (1842; reprint, Bowie, Md.: Heritage Books, 1999), 526.

4. Margaret Stanton Lawrence noted that her mother often took the river road in "Elizabeth Cady Stanton, 1815–1915, A Sketch of Her Life by her Elder Daughter," typescript, Stanton Papers, Vassar, 32.

5. William Harrison Beach, "The Old Farm and the New," *Papers of the Seneca Falls Historical Society* (1907): 22, hereafter cited as *Papers, SFHS;* Benjamin F. Beach, "Early Transportation," *Papers, SFHS* (1905): 25.

6. Harrison Chamberlain, "Early Flouring Mills," *Papers, SFHS* (1905): 33–34; Beach, "Old Farm and New," 25.

7. Harrison Chamberlain, "Water Transportation and Packets," *Papers, SFHS* (1907): 5–6; Harrison Chamberlain, "Early Barrel and Boat Industries," *Papers, SFHS* (1908): 10.

8. [Harrison Chamberlain?], "Jacob P. Chamberlain," *Papers, SFHS* (1906): 54–58.

9. Mrs. L. R. Sanford, "Early Industries," *Papers, SFHS* (1903): 39; *Seneca County Courier,* April 7, 1841; U.S. Manuscript Census, 1850.

10. *Seneca County Courier,* June 13, 1848.

11. *New York Tribune,* July 19, 1848, noted that Henry was speaking in Canandaigua, New York.

12. Samuel Kline, "Saw Mills of Seneca Falls," *Papers, SFHS* (1905): 29.

13. ECS to Martha Coffin Wright, [c. 1852], Garrison Papers, Smith.

14. "Membership List," Trinity Episcopal Church, Seneca Falls, N.Y. Microfilm, Cornell; U.S. Manuscript Census, 1850; Deed, James and Margaret Clark to Patrick Quinn, March 24, 1843, Seneca County Clerk's Office, Waterloo, New York. Patrick Quinn signed this deed with his mark.

15. Harrison Chamberlain, "Early Industries," *Papers, SFHS* (1906): 36; [Harrison Chamberlain?], "Jacob P. Chamberlain," 57; *Seneca Falls Union Advertiser,* July 11, 1848.

16. Chamberlain, "Early Flouring Mills," 32; *Seneca Falls Union Advertiser,* July 11, 1848.

17. Sanford, "Early Industries," 40–41.

18. Chamberlain, "Early Barrel and Boat Industries," 10–11. The ravine across Fall Street may have been filled in by 1848. Advertisements, *Seneca County Courier,* February 15, 1848; June 13, 1848; June 20, 1848; July 18, 1848; February 2, 1849. *Seneca County Courier,* February 15, 1848. Credit ratings for S. E. Woodworth, New York, vols. 58–60, 75, 85, 88, R. G. Dun and Co. Collection, Baker Library, Harvard Business School.

19. This advertisement appeared several times in the *Seneca County Courier* in 1848. See, for example, February 15, 1848.

20. *Seneca County Courier,* September 30, 1847.

21. "Charles L. Hoskins," *Portrait and Biographical Record of Seneca and Schuyler Counties, New York* (New York: Chapman Publishing Co., 1895), 269–70; B. F. Beach, "Early Merchants of Seneca Falls," *Papers, SFHS* (1907): 9; Sanford, "Early Industries," 36–37; obituary for Charles Hoskins, *Seneca Falls Reveille,* April 23, 1897; Stephen Monroe, "Seneca Falls in Earlier Days, Should Old Acquaintance Be Forgot," *Papers, SFHS* (1911–12): 33–45.

22. Frederick W. Lester, "The Latham Family," *Papers, SFHS* (1948): 172–73, 176; Monroe, "Seneca Falls in Earlier Days," 33.

23. Monroe, "Seneca Falls in Earlier Days," 39.

24. U.S. Manuscript Census, 1850; "Charles L. Hoskins," 269–70.

25. Harrison Chamberlain, "Early Taverns of Seneca Falls," *Papers, SFHS* (1903): 71–72.

26. Earliest extant photograph of Fall Street, 1850s, reprinted in *As We Were,* 1: 9, shows small wooden houses and stores, with only a few brick buildings.

27. *Seneca County Courier,* July 18, 1848, and elsewhere. U.S. Manuscript Census, 1850, lists occupations; ECS to *Lily,* [June 1852], in Ann D. Gordon, ed., *The Selected Papers of Elizabeth Cady*

Stanton and Susan B. Anthony, vol. 1, *In the School of Anti-Slavery, 1840 to 1866* (New Brunswick, N.J.: Rutgers University Press, 1997), 200.

28. ECS, *Eighty Years and More* (1898; reprint, Boston: Northeastern University Press, 1993), 145.

29. Harrison Chamberlain, "Five Pivotal Years of Our History," *Papers, SFHS* (1908): 23; Gilbert Wilcoxen, "The Legal Profession," *Papers, SFHS* (1908): 15; David Lum, typescript, [n.d.], SFHS, 11.

30. Monroe, "Seneca Falls in Earlier Days," 35–36.

31. Samuel Taylor was instructed to procure lumber for a new boardwalk in front of the Wesleyan Chapel in the *Seneca County Courier,* April 3, 1848; *History of Woman Suffrage,* ed. Elizabeth Cady Stanton, Susan B. Anthony, and Matilda Joslyn Gage, vol. 1 (New York: Fowler and Wells, 1881–82), 69.

32. Interview with Rhoda Palmer, *Geneva Daily Times,* June 24, 1916.

33. LCM to ECS, July 16, 1848, Stanton Papers, LC; David Wright, "Account Book, July 19, 1847–November 29, 1848," July 19, 1848, Osborne Papers, SyU.

34. ECS, SBA, and Gage, *History of Woman Suffrage,* 1: 69; *Report of the Woman's Rights Convention Held at Seneca Falls, N.Y., July 19th and 20th, 1848* (Rochester: John Dick at the North Star Office, [1848]).

35. ECS, SBA, and Gage, *History of Woman Suffrage,* 1: 67–69; Arch Merrill, quoted in Michael Zeigler, "Falls Fever," *Upstate Magazine, Sunday Democrat and Chronicle,* July 11, 1982.

36. Theodore Stanton and Harriot Stanton Blatch, eds., *Elizabeth Cady Stanton as Revealed in Her Letters, Diary, and Reminiscences,* vol. 1 (New York: Harper and Bros., 1922); Alma Lutz, *Created Equal: A Biography of Elizabeth Cady Stanton* (New York: John Day, 1940); Mary Ritter Beard, *Woman as Force in History* (New York: Macmillan, 1946); Eleanor Flexner, *Century of Struggle* (Cambridge, Mass.: Harvard University Press, 1959).

37. References in alphabetical order are Bonnie Anderson, *Joyous Greetings: The First International Women's Movement, 1830–1860* (New York: Oxford University Press, 2000); Margaret Hope Bacon, *Valiant Friend: The Life of Lucretia Mott* (New York: Walker and Co., 1980); Lois Banner, *Elizabeth Cady Stanton: A Radical for Woman's Rights* (Boston: Little, Brown, 1980); Virginia Bernhard and Elizabeth Fox-Genovese, eds., *The Birth of American Feminism: The Seneca Falls Woman's Convention of 1848* (St. James, N.Y.: Brandywine Press, 1995); Christine Bolt, *The Women's Movements in the United States and Britain from the 1790s to the 1920s* (Amherst: University of Massachusetts Press, 1993); Steven M. Buechler, *Women's Movements in the United States* (New Brunswick, N.J.: Rutgers University Press, 1990); Ken Burns and Geoffrey C. Ward, *Not for Ourselves Alone: The Story of Elizabeth Cady Stanton and Susan B. Anthony* (New York: Alfred Knopf, 1999); Karlyn Kohrs Campbell, *Man Cannot Speak for Her,* 2 vols. (Westport, Conn.: Praeger, 1989); Ellen Carol DuBois, *Feminism and Suffrage: The Emergence of an Independent Women's Movement in America, 1848–1869* (Ithaca, N.Y.: Cornell University Press, 1978), and *Woman Suffrage and Women's Rights* (New York: New York University Press, 1998); Richard J. Evans, *The Feminists: Women's Emancipation Movements in Europe, America, and Australia, 1840–1920* (New York: Barnes and Noble, 1977); Ann D. Gordon, ed., *The Selected Papers of Elizabeth Cady Stanton and Susan B. Anthony,* 4 vols. (New Brunswick, N.J.: Rutgers University Press, 1997–); Elisabeth Griffiths, *In Her Own Right: The Life of Elizabeth Cady Stanton* (New York: Oxford, 1984); Nancy Hewitt, *Women's Activism and Social Change: Rochester, New York, 1822–1872* (Ithaca, N.Y.: Cornell University Press, 1984); Nancy Isenberg, *Sex and Citizenship in Antebellum America* (Chapel Hill: University of North Carolina Press, 1998); Estelle C. Jelinek, *The Tradition of Women's Autobiography* (Boston: Twayne Publishers, 1986), 108–27; Kathi Kern, *Mrs. Stanton's Bible* (Ithaca, N.Y.: Cornell University Press, 2001); James Livingston and Sherry Penney, *Martha Wright* (Amherst: University of Massachusetts Press, 2004); Alma Lutz, "Elizabeth Cady Stanton," *Notable American Women, 1607–1950,* eds. Edward T. James, Janet Wilson James, and Paul S. Boyer, vol. 3 (Cambridge, Mass.: Belknap Press, 1971), 342–47; Suzanne M. Marilley, *Woman Suffrage and the Origins of Liberal Feminism in the United States, 1820–1920* (Cambridge, Mass.: Harvard University Press, 1996); Nancy E. McGlen and

Karen O'Connor, *Women's Rights: The Struggle for Equality in the Nineteenth and Twentieth Centuries* (New York: Praeger, 1983); Keith Melder, *Beginnings of Sisterhood: The American Woman's Rights Movement, 1800–1850* (New York: Schocken Books, 1977); Beverly Wilson Palmer, ed., *Selected Letters of Lucretia Coffin Mott* (Urbana: University of Illinois Press, 2002); Ross Evans Paulson, *Women's Suffrage and Prohibition: A Comparative Study of Equality and Social Control* (Glenview, Ill.: Scott, Foresman, 1973); Barbara Ryan, *Feminism and the Women's Movement: Dynamics of Change in Social Movement Ideology and Activism* (New York: Routledge, 1992); Rita J. Simon and Gloria Danziger, *Women's Movements in America: Their Successes, Disappointments, and Aspirations* (New York: Praeger, 1991); Kathryn Kish Sklar, *Women's Rights Emerges within the Antislavery Movement, 1830–1870: A Brief History with Documents* (Boston: Bedford/St. Martin's, 2000).

38. For a pioneering exploration of this approach, see Katherine Milton, "The Signers of Seneca Falls" (independent study paper for Ross Evans Paulson, Augustana College, April 1970). Looking at the convention from the perspective of local history helps to pin down Stanton's own somewhat haphazard historical memory, a problem compounded by the work of Harriot Stanton Blatch and Theodore Stanton, who edited ECS's papers in the early twentieth century and may have destroyed many of them. For discussions of this, see Amy Dykeman, "'To Pour Forth from My Own Experience': Two Versions of Elizabeth Cady Stanton," *Journal of the Rutgers University Libraries* 44(1) (June 1982): 1–16; Griffiths, *In Her Own Right;* Ann Gordon, Afterword, in ECS, *Eighty Years and More* (1893; reprint, Boston: Northeastern University Press, 1993). The first announcement of the convention appeared in the local newspaper eight days before the meeting, for example, instead of, as Stanton claimed, five. No men participated in the discussions on the first day, and both Thomas M'Clintock and James Mott chaired the convention on the second day.

39. For more on these networks, see Judith Wellman, "The Seneca Falls Women's Rights Convention: A Study of Social Networks," *Journal of Women's History* 3(1) (Spring 1991). I am indebted to Elizabeth Griffiths for her insights on this issue.

40. Nathan Milliken, *Seneca County Courier,* July 21, 1848.

Chapter 1: Elizabeth Cady Stanton

1. ECS, *Sunday Herald,* January 22, 1899, in Scrapbook II: 305–7, Stanton Papers, LC.

2. "Daniel Cady," *Dictionary of American Biography* (New York: Scribner, 1990), 2: 401; James Livingston to Peter Smith, March 1, 1801, Gerrit Smith Papers, SyU; U.S. Manuscript Census, 1850.

3. Franklin Ellis, *History of Columbia County, New York* (Philadelphia: Everts and Ensign, 1878), 104; William Raymond, *Biographical Sketches of the Distinguished Men of Columbia County* (Albany, N.Y.: Weed, Parsons, and Co., 1851), 45; John Wells and James Dudley, "Death of Hon. Daniel Cady. Meeting of the Fulton County Bar," *Johnstown Independent,* November 25, 1859; [John R. L. Jeffers], biographical sketch of Daniel Cady in [Fulton County] *Republican,* n.d., from files in Johnstown Public Library, Johnstown, New York; Washington Frothingham, *History of Fulton County* (Syracuse: D. Mason, 1892), 200; "Daniel Cady," *Dictionary of American Biography,* 2: 401; DeAlva Stanwood Alexander, *A Political History of the State of New York,* vol. 1 (New York: Henry Holt, 1906), 169; L. B. Procter, *Lives of Eminent Lawyers and Statesmen of the State of New York,* vol. 1 (New York: S. S. Peloubet and Co., 1882), 110; Judith Wellman, "Daniel Cady," *American National Biography* (New York: Oxford University Press, 1999), 4: 171–72.

4. ECS, *Eighty Years,* 3; Theodore Tilton, "Mrs. Elizabeth Cady Stanton," in James Parton, ed., *Eminent Women of the Age* (Hartford, Conn.: S. M. Betts, 1868), 334. Much of this chapter relies on information from Stanton's recollections written in the 1880s and 1890s. By this time, Stanton had converted personal stories into effective political tools to win support for woman's rights. This basic purpose made her a powerful storyteller but a less reliable historian. Nevertheless, I have assumed that key incidents and details (although often not dates) are reliable enough to include here. Where possible, I have compared various versions of Stanton's stories and have used other sources to put her recollections into a larger context. For more discussion of problems with Stan-

ton's recollections, see Dykeman, "'To Pour Forth from My Own Experience,'" 1–16; Gordon, Afterword, 469–83; Jelinek, *Tradition of Women's Autobiography,* 108–27; Kern, *Mrs. Stanton's Bible,* 1–4.

5. ECS, *Eighty Years,* 3; Tilton, "Elizabeth Cady Stanton," 334; Laura Curtis Bullard, "Elizabeth Cady Stanton," in *Our Famous Women,* ed. Elizabeth Stuart Phelps (Hartford, Conn., 1884), 603–4. Harriot Stanton Blatch, *Challenging Years: The Memoirs of Harriot Stanton Blatch* (New York: G. P. Putnam's Sons, 1940), 19, noted that Margaret Cady was five feet eleven inches tall.

6. Frothingham, *History of Fulton County,* 190, 194–96, 224–25; Franklin B. Hough, *Census of the State of New York for 1855* (Albany: C. Van Benthuysen, 1857), xi; John Taylor, "Journal of the Rev. John Taylor," *Documentary History of the State of New-York,* ed. E. B. O'Callaghan (Albany: Weed, Parsons and Co., 1850), 3: 1129; Tilton, "Elizabeth Cady Stanton," 334; Horatio Gates Spafford, *A Gazetteer of the State of New York* (Albany, N.Y.: H. C. Southwick, 1813), 217; "Elizabeth Gilpin's Journal of 1830," Marjorie McNinch, ed., *Delaware History* 20(4) (1983): 241.

7. Theodore Tilton quoted in ECS, *Eighty Years,* 6.

8. James Livingston to Peter Smith, March 1, 1801, Smith Papers, SyU; Index to records of First Presbyterian Church, Johnstown, in Johnstown Public Library, Johnstown, N.Y.; U.S. Manuscript Census, 1800.

9. "Daniel Cady," *Dictionary of American Biography,* 2: 401.

10. Winthrop Hudson, *American Protestantism* (Chicago: University of Chicago Press, 1961), 14–15.

11. "Daniel Cady," *Dictionary of American Biography,* 2: 401; Wellman, "Daniel Cady," *American National Biography,* 4: 171–72; ECS, *Eighty Years,* 3; Sallie Holley to C. L. Holley, February 4, 1854, in Stanton and Blatch, *Elizabeth Cady Stanton,* 1: 56; McNinch, "Elizabeth Gilpin's Journal of 1830," 244.

12. Daniel Cady to Gerrit Smith, April 4, 1833, Smith Papers, SyU, noted his "passion" for lands. Seneca County deeds recorded Cady's purchase and sale of several lots in the New Military Tract in the early nineteenth century. Cady to Gerrit Smith, March 21, 1834, Smith Papers, SyU, also listed several lots in Cortland, Oswego, Wayne, Onondaga, Cayuga, and Herkimer Counties. Daniel Cady's will in 1859 listed several farms in Fulton, Montgomery, and Columbia Counties. Frothingham, *History of Fulton County,* 193, 200.

13. Wells, Dudley, and Resolutions of the Montgomery County Bar Association, in "Death of Hon. Daniel Cady," *Johnstown Independent,* November 25, 1859.

14. ECS, *Eighty Years,* 25; Wells et al., "Death of Hon. Daniel Cady," *Johnstown Independent,* November 25, 1859; Daniel Stewart, *A Discourse Delivered Lord's Day, Nov. 19, 1865, on Occasion of the Last Public Service Held in the Old House of Worship of the Presbyterian Church, Johnstown, N.Y.* (Albany: Weed, Parsons, and Co., 1866), 18–24, 29–32, 33–36; Leah Ireland, comp., *A History of the First Presbyterian Church of Johnstown, N.Y.* (n.p., 1965), 39; McNinch, "Elizabeth Gilpin's Journal of 1830," 241.

15. ECS, *Eighty Years,* 4.

16. ECS, *Eighty Years,* 8, 9.

17. ECS, *Eighty Years,* 2–11.

18. ECS, *Eighty Years,* 8, 25–26.

19. U.S. Manuscript Census, 1820; ECS, *Eighty Years,* 6, 10, 14–18; ECS to Harriot Stanton Blatch, October 1, 1889, Stanton Papers, Rutgers; Blatch, *Challenging Years,* 24–25; Lawrence, "Elizabeth Cady Stanton," 6.

20. Sallie Holley to C. L. Holley, February 4, 1854, Stanton and Blatch, *Elizabeth Cady Stanton,* 1: 56–57, and Stanton Papers, Rutgers; ECS, *Eighty Years,* 4–5; Daniel Cady to Peter Smith, November 24, 1816, Smith Papers, SyU. Rhoda Barney Jenkins, Stanton's great-granddaughter, owns one painting of the Cady house and one photograph (after its remodeling in the 1840s).

21. ECS, *Eighty Years,* 4–5, 11; Lawrence, "Elizabeth Cady Stanton," 4, noted that there were two kitchens; Daniel Cady in his will bequeathed to Margaret, his wife, "my dwelling house & garden . . .

also my barns & carriage houses with the land attached thereto." Will book, 196–98, Surrogate's Court, Johnstown, N.Y.

22. Newspaper picture of "Cady homestead," n.d., no source, in Cady file, Johnstown Historical Society, Johnstown, N.Y.; Blatch, *Challenging Years,* 8.

23. ECS, *Eighty Years,* 5, 16. Daniel Cady's will listed three farms in the area.

24. Sallie Holley to C. L. Holley, February 4, 1854, Stanton and Blatch, *Elizabeth Cady Stanton,* 1: 56–57. Information about piano price and cover were found in an unsigned note in the piano stool, Johnstown Historical Society, Johnstown, N.Y. Note on books comes from typescript in Cady file at Johnstown Historical Society signed "MVVP/1979."

25. ECS, *Eighty Years,* 4, 9–10.

26. ECS, *Eighty Years,* 29, 9, 12.

27. ECS, *Eighty Years,* 5.

28. ECS, *Eighty Years,* 5; Lawrence, "Elizabeth Cady Stanton."

29. ECS, *Eighty Years,* 5, 14–15, 17.

30. ECS, *Eighty Years,* 6, 19.

31. ECS, *Eighty Years,* 11.

32. ECS, *Eighty Years,* 14, 17.

33. ECS, *Eighty Years,* 14, 17; Lawrence, "Elizabeth Cady Stanton," 5; Theodore Stanton and Harriot Stanton Blatch, *Elizabeth Cady Stanton,* vol. 2 (1922; reprint, New York: Arno Press, 1969), xvi–xvii. While Stanton remembered Peter as "the only colored member of the church," others appear in the records of St. John's Church, Johnstown Public Library, Johnstown, N.Y.

34. Stanton and Blatch, *Elizabeth Cady Stanton,* 2: xvi–xvii.

35. ECS, *Eighty Years,* 12.

36. ECS, *Eighty Years,* 9–11.

37. Griffiths, *In Her Own Right,* 227.

38. Daniel Cady to Gerrit Smith, August 17, 1826, Smith Papers, SyU; ECS, *Eighty Years,* 20, 22.

39. ECS, *Eighty Years,* 20–21.

40. ECS, *Eighty Years,* 21–22.

41. Daniel Cady to Peter Smith, January 29, 1827, Smith Papers, SyU; ECS, *Eighty Years,* 20, 22.

42. Many years later, Stanton also recalled a public hanging when she was eleven years old. This public hanging may have been particularly significant to Stanton because it happened the same summer that her brother died. Death must have seemed all around her that summer, in one way or another. For an impressionable preteenager, the public hanging must have made a special impression. She never did talk about the hanging, a gruesome spectacle, in her autobiography, but she discussed it when she wanted particularly to speak out against capital punishment, another example of how she shaped her writing to fit her audience. ECS, *Reasons for Abolishing Capital Punishment* (Chicago: Cox and Company, 1878), 173–75. See also Blatch, *Challenging Years,* 24–25.

43. ECS to Theodore Stanton, April 29, 1879, Stanton Papers, Rutgers.

44. ECS, *Eighty Years,* 26–28; Index to records of Presbyterian Church, Johnstown Public Library, Johnstown, N.Y.

45. ECS, *Eighty Years,* 31; Lawrence, "Elizabeth Cady Stanton," 6–7.

46. ECS, *Eighty Years,* 31–32.

47. Norma Basch, *In the Eyes of the Law: Women, Marriage, and Property in Nineteenth-Century New York* (Ithaca, N.Y.: Cornell University Press, 1982), 79–83.

48. A person named Campbell, aged thirty-one, whose first name is illegible on the gravestone, died November 9, 1831, and is buried immediately next to the Cady family plot in the old Johnstown cemetery. ECS, *Eighty Years,* 32.

49. ECS, *Eighty Years,* 28–31.

50. ECS, *Eighty Years,* 33; Broadside dated Johnstown, October 12, 1818, in Johnstown Historical Society, Johnstown, N.Y.

51. ECS, *Eighty Years,* 23.

52. ECS, *Eighty Years,* 13.

53. ECS, *Eighty Years,* 33–34.

54. Frederick Rudolph, "Emma Willard," in James, James, and Boyer, *Notable American Women,* 3: 612; Anne Firor Scott, "What, Then, Is the American: This New Woman?" *Journal of American History* 65(3) (1978): 679–703.

55. Rudolph, "Emma Willard," 3: 612.

56. "Register, Troy Female Seminary," March 2, 1831, and September 21, 1831; "Ledger, Troy Female Seminary," March 14 to August 8, 1832, Emma Willard School, Troy, New York, in Patricia G. Holland and Ann D. Gordon, eds., *Papers of Elizabeth Cady Stanton and Susan B. Anthony: Guide and Index to the Microfilm Edition* (Wilmington, Del.: Scholarly Resources, 1991), 8; ECS, *Eighty Years,* 35–36; Lawrence, "Elizabeth Cady Stanton," 11.

57. ECS, *Eighty Years,* 41.

58. ECS, *Eighty Years,* 43.

59. "Ledger, Troy Female Seminary," March 14 to August 8, 1832, Emma Willard School, Troy, New York, in Holland and Gordon, *Papers of Elizabeth Cady Stanton and Susan B. Anthony: Guide;* John D. Davies, *Phrenology: Fad and Science, a Nineteenth Century Crusade* (New Haven: Yale University Press, 1955), 3–9.

60. ECS, *Eighty Years,* 44.

61. ECS, *Eighty Years,* 48; Daniel Cady to Peter Smith, April 4, 1833, Smith Papers, SyU.

62. ECS, *Eighty Years,* 45–46.

63. ECS, *Eighty Years,* 45; Harriot Stanton Blatch to Alma Lutz, May 16, 1930, in Alma Lutz Papers, Vassar.

64. ECS, *Eighty Years,* 49–50. Tryphena married Edward Bayard on May 21, 1827; Harriet married Daniel Eaton on January 3, 1831. Index to records of Presbyterian Church, Johnstown Public Library, Johnstown, N.Y.

65. ECS, *Eighty Years,* 47.

66. Stanton and Blatch, *Elizabeth Cady Stanton,* 2: xiii; ECS to Harriot Stanton Blatch, August 20, 1880, Stanton Papers, Rutgers, and ECS diary, February 4, 1899, in Stanton and Blatch, *Elizabeth Cady Stanton,* 2: 337, quoted in Griffiths, *In Her Own Right,* 216.

67. Sallie Holley to C. L. Holley, February 4, 1854, in Stanton and Blatch, *Elizabeth Cady Stanton,* 2: 56–57, and Stanton Papers, Rutgers.

68. Interview with ECS in *Sunday Herald,* January 22, 1899, in Scrapbook II: 305–7, Stanton Papers, LC.

69. ECS, "Reminiscences in the *Tribune,* XVI," 1, Stanton Papers, Rutgers.

70. ECS, *How to Make an Ideal Sunday for a Cosmopolitan American City* (New York: W. R. Hearst, 1901).

71. [Wealtha Tyler?], "Elizabeth Cady Stanton, Some Reminiscences of her Family Life, at Seneca Falls, N.Y., by an Old Acquaintance," typescript, SFHS, 4–7.

72. Index to records of Presbyterian Church, Johnstown Public Library, Johnstown, N.Y.

Chapter 2: Entering the World of Reform

1. ECS to Peter Smith, January 27, [c. 1834–37], Smith Papers, SyU. This interpretation of Stanton's use of Smith, Stanton, and Mott as role models and as anchors for reform networks owes much to discussions with Elisabeth Griffith.

2. Sarah Grimké, Angelina Grimké Weld, and Theodore Weld to Gerrit and Ann Smith, June 18, 1840, printed in Gilbert H. Barnes and Dwight L. Dumond, eds., *Letters of Theodore Dwight Weld, Angelina Grimké Weld, and Sarah Grimké,* 2 vols. (1934; reprint, Gloucester, Mass.: Peter Smith, 1965), 2: 840; Octavius Brooks Frothingham, *Gerrit Smith: A Biography,* 2d ed. (New York: G. P. Putnam, 1879), 140–43; ECS, *Eighty Years,* 51.

3. ECS, *Eighty Years,* 52–55.

4. "Autobiographical Sketch of the Life of Gerrit Smith," [after 1861], Smith Papers, SyU; Gerrit Smith, *Sermons and Speeches* (1861; reprint, New York: Arno Press and the New York Times, 1969); Ralph Volney Harlow, *Gerrit Smith: Philanthropist and Reformer* (New York: Holt and Company, 1939), chap. 3 and 4.

5. "Autobiographical Sketch," Smith Papers, SyU; Luna M. Hammond, *History of Madison County* (Syracuse, N.Y.: Truair, Smith, and Co., 1872), 703, 717; "Town of Smithfield," newspaper clipping, undated, Smith Papers, SyU; Frothingham, *Gerrit Smith,* 5, 21.

6. "Bill of Sale of Slaves. Peter Smith to Jesse Ives," August 17, 1801, fly-leaf of Peter Smith's Bible, Smith Papers, SyU; Edgar McManus, *A History of Negro Slavery in New York* (Syracuse, N.Y.; Syracuse University Press, 1966).

7. Harlow, *Gerrit Smith,* 914–15; "Autobiographical Sketch of the Life of Gerrit Smith," Smith Papers, SyU; Hammond, *History of Madison County,* 720–26; Frothingham, *Gerrit Smith,* 7–8, gives details of land prices; "Town of Smithfield," newspaper article, n.p., n.d., Smith Papers, SyU; Carlton Rice, "Early Settlement of Smithfield," *Madison Observer,* September 20, 1893, Smith Papers, SyU.

8. "Obituary: Gerrit Smith," *New York Times,* December 29, 1874; Harlow, *Gerrit Smith,* 22–34; Frothingham, *Gerrit Smith,* 32.

9. Frothingham, *Gerrit Smith,* 27; "Scenes in Johnstown, A.D. 1838," newspaper clipping, Smith Papers, SyU.

10. Frothingham, *Gerrit Smith,* 137–38.

11. Ann Smith to Gerrit Smith, May 2, 1838, April 26, 1850, Smith Papers, SyU; Frothingham, *Gerrit Smith,* 39, 138.

12. Harlow, *Gerrit Smith,* 193–217; Gerrit Smith to Rev. John C. Smith, November 24, 1852, in Harlow, *Gerrit Smith,* 217.

13. Leonard L. Richards, *"Gentlemen of Property and Standing": Anti-Abolition Mobs in Jacksonian America* (New York: Oxford University Press, 1970); Howard Alexander Morrison, "Gentlemen of Proper Understanding: A Closer Look at Utica's Anti-Abolitionist Mob," *New York History* 62(1) (1981): 61–82; Benjamin Sevitch, "The Well-Planned Riot of October 21, 1835: Utica's Answer to Abolitionism," *New York History* 50(3) (1969): 251–63.

14. ECS to Peter Smith, January 27, [1835–37], Smith Papers, SyU; Frothingham, *Gerrit Smith,* 165–66; Gerrit Smith to R. R. Gurley, November 24, 1835, in Frothingham, *Gerrit Smith,* 167–68.

15. Frothingham, *Gerrit Smith,* 113–22.

16. ECS, *Eighty Years,* 62–64; Barbara Sheklin Davis, *A History of the Black Community of Syracuse,* exhibit catalog for an exhibit of the same name at Onondaga Community College, October 1980 (n.p., n.d.), 6.

17. ECS, *Eighty Years,* 63–64; Smith to Marcus Smith, December 9, 1839, Smith Papers, SyU; Gerrit Smith to William Goodell, October 31, 1839, *Friend of Man,* November 6, 1839.

18. Ann Smith to Gerrit Smith, December 13, 1836; Elizabeth Smith and Ann Smith to Gerrit Smith, February 6, 1837; Ann Smith to Gerrit Smith, February 8, 1837; November 15, 1839; and November 23, 1839. Preceding letters in Smith Papers, SyU.

19. ECS to Peter Smith, January 27, [1835–37], Smith Papers, SyU.

20. Daniel Cady to Gerrit Smith, April 19, 1838, Smith Papers, SyU.

21. Ann Smith to Gerrit Smith, January 6, 1837, Smith Papers, SyU; "Genealogy Charts," in *Gerrit Smith Papers,* 1775–1924 (n.p., n.d.), 84; Harlow, *Gerrit Smith,* 41, 131; Gerrit Smith to Elizur Wright, March 14, 1840, Elizur Wright Papers, LC; Frothingham, *Gerrit Smith,* 38–43.

22. Gerrit Smith to Elizur Wright, April 20, 1840, Wright Papers, LC; "Obituary: Gerrit Smith," *New York Times,* December 19, 1874, quoting from Smith's obituary in the *Sun* (probably written by Henry B. Stanton); Gerrit Smith to Ann Smith, December 11, 1839, quoted in Frothingham, *Gerrit Smith,* 31, 115.

23. Lydia Fuller to Samuel Fuller, September 7, 1841, courtesy of Jack Fuller; Milton Sernett, *North Star County: Upstate New York and the Crusade for African American Freedom* (Syracuse, N.Y.: Syracuse University Press, 2001), 169–70.

24. ECS, *Eighty Years,* 55.

25. ECS, *Eighty Years,* 59.

26. ECS, *Eighty Years,* 59–60.

27. Arthur Harry Rice, "Henry B. Stanton as a Political Abolitionist" (Ph.D. diss., Columbia University, 1968), 6–10. Robert B. Stanton, "Reminiscences," 7, New York Public Library; Henry B. Stanton, *Random Recollections,* 3rd ed. (New York: Harper and Brothers, 1887), 5, 11.

28. Obituary for Henry Stanton in *New York Tribune,* January 15, 1887, quoted in William A. Stanton, *A Record, Genealogical, Biographical, Statistical, of Thomas Stanton, of Connecticut, and His Descendants, 1635–1891* (Albany, N.Y.: Joel Munsell, 1891), 458; Rice, "Henry B. Stanton," 3–4, 14, 16, 25; HBS, *Random Recollections,* 35–36, 27–28.

29. HBS, *Random Recollections,* 41–42, quoted in Rice, "Henry B. Stanton," 18–19.

30. Robert H. Abzug, *Passionate Liberator: Theodore Dwight Weld and the Dilemma of Reform* (New York: Oxford University Press, 1980), 81; "Robert Livingston Stanton," in William A. Stanton, *Record,* 463–64.

31. Daniel Cady to Gerrit Smith, December 14, 1839, Smith Papers, SyU.

32. Gerrit Smith to Ann and Elizabeth Smith, November 13, 1839, Smith Papers, SyU; ECS, *Eighty Years,* 61.

33. HBS to Gerrit Smith, December 25, [1839], Smith Papers, SyU; HBS to Elizur Wright, December 25, [1839], Wright Papers, LC, contained the same request.

34. ECS, *Eighty Years,* 62; HBS to ECS, January 1, 1840, Stanton Papers, LC; poet identified as Thomas Moore in Gordon, *Selected Papers,* 1: 3.

35. HBS to ECS, January 4, 1840, Stanton and Blatch, *Elizabeth Cady Stanton,* 2: 4–5.

36. ECS to Ann Smith, March 4, 1840, Stanton Papers, LC; HBS to Gerrit Smith, February 27, 1840, Smith Papers, SyU. On March 5, 1840, ECS witnessed a loan agreement between Daniel Cady, on the one hand, and Edward Bayard and Elisha Foote, on the other.

37. ECS to Ann Smith, March 4, 1840, in Gordon, *Selected Papers,* 1: 4–7.

38. HBS to Gerrit Smith, February 27, 1840, and April 17, 1849, Gerrit Smith Papers, SyU.

39. ECS, *Eighty Years,* 71–72; ECS to her granddaughter and namesake, Elizabeth Cady Stanton (daughter of Theodore Stanton and Marguerite Berry), June 16, [1882], Stanton Papers [Vassar]; John G. Whittier to his sister Elizabeth, May 4, 1840, quoted by Alma Lutz, Lutz Papers, Vassar.

40. HBS to Gerrit Smith, February 27, 1840; ECS to Ann Smith, March 4, 1840, in Gordon, *Selected Papers,* 1: 4–7.

41. HBS to Gerrit Smith, May 10, 1840, Smith Papers, SyU. Elizabeth's attempts to assert her own independence from Henry come through in many ways in the early 1840s. Writing to Elizabeth J. Neall on November 16, [1841], for example, she noted, "You need not direct my letters to Henry unless you intend them for both of us. I am as well known here as he is." Henry continued to try to assert his authority, at least indirectly, however. On June 23, 1842, he addressed a letter to Elizabeth as "My dearest daughter." Gordon, *Selected Letters,* 1: 26, 35.

42. Abzug, *Passionate Liberator;* Gilbert Barnes, *Anti-Slavery Impulse, 1830–1844* (1933; reprint, New York: Harcourt, Brace, and World, 1964).

43. ECS, *Eighty Years,* 58–59; Merton Dillon, *The Abolitionists: The Growth of a Dissenting Minority* (1974; reprint, New York: W. W. Norton, 1979), 76.

44. Richards, *"Gentlemen of Property and Standing";* John L. Myers, "The Beginning Of Anti-Slavery Agencies in New York State, 1833–1836," *New York History* 43(2) (1962): 149–81; John L. Myers, "The Major Effort of National Anti-Slavery Agents in New York State, 1836–1837," *New York History* 46(2) (1965): 162–86.

45. Barnes, *Anti-Slavery Impulse,* 89, 104, 106; William Lloyd Garrison to Lewis Tappan, February 29, 1836, and Garrison to George W. Benson, June 14, 1837, in Louis Ruchames, eds., *Letters of William Lloyd Garrison,* vol. 2, *A House Dividing against Itself, 1836–1840* (Cambridge, Mass.: Belknap Press, 1971), 52, 268.

46. Dwight Lowell Dumond, "Petitions," in *Antislavery: The Crusade for Freedom in America* (Ann Arbor: University of Michigan Press, 1961), 242–48; Richard H. Sewall, *Ballots for Freedom:*

Antislavery Politics in the United States, 1836–1860 (New York: W. W. Norton, 1976), 3–23; Judith Wellman, *Grass Roots Reform in the Burned-over District of Upstate New York: Religion, Abolitionism, and Democracy* (New York: Garland, 2000), 129–208.

47. National Archives, HR23A-Hl.2, received February 16, 1835.

48. "Fourth Annual Report of the New York State Antislavery Society," *Friend of Man,* October 2, 1839; Judith Wellman, "Women and Radical Reform in Antebellum Upstate New York: A Profile of Grassroots Female Abolitionists," in Mabel E. Deutrich and Virginia C. Purdy, eds., *Clio Was a Woman: Studies in the History of American Women* (Washington, D.C.: Howard University Press, 1980), 113–27.

49. *Friend of Man,* April 11, 1838; Barnes, *Anti-Slavery Impulse,* 266.

50. "Auxiliaries to the American Anti-Slavery Society, 1836," Wright Papers, LC; Wellman, "Women and Radical Reform," 118.

51. Marilyn Richardson, ed., *Maria W. Stewart, America's First Black Woman Political Writer: Essays and Speeches* (Bloomington: Indiana University Press, 1987).

52. Maria Weston Chapman to Elizabeth Pease, April 29, 1840, BPL. "Ultra Barn Burning" quote in *Buffalo Commercial Advertiser,* Scrapbook II, Stanton Papers, LC; "Radical of radicals" quote in Eliza M. Estabrook to [Maria Mott] Davis, n.d., quoting Longfellow's sermon of "the 14th inst," Lucretia Mott Papers, FHL, and in Phoebe Couzins, "Lucretia Mott," November 22, 1880, newspaper clipping, Mott Papers, FHL.

53. *Proceedings of the First Anniversary of the American Equal Rights Association* (New York: Robert J. Johnston, 1867), 7. Biographies of Mott include Mary Clemmer, "Lucretia Mott," in Stuart Phelps Ward, *Our Famous Women,* 462–97; ECS, "Lucretia Mott," in ECS, SBA, and Gage, *History of Woman Suffrage,* 1: 407–31; *James and Lucretia Mott: Life and Letters,* ed. A. D. Hallowell, 5th ed. (Boston: Houghton, Mifflin, and Co., 1896); Otelia Cromwell, *Lucretia Mott* (Cambridge, Mass.: Harvard University Press, 1958); and Bacon, *Valiant Friend.* For Mott's writings, see Dana Greene, ed., *Lucretia Mott: Her Complete Speeches and Sermons* (New York: Edwin Mellon Press, 1980); Palmer, *Selected Letters of Lucretia Coffin Mott.*

54. Bacon, *Valiant Friend,* 55–57; ECS, SBA, and Gage, *History of Woman Suffrage,* 1: 324; Ira V. Brown, "Cradle of Feminism: The Philadelphia Female Anti-Slavery Society, 1833–1840," *Pennsylvania Magazine of History and Biography* 103 (1978): 143–66.

55. Janice Sumler-Lewis, "The Forten-Purvis Women of Philadelphia and the American Anti-Slavery Crusade," *Journal of Negro History* 66 (1981–82): 281–88; Ray Allen Billington, ed., *The Journal of Charlotte L. Forten: A Free Negro in the Slave Era* (New York, 1981); Bacon, *Valiant Friend,* 61; Mary Grew's final report for the Philadelphia Female Anti-Slavery Society, 1870, excerpted in ECS, SBA, and Gage, *History of Woman Suffrage,* 1: 325–26.

56. Gerda Lerner, *Grimké Sisters from South Carolina: Rebels against Slavery* (Boston: Houghton Mifflin, 1967); Katherine Du Pre Lumpkin, *The Emancipation of Angelina Grimké* (Chapel Hill: University of North Caroline Press, 1974); Barnes and Dumond, *Letters of Theodore Dwight Weld, Angelina Grimké Weld, and Sarah Grimké;* Larry Ceplair, ed., *The Public Years of Sarah and Angelina Grimké: Selected Writings, 1835–1839* (New York: Columbia University Press, 1989); Gerda Lerner, *The Feminist Thought of Sarah Grimké* (New York: Oxford University Press, 1998).

57. Angelina Grimké to Jane Smith, September 18, [1836], and November 19, 1836, in Ceplair, *Public Years,* 81–84; Susan Zaeske, "The 'Promiscuous Audience'": Controversy and the Emergence of the Early Woman's Rights Movement," *Quarterly Journal of Speech* 81(2) (1995): 191–207.

58. Angelina Grimké to Jane Smith, December 17, [1836], in Ceplair, *Public Years,* 87–90.

59. Angelina Grimké to Jane Smith, December 17, [1836], in Ceplair, *Public Years,* 87–90.

60. Angelina Grimké to Jane Smith, February 4, 1837; Angelina Grimké to Sarah Douglass, April 3, 1837; A. E. Grimké to Jane Smith, June [1837]. In Ceplair, *Public Years,* 116–17, 127, 144–46.

61. Angelina Grimké, Letter XII, "Human Rights Not Founded On Sex," in *Letters to Catherine E. Beecher, in reply to* An Essay on Slavery and Abolitionism, *addressed to A. E. Grimké. Revised by the author* (Boston: Isaac Knapp, 1838), reprinted in Ceplair, *Public Years,* 194. Sarah Grimké, Let-

ter III, "The Pastoral Letter of the General Association of Congregational Ministers of Massachusetts," in *Letters on the Equality of the Sexes and the Condition of Woman, addressed to Mary S. Parker, President of the Boston Female Anti-Slavery Society* (Boston: Isaac Knapp, 1838), reprinted in Ceplair, *Public Years,* 213.

62. Angelina Grimké to Jane Smith, July [August] 10, [1837]; Angelina E. Grimké to Jane Smith, [February 7, 1838]. In Ceplair, *Public Years,* 287, 275–76, 306–7. Barnes, *Anti-Slavery Impulse,* 155, 160, 176, 274; Angelina Grimké to Theodore Weld, February 11, 1838, Weld-Grimké Papers, quoted in Barnes, *Anti-Slavery Impulse,* 156.

63. John G. Whittier to Grimkés, August 14, 1837, in Ceplair, *Public Years,* 280.

64. "A Friend of Woman," "Lyceum Meeting at the Odeon," *Liberator,* January 19, 1838, 10, in Ceplair, *Public Years,* 104; *The True History of the Late Division in the Anti-Slavery Societies, Being Part of the Second Annual Report of the Executive Committee of the Massachusetts Abolition Society* (Boston: Devaid H. Ela, 1841).

65. Theodore Weld to Sarah and Angelina Grimké, August 15, 1837; Angelina E. Grimké to Theodore Weld and John G. Whittier, August 20, [1837]; and Sarah and Angelina Grimké to Theodore Weld, September 20, 1837. In Ceplair, *Public Years,* 281–85 and 289–94.

66. [Minutes of the Convention], reprinted in *Turning the World Upside Down: The Anti-Slavery Convention of American Women Held in New York City, May 9–12, 1837,* Dorothy Sterling, ed. (New York: Feminist Press, 1987); Ira V. Brown, "'Am I Not a Woman and a Sister?': The Anti-Slavery Conventions of American Women, 1837–1839," *Pennsylvania History* 50 (1983): 1–19.

67. *Proceedings of the Antislavery Convention of American Women* (New York: William S. Dorr, 1837), 4–6; Angelina Grimké, *An Appeal to the Women of the Nominally Free States* (Boston: Isaac Knapp, 1838), 6, 19.

68. *Proceedings of the Antislavery Convention of American Women,* 36; Angelina Grimké, *Appeal,* 58–64.

69. "Circular of the Antislavery Convention of American Women," *Proceedings of the Third Antislavery Convention of American Women* (Philadelphia: Merrihew and Thompson, 1839), 26; "Petitions! Petitions! Petitions!" *Friend of Man,* November 14, 1838.

70. Wellman, "Women and Radical Reform," 118; "Auxiliaries to the American Anti-Slavery Society, 1836," Wright Papers, LC; "Address of Farmington Female Anti-Slavery Society, to Females Residing in the Western Part of the State of New York," *Friend of Man,* July 4, 1838. For more on women and antislavery petitions, see Deborah Bingham Van Broekhoven, *The Devotion of These Women: Rhode Island in the Antislavery Network* (Amherst: University of Massachusetts Press, 2002).

71. Theodore Weld to Angelina Grimké, February 8, 1838; Angelina Grimké to Theodore Weld, February 11, [1838]; Sarah Grimké to Theodore Weld, [February 11, 1838]. In Ceplair, *Public Years,* 307–9.

72. Angelina Grimké to Jane Smith, March 27, [1838]; Angelina Grimké to Theodore Weld, [April 29, 1838]; and Sarah Grimké to Elizabeth Pease, [May 20?, 1838]. In Ceplair, *Public Years,* 315–18. Maria M. Davis to Edward M. Davis, May 7, 1838, Mott Papers, FHL.

73. Bacon, *Valiant Friend,* 75–78.

74. Bacon, *Valiant Friend,* 78; LCM to E. M. Davis, June 18, 1838, Houghton Library, Harvard.

75. In 1836, according to Dorothy Sterling, "almost half the women in Lynn had signed one or more [antislavery] petitions." Sterling, *Ahead of Her Time: Abby Kelley and the Politics of Antislavery* (New York: W. W. Norton and Co., 1991), 35. Abby Kelley to Maria Weston Chapman noted that 1,500 women signed petitions from Lynn, November 25, 1837, William Lloyd Garrison Papers, BPL.

76. Bacon, *Valiant Friend,* 79–80.

77. *Liberator,* December 15, 1837, in George M. Frederickson, ed., *William Lloyd Garrison* (Englewood Cliffs, N.J.: Prentice-Hall, 1968), 48.

78. Wendell Phillips Garrison, ed., *William Lloyd Garrison* (New York: Century Co., 1885–89), 1: 204, quoted in Kathryn Kish Sklar, "'Women Who Speak for an Entire Nation': American and

British Women Compared at the World Anti-Slavery Convention, London, 1840," *Pacific Historical Review* 59(4) (1990): 488; William Lloyd Garrison to Helen Garrison, May 12, 1838, in Ruchames, *Letters of William Lloyd Garrison,* 2: 359.

79. C. C. Burleigh to J. Miller McKim, May 28, June 6, 1838, Mott Papers, FHL.

80. Angelina Grimké to Jane Smith, July 25, [1837], in Ceplair, *Public Years,* 272; Sterling, *Abby Kelley,* 69; Charles Stuart to Gerrit Smith, August 15, 1841, Smith Papers, SyU. For more on Stuart, see Anthony J. Barker, *Captain Charles Stuart: Anglo American Abolitionist* (Baton Rouge: Louisiana State University Press, 1986).

81. William Lloyd Garrison to Mary Benson, September 22, 1838, in Ruchames, *Letters of William Lloyd Garrison* 2: 395; Frederickson, *William Lloyd Garrison,* 51.

82. William Lloyd Garrison to James Mott and LCM, quoted in James Mott to E. M. Davis, March 7, 1839, Houghton Library, Harvard; HBS to James G. Birney, January 16, 1839, in Frederickson, *William Lloyd Garrison,* 81.

83. LCM to J. Miller McKim, December 29, 1839, Mott Papers, FHL; Maria Weston Chapman to Elizabeth Pease, April 20, 1840, Garrison Papers, BPL.

84. LCM to J. Miller McKim, December 29, 1839, Mott Papers, FHL.

85. For several years, Garrison made considerable political capital out of the sale of the American Anti-Slavery Society's assets. See, e.g., *Liberator,* October 20, 1843; October 27, 1843; November 3, 1843; and November 3,1848. In Barnes and Dumond, *Weld-Grimké Letters,* 842, 848.

86. HBS to Gerrit Smith, February 27, 1840, Smith Collection, SyU; HBS to Charles Torrey, February 2, 1840, typescript in Alma Lutz Papers, Vassar.

87. "Convention of Western New York," *Friend of Man,* March 20, 1839.

88. Sarah Grimké, Angelina Grimké Weld, and Theodore Weld to Gerrit and Ann Smith, June 18, 1840; Gerrit Smith to Theodore Weld, [July 11, 1840]. In Barnes and Dumond, ed., *Weld-Grimké Letters,* 843, 849.

89. Sarah Grimké and Angelina and Theodore Weld to Gerrit and Ann Smith, June 18, 1840; ECS to Angelina Grimké Weld and Sarah Grimké, June 25, 1840. In Barnes and Dumond, *Weld-Grimké Letters,* 842, 848.

90. HBS to John G. Whittier, April 18, 1840, Harvard. Lewis Tappan to Maria Waring, *Liberator,* November 3, 1848.

91. HBS to Gerrit Smith, May 10, 1840, Smith Papers, SyU.

92. ECS, *Eighty Years,* 73–74; ECS to Gerrit Smith, August 3, [1840], Smith Papers, SyU; ECS to Angelina Grimké Weld and Sarah Grimké, June 25, 1840, in Barnes and Dumond, *Weld-Grimké Letters,* 848.

93. William Lloyd Garrison to Helen Garrison, June 29, 1840, Garrison Papers, BPL; ECS, SBA, and Gage, *History of Woman Suffrage,* 1: 54–62, 419–27, and 432–40, carried a detailed account of this meeting. For recent studies of the World Anti-Slavery Convention, see Donald R. Kennon, "'An Apple of Discord': The Woman Question at the World's Anti-Slavery Convention of 1840," *Slavery and Abolition,* 5 (1984): 244–66; Sklar, "'Women Who Speak for an Entire Nation,'" *Pacific Historical Review,* 453–99; Karen I. Halbersleben, *Women's Participation in the British Antislavery Movement, 1824–1865* (Lewiston: E. Mellen Press, 1993).

94. ECS, SBA, and Gage, *History of Woman Suffrage,* 1: 54–55; Wendell Phillips, "The Right Arm of Our Enterprise," from Oscar Sherwin, *Prophet of Liberty: the Life and Times of Wendell Phillips* (New York: Bookman Associates, 1958), 112–13, quoted in Herbert Aptheker, *And Why Not Every Man?* (New York: International Publishers, 1970), 143–45. Thanks to Sally Roesch Wagner for this citation. For biographies of Phillips, see James Brewer Stewart, *Wendell Phillips: Liberty's Hero* (Baton Rouge: Louisiana State University Press, 1986), and Irving H. Bartlett, *Wendell and Ann Phillips: The Community of Reform, 1840–1880* (New York: Norton, 1979).

95. Sklar, "'Women Who Speak for an Entire Nation,'" *Pacific Historical Review,* 463; Richard D. Webb to Elizabeth Pease, November 4, 1840, Garrison Papers, BPL.

96. William Howitt to LCM, June 27, 1840, quoted in James Mott, *Three Months in Great Brit-*

ain (Philadelphia, 1841), 4; LCM to John Morgan, quoted in Frederick B. Tolles, ed., *Slavery and "The Woman Question": Lucretia Mott's Diary of Her Visit to Great Britain to Attend the World's Anti-Slavery Convention of 1840* (Haverford, Pa., 1952), 58; ECS to Sarah Grimké and Angelina Grimké Weld, June 25, 1840, in Gordon, *Selected Papers,* 1: 8–15.

97. Maria Waring to members of the Webb family, [June 1840], in Clare Taylor, comp., *British and American Abolitionists: An Episode in Transatlantic Understanding* (Edinburgh: Edinburgh University Press, 1974), 96.

98. ECS, *Eighty Years,* 79, 81; William Lloyd Garrison to Helen Garrison, June 29, 1840, Garrison Papers, BPL; Cromwell, *Lucretia Mott,* 79, 85; LCM, diary, [June] 23, [1840], in Tolles, *Slavery and "The Woman Question,"* 44; Kennon, "'Apple of Discord,'" 260, disputes Henry's support for the women delegates.

99. ECS, SBA, and Gage, *History of Woman Suffrage,* 1: 61–62; ECS, *Eighty Years,* 71–91.

100. Mary Grew, "Diary, 1840," typescript, Schlesinger, 35; extract from the Minutes of the Seventh Annual Meeting of the American Anti-Slavery Society, May 12–15, 1840, Garrison Papers, BPL; William Lloyd Garrison to Helen Garrison, June 29, 1840, Garrison Papers, BPL.

101. [Richard D. Webb], "Sketches of the Anti-Slavery Convention, No. VIII: Lucretia Mott," *Liberator,* October 23, 1840; LCM to Elizabeth Pease, April 28, 1846, Mott Papers, FHL; Bacon, *Valiant Friend,* 99.

102. ECS to Angelina Grimké Weld and Sarah Grimké, June 25, 1840, in Gordon, *Selected Papers,* 1: 8–15.

103. Grew, "Diary, 1840"; ECS, *Eighty Years,* 82–83.

104. LCM to Richard and Hannah Webb, April 2, 1841, and Richard D. Webb to Elizabeth Pease, November 4, 1840, Garrison Papers, BPL; Richard and Hannah Webb to Sarah Pugh, quoted in Lutz, *Created Equal,* 34; LCM, Diary, in Tolles, *Slavery and the "Woman Question";* "Lucretia Mott's Diary of Her Visit to Great Britain to Attend the World's Anti-Slavery Convention of 1840," Supplement No. 23 to the *Journal of the Friends Historical Society* (Haverford, Pa., 1952): 41.

105. William Lloyd Garrison to Helen Garrison, June 29, 1840, Garrison Papers, BPL; ECS to Angelina Weld and Sarah Grimké, June 25, 1840, in Gordon, *Selected Letters,* 1: 8–15.

106. LCM to Richard and Hannah Webb, April 2, 1841, Garrison Papers, BPL.

107. ECS, SBA, and Gage, *History of Woman Suffrage,* 1: 62.

108. ECS, SBA, and Gage, *History of Woman Suffrage,* 1: 61.

109. LCM to Richard and Hannah Webb, February 25, 1842, Mott Papers, FHL.

110. The *Liberator* subscription list noted that she subscribed in Johnstown from November 1841 to March 1844; moved her subscription from Albany to Chelsea, Massachusetts, in July 1844; and then to Seneca Falls in October 1847. Garrison Papers, BPL.

Chapter 3: Communities in Transition

1. Carol Sheriff, *The Artificial River: The Erie Canal and the Paradox of Progress, 1817–1862* (New York: Hill and Wang, 1996).

2. New York (State), Secretary of State, "Journal of Serg't Major George Grant," *Journals of the Military Expedition of Major General John Sullivan against the Six Nations of Indians in 1779* (1887; reprint, Freeport, N.Y.: Books for Libraries Press, 1972), 111; Alan Taylor, *William Cooper's Town: Power and Persuasion on the Frontier of the Early American Republic* (New York: A. A. Knopf, 1996).

3. John Delafield, "A General View and Agricultural Survey of the County of Seneca," *Transactions of the N.Y. State Agricultural Society* 10 (1850): 380–81; Barbara Graymont, *The Iroquois in the American Revolution* (Syracuse, N.Y.: Syracuse University Press, 1972).

4. D. W. Meinig, "Geography of Expansion, 1785–1855," in John Thompson, ed., *Geography of New York State* (Syracuse: Syracuse University Press, 1966), 140–71; Jack Campisi, "From Stanwix to Canandaigua: National Policy, States' Rights and Indians," in Christopher Vecsey and William A. Starna, eds., *Iroquois Land Claims* (Syracuse, N.Y.: Syracuse University Press, 1988), 49–65; Lau-

rence M. Hauptman, *Conspiracy of Interests: Iroquois Dispossession and the Rise of New York State* (Syracuse, N.Y.: Syracuse University Press, 1999).

5. Henry O'Reilly, *Sketches of Rochester* (Rochester, N.Y.: William Alling, 1838; reprint, Geneseo, N.Y.: James Brunner, 1984), 110–12, 120. Note by unidentified person on back of photograph of Bascom property, SFHS, identified the apple orchards as Cayuga in origin; Beach, "The Old Farm and the New," 23, noted the peach orchards on his family's farm. Delafield, "General View," 394, noted that Silas Halsey started the first nursery of fruit trees in Seneca County from apple seeds from an Indian orchard. Harrison Chamberlain, "Early Barrel and Boat Industries," *Papers, SFHS* (1908): 7; James Sanderson, "Some Early Recollections of Seneca Falls," *Papers, SFHS* (1911–12): 58; Stephen Burritt, "Early History," *Seneca Falls Reveille,* November 12, 1875.

6. Betty Auten, Seneca County Historian, noted that an Iroquois officer claimed land where the Polar Freeze ice cream stand stood along Route 20 in the 1980s; Sanford, "Early Industries," 42; Henry Stowell, "Historical Sketches of Seneca Falls," *Seneca Falls Reveille,* July 8, 1887; Delafield, "General View," 398.

7. Stowell, "Historical Sketches."

8. Chamberlain, "Early Flouring Mills," 31; Spafford, *Gazetteer* (Albany, N.Y.: B. D. Packard, 1824), 259–60; Winslow C. Watson, [Letter to Centennial Celebration], *Journals of the Military Expedition,* 512.

9. Whitney Cross, *The Burned-over District* (Ithaca, N.Y.: Cornell University Press, 1950), 67, noted that "the triangle of Pennsylvania migration extended into the heart of the region. Seneca County, for example, had the lowest percentage of Yankee nativity in western New York." See also James W. Darlington, "Peopling the Post-Revolutionary New York Frontier," *New York History* 74 (October 1993): 360–66.

10. Elizabeth M'Clintock to Mary Truman, July 9, 1838, WRNHP. Thanks to Anne Derousie and Vivien Rose for locating this letter. In 1856, rail connections reinforced the direct north-south route from Seneca Falls to Elmira to Philadelphia. *American Reveille,* April 5, 1856. Thanks to Marjorie Waters for sharing her research on her own family members who migrated from Ardee to Seneca Falls.

11. Caroline Lester, "Negro Residents of Seneca Falls in Bygone Days," *Papers, SFHS* (1943): 85–92; Hough, *Census of the State of New York for 1855,* xi; Judith Wellman, "This Side of the Border: Fugitives from Slavery in Three Central New York Communities," *New York History* 79(4) (1998): 359–92.

12. Fred Teller, "Early Roads," *Papers, SFHS* (1903): 1–10.

13. The Cayuga Bridge fell into the lake in 1807, was rebuilt in 1812–13, rebuilt again in 1833, and finally became unusable in 1854. Edward C. Eisenhart, "A Century of Seneca Falls History" (B.A. thesis, Princeton University, 1942), 28; Delafield, "General View," 411; B. F. Beach, "Seneca Falls Sixty or More Years Ago," *Papers, SFHS* (1903): 51; Stowell, "Historical Sketches"; Beach, "The Old Farm and the New," 25; Anna Henion, "The Old Stage Coach," *Papers, SFHS* (1913): 26–28.

14. Chamberlain, "Early Flouring Mills"; Letter from "Veridicus" [Robert Troup], July 22 or 23, 1810, in Blandina Dudley Miller, ed., *Observer* (n.p., n.d.), clipping in the Smith Papers, SyU.

15. Spafford, *Gazetteer* (1823): 259–60.

16. For general discussions of agriculture in upstate New York before the Civil War, see David Maldwyn Ellis, *Landlords and Farmers in the Hudson-Mohawk Region, 1790–1850* (1946; reprint, New York: Octagon Books, 1967); Neil McNall, *An Agricultural History of the Genesee Valley, 1790–1860* (Philadelphia: University of Pennsylvania Press, 1952, 1971); Percy Bidwell and John I. Falconer, *History of Agriculture in the Northern United States, 1620–1860* (1925; reprint, New York: P. Smith, 1941); Paul W. Gates, *The Farmer's Age—Agriculture, 1850–1860* (New York: Holt, Rinehart, Winston, 1960).

17. Delafield, "General View," 411, 418, 423, 493–98, 586; David C. Smith, "Middle Range Farming in the Civil War Era: Life on a Farm in Seneca County, 1862–1866," *New York History* 18 (October 1967): 352–69.

18. Delafield, "General View," 418, 530, 543–44.

19. Printed U.S. Censuses for 1840, 1850, 1860; *Census of the State of New York for 1845* (Albany: Carroll & Cook, 1846).

20. Chamberlain, "Five Pivotal Years," 19–25.

21. Stowell, "Historical Sketches."

22. *Seneca Farmer and Seneca Falls Advertiser,* August 15, 1832.

23. Deeds cited in Wellman, "Boundaries of the Stanton Lot," typescript, WRNHP, December 1986, 6.

24. Chamberlain, "Five Pivotal Years," 19–25; Burritt, "Early History"; David B. Lum, typescript, SFHS, 10.

25. Chamberlain, "Water Transportation and Packets."

26. "Seneca Falls in 1831," *Seneca Farmer and Seneca Falls Advertiser,* August 15, 1832; Spafford, *Gazetteer* (1824): 259–60; Thomas Gordon, *Gazetteer* (1836; reprint, Salem, Mass.: Higginson Book Co., 1990).

27. New mills included the Clinton Mills (1825–26), the Empire Mills (1830), the Stone Mills (1833), and the City Mills (1837), all on the north side. The Globe Mills were built on the south side in 1833; in the 1840s, two more were added. This count is based primarily on Chamberlain, "Early Flouring Mills."

28. "County of Seneca," *Census of the State of New York for 1835* (Albany: Croswell, Van Benthuysen, and Burt, 1836); J. D. B. De Bow, U.S. Census Office, *Statistical View of the United States: Embracing its Territory, Population—White, Free Colored, and Slave—Moral and Social Condition, Industry, Property, and Revenue* (1854; reprint, New York: Norman Ross Publications, 1990).

29. "County of Seneca," *Census of the State of New York for 1835;* "County of Seneca," *Census of the State of New York for 1845.*

30. Chamberlain, "Early Barrel and Boat Industries," 6–11.

31. Chamberlain, "Early Flouring Mills," 13, and "J. P. Chamberlain," 57.

32. Gordon, *Gazetteer,* 700; "County of Seneca," *Census of the State of New York for 1835;* Sanford, "Early Industries," 43.

33. Beach, "The Old Farm and the New," 23.

34. For general discussions of factory women, see Thomas Dublin, *Women at Work: The Transformation of Work and Community in Lowell, Massachusetts, 1825–1860* (New York: Columbia University Press, 1979), and Daniel Walkowitz, *Worker City: Company Town: Iron and Cotton-Worker Protest in Troy and Cohoes, New York, 1855–84* (Urbana: University of Illinois Press, 1978).

35. Mrs. S. A. Wetmore, "The Bayard Family," *Papers, SFHS* (1911–12): 67; Chamberlain, "Water Transportation and Packets," 5.

36. Chamberlain, "Five Pivotal Years," 24, noted that Hezekiah Kelley took the machinery and business to Buffalo, New York, in 1844; Claribel Teller, "An Historical Sketch of Horace Silsby," *Papers, SFHS* (1905): 19. *Census of the State of New York for 1855,* xxix, gives a summary of population statistics for each town in New York. The town of Seneca Falls grew 45 percent from 1830 to 1835 (from 2,603 to 3,786) and 13 percent from 1835 to 1840 (from 3,786 to 4,281). It then declined by 7 percent to 3,997 in 1845. From 1845 to 1850, it gained 9 percent to reach 4,297, just about its size a decade before.

37. J. H. French, *Gazetteer of the State of New York* (Syracuse, New York: R. P. Smith, 1860), 618.

38. *Census of the State of New York for 1855,* xxix.

39. In 1845, Seneca Falls grist mills earned only 42 percent of what they had earned in 1835, $21,018 in value added by manufacture in 1835, compared with $9,350 in 1845. "County of Seneca," *Census for the State of New York for 1835;* "County of Seneca," *Census for the State of New York for 1845.*

40. Walter Rostow, *Stages of Economic Growth: A Non-Communist Manifesto,* 2d ed. (Cambridge, England: Cambridge University Press, 1971).

41. *History of Seneca County* (Philadelphia: Everts, Ensign, and Everts, 1876), 109; incorporation records in Minute Book, SFHS; "County of Seneca," *Census of the State of New York for 1845;* Hen-

ry Stowell, "History of Seneca Falls, N.Y.," in *Brigham's Geneva, Seneca Falls and Waterloo Directory* (1862; reprint, Seneca Falls: Seneca Falls Historical Society, 1975), 22–23.

42. Chamberlain, "Early Industries," 36; *Union Advertiser,* July 11, 1848; Lum, typescript, SFHS, 15.

43. Stowell, "Historical Sketches"; *Seneca Falls Reveille,* July 8, 1887; *Census of the State of New York for 1845.*

44. Teller, "Horace Silsby," 19.

45. Chamberlain, "Five Pivotal Years," 1.

46. "Classification by Age and Sex," [Seneca County], *Census of the State of New York for 1855,* 48–49. In Seneca Falls, the number of women and men were just about equal for age groups between twenty and forty. In Waterloo, women outnumbered men through age thirty-four (from ages 20–24, 56 percent were women; 25–29, 54 percent; 30–34, 53 percent; and 35–39, 47 percent). Larger numbers of women than men often characterized mature areas as well as communities with textile factories.

47. "Industrial Schedule," Paris Township, Oneida County, New York State Manuscript Census, 1855.

48. These items were all advertised for sale at Woodworth's store and at Thomas and Ditmars (No. 2 Sackett's block, south side), *Seneca County Courier,* February 15, 1848, April 25, 1848, and elsewhere.

49. Spafford, "Seneca County," in *Gazetteer* (1813), 103; *New York State Census, 1835.*

50. Catherine Beecher, *Treatise on Domestic Economy* (Boston: T. H. Webb, 1842); Jane Nylander, *Our Own Snug Fireside: Images of the New England Home, 1760–1860* (New York: Alfred Knopf, 1993).

51. Joan M. Jensen, *Loosening the Bonds: Mid-Atlantic Farm Women, 1750–1850* (New Haven, Conn.: Yale University Press, 1986).

52. Sanderson, "Some Early Recollections of Seneca Falls," 58; Fred Teller, "Union Hall, Daniels Hall, Daniels Opera House and Other Amusement Halls of Seneca Falls," *Papers, SFHS* (1905): 37; Teller, "Horace Silsby," 19.

53. Patricia C. Rupert, "Working Women in Oswego, 1915 and 1925" (M.A. thesis, State University of New York at Oswego, 1979).

54. Ruth Schwartz Cowan, *More Work for Mother: The Ironies of Household Technology from the Open Hearth to the Microwave* (New York: Basic Books, 1983).

55. William Keith, "Account Book," SFHS; Janet McKay Cowing, "Some Early Advertisements," *Papers, SFHS* (1913): 61.

56. Chamberlain, "Early Barrel and Boat Industries," 7; Sanford, "Early Industries," 43 and 38, mentioned Joshua Martin and Jedidiah Coleman; Stowell, "Historical Sketches"; Chamberlain, "Five Pivotal Years," 21.

57. Janet Cowing and Sheldron F. Frazier, "Early Churches," *Papers, SFHS* (1903): 27–34; *History of Seneca County,* 113–14. Cornell University has a microfilm collection of many of the manuscript records for these churches, including records for the Waterloo Missionary Society, 1817–24.

58. Thomas Kane, *A Lasting City* (Seneca Fall, N.Y.: [St. Patrick's Church], 1956), 12.

59. *The New York Catholic Diary,* May 21, 1835, quoted in Kane, *A Lasting City,* 13; Albert W. Golder, "Records of the Methodist Church in Seneca Falls," *Papers, SFHS* (1906): 1–3. Presbyterians sold slips in their new church when it opened in November 1842, although it is not clear whether most of the purchasers were church members. See *Seneca Falls Democrat,* November 24, 1842. The Wesleyan Methodists kept the seats in their new building, completed in October 1843, open and free, partly at the insistence of a major donor, Joseph Metcalf.

60. Cross, *Burned-over District;* Charles Grandison Finney, *Memoirs of Rev. Charles G. Finney* (New York: A. S. Barnes, 1876); Anne Boylan, *Sunday School: The Formation of an American Institution, 1790–1880* (New Haven, Conn.: Yale University Press, 1988); Lois Banner, "Religious Benevolence as Social Control: A Critique of an Interpretation," *Journal of American History* 60(1) (1973): 23–41.

61. Proceedings of Waterloo Missionary Society, 1817–1824, microfilm, Olin Library, Cornell.

62. Newland, "The First Baptist Church," 75, reported Knapp's work in Seneca Falls and Sunday School attendance; Golder, "Methodist Church in Seneca Falls." See also "Records of the Baptist Sunday School," manuscript, SFHS, and typescript of Methodist Episcopal Church records, SFHS. For a regional context for women's benevolent reform work, see Carol Brown Kaulfuss, "'Remember the Cause': The Female Missionary Society of the Western District, A Study in Women's Involvement in Early Antebellum Benevolent Reform, 1806–1832" (M.A. thesis, State University of New York at Oswego, 1977).

63. For a discussion of debates about women praying in public, see Keith J. Hardman, *Charles Grandison Finney, 1972–1875* (Syracuse, N.Y.: Syracuse University Press, 1987), 88, 101–3, 127, 138.

64. Proceedings of Waterloo Missionary Society, and Records, Female Sewing Society, 1837–38, microfilm, Olin Library, Cornell.

65. "The Fourth of July," July 9, 1840, *Seneca Falls Democrat;* July 8, 1841, *Seneca County Courier.*

66. "Celebration of the 4th of July in Seneca Falls by the Sunday Schools," July 7, 1841, *Seneca Falls Democrat.*

67. *Water Bucket,* May 6, 1842; June 10, 1842.

68. *Water Bucket,* March 11, 1842; March 25, 1842. Dexter Bloomer, ed., *Life and Writings of Amelia Bloomer* (1895; reprint, New York: Schocken Books, 1975), 16, 20.

69. *Water Bucket,* April 8, 1842; May 6, 1842.

70. *Water Bucket,* February 25, 1842.

71. *Water Bucket,* February 24, 1843. John Timmerman is identified in Glen Altschuler and Jan Saltzgaber, eds., *Revivalism, Social Conscience, and Community in the Burned-over District: The Trial of Rhoda Bement* (Ithaca, N.Y: Cornell University Press, 1983), 86.

72. *Water Bucket,* August 5, 1842.

73. Quotation from Methodist Church records, in "Historical Record," *Seneca Falls Reveille,* May 3, 1929; Newland, "The First Baptist Church," 75.

74. *Water Bucket,* March 11, 1842; April 1, 1842.

75. *Water Bucket,* March 25, 1842.

76. *Water Bucket,* July 8, 1842.

77. *Water Bucket,* July 8, 1842.

78. *Water Bucket,* July 8, 1842.

79. *Seneca Falls Democrat,* December 24, 1840; April 22, 1841.

80. *Seneca Falls Democrat,* March 25, 1841; December 22, 1842; December 19, 1842. Other phrenologists also lectured in Seneca Falls, including Mr. Rousmaniere, in March 1842 (*Seneca Falls Democrat,* March 31, 1842) and C. S. Chase, in 1846 and 1847 (*Seneca County Courier,* February 23, 1847).

81. Elias Lester, "The Medical Profession," *Papers, SFHS* (1908). Discussions of debates about the merits of homeopathy appeared regularly in the *Seneca Falls Democrat.* See, for example, July 29, 1841, and June 15, 1843.

82. *Seneca Falls Democrat,* August 15, 1842.

83. *Seneca Falls Democrat,* January 19, 1843.

Chapter 4: Minding the Light

1. Ora B. Kearns, "McClintock Family Records," 2 vols., typescript (Syracuse, N.Y., 1985), Onondaga County Public Library; Minutes, Women's Meeting of Junius Monthly Meeting of Friends, March 26, 1845, FHL. All minutes of Quaker meetings are in Friends Historical Library, Swarthmore College, unless otherwise noted.

2. Minutes, Women's Meeting, Junius, March 26, 1846.

3. Giles B. Stebbins, "Henry Bonnell and the Waterloo Meeting of the Friends of Human Progress," *Free Thought Magazine* 13 (1895): 49. Thanks to Christopher Densmore for finding this.

4. *Seneca County Courier,* July 11 and July 14, 1848.

5. Nathaniel Potter to Amy Post, October 7, 1843, Post Family Papers, UR.

6. Nathaniel Potter to Amy Post, October 7, 1843, Post Family Papers, UR. Nancy Hewitt developed the idea that withdrawal from Quaker meetings led to new energy in larger reform movements in "The Fragmentation of Friends: The Consequences for Quaker Women in Antebellum America," in Elisabeth Potts Brown and Susan Mosher Stuard, eds., *Witnesses for Change: Quaker Women Over Three Centuries* (New Brunswick, N.J.: Rutgers University Press, 1989), 93–108. For a general discussion of Quakerism within New York Yearly Meeting, see Hugh Barbour, Christopher Densmore et al., eds., *Quaker Crosscurrents: Three Hundred Years of Friends in the New York Yearly Meetings* (Syracuse, N.Y.: Syracuse University Press, 1995). In this volume, Nancy Hewitt and others focused on issues relating to women, 165–82.

7. John Becker, comp., *Some Waterloo Citizens of Yesterday* (Waterloo, 1950), unpublished typescript, Waterloo Historical Society, partly based on an article in the *Waterloo Observer,* June 21, 1876; "Mansion House," *History of Seneca County,* opposite p. 81. For a detailed study of Hunt's land holdings, see Chad Garrett Randl, "Richard P. Hunt: Leader in Waterloo Real Estate and Business," paper presented to WRNHP, December 15, 1999.

8. Although earlier accounts consistently identified Sarah M'Clintock as Thomas's sister, Gene Ballentine Rooks has argued that she was the daughter of Thomas's brother Samuel. Rooks, "M'Clintock Genealogy," e-mail to Anne Derousie, historian, WRNHP, August 2001. Thomas M'Clintock, *Observations on the Articles Published in the Episcopal Recorder Over the Signature of "A Member of the Society of Friends"* (New York: Isaac T. Hopper, 1837).

9. Kearns, "McClintock Family Records"; M'Clintock marriage certificate, in possession of Charles W. M'Clintock; Christopher Densmore and Judith Wellman, "The M'Clintock Family," in *American National Biography* (New York: Oxford University Press, 1999), 15: 148–49.

10. *Seneca Observer,* December 15, 1836, quoted in John E. Becker, *A History of the Village of Waterloo, New York* (Waterloo, N.Y.: Waterloo Library and Historical Society, 1949), 135.

11. *Seneca Observer,* December 2, 1839; Giles B. Stebbins, *Upward Steps of Seventy Years* (New York: United States Book Co., 1890), 70; *Seneca County Courier,* October 10, 1850 (comment dated December 31, 1849); Susan Mooring Hollis, *Historic Resources Survey, Village of Waterloo, Seneca County, New York* (Ithaca, N.Y.: Cornell University College of Architecture, Art, and Planning, 1982). Elizabeth M'Clintock listed her occupation for the census taker in 1850 as "clerk." This is the only woman, among thousands of names I have looked at in the 1850 census, whose occupation was listed. New York, vols. 69, 140, R. G. Dun and Co. Collection, Baker Library, Harvard Business School; *New York Tribune,* June 16, 1855.

12. *Seneca Observer,* October 30, 1839; letter to author from Betty Auten, December 5, 1980; *Annual Catalogue of the Officers and Students of Waterloo Academy, for the Year, Ending June, 1844* (Waterloo: Pew and Marsh, 1844).

13. Joseph Schuchman, "McClintock House/Waterloo Baptist Church Nursery," in Hollis, *Historic Resources Survey,* 368–70; Barbara A. Yocum, *The M'Clintock House: Historic Structure Report, Women's Rights National Historical Park, Waterloo, New York* (Lowell, Mass.: U.S. Department of the Interior, National Park Service, 1993).

14. Gilbert Cope, ed. and comp., *Genealogy of the Darlington Family* (West Chester, Pa., 1900), 99–100; Elisabeth Dunbar, "Unity of Purpose, Freedom for the Individual: The M'Clintock Family of Philadelphia, Pennsylvania and Waterloo, New York" (unpublished paper, State University of New York at Oswego, 1997).

15. Nancy A. Hewitt, "Amy Kirby Post," *University of Rochester Library Bulletin* 37 (1984): 4–21; "Mrs. Amy Post at Rest," *Rochester Democrat and Chronicle,* January 30, 1889; "Isaac Post," *Dictionary of American Biography* 8 (1935): 117; "Death of Isaac Post," *Rochester Democrat and Chronicle,* May 10, 1872.

16. "Register," Rochester Monthly Meeting, noted that Amy and Isaac Post were received as members by certificate on June 24, 1836, along with children Mary, Jacob, Joseph, and Henry.

17. R. G. Dun and Co. Collection, Baker Library, Harvard Business School; Hewitt, "Amy Kirby Post," 9.

18. J. M. Parker, *Rochester: A Story Historical* (1884), 258, quoted in "Isaac Post," *Dictionary of American Biography*, 8: 117.

19. Catharine W. Morris and Mary Elliott to Martha Pelham, January 17, 1825, reprinted in Eliza Wright Osborne, "A Recollection of Martha Coffin Wright by her Daughter," typescript in possession of L. Devens Osborne (great-great-grandson of Martha Wright), 7; M. C. Pelham [Wright] to "Dear friends," April 4, 1825, Garrison Papers, Smith.

20. Paul Messbarger, "Martha Coffin Pelham Wright," in James, James, and Boyer, *Notable American Women*, 3: 684–65; Eliza Wright Osborne, "My Mother, Martha Coffin," n.d., Osborne Papers, SyU; David Wright, [Sketch of His Own Life], typescript, Garrison Papers, Smith; Theodore M. Pomery, "Sketch of the Life and Character of Mr. David Wright" (1898), typescript, Garrison Papers, Smith; Anne L. Hoblitzelle, "The Ambivalent Message: Sex-role Training in Mid-19th Century United States as Reflected in the Correspondence of Martha Coffin Wright to Ellen Wright Garrison" (M.A. thesis, Sarah Lawrence College, May 1974). See also Amy Cardamone, "A Commitment to Practical Righteousness," and Alan D. Myers, "The Writings of Martha Coffin Pelham Wright" (unpublished papers, State University of New York at Oswego, 1982); Connie Hasto, "Martha Wright: A Restricted Analysis of True Love and Perfect Union" (unpublished paper, Binghamton University, 1982).

21. Osborne, "My Mother, Martha Coffin"; W.L.G. [perhaps William Lloyd Garrison, Jr.], "A Sharp Bereavement," *Woman's Journal*, January 9, 1875; ECS, "Martha C. Wright," typescript, Osborne Papers, SyU.

22. ECS, "Martha C. Wright."

23. Osborne, "My Mother, Martha Coffin."

24. Steven Mintz and Susan Kellogg, *Domestic Revolutions: A Social History of American Family Life* (New York: Free Press, 1988); Stephanie Coontz, *The Social Origins of Private Life: A History of American Families, 1600–1900* (London: Verso, 1988).

25. Karen Sacks [Brodkin], *Sisters and Wives: The Past and Future of Sexual Equality* (Urbana: University of Illinois Press, 1982); Francis L. K. Hsu, *Kinship and Culture* (Chicago: Aldine Publishing Co., 1971).

26. Notes made by Charles and Doris McClintock for Christopher Densmore, November 24, 1993; Herbert Gutman, *Black Family in Slavery and Freedom, 1750–1925* (New York: Pantheon Books, 1976).

27. Phoebe Post Willis to Isaac and Amy Post, October 14, 1838, Post Family Papers, UR.

28. Mary Kirby to Amy Post, February 20, 1838, Post Family Papers, UR.

29. Osborne, "My Mother, Martha Coffin"; Martha Wright to LCM, March 11, 1844, Garrison Papers, Smith.

30. Bacon, *Valiant Friend*, 109.

31. Thanks to John Genung for his assistance with Hunt family genealogy. "Hannah Hunt," and "Lydia Hunt," Weltha Bacon Woodward, *Bacon-Woodward, Pedigree of Paternal Branch*, vol. 1, series 6, unpublished typescript (1968), 409–13. After Lydia's husband, Randolph Mount, died of consumption in 1842, Lydia moved to 100 East Williams Street, Waterloo, with her three children, all young girls. The oldest daughter, Mary Elenor Mount, married Gilbert Vail in 1844 when she was only seventeen years old. Richard P. Hunt helped to educate the other two at a boarding school in Ithaca. In 1850, Lydia Hunt Mount owned $13,800 worth of real estate.

32. William C. Nell to Posts, March 16, 1855, Post Family Papers, UR; Wright to LCM, April 1, 1849, Garrison Papers, Smith; Osborne, "My Mother, Martha Coffin."

33. [Thomas Mumford], "Thomas M'Clintock," *Christian Register*, March 25, 1876. Thanks to Christopher Densmore for this citation.

34. For more on European American colonial families, see David Hackett Fischer, *Albion's Seed: Four British Folkways in America* (New York: Oxford, 1989), 432–33; Mintz and Kellogg, *Domestic Revolutions;* Barry Levy, *Quakers and the American Family: British Settlement in the Delaware Valley* (New York: Oxford University Press, 1988); J. William Frost, *The Quaker Family in Colonial America* (New York: St. Martin's Press, 1973).

35. [Thomas Mumford], "Thomas M'Clintock," *Christian Register,* March 25, 1876. Thanks to Christopher Densmore for finding this article. Margaret Hope Bacon, *Mothers of Feminism: The Story of Quaker Women in America* (San Francisco: Harper and Row, 1986), 112.

36. "Marriage Certificate, Thomas M'Clintock and Mary Ann Wilson, Recorded at Burlington in Book B," manuscript in possession of Charles W. McClintock.

37. Charles Bonnel and Deanna Dell marriage certificate, Junius Monthly Meeting, "A Record"; Joni Masuicca, "Notes on M'Clintock Family," typescript, WRNHP; gravestone for Rachel Dell Bonnell, Junius Monthly Meeting cemetery, Nine-Foot Road, Waterloo.

38. Nell to Amy Post, March 11, 1853, Post Family Papers, UR; Martha Coffin Wright to David Wright, October 23, 1839, Garrison Papers, Smith.

39. Extant records for the Junius Monthly Meeting of Friends are incomplete, but they do not include Richard P. Hunt's name. Local people always identified him as a Quaker, however, and he was originally buried in the Quaker cemetery in Waterloo. His body was later removed to Maple Grove Cemetery. ECS, "Henry Bonnell and the Waterloo Meeting of the Friends of Human Progress," *Free Thought Magazine* 13 (1895): 49–50. Hunt's sisters joined St. Paul's Episcopal Church in Waterloo. About 1950, John E. Becker talked to Hunt's grandson Richard P. Hunt and noted that "Richard P. Hunt was a Quaker, a rather belligerent Quaker who believed in accomplishment." Becker, *Some Waterloo Citizens of Yesterday.* Woodward, *Bacon-Woodward, Pedigree of Paternal Branch,* 413.

40. Wright to LCM, March 11, 1844, Garrison Papers, Smith.

41. LCM to Phoebe Post Willis, March 10, 1835, Post Family Papers, UR.

42. George Fox, *Journal of George Fox,* John L. Nickalls, ed. (London: Religious Society of Friends, 1975), 11; Margaret Fell Fox, quoting George Fox, 1694, in London Yearly Meeting, *Christian Faith and Practice* (Richmond, Ind.: Friends United Press, c. 1960); Howard H. Brinton, *Friends for 300 Years* (Philadelphia: Pendle Hill Publications, 1952), 20.

43. Brinton, *Friends,* 14.

44. "Every creature under heaven" from Col. 1:23; "Light and Spirit of God," from Fox, quoted in Brinton, *Friends,* 185; "wars," quoted in Margaret Hope Bacon, *The Quiet Rebels: The Story of the Quakers in America* (New York: Basic Books, 1969), 17; "unity with the creation," Fox, *Journal,* 2. For more on Quaker universalism, see Brinton, *Friends,* 36–39; General Meeting at Skipton for Friends in the North, 1659, *Letters Etc. of Early Friends,* 282, quoted in Brinton, *Friends,* 100.

45. Bacon, *Quiet Rebels,* 94–121.

46. Bacon, *Mothers of Feminism,* 11–17.

47. Hewitt, "Fragmentation of Friends," 93–108; Rufus M. Jones, *The Later Periods of Quakerism,* 2 vols. (London: Macmillan and Co., 1921; reprint, Westport, Conn.: Greenwood Press, 1970), 488; Elbert Russell, *The History of Quakerism* (Richmond, Ind.: Friends United Press, 1979).

48. Robert W. Doherty, *The Hicksite Separation: A Sociological Analysis of Religious Schism in Early Nineteenth Century America* (New Brunswick, N.J.: Rutgers University Press, 1967); H. Larry Ingle, *Quakers in Conflict: The Hicksite Reformation* (Knoxville: University of Tennessee Press, 1986); J. William Frost, "Years of Crisis and Separation: Philadelphia Yearly Meeting, 1790–1860," in *Friends in the Delaware Valley,* John M. Moore, ed. (Haverford, Pa.: Friends Historical Association, 1981), 57–102; Thomas D. Hamm, *The Transformation of American Quakerism, Orthodox Friends, 1800–1907* (Bloomington: Indiana University Press, 1992); *The Testimony of the Society of Friends [Orthodox], on the Continent of America* (Philadelphia, 1830). See also Kathryn Kish Sklar, "'Women Who Speak for an Entire Nation': American and British Women at the World Anti-Slavery Convention, London, 1840," in Jean Fagan Yellin and John C. Van Horne, eds., *The Abolitionist Sisterhood* (Ithaca, N.Y.: Cornell University Press, 1994).

49. Ingle, *Quakers in Conflict,* 63, 53; M'Clintock correspondence with William Poole, Swarthmore, one of which is printed in H. Larry Ingle, "The Hicksite Die Is Cast: A Letter of Thomas McClintock, February 1827," *Quaker History* 75(2) (Fall 1986): 115–22; Densmore and Wellman, "The M'Clintock Family"; LCM to Phoebe Post Willis, March 10, 1835, Post Family Papers, UR.

50. M'Clintock, *Observations on the Articles Published in the Episcopal Recorder,* 34–36.

51. Cowing and Frazier, "Early Churches," 28–29; Adah Brown Adams, in Mrs. Sidney A. Eshenour, *Seneca County News,* January 25, 1934.

52. "History of the Bonnel Family," typescript, Waterloo Library and Historical Society; Frothingham, *Gerrit Smith,* 56; U.S. Manuscript Census, 1850.

53. Catharine Fish Stebbins was received into Rochester Monthly Meeting May 29, 1829, Rochester MM Records; "Mrs. Catharine A. F. Stebbins," *American Women,* vol. 2 (1973), 681. Giles B. Stebbins to William R. Hallowell, August 7, 1846, Post Family Papers, UR.

54. Martha Wright to LCM, April 5, 1841, Garrison Papers, Smith.

55. *Seneca Falls Democrat,* November 16, 1843. Abby Kelley to Stephen S. Foster, August 13, 1843, Abby Kelley Foster Papers, AAS.

56. John A. Collins, John Orvis, N. H. Whiting, John O. Wattles, *Syracuse Standard,* August 23, 1843, and *Liberator,* October 13, 1843. Thanks to Sally Roesch Wagner for the citation in the *Standard.* Thomas M'Clintock to J. A. Collins, June 22, 1843, *Liberator,* September 29, 1843; Joseph Savage, Lydia P. Savage, Stephen Shear, George Pryor, Margaret Pryor, Charles White, and Charles Hart to John A. Collins, August 16, 1843, *Liberator,* September 29, 1843.

57. Martha Wright to LCM, March 11, 1844, and September 23, 1844, Garrison Papers, Smith; H. Roger Grant, ed., "The Skaneateles Community: A New York Utopia," *Niagara Frontier* 222(3) (1975): 68–72; Lester Grosvenor Wells, *The Skaneateles Communal Experiment, 1843–1846* (Syracuse, N.Y.: Onondaga Historical Association, 1953).

58. *Friend; or Advocate of Truth* 4(10) (October, 1831): 153.

59. "Women's Meetings for Discipline," *Discipline of the Yearly Meeting of Friends, Held in New-York For the State of New-York, and parts adjacent, revised, in the sixth month, 1810* (New York, 1830), 16–19.

60. Genesee Yearly Meeting Minutes, June 11, 1838, FHL; *Discipline of Genesee Yearly Meeting* (Rochester, N.Y., 1842), 11; Christopher Densmore, "The Quaker Tradition: Sustaining Women's Rights," National Women's Studies Association, 1998, available at <http://ublib.buffalo.edu/libraries/units/archives/urr/>.

61. Mary Robbins Post to Isaac Post, 1838, Post Family Papers, UR.

62. "Letter from Jacob Ferris," *National Anti-Slavery Standard,* July 22, 1841, cited in Christopher Densmore, "Quaker Comeouters and the Seneca Falls Women's Rights Convention of 1848" (paper presented at the Conference on New York State History, June 4–5, 1993).

63. Bacon, *Valiant Friend,* 39; Martha Wright to LCM, n.d., [early 1850s], Garrison Papers, Smith.

64. Martha Wright to LCM, May 13, 1846, Garrison Papers, Smith.

65. Martha Wright to LCM, January 27, 1846, Garrison Papers, Smith.

66. Martha Wright to LCM, January 1, 1846, Garrison Papers, Smith.

67. Anthony F. C. Wallace, *Death and Rebirth of the Seneca* (New York: Alfred Knopf, 1970); Judith Brown, "Economic Organization and the Position of Women Among the Iroquois," *Ethnohistory* 17:3–4 (1970); Joan Jensen, "Native American Women and Agriculture: A Seneca Case Study," *Sex Roles* 3 (1977): 423–41; M. Holly, "Handsome Lake's Teaching: The Shift from Female to Male Agriculture in Iroquois Culture: An Essay in Ethnophilosophy," *Agriculture and Human Values* 7:3–4 (1990): 80–94. Significant articles relating to Iroquois women have been reprinted in W. G. Spittal, ed., *Iroquois Women: An Anthology* (Ohsweken, Ontario: Iroqrafts, 1990).

68. "Friends in Commotion," E.W.C. to William Lloyd Garrison, Walworth, N.Y., October 28, 1842, *Liberator,* December 2, 1842; petition from Rush, New York, February 5, 1841, National Archives, [petition sent to the House of Representatives], Box 74; petitions from Cayuga County, National Archives, HR 27A-H1.6.

69. Minerva BlackSmith and others to John Tyler, Tonawanda, March 14, 1842, Post Family Papers, UR. Christopher Vecsey and William A. Starna, eds., *Iroquois Land Claims* (Syracuse, N.Y.: Syracuse University Press, 1988), 9–10. "Mrs. Amy Post at Rest," *Democrat and Chronicle,* January 30, 1889, noted, "She was especially interested in the condition of the Indians on the state reserva-

tions, and an Indian named Blind John has annually visited her house from the Cattaraugus Reservation." Letters from fellow Quakers to the Posts often adopted Iroquois phrases. John Ketcham spoke of "the great Council fire of the A.A.S. Society in N. York," for example (Ketcham to Posts, June 1, 1842, Post Family Papers, UR). Oliver Johnson closed one letter with "let the chain of friendship between us be kept bright" (Johnson to Isaac Post, June 7, 1842, Post Family Papers, UR). For a less sanguine view of Quakers and the 1842 treaty, see Laurence M. Hauptman, "The State's Men, the Salvation Seekers, and the Seneca: The Supplemental Treaty of Buffalo Creek, 1842," *New York History* (January 1997): 51–82.

70. Ruth Ketring Nuermberger, *The Free Produce Movement* (Durham, N.C.: Duke University Press, 1942), 14; M'Clintock advertisements in the *Seneca Observer,* noted in Becker, *History of Waterloo,* 135; obituary of Sarah Hunt, *National Anti-Slavery Standard,* October 30, 1842, cited in Christopher Densmore, "Quaker History and Woman's Rights Tour, Friends General Conference Gathering at Rochester, New York, July 3–5, 2000," unpublished typescript.

71. "Auxiliaries to the American Anti-Slavery Society, 1836," in Wright Papers, LC; J. C. Hathaway to *National Anti-Slavery Standard,* July 30, 1846; Christopher Densmore, "The Dilemma of Quaker Anti-Slavery: The Case of Farmington Quarterly Meeting, 1836–1860," *Quaker History* 82(2) (Fall 1993): 80–91; *Seneca Observer,* November 11, 1843, noted that temperance meetings were held at "T. M'Clintock's School Room," quoted in "Thomas McClintock," in Becker, *Some Waterloo Citizens of Yesterday;* "Convention of Western New York," *Friend of Man,* March 20,1839.

72. "Auxiliaries to the American Anti-Slavery Society, 1835," Wright Papers, LC; *Liberator,* June 23, 1837, and September 30, 1837, noted in Hewitt, *Women's Activism,* 92.

73. Petitions dated February 4,10, and 18, 1839, National Archives, HR25-H1.8; membership list of First Presbyterian Church of Waterloo, in Records, 1817–1935, Olin Library, Cornell; St. Paul's Episcopal Church of Waterloo, Records, 1817–1893, Olin Library, Cornell University.

74. There may also have been another petition, received from 248 males in 1850. It is not clear whether this was from the Waterloo area. These petitions are all in the National Archives, in Congressional petition boxes 108 and 137 from the Library of Congress or filed under Sen. 25A-H. 80, HR25-H1.8, HR30A-G9.2, HR31A-G4.1, or HR31A-G23.1.

75. National Archives, HR24A-H1.8, February 27, 1836; Petition of the Women of Western New York, HR25A-H1.7, box 83, September 19, 1837, noted in Hewitt, "Amy Kirby Post," 20; HR25A-H1.7, dated December 22, 1838, and received in the House on January 7, 1839.

76. "Mr. Garrison—His Past Course and Present Position," Thomas M'Clintock to Oliver Johnson, Waterloo, September 12, 1839, and James C. Jackson to "two women of this vicinity," Peterboro, August 18, 1839, *Liberator,* September 27, 1839; Garrison to M'Clintock, May 1, 1840, McClintock-Neeley Papers, WRNHP.

77. William Lloyd Garrison to Richard P. Hunt, May 1, 1840, No. 1818, in Ruchames, *Letters of William Lloyd Garrison,* 2: 594–95; Garrison to Thomas M'Clintock, May 1, 1840, McClintock-Neeley Collection, WRNHP; *Liberator,* January 6, 1843; Gerrit Smith to Richard P. Hunt, October 28, 1842, Smith Papers, SyU; Oliver Johnson to [James C.? or Francis?] Jackson, December 8, 1847, with enclosure to Richard P. Hunt, Garrison Papers, BPL.

78. Thomas M'Clintock, "To the Association of Friends for advocating the cause of the slave, and improving the condition of the Free People of Color," Waterloo, May 9, 1840, reprinted in *National Anti-Slavery Standard,* July 16, 1840; M'Clintock to the Editors of the *National A.S. Standard,* Waterloo, July 23, 1840.

79. List of agents in the *Liberator,* June 3, 1842.

80. [Thomas Mumford], "Thomas M'Clintock"; Stebbins, *Upward Steps of Seventy Years,* 70–71; *Seneca County Reveille,* July 7, 1856.

81. Bacon, *Valiant Friend,* 40, 52, 84, 101, 103; Isaac Hopper to Joseph Dugdale, September 3, 1841, Dugdale Papers, Swarthmore; ECS, "Lucretia Mott," in ECS, SBA, and Gage, *History of Woman Suffrage,* 1: 414.

82. John Ketcham to Amy and Isaac Post, March 11, 1841, Post Family Papers, UR.

83. Abby Kelley to Uxbridge Monthly Meeting of Friends, March 22, 1841, copy enclosed in Abby Kelley to William Lloyd Garrison, September 30, 1841, Garrison Papers, BPL.

84. Sterling, *Ahead of Her Time,* 139–44, 147–48; *Liberator,* August 12, 1842, and several other issues published notices of the conventions.

85. *Liberator,* July 15, 1842, July 29, 1842, August 5, 1842, August 12, 1842.

86. *Liberator,* August 12, 1842; *New York Express* report of the American Anti-Slavery Society's annual meeting, quoted in the *Liberator,* May 13, 1843.

87. Abby Kelley to Maria Weston Chapman, August 13, 1843, Kelley Foster Papers, AAS.

88. Abby Kelley to Maria Weston Chapman, August 13, 1843, Kelley Foster Papers, AAS.

89. *Liberator,* August 12, 1842, September 2, 1842, and September 23, 1842.

90. "Our Cause in Western New-York," *Liberator,* September 30, 1842. "Letter from Abby Kelley," April 10, 1843, reprinted from the *National Anti-Slavery Standard* in the *Liberator,* May 5, 1843.

91. November 21, 1842, No. 47, in Walter Merrill ed., *Letters of William Lloyd Garrison,* vol. 3, *No Union with the Slaveholders, 1841–1849* (Cambridge, Mass.: Belknap Press, 1974), 108–10.

92. "Convention at Utica," *Liberator,* December 23, 1842; "Interesting Report of the Anti-Slavery Convention," "Utica Convention," and "The Abolition Convention," *Liberator,* December 30, 1842; "American Anti-Slavery Society," *Liberator,* January 6 [5], 1843; Hewitt, *Women's Activism,* 108; *Liberator,* February 3, 1843.

93. William Lloyd Garrison to Helen E. Garrison, November 21, 1842, *Garrison Papers,* 3(47) (1973): 108–10.

94. *Liberator,* January 5, 1843.

95. "American Anti-Slavery Society," *Liberator,* January 5, 1843; Sarah Burtis to Abby Kelley, January 17, 1843; E. I. Neall to Abby Kelley, March 12, 1843, Abby Kelley Foster Papers, AAS.

96. Elizabeth M'Clintock to Abby Kelley, January 10, 1843; Sarah Burtis to Abby Kelley, January 17, 1843, Abby Kelley Foster Papers, AAS. For more on fairs, see Van Broekhoven, *Devotion of These Women,* and Lee Chambers-Shiller, "'A Good Work Among the People': The Political Culture of the Boston Antislavery Fair," in Jean Fagan Yellin and John C. Van Horne, eds., *The Abolitionist Sisterhood* (Ithaca, N.Y.: Cornell University Press, 1994): 249–74.

97. "Western New-York Anti-Slavery Fair, to Be Held in Rochester, February 22d, 1843," *National Anti-Slavery Standard,* February 2, 1843.

98. John C. Hathaway to Abby Kelley, February 16, 1843; Elizabeth Neall to Abby Kelley, March 12, 1843, Abby Kelley Foster Papers, AAS.

99. "Western New-York Anti-Slavery Fair, to Be Held in Rochester, February 22d, 1843," *National Anti-Slavery Standard,* February 2, 1843.

100. *National Anti-Slavery Standard,* February 2, 1843; Lucy Colman, *Reminiscences* (Buffalo: H. L. Green, 1891), 84, quoted in Hewitt, "Amy Kirby Post," 9; Nathaniel Potter to Amy Post, October 7, 1843, Post Family Papers, UR.

101. Amy Post to Abby Kelley, December 4, 1843, Abby Kelley Foster Papers, AAS.

102. *Seneca Observer,* October 3, 1843.

103. Mary [M'Clintock, probably the daughter] to Amy Post, February 9, 1847, Post Family Papers, UR; William H. Seward to Thomas M'Clintock, March 20, 1847, McClintock-Neeley Papers, WRNHP.

104. Amy Post to Elizabeth Pease, March 25, 1846, Garrison Papers, BPL.

105. Amy Post to Maria W. Chapman, May 1, 1846, Garrison Papers, BPL.

106. Amy Post to Abby Kelley, December 4, 1843, Abby Kelley Foster Papers, AAS; Post to Chapman, May 1, 1846, Garrison Papers, BPL; advertisement for Rochester Anti-Slavery Fair, *North Star,* December 3, 1847.

107. Sterling, *Ahead of Her Time,* 169; report on the May meeting from the *New York Express,* reprinted in the *Liberator,* May 19, 1843; report from the *National Anti-Slavery Standard,* printed in the *Liberator,* May 26, 1843; Densmore and Wellman, "The M'Clintock Family."

108. Frederick Douglass, *Life and Times of Frederick Douglass* (1892; reprint, New York: Macmil-

lan, 1962), 266; Amy Post, "The Underground Railroad," in William F. Peck, *Semi-Centennial History of the City of Rochester* (Syracuse, N.Y.: Mason and Co., 1884), 458–62; Harriet Jacobs, *Incidents in the Life of a Slave Girl,* ed. Jean Fagan Yellin (Cambridge, Mass.: Harvard University Press, 1987).

109. Martha Wright to LCM, November 19, 1841, Garrison Papers, Smith; Judith Wellman, "This Side of the Border: Fugitives from Slavery in Three Central New York Communities," *New York History* 79(4) (1998): 359–92.

110. Becker, "Richard P. Hunt," *Waterloo Citizens of Yesterday;* Anonymous to the *Journal,* 8 mo. 30, 1876, reprinted from *Christian Register,* [3 mo 25, 1876]. Thanks to Christopher Densmore for locating this.

111. Martha Wright to LCM, January 11, 1843, Garrison Papers, Smith.

112. Samuel Lundy to Isaac and Amy Post, August 16, 1837, Post Family Papers, UR; Thomas M'Clintock to Isaac Post, September 28, 1839, Post Family Papers, UR; M'Clintock to Garrison, October 1, 1847, Garrison Papers, BPL; and M'Clintock to H. C. Wright and Garrison, January 8, 1848, Garrison Papers, BPL.

113. Jeremiah B. Sanderson to Amy Post, April 8, 1845, and William C. Nell to Amy Post, August 11, 1849, Post Family Papers, UR. Benjamin Quarles, *Frederick Douglass* (New York: Athenaum, 1970), 27; Douglass, *Life and Times,* 229.

114. Sanderson to Amy Post, May 8, 1845, and William C. Nell to Amy Post, August 11, 1849, Post Family Papers, UR; Philip S. Foner, ed., *Frederick Douglass on Women's Rights* (Westport, Conn.: Greenwood Press, 1976); Philip S. Foner, *The Life and Writings of Frederick Douglass, Early Years, 1817–1849* (New York: International Publishers, 1950).

115. E. W. Capron to William Lloyd Garrison, January 21, 1842, *Liberator,* February 10, 1843; Nathaniel Potter to Amy Post, November 19, 1844, also referred to "thy trial about going to meeting"; Phoebe Post Willis to Isaac Post, March 7, 1845. The *Liberator* carried many articles about the impact of abolitionism on Quakers in these years. See, for example, "Quakerism, Church Discipline," April 1, 1842; "Scenes in a Quaker Meeting-House in Lynn," July 15, 1842; "New-York Yearly Meeting of Friends," July 22, 1842; "Religious Formalities," September 9, 1842; "The Quaker," October 7, 1842; "Friends in Commotion," December 2, 1842.

116. Charles Remond to William Lloyd Garrison, August 30, 1843, *Liberator,* September 23, 1843.

117. E.W.C. [probably Eliab W. Capron] to *Liberator,* written October 28, 1842 and printed December 2, 1842.

118. Mary Kirby to Amy Post, January 9, 1845, Post Family Papers, UR.

119. Phoebe Post Willis to Isaac Post, March 7, 1845, Post Family Papers, UR; Rochester Monthly Meeting recorded Isaac's "release" on March 28, 1845. The Women's Minutes recorded Amy's death, "date not ascertained," as if they still counted her a member of meeting, "Register," Rochester Monthly Meeting.

120. Joseph Post to Edmund and Julia Willis, September 17, 1845, Post Family Papers, UR.

121. Daniel Anthony to SBA, June 4, 1848, Anthony Papers, Schlesinger.

122. *Liberator,* August 25, 1843.

Chapter 5: Seneca Falls

1. Bull, "Women's Rights and Other 'Reforms'"; Eliza Bascom, quoted in Altschuler and Saltzgaber, *Revivalism, Social Conscience, and Community,* 118.

2. For comments on Bascom, see Lum, typescript, SFHS, 11; Gilbert Wilcoxen, "The Legal Profession," *Papers, SFHS* (1908): 15; Chamberlain, "Five Pivotal Years," 23; Monroe, "Seneca Falls in Earlier Days," 34.

3. Reconstructed from testimony given in the trial of Rhoda Bement in the Presbyterian Church, reprinted in Altschuler and Saltzgaber, *Revivalism, Social Conscience, and Community,* 109–23.

4. Jonathan Metcalf quoted in Altschuler and Saltzgaber, *Revivalism, Social Conscience, and Community,* 113.

5. Cross, *Burned-over District*; Judith Wellman, "Crossing over Cross: Whitney Cross and *The Burned-over District* as Social History," *Reviews in American History* 17(1) (March 1989): 159–74.

6. The lack of extant antislavery petitions to Congress is based on a survey of petitions now in the National Archives, sent to Congress from 1834 to 1844 and in 1850. Some petitions may have been burned, as Barnes, *Anti-Slavery Impulse,* noted in chap. 13, fn. 40, p. 266.

7. Statistical information for 1850 comes from the U.S. Manuscript Census, 1850; Wellman, "This Side of the Border." Thanks to Betty Auten, Seneca County historian, for sharing her work on African Americans in Seneca County.

8. U.S. Manuscript Census, 1850; *Seneca Falls Democrat,* December 26, 1844.

9. "Assessment Records, 1851, Seneca Falls," in Seneca Falls Village Hall, Seneca Falls, New York.

10. "Assessment Records, 1851, Seneca Falls"; "Minutes of the Annual Meeting of the Wesleyan Methodist Society, April 1, 1850"; "Book No. 1, The Property of the First Wesleyan Methodist Church, Seneca Falls, New York," microfilm, Olin Library, Cornell.

11. *Seneca County Courier,* September 24, 1839.

12. *Seneca Falls Democrat,* October 31, 1839; November 21, 1839.

13. *Seneca Falls Democrat,* August 27, 1840.

14. *Seneca Falls Democrat,* April 2, 1840.

15. *Seneca Falls Democrat,* April 2, 1840; October 15, 1840; "Letter of a Whig Elector, to Ansel Bascom, Esq.," October 17, 1840, printed in the *Seneca Falls Democrat,* October 22, 1840; November 5, 1840.

16. *Seneca Falls Democrat,* November 5, 1840; November 19, 1840, contained the official election returns. In Seneca Falls, 789 people voted for assemblyman. *Seneca County Courier,* November 10, 1840.

17. *Seneca Falls Democrat,* September 2 and 25, 1841; October 14, 1841; November 4, 1841; September 5, 1842; April 7, 1842; October 5, 1843.

18. *Seneca Falls Democrat,* May 3[?], 1842.

19. *Seneca Falls Democrat,* May 3[?], 1842; August 11, 1842; November 24, 1842.

20. Abby Kelley to Stephen S. Foster, August 13, 1843, Abby Kelley Foster Papers, AAS.

21. Abby Kelley to Stephen Foster, August 13, 1843, Abby Kelley Foster Papers, AAS; Abby Kelley to Maria Weston Chapman, August 13, 1843, Garrison Papers, BPL; B [Ansel Bascom] to William Lloyd Garrison, Seneca Falls, October 30, 1843, printed in the *Liberator,* November 24, 1843.

22. Michael Barkun, *Crucible of the Millennium: The Burned-over District of New York State in the 1840s* (Syracuse, N.Y.: Syracuse University Press, 1986); David L. Rowe, *Thunder and Trumpets: Millerites and Dissenting Religion in Upstate New York, 1800–1850* (Chico, Calif.: Scholars Press, 1985).

23. O. R. Fassett to William Miller, September 2, 1846, quoted in Rowe, *Thunder and Trumpets,* 44.

24. Newland, "The First Baptist Church," 75–76. Note on Pinney printing his pamphlet in Rowe, *Thunder and Trumpets,* 45, and *Seneca Falls Democrat,* January 12, 1843. The *Seneca Falls Democrat* continued to print letters and editorial comments on Millerism throughout this period. See, for example, January 19 and 26, 1843, and February 2, 1843. The *Seneca County Courier* carried an article on November 13, 1844. Rowe, *Thunder and Trumpets,* 42, listed four Millerite lecturers in the Seneca Falls area. Methodist Church Records, "Old Brown Book, Members 1841 to 1846," compiled and typed by Ruth Larsen Kelly and Shirley Minard, given to SFHS, July 2, 1984.

25. E. R. Pinney's lecture quoted in Rowe, *Thunder and Trumpets,* 44.

26. Abby Kelley to Stephen Foster, August 13, 1843, Abby Kelley Foster Papers, AAS.

27. Galatians 3:28.

28. Newland, "The First Baptist Church," 75.

29. "Historical Record," quoted in the *Seneca Falls Reveille,* May 3, 1929.

30. Donald G. Mathews, *Slavery and Methodism: A Chapter in American Morality, 1780–1845* (Princeton, N.J.: Princeton University Press, 1965), 230–31; *One Hundred Years of Service for Christ in the Wesleyan Methodist Church, 1844–1944* (n.p., n.d.), 7–8; "A New Methodist Organization," in the *Herkimer Journal,* reprinted in the *Liberator,* July 21, 1843. For a general overview of Meth-

odist history, see Russell E. Richey, *Early American Methodism* (Bloomington: Indiana University Press, 1991).

31. See resolutions of the Western New York Conference of the Wesleyan Methodists in *One Hundred Years of Service,* 10–20.

32. *One Hundred Years of Service,* 41; "Book No. 1. The Property of the First Wesleyan Methodist Church, Seneca Falls, N.Y."; George Pegler, *Autobiography of the Life and Times of the Rev. George Pegler* (Syracuse, N.Y.: Wesleyan Methodist Publishing House, 1879), 408–11; Paul W. Thomas, director of Archives for the Wesleyan Church, letter to author, September 15, 1982.

33. "List of Subscribers, Seneca Falls, April 20, 1843," in "Book No. 1. The Property of the First Wesleyan Methodist Church, Seneca Falls, N.Y."; Pegler, *Autobiography,* 409, 412, 414–15; *One Hundred Years of Service,* 41.

34. On January 14, 1844, the trustees resolved "that this House of worship shall not be opened for the purpose of Speaking or preaching in favor of elevating to Power either of the political parties of the Country." On March 27, 1845, however, they rescinded this resolution. See "Book No. 1. The Property of the First Wesleyan Methodist Church, Seneca Falls, N.Y." Abby Kelley to Stephen Foster, August 13, 1843, Abby Kelley Foster Papers, AAS, quoted the Wesleyans as calling their building "a free discussion house." J. C. Hathaway to Sydney Howard Gay, July 1846, in the *National Anti-Slavery Standard,* July 30, 1846. Thomas James was mentioned in minutes of a Trustees' meeting, April 1, 1850, in "Book No. 1. The Property of the First Wesleyan Methodist Church, Seneca Falls, N.Y."

35. James Hotchkins, *A History of the Purchase and Settlement of Western New York and of the Rise, Progress, and Present State of the Presbyterian Church in that Section* (New York: W. W. Dodd, 1848); "Presbyterian General Assembly," *Liberator,* July 15, 1842.

36. Session minutes, October 2, 1843, printed in Altschuler and Saltzgaber, *Revivalism, Social Conscience, and Community,* 89–91.

37. "American Anti-Slavery Society," *Liberator,* January 5, 1843.

38. Ansel Bascom to Abby Kelley, February 16, 1844, Abby Kelley Foster Papers, Worcester Historical Society, Worcester, Mass.

39. Testimony of Rhoda Bement before a committee appointed to visit her, recorded in Session minutes, October 13, 1843, Records of First Presbyterian Church of Seneca Falls, printed in Altschuler and Saltzgaber, *Revivalism, Social Conscience, and Community,* 91–93.

40. Charges brought by Alexander S. Platt and "Brother Race" and recorded in session minutes on December 11, 1843, Altschuler and Saltzgaber, *Revivalism, Social Conscience, and Community,* 96–97; Bogue's comments, as they appeared in trial testimony, Altschuler and Saltzgaber, 128.

41. Altschuler and Saltzgaber, *Revivalism, Social Conscience, and Community,* 101, 106–8.

42. Altschuler and Saltzgaber, *Revivalism, Social Conscience, and Community,* 99.

43. This version of the pledge was introduced at the Syracuse antislavery convention, held November 22–24, 1842, "Interesting Report of the Anti-Slavery Convention," *Liberator,* December 30, 1842. Sterling, *Ahead of Her Time,* 168, noted that although this pledge was adopted at the American Anti-Slavery Society meeting in May 1843, even so committed an abolitionist as Lydia Maria Child, editor of the *National Anti-Slavery Standard,* found it objectionable.

44. *Liberator,* May 5, 1843.

45. Altschuler and Saltzgaber, *Revivalism, Social Conscience, and Community,* 121; Bascom to Kelley, February 16, 1844, Kelley Foster Papers, Worcester Historical Society, Worcester, Mass.

46. Altschuler and Saltzgaber, *Revivalism, Social Conscience, and Community,* 116–17.

47. Altschuler and Saltzgaber, *Revivalism, Social Conscience, and Community,* 139–40; Bascom to Kelley, February 16, 1844, Kelley Foster Papers, Worcester Historical Society, Worcester, Mass.

48. Daniel W. Forman was mentioned in minutes of a trustees' meeting, April 1, 1850, in "Book No. 1. The Property of the First Wesleyan Methodist Church, Seneca Falls, N.Y."; Altschuler and Saltzgaber, *Revivalism, Social Conscience, and Community,* 83, 97, 140; *Seneca Falls Democrat,* October 31, 1839; November 21, 1839.

49. *History of Seneca County,* 113–14; Wellman, *Grass Roots Reform in the Burned-over District of Upstate New York.*

50. Grimké, *Letters on the Equality of the Sexes,* 122–23.

Chapter 6: Women and Legal Reform in New York State

1. Frances Seward's copy of this lecture is still in the library of the William Henry Seward House, where Betty Lewis, curator, called my attention to it. Martha Wright to LCM, March 11, 1841, Garrison Papers, Smith.

2. For further discussion of these arguments, see Aileen Kraditor, *The Ideas of the Woman Suffrage Movement, 1890–1920* (New York: Columbia University Press, 1965), especially 43–74, 249–54; Kristi Anderson, *After Suffrage: Women in Partisan and Electoral Politics before the New Deal* (Chicago: University of Chicago Press, 1996), 21–25.

3. William Blackstone, *Commentaries on the Laws of England,* vol. 1 (Oxford: Clarendon Press, 1765–69), 1: 356, quoted in J. H. Ehrlich, *Ehrlich's Blackstone* (Westport, Conn.: Greenwood Press, 1959), 83.

4. Abigail Adams to John Adams, March 31, 1776, in Alice Rossi, ed., *The Feminist Papers* (New York: Bantam, 1974), 10–11.

5. Linda Kerber, *Women of the Republic: Intellect and Ideology in Revolutionary America* (Chapel Hill: University of North Carolina Press, 1980), 30–31; Flexner, *Century of Struggle,* 14–15; Rossi, *Feminist Papers,* 16–85.

6. Kerber, *Women of the Republic,* 283.

7. Charles Brockden Brown, *Alcuin* (1793, 1815; reprint, New York: Grossman Publishers, 1971), 29–33.

8. Lucy Stone, *Woman Suffrage in New Jersey, An Address Delivered by Lucy Stone at a Hearing Before the New Jersey Legislature, March 6th, 1867* (Boston: C. H. Simonds, [1867]); Judith Apter Klinghoffer and Lois Elkis, "'The Petticoat Electors' Women's Suffrage in New Jersey, 1776–1807," *Journal of the Early Republic* 12(2) (1992): 159–93.

9. Sections 7 and 10 of the 1777 constitution, in Nathaniel Carter and William L. Stone, eds., *Reports of the Proceedings and Debates of the Convention of 1821* (Albany, N.Y.: E. and E. Hosford, 1821), 2–21.

10. Alexander, *Political History,* 1: 295–311; John S. Jenkins, *History of Political Parties in the State of New York,* 2d ed. (Auburn, N.Y.: Alden and Parsons, 1849), 242–59; Carter and Stone, *Reports of the Proceedings,* 2–21. The referendum on whether or not to call a constitutional convention allowed "all free male citizens," with few restrictions, to vote, and no one really expected black or white suffrage to be further limited. Carter and Stone, *Reports,* 22, 183, 194.

11. E. Williams in Carter and Stone, *Reports of the Proceedings,* 369.

12. Carter and Stone, *Reports of the Proceedings,* 215, 220.

13. John Locke, *Two Treatises of Government,* 2, paragraph 123, in Peter Laslett, *Two Treatises of Government,* 2d ed. (Cambridge: Cambridge University Press, 1967), 368. Laslett argued that Locke thought of property generally in this larger sense, as incorporating life and liberty as well as material possessions. Nineteenth-century theorists who spoke of government's purposes to protect property usually used the term in its narrower sense. Carter and Stone, *Reports of the Proceedings,* 265.

14. Carter and Stone, *Reports of the Proceedings,* 266.

15. Carter and Stone, *Reports of the Proceedings,* 279–80, 362, 285, 278. Judge Van Ness expressed similar sentiments, 268–69; so did General J. R. Van Rensellaer, 360–63.

16. Carter and Stone, *Reports of the Proceedings,* 278, 248–49.

17. Carter and Stone, *Reports of the Proceedings,* 235, 239, 243.

18. Initial report of committee on suffrage, Carter and Stone, *Reports of the Proceedings,* 180–81, 186, 198–99. Philip S. Foner and George E. Walker, eds., *Proceedings of the Black State Conventions, 1840–1865,* vol. 1 (Philadelphia: Temple University Press, 1979).

19. Carter and Stone, *Reports of the Proceedings,* 190, 180, 375.

20. Carter and Stone, *Reports of the Proceedings,* 180–81, 189, 190.

21. Carter and Stone, *Reports of the Proceedings,* 181, 190, 191.

22. Carter and Stone, *Reports of the Proceedings,* 184, 186–87, 191–94.

23. Carter and Stone, *Reports of the Proceedings,* 187.

24. Carter and Stone, *Reports of the Proceedings,* 197, 201.

25. Carter and Stone, *Reports of the Proceedings,* 194, 201, 183.

26. Carter and Stone, *Reports of the Proceedings,* 365.

27. Carter and Stone, *Reports of the Proceedings,* 375, 376.

28. Carter and Stone, *Reports of the Proceedings,* 557.

29. William Ray, *Poems, on Various Subjects, Religious, Moral, Sentimental, and Humorous* (Auburn, N.Y.: U. F. Doubleday, 1821), 174–76. Many thanks to the late Richard Wright for finding this volume.

30. Abraham Lincoln to Editor of the *Journal,* June 13, 1836, in Roy P. Basler, ed., *The Collected Works of Abraham Lincoln,* vol. 1 (New Brunswick, N.J.: Rutgers University Press, 1953–55), 1: 48.

31. Angelina Grimké, *Appeal,* 19.

32. Harriet Martineau quoted in Gayle Graham Yates, ed., *Harriet Martineau on Women* (New Brunswick, N.J.: Rutgers University Press, 1985), 134.

33. John Greenleaf Whittier, quoted in ECS, SBA, and Gage, *History of Woman Suffrage,* 1: 84.

34. Basch, *Eyes of the Law;* George Geddes to Matilda Joslyn Gage, November 25, 1880, in ECS, SBA, and Gage, *History of Woman Suffrage,* 1: 65.

35. Basch, *Eyes of the Law,* 73–79; Elizabeth Bowles Warbasse, *The Changing Legal Rights of Married Women, 1800–1861* (New York: Garland, 1987), 4; Peggy A. Rabkin, *Fathers to Daughters: The Legal Foundations of Female Emancipation* (Westport, Conn.: Greenwood, 1980); Kerber, *Women of the Republic,* 154–55.

36. Basch, *Eyes of the Law,* 79–112; Warbasse, *Changing Legal Rights,* 5–6; Randy Rabinowitz, "The Impact of Codification on the Equitable Property Rights of Married Women" (paper presented at the Berkshire Conference on Women's History, 1981).

37. Paul S. Boyer, "Fanny Wright," in James, James, and Boyer, *Notable American Women,* 3: 678. Historians have probably underestimated the influence of Frances Wright on subsequent woman's rights activity. Her significance is difficult to define clearly, partly because she was not as prolific a writer as many reformers were. Stanton, Anthony, and Gage, however, placed Wright's picture on the frontispiece of volume 1 of their 1881 *History of Woman Suffrage.* They also listed the lectures of Fanny Wright, as well as those of her successor, Ernestine Rose, as one of the three most important causes of the organized demand for women's political rights. ECS, SBA, and Gage, *History of Woman Suffrage,* 1: 51–52.

38. [Solomon Southwick], *A Layman's Apology for the Appointment of Clerical Chaplains by the Legislature of the State of New-York* (Albany, N.Y.: Hoffman and White, 1834), 43, 189, 190.

39. L. E. Barnard, "Ernestine L. Rose," in ECS, SBA, and Gage, *History of Woman Suffrage,* 1: 95–98; Ernestine Rose to SBA, January 9, 1877, in ECS, SBA, and Gage, *History of Woman Suffrage,* 1: 98–100.

40. Thomas Herttell, *Remarks Comprising in Substance Judge Herttell's Argument in the House of Assembly of the State of New-York, in the Session of 1837, in Support of the Bill to Restore to Married Women "The Right of Property," as Guarantied by the Constitution of this State* (New York: Henry Durell, 1839), 5–6; Rose to SBA, January 9, 1877, in ECS, SBA, and Gage, *History of Woman Suffrage,* 1: 98–100. For more on Rose, see Alice Felt Tyler, "Ernestine Rose," *Notable American Women,* 3: 195–96.

41. *Evening Star,* January 18, 1838, quoted in Herttell, *Remarks,* 5; Herttell, *Remarks,* 6.

42. Herttell, *Remarks,* 15–17, 20.

43. Herttell, *Remarks,* 79–80.

44. Warbasse, *Changing Legal Rights,* 7.

45. "Report of the committee on the judiciary, on the petitions to extend and protect the rights of property of married women," April 12, 1842, No. 189 in *Documents of the Assembly of the State of New York, 64th* (1842), vol. 7.

46. "Report of the committee on the judiciary, in relation to divorce and the separate property of married women," May 9, 1846, No. 219 in *Documents of the Assembly of the State of New York, 69th* (1846), vol. 6.

47. ECS, SBA, and Gage, *History of Woman Suffrage,* 1: 51–52.

48. ECS, SBA, and Gage, *History of Woman Suffrage,* 1: 52; and ECS, *Eighty Years,* 150; "Report of the committee on the judiciary, on the petitions to extend and protect the rights of property of married women," No. 189 in *Documents of the Assembly of the State of New York, 64th* (1842), vol. 7, noted the referral of "sundry petitions"; the "Report of the committee on the judiciary, in relation to divorce and the separate property of married women" noted "sundry petitions of the inhabitants of the city of Albany"; the quotation about Stanton's work and the reference to Frances Seward's assistance comes from Lawrence, "Elizabeth Cady Stanton."

49. *Seneca Falls Democrat,* September 14, 1843; *New York Herald,* January 25, 1843, noted in Elizabeth Warbasse, "Legal Status of Women from Blackstone to 1848" (paper presented at Seneca Falls Women's History Conference, June 1979).

50. *Seneca Falls Democrat,* April 10, 1846. The Seneca Falls Historical Society owns the loving cup.

51. William G. Bishop and William H. Attree, *Report of the Debates and Proceedings of the Convention for the Revision of the Constitution of the State of New-York, 1846* (Albany, N.Y.: Albany Argus, 1847), 1038–42.

52. Bishop and Attree, *Report of the Debates,* 1057–60. A slightly different version of O'Conor's speech appeared in Charles Z. Lincoln, *The Constitutional History of New York, Vol. 2: 1822–1894* (Rochester, N.Y.: Lawyers Co-operative Publishing Co., 1906), 112–13. Unless otherwise noted, biographical information about convention delegates comes from Bishop and Attree, *Report of the Debates,* "Members and Officers of the Convention."

53. "Address of the New York State Convention of Colored Citizens, to the People of the State," in Philip S. Foner and George E. Walker, eds., *Proceedings of the Black State Conventions, 1840–1865,* Vol. 1 (Philadelphia: Temple University Press, 1979), 22–23.

54. *New York Tribune,* July 21, 1846.

55. Bishop and Attree, *Report of the Debates,* 196.

56. Bishop and Attree, *Report of the Debates,* 453.

57. Bishop and Attree, *Report of the Debates,* 539.

58. Bishop and Attree, *Report of the Debates,* 539–40.

59. Bishop and Attree, *Report of the Debates,* 540. The tactic here is very similar to that used by Senator Howard K. Smith of Virginia in 1964. Trying to stop passage of the Civil Rights Act, he proposed an amendment to prohibit sexual discrimination as well as racial and religious discrimination. To Smith's surprise, the bill passed, including his amendment. Charles and Barbara Whalen, authors of *The Longest Debate: A Legislative History of the 1964 Civil Rights Act* (New York: New American Library, 1985), 117, argued that this made the act "one of the most radical civil rights amendments in U.S. history."

60. Bishop and Attree, *Report of the Debates,* 540–41.

61. Petition dated August 8, 1846, in Bishop and Attree, *Report of the Debates,* 646. A petition "numerously and respectably signed by some of the first citizens of Albany" was referred to the committee on the elective franchise on July 11. Another from women in Covington, Wyoming County, was received on August 27. Bishop and Attree, 284, 763. For more on the Jefferson County petition, see Jacob Katz and Lori D. Ginzberg, "1846 Petition for Woman's Suffrage, New York State Constitutional Convention," *Signs* 22 (1997): 427–39. Diane Turo-Hughes has identified these women as farm women from the area of Depauville, Town of Clayton. Correspondence with author, March 13, 2001.

62. Bishop and Attree, *Report of the Debates,* 1027.

63. Bishop and Attree, *Report of the Debates,* 1031.

64. Bishop and Attree, *Report of the Debates,* 1029–31.

65. M. E. Mills to Gerrit Smith, September 18, 1846, Smith Papers, SyU.

66. Samuel J. May, "The Rights and Condition of Women," in *Woman's Rights Tract No. 1: Commensurate with her capacities and obligations, are Woman's Rights* (Syracuse, N.Y.: N. M. D. Lathrop, 1853), 1–2, 13.

67. May, "Rights and Condition of Women," 1–2, 13.

68. Elisha P. Hurlbut, *Essays on Human Rights, and Their Political Guaranties* (New York: Fowlers and Wells, 1848), 117, 123.

69. Franklin B. Hough, *A History of St. Lawrence and Franklin Counties, New York* (Albany: Little and Co., 1853; reprint, Baltimore: Regional Publishing Co., 1970), 586.

70. [John Fine], *Lecture Delivered Before the Ogdensburgh Lyceum, on the Political Rights of Women* (Ogdensburgh, N.Y.: Tyler and James, n.d.), 2–3.

71. This account of the bill's passage comes primarily from George Geddes to Matilda Joslyn Gage, November 25, 1880, in *History of Woman Suffrage,* 1: 64–67.

72. ECS, SBA, and Gage, *History of Woman Suffrage,* 1: 64–67.

73. *Documents of the Assembly of New York* (Albany: E. Crosswell, 1848), March 15, 1848, No. 129, 1–2; George Geddes to Matilda Joslyn Gage, in ECS, SBA, and Gage, *History of Woman Suffrage,* 1: 65. For a collective biography of women who signed this petition, see Carolyn Wright-Dauenhauer, "With All My Worldly Goods I Thee Endow: The Married Women's Property Act of 1848 and Its Petitioners from Darien and Covington" (unpublished paper, State University of New York at Oswego, 1984); *New York Assembly Documents,* March 15, 1848, No. 129, 1–2.

74. ECS, SBA, and Gage, *History of Woman Suffrage,* 1: 64.

75. Stanton and Blatch, *Elizabeth Cady Stanton,* 1: 149.

Chapter 7: Adversity and Transcendence, June 1847–June 1848

1. ECS to Elizabeth Smith Miller, [February? 1847], Smith Papers, SyU; ECS, *Eighty Years,* 144.

2. For a recent discussion of network theory, see Albert-Laszlo Barabasi, *Linked: The New Science of Networks* (Cambridge, Mass.: Perseus Press, 2002).

3. ECS, *Eighty Years,* 111–12; ECS to Elizabeth Smith Miller, March 17, [1841], Stanton Papers, Rutgers. Henry dated the beginning of his law studies as February 23, 1841, HBS to ECS, June 23, 1842, Stanton Papers, LC.

4. ECS to Elizabeth Neall, Johnstown, November 26, [1841], Sydney Howard Gay Papers, Columbia; ECS to Elizabeth Pease, February 12, 1842, Garrison Papers, BPL.

5. LCM to ECS, March 23, 1841, Stanton Papers, LC; LCM to Richard and Hannah Webb, Philadelphia, April 2, 1841, Garrison Papers, BPL.

6. HBS to Elizur Wright, August 25, 1841, Wright Papers, LC; HBS to Gerrit Smith, September 9, 1841, and [November 1841 or 1842], Smith Papers, SyU.

7. ECS to Elizabeth Neall, November 26, [1841], Gay Papers, Columbia.

8. ECS to Elizabeth Pease, February 12, 1842, Garrison Papers, BPL.

9. Sarah Pugh to ECS, Philadelphia, February 24, 1841, quoting a letter from Hannah Webb, Stanton Papers, LC; ECS to Elizabeth Neall, November 26, [1841], Gay Papers, Columbia.

10. LCM, before February 25, 1842, quoted in Hallowell, *James and Lucretia Mott,* 228. ECS to Elizabeth Neall, November 26, [1841], Gay Papers, Columbia; Sarah Grimké to ECS, April 9, 1842, transcript for Theodore Stanton and Harriot Stanton Blatch, Stanton Papers, Rutgers; *Liberator* subscription list, Garrison Papers, BPL.

11. ECS to Elizabeth Neall, November 26, [1841], Gay Papers, Columbia.

12. HBS to ECS, June 23, 1842, Stanton Papers, LC.

13. LCM to Richard and Hannah Webb, February 25, 1842, Garrison Papers, BPL.

14. ECS to Elizabeth Neall, February 3, [1843], Gay Papers, Columbia. For references to Boston, see, e.g., ECS to the Smith family, Albany, February 3, [1845], Stanton Papers, Vassar; Ann Smith to Gerrit Smith, Albany, February 20, 1846, Smith Papers, SyU.

15. ECS, *Eighty Years*, 127–42.

16. ECS, *Washington Evening Star*, February 25, 1895, 2, quoted in Rayford W. Logan, Introduction, in Douglass, *Life and Times*, 19; Douglass, *Life and Times*, 473; Alma Lutz, *Created Equal*, 39; Frederick Douglass, "Address before Woman Suffrage Association, April 1888," in Foner, *Douglass on Women's Rights*, 113; Frederick Douglass to ECS, October 22, 1885, in Foner, *Douglass on Women's Rights*, 163.

17. Lucretia Mott to ECS, March 16, 1855, Stanton Papers, LC. Mott recalled this was the first time they had discussed a convention and the meeting was Stanton's idea. Mott may not have remembered conversations in London, or Stanton may have fused her memories of the walk in Boston with her memories of the London walk. Or there may indeed have been two discussions, as reported in ECS, SBA, and Gage, *History of Women's Suffrage*, 1: 68.

18. HBS to Gerrit Smith, July 6, 1844, and November 12, 1844, Smith Papers, SyU.

19. ECS, *Eighty Years*, 133. HBS to Gerrit Smith, July 6, 1844; November 12, 1844; November 23, 1844; and December 2, 1844. Preceding letters in Smith Papers, SyU. ECS to Margaret Livingston Cady, July 17, 1845, Stanton Papers, Rutgers.

20. ECS, *Eighty Years*, 136.

21. ECS, *Eighty Years*, 137.

22. ECS, *Eighty Years*, 137; Ann Smith to Gerrit Smith, Albany, February 29, 1846, Smith Papers, SyU; HBS to Gerrit Smith, December 2, 1844, Smith Papers, SyU.

23. HBS to Gerrit Smith, August 4, 1843; Ann Smith to Gerrit Smith, Albany, [October 1843]; and HBS to Gerrit Smith, December 20, 1843. Preceding letters in Smith Papers, SyU. ECS to John Greenleaf Whittier, October 10, 1843, in Stanton and Blatch, *Elizabeth Cady Stanton*, 2: 9–10. ECS, *Eighty Years*, 135.

24. ECS, *Eighty Years*, 138; HBS to Gerrit Smith, December 18, 1845, Smith Papers, SyU.

25. ECS to John Greenleaf Whittier, October 10, 1843, Stanton and Blatch, *Elizabeth Cady Stanton*, 2: 9–10; poem printed in Thomas Moore, *The Poetical Works of Thomas Moore*, 10 vols. (London: Longman, Orme, Brown, Green, and Longmans, 1840–41).

26. LCM to ECS, March 23, 1841, Stanton Papers, LC.

27. ECS, *Eighty Years*, 132–34.

28. This manuscript, in ECS's own hand, is in the Stanton Papers at Rutgers. A note in Theodore Stanton's handwriting dates it to the late 1840s or 1850s. Certainly, references to slavery (12) and to stagecoaches (15) put the speech before 1860. Internal evidence suggests a date of about 1846 or 1847. Stanton's reference to Theodore Parker's sermon on what is permanent and transient in religion places this speech after 1841. Parker delivered this sermon in the Hawes Place Church of South Boston on May 10, 1841. See Sydney E. Ahlstrom, *A Religious History of the American People* (New Haven, Conn.: Yale University Press, 1972), 606. Stanton's emphasis on reason suggests that she was also influenced by Emerson, whose essay "Nature" was published in 1837. As Ann Gordon has suggested, Stanton's manuscript apparently was given as a speech rather than prepared for publication, for it refers to an audience "in this house" (10). Further references to "a free church with no creed or authority or ecclesiastical discipline" (22) and to "an unpretentious house" (23) make it plausible that she prepared this talk for a meeting of the Peterboro Free Church. This church was organized in 1843, but Frothingham, *Gerrit Smith*, 57–66, noted that the first meetings were held in a room of the local hotel. About 1846 or 1847, Smith built a simple house of worship, perhaps "this house" of Stanton's speech, where the group met until it finally disbanded. Stanton's discussion of "a pattern man," "who by suffering has secured this boon [i.e., religious freedom in this house] for you" (25) probably referred to Gerrit Smith, whose controversy with the Presbyterian minister Asa Rand had been public and bitter since 1845 (see Harlow, *Gerrit Smith*, 208–12). Stanton called Smith a "pattern man" in a poem she wrote for him dated April 1, 1860, copy, SFHS.

Stanton's writings for the Congregational Friends in the 1850s (who also met in unpretentious houses) focused primarily on woman's rights rather than on overtly theological issues. A date of c. 1846–47 therefore seems most reasonable for "Fear." The topic itself, as suggested earlier, was a major preoccupation for her. Many thanks to Ann Gordon for her thoughts on this issue.

29. ECS, "Fear," 8–10.

30. ECS, "Fear," 12–13.

31. ECS, "Fear," 13–15, 18.

32. ECS, "Fear," 26–27.

33. HBS to Gerrit Smith, May 20, 1844, Smith Papers, SyU. Harriot Stanton Blatch to Alma Lutz, August 1931, Lutz Papers, Vassar.

34. HBS to Gerrit Smith, May 20, 1844, Smith Papers, SyU; Gordon, *Selected Papers,* 1: 40, noted that "ECS spent nearly equal amounts of time with her sisters and parents in New York and with her husband in Boston between the end of 1842 and 1846."

35. Wetmore, "The Bayard Family," 65–67.

36. We can infer that William married Romainea sometime between April 1835, when William's name appears on a deed without that of his wife (Samuel I. Bayard and Jane A. his wife and William M. Bayard to Richard Richardson, April 1, 1835, Seneca County Clerk's Office, C2-339), and November 2, 1836, when Romainea's name first appeared in a deed (Samuel I. Bayard and Jane A. his wife and William M. Bayard and Romainea C. his wife to David Bedell, Seneca County Clerk's Office, H2-38). The first recorded reference to what would become the Stanton house appeared in Samuel I. Bayard and wife and William M. Bayard and wife to Joseph D. Beers, December 5, 1838, copy made in Seneca County Clerk's Office on October 3, 1857, now in Bayard Box, SFHS, so we know that some structure, probably the one that Stanton would later acquire, already existed on that site. Corinne Guntzel, "History of the Stanton House," [June 1982]; Hanns Kuttner, "The Stanton House Property" (c. 1978); Corinne Guntzel and Paul Grebinger, "The Domestic Economy of Elizabeth Cady Stanton, Her House and Its Artifacts" (1981); Barbara Pearson, "The Stanton House: Preliminary Historic Structure Report" (October 1982); Judith Wellman, "Elizabeth Cady Stanton's House: Some Thoughts" (September 1982) and "Boundaries of the Stanton Lot" (December 1986). Special thanks to Margaret McFadden, who located many of these deeds, and to the late Corinne Guntzel, who first organized many of these sources into coherent form. All on file in WRNHP.

Susan Bradford and others to William and Samuel Bayard, December 1833 (Seneca County Clerk's Office, Liber D, p. 150), cited in Pearson, "The Stanton House," 1. Samuel Bayard's farm is mentioned in other deeds. See, for example, Elisha Foote and Edward Bayard to Daniel Cady, February 12, 1841, Liber L2, pp. 275–76, Seneca County Clerk's Office, Waterloo, N.Y.

37. The disposition of this property was summarized in Nathaniel Hoyt to Elisha Foote, Junior, March 11, 1844, Liber P2, p. 225, Seneca County Clerk's Office, Waterloo, N.Y. Samuel Bayard to Thurlow Weed, January 12, 1843, Thurlow Weed Collection, Rush Rhees Library, UR. Samuel and Jane's residence in Iowa is documented in Jane A. Bayard's relinquishment of her dower rights in the Stanton house to Daniel Cady, August 20, 1845, Liber 58, p. 130, Seneca County Clerk's Office, Waterloo, N.Y.

38. Nathaniel Hoyt to Elisha Foote, Junior, March 11, 1844; Elisha Foote and Edward Bayard to Daniel Cady, February 12, 1841, Liber L2, 275; Edward Bayard to Daniel Cady, November 23, 1842, Liber N2, 416. All in Seneca County Clerk's Office, Waterloo, N.Y.

39. ECS, *Eighty Years,* 144.

40. We do not know exactly when William and Romainea Bayard left their honeymoon house. Harrison Chamberlain, "Early Flouring Mills," 34, noted that the Bayards lived in Seneca Falls from 1830 until 1845. See also, ECS, *Eighty Years,* 144, and Pearson, "The Stanton House," 4.

41. Janet Cowing, "Mrs. Stanton Our Pioneer Suffragist," *State Service: The New York State Magazine* 3 (May 1919), 18; Carol Petravage, "Historic Furnishings Study, Stanton House, Wesleyan Chapel, and McClintock House" (Harper's Ferry, W.V.: U.S. Department of the Interior, 1989).

42. ECS, *Eighty Years,* 145, 166; Pearson, "The Stanton House." Like many Greek Revival houses, this one had been built in stages. Several features suggest that it had been put into this form before the late 1830s, just about the time that William Bayard would have needed a new house.

43. Gerrit Smith Stanton, "How Aged Housekeeper Gave Her All to Cause of Woman's Suffrage," newspaper article (n.p., [c. 1930]) on file in SFHS.

44. Seneca Falls Assessment Records, 1860, Town Clerk's Office, Seneca Falls, N.Y.

45. Delevan, "Elizabeth Cady Stanton," 1938 typescript, SFHS, 6, 10; Pearson, "The Stanton House," 7; SBA to Henry B. Stanton Jr. and Gerrit S. Stanton, September 27, 1860, Stanton Papers, Vassar; Stanton, "How Aged Housekeeper Gave Her All"; Romainea C. Bayard to ECS, May 22, 1856, Liber 58, p. 131, Seneca Falls County Clerk's Office; Henry B. Stanton to Gerrit Smith, May 2, 1849, Smith Papers, SyU; ECS, quoted in obituary for Henry B. Stanton, *New York Tribune,* January 15, 1887; "Henry Brewster Stanton," *A Record, Genealogical, Biographical, Statistical, of Thomas Stanton, of Connecticut* (Albany, N.Y.: Joel Munsell, 1891), 461; Blatch, *Challenging Years,* 4.

46. ECS, *Eighty Years,* 90, 194; ECS to Elizabeth M'Clintock, [July 14, 1848], WRNHP.

47. Beach, "Early Transportation," 25.

48. Daniel Cady to Elizabeth Cady Stanton, June 22, 1847, Deeds, Liber 52, pp. 479–80, recorded July 19, 1853, Seneca County Clerk's Office, Waterloo, N.Y.

49. Later in her life, Stanton would use her own experience as a home owner and homemaker as the basis for advice to others. See ECS,"Home Life," given on the lecture circuit in the 1870s, manuscript notes, Stanton Papers, Rutgers.

50. ECS, *Eighty Years,* 145. One possible letter, tentatively dated in the Stanton-Anthony Papers, *Film,* as May? 1?, 1847? is from ECS to Rebecca R. Eyster. This letter exists only as a transcript in the Stanton Papers, Rutgers, and deals with married women's use of their husband's names, a topic that concerned Stanton most obviously about 1859–60, not in 1847. The other letter, from ECS to John Pierpont, September 2, 1847, appeared in Stanton and Blatch, *Elizabeth Cady Stanton,* 2: 16–17.

51. ECS, *Eighty Years,* 145–47.

52. ECS, *Eighty Years,* 147.

53. William A. Stanton, *Record,* 462–63.

54. Kathryn Kish Sklar, "Victorian Women and Domestic Life: Mary Todd Lincoln, Elizabeth Cady Stanton, and Harriet Beecher Stowe," in Cullom Davis et al., eds., *The Public and the Private Lincoln* (Carbondale: Southern Illinois University Press, 1979), 20–37.

55. ECS to Abby Kelley Foster, [January] 12, [1851], Abby Kelley Foster Papers, AAS; Martha Wright to LCM, December 9, 1850, and March 5, 1849, Garrison Papers, Smith.

56. William A. Stanton, *Record,* 464; Martha Wright to LCM, August 5, 1848, Garrison Papers, Smith.

57. Harlene Gilbert pointed out the similarities in dress in the portraits of Stanton and her mother.

58. *North Star,* March 24, 1848; *North Star,* April 28, 1848, noted Frederick Douglass's lecture there on May 4.

59. Advertisement in the *Seneca County Courier,* June 13, 1848, for a show on June 23.

60. See, for example, a reprint of this series from the *National Era* in the *North Star,* June 9, 1848.

61. ECS, *Eighty Years,* 145. Stanton noted that the convention was then in session, when actually it had occurred the year before.

62. ECS, *Eighty Years,* 150–51; ECS, SBA, and Gage, *History of Woman Suffrage,* 1: 67; ECS, typescript, 1898, UR, 4–5.

63. Charles Sumner to George Sumner, quoted in Sewall, *Ballots for Freedom,* 131–32.

64. *Address of the Macedon Convention, by William Goodell; and Letters of Gerrit Smith* (Albany, N.Y.: S. W. Green, 1847); Gerrit Smith, "To the Editors of the *Emancipator,*" Boston, August 23, 1847.

65. *Letter of Gerrit Smith to S. P. Chase, "on the Unconstitutionality of Every Part of American Slavery"* (Albany, N.Y.: S. W. Green, 1847), 3–4.

66. Stanton to Salmon P. Chase, August 1, 1847, and August 6, 1847, Salmon P. Chase Papers, LC, quoted in Arthur H. Rice, "Henry B. Stanton," 276; *Emancipator,* September 1, 15, 1847, quoted in Sewall, *Ballots for Freedom,* 134, and in Rice, "Henry B. Stanton," 276–77.

67. Rice, "Henry B. Stanton," 278; Sewall, *Ballots for Freedom,* 136–37; James B. Kent, *Commentaries on American Law* (New York: Printed by the author, 1836).

68. Rice, "Henry B. Stanton," 279.

69. John Duer and Benjamin F. Butler, *Revised Statutes of the State of New York* (Albany: Packard and Van Benthuysen, 1829); Henry B. Stanton, *Random Recollections,* 159–60; *Emancipator,* March 22, 1848, 1, quoted in Rice, "Henry B. Stanton," 290–91; Sewall, *Ballots for Freedom,* 146.

70. March 2, 1848, John P. Hale Papers, New Hampshire Historical Society, Concord, N.H., noted in Rice, "Henry B. Stanton," 292, 194–95; Sewall, *Ballots for Freedom,* 148–49.

71. *Seneca County Courier,* June 13, 1848.

72. Sewall, *Ballots for Freedom,* 152; *Emancipator,* February 24, 1847, quoted in Rice, "Henry B. Stanton," 293.

73. Thanks to the late Corinne Guntzel for sharing this research.

74. Throughout 1847 and early 1848, Liberty League publications, as well as Smith's own writings, discuss the "right of all men." While they include specific references to "colored men," they do not mention women.

75. Report on the Liberty League convention from the *Liberator,* June 23, 1848, copied from the *New York Commercial Advertiser; Proceedings of the National Liberty Convention, Held at Buffalo, N.Y., June 14th and 15th, 1848* (Utica, N.Y.: S. W. Green, 1848), 14.

76. *Proceedings of the National Liberty Convention.*

77. Sewall, *Ballots for Freedom,* 148–50; Rice, "Henry B. Stanton," 295; Oliver Cromwell Gardiner, *The Great Issue: or, The Three Presidential Candidates Being a Brief Historical Sketch of the Free Soil Question in the United States* (New York, 1848), 107–21, quoted in Sewall, *Ballots for Freedom,* 149.

78. Sewall, *Ballots for Freedom,* 153; HBS to John G. Whittier, July 31, 1848, in John Albree, ed., *Whittier Correspondence from the Oak Knoll Collections, 1830–1892* (Salem: Essex Book and Print Club, 1911), 102–4, quoted in Rice, "Henry B. Stanton," 297–98.

79. *New York Tribune,* July 19, 1848; Rice, "Henry B. Stanton," 295; the *New York Tribune,* July 12, 1848, reported a speech by Ansel Bascom before "a large and enthusiastic Van Buren Ratification Meeting" at Syracuse; *Seneca County Courier,* August 4, 1848.

80. Meeting in Mendon held on December 4, 1847, and reported in the *North Star,* January 8, 1848.

81. Daniel Anthony to SBA, June 4, 1848, Anthony Papers, Schlesinger.

82. *Pennsylvania Freeman,* September 14, 1848, quoted in Albert J. Wahl, "The Progressive Friends of Longwood," *Friends' Historical Association Bulletin* 42(1) (1953): 14; *An Address to Friends of Genesee Yearly Meeting and Elsewhere* (Seneca Falls, N.Y.: Milliken and Mumford, 1848), 2.

83. Manuscript Minutes of Genesee Yearly Meeting for Women, and Minutes of Genesee Yearly Meeting for Men, 1847, FHL; *Address to Friends,* 3–4. This issue had special urgency for Genesee Yearly Meeting because so many Friends from Michigan were migrants from central New York, especially from Scipio Yearly Meeting, as noted in Carlisle G. Davidson, "A Profile of Hicksite Quakerism in Michigan, 1830–1860," *Friends' Historical Association Bulletin* 59 (1970): 106–12.

84. A. Day Bradley, "Progressive Friends in Michigan and New York," *Quaker History* 52 (Autumn 1963): 95–101; John J. Cornell, *Autobiography* (Baltimore: Lord Baltimore Press, 1906); Katharine Anthony, *Susan B. Anthony* (Garden City, N.Y.: Doubleday, 1954), 92–93; Benjamin Gue, "Journal," typescript at New York State Library, Albany, N.Y., 40–41. Gue's diary was also published as *Diary of Benjamin Gue in Rural New York and Pioneer Iowa, 1847–1856,* ed. Earle D. Ross (Ames: Iowa State University Press, c. 1962); *Address to Friends; New York Tribune,* June 16, 1855; Carolyn Stefanco-Schill, "Congregational Friends and the Nineteenth Century Woman's Rights Movement in West-Central New York" (paper presented at Quaker History Conference, 1980); Densmore, "The

Quaker Tradition: Sustaining Women's Rights." For a hostile view of the Congregational Friends, see "A New Society," *Friend,* June 30, 1849.

85. Minutes of the Men's Meeting of Genesee Yearly Meeting, June 1847, FHL. The committee's statement as reported here is virtually identical to the report from the Women's Meeting Minutes. Exclamation points appeared in the Men's Meeting Minutes only. I have standardized spelling and punctuation.

86. Manuscript Minutes of the Men's Meeting of Genesee Yearly Meeting of Men, June 12–16, 1848, FHL; *Address to Friends,* 5.

87. *Address to Friends,* 6.

88. *Address to Friends,* 6–7. Like the official minutes from the men's meeting, those from the women's meeting on June 14 generally recorded the results of the discussion, alluding only briefly to its nature.

89. *Address to Friends,* 8; Gue, "Journal," 40.

90. LCM to George W. Julian, November 14, 1848, Mott Papers, FHL.

91. Daniel Anthony to SBA, July 16, 1848, Anthony Papers, Schlesinger; LCM to Richard D. Webb [etc.], September 10, 1848, Garrison Papers, BPL.

92. *Basis of Religious Association. Adopted by the Conference Held at Farmington, in the State of New York, on the Sixth and Seventh of Tenth Month, 1848* in *Proceedings of the Yearly Meeting of Congregational Friends* (Auburn, N.Y.: Henry Oliphant, 1850), 44–48; *New York Tribune,* June 16, 1855; Densmore and Wellman, "Thomas and Mary Ann M'Clintock." LCM to George W. Julian, November 14, 1848, noted, "We have only received the 'Preceedings' of Farmington, N. York, which I will send as a sample of a broad 'Basis.' Thos. McClintock, before spoken of[,] is the writer of that document. About 200 persons adopted it." For a discussion of the turmoil in New York state Quakerism in this period, see Barbour, Densmore et al., *Quaker Crosscurrents,* 100–145.

93. *Address to Friends,* 2, 8.

Chapter 8: Declaring Woman's Rights, July 1848

1. *Liberator,* May 26, 1848; *North Star,* July [?], 1848. For a discussion of the French Revolution and its impact on French women, see Anderson, *Joyous Greetings.*

2. *Seneca County Courier,* July 7, 1848.

3. *North Star,* July 7, 1848.

4. *Seneca County Courier,* July 11, 1848.

5. ECS, SBA, and Gage, *History of Woman Suffrage,* 1: 68; *Report of the International Council of Women* (Washington, D.C.: National Woman Suffrage Association, 1888), 32.

6. *New York Tribune* article reprinted in *Pennsylvania Freeman,* June 29, 1848. Thanks to Christopher Densmore for locating this. LCM to ECS, July 16, 1848; LCM to Richard D. Webb, September 10, 1848, Garrison Papers, BPL.

7. James Mott to "Dear Friend," July 2, 1848, printed in *Pennsylvania Freeman,* July 27, 1848. Thanks to Christopher Densmore for finding this citation. LCM to E.Q. [Edmund Quincy], August 24, 1848, printed in the *Liberator,* October 6, 1848.

8. LCM to E.Q. [Edmund Quincy], August 24, 1848, printed in the *Liberator,* October 6, 1848.

9. LCM to E.Q. [Edmund Quincy], August 24, 1848, printed in the *Liberator,* October 6, 1848.

10. For a different and more lengthy discussion of the influence of Haudenosaunee women on the nineteenth-century woman's rights movement, see Sally Roesch Wagner, *The Untold Story of the Iroquois Influence on Early Feminists* (Aberdeen, S.D.: Sky Carrier Press, 1996), and *Sisters in Spirit: Haudenosaunee (Iroquois) Influence on Early American Feminists* (Summertown, Tenn.: Native Voices, 2001).

11. Stanton gives several different lists of those who attended this tea party. In many of them, she collapsed this tea party at the Hunt house, where she and others wrote the call to the convention, with the tea party at the M'Clintock house a few days later, where Stanton and the M'Clintocks

worked on the Declaration of Sentiments and resolutions. For the tea party at the Hunt house, Stanton in *History of Woman Suffrage,* 1: 67, listed four women—Lucretia Mott, Martha C. Wright, Elizabeth Cady Stanton, and Mary Ann M'Clintock—as authors of the call. In her obituary for Elizabeth M'Clintock Phillips in *Woman's Journal* 27(47) (November 21, 1896): 373, Stanton added several names to the organizing process. She noted that "the discussions as to the wisdom of calling a convention took place at their home. The historic table round which the moving spirits, Lucretia Mott, Martha Wright, Mary Ann M'Clintock, Jane Hunt, James Mott, Thomas M'Clintock, Richard Hunt, the two daughters and myself drew up the declaration and resolutions, is still in possession of the family." Yet we know that neither Martha Wright nor Lucretia and James Mott drank tea at the M'Clintock house that day, for Mott wrote to Stanton from Auburn, dating the letter Sunday, July 16, saying that James was sick. David Wright confirmed that Lucretia Mott was in Auburn, noting that she held a meeting in the Universalist Church in the afternoon (Wright, "Account Book," July 16, [1848], Osborne Papers, SyU). By 1898, in *Eighty Years,* 148–49, Stanton included five women, the four she had mentioned in *History of Woman Suffrage* plus Jane Hunt. "The call," she wrote, "was inserted without signatures . . . but the chief movers and managers were Lucretia Mott, Mary Ann M'Clintock, Jane Hunt, Martha C. Wright, and myself." In "Mrs. Stanton's Letter to the Suffrage Convention. Held in Washington, D.C., in 1898" (Scrapbook 3, Stanton Papers, Vassar), she noted that "the seven women who inaugurated this movement, were Lucretia Mott, Elizabeth Cady Stanton, Martha C. Wright, Jane Hunt, Mary Ann M'Clintock and her two daughters," presumably Elizabeth and Mary Ann Jr. (A typescript that seems to be a version of this letter is now at the University of Rochester.) In an undated "Reminiscences" at the Minnesota Historical Society, Stanton noted that "this committee consisted of five quakeresses and myself."

12. Probate File for Richard P. Hunt, #572, Surrogate's Court, Seneca County Courthouse, Waterloo, New York, December 8, 1856; Probate File for Jane Hunt, #2214, Surrogate's Court, Seneca County Courthouse, Waterloo, New York, February 7, 1890.

13. U.S. Manuscript Census, 1850; Woodward, *Bacon-Woodward Pedigree,* 430.

14. ECS, *Eighty Years,* 147–48.

15. Richard P. Hunt, grandson of Richard P. Hunt, interview with John Becker, March 19, 1948, quoted in Becker, *History of Waterloo,* 155.

16. ECS, SBA, and Gage, *History of Woman Suffrage,* 1: 68; *Seneca County Courier,* July 11, 1848.

17. *Report of the Woman's Rights Convention,* [3].

18. Stanton noted in *Eighty Years,* 149, that "[w]e wrote the call that evening and published it in the *Seneca County Courier* the next day, the 14th of July, 1848, giving only five days' notice, as the convention was to be held on the 19th and 20th." The first notice, however, clearly appeared in the *Courier* on July 11.

19. LCM to ECS, July 16, 1848, Stanton Papers, LC; ECS to Elizabeth M'Clintock, Grassmere, Friday morning [July 14, 1848], WRNHP. ECS, "In Memoriam" [obituary for Elizabeth M'Clintock Phillips], *Woman's Journal,* 27(47) (November 21, 1896): 373. Stanton never gave a "great speech" at Seneca Falls, so Mott's note probably refers to what would become a draft of the declaration itself.

20. Bull, "Woman's Rights and Other 'Reforms,'" 1; LCM to ECS, July 16, 1848, Stanton Papers, LC.

21. ECS to Elizabeth M'Clintock, Grassmere, Friday morning [July 14, 1848], WRNHP. Frederick Douglass to Elizabeth M'Clintock, Rochester, July 14, [1848], WRNHP; "Subscribers" (manuscript list of subscribers to newspapers and periodicals in Seneca Falls, c. 1850), SFHS.

22. LCM to ECS, July 16, 1848, Stanton Papers, LC.

23. This tea table was in the possession of the M'Clintock family in 1881 (ECS, SBA, and Gage, *History of Woman Suffrage,* 1: 68); in 1888 (*International Council of Women,* 323); and in 1896 (ECS, "In Memoriam," 373). Sarah J. M'Clintock gave it to Stanton in 1898. Stanton presented it to Susan B. Anthony on her eightieth birthday, February 15, 1900. After Anthony's death, the table went to Anthony's niece Lucy Anthony and Anna Howard Shaw, both active in the National American

Woman's Suffrage Association (NAWSA). On February 11, 1920, the NAWSA gave it to the Smithsonian Institution. See letter from the Smithsonian to Mrs. David St. George, copied "for our files" December 11, 1973, SFHS.

24. ECS, SBA, and Gage, *History of Woman Suffrage,* 1: 68.

25. ECS, *Revolution* (September 17, 1868): 161–62. Thanks to Christopher Densmore for locating this. Stanton never took personal credit for the idea of using the Declaration of Independence as a model. Harriot Stanton Blatch to Alma Lutz, August 11, 1933, Lutz Papers, Vassar.

26. ECS, SBA, and Gage, *History of Woman Suffrage,* 1: 68.

27. ECS, SBA, and Gage, *History of Woman Suffrage,* 1: 68; ECS, *Revolution* (September 17, 1868): 161–62. Ann Gordon in *Selected Papers,* 1: 86, suggested that Elisha Hurlbut, *Essays on Human Rights, and Their Political Guaranties* (New York: Fowler and Wells, 1848), was a particularly important influence on the authors of the declaration, who "followed Hurlbut in all their examples."

28. ECS, SBA, and Gage, *History of Woman Suffrage,* 1: 67–69; *History of Woman Suffrage,* 1: 69, mentioned "one youthful lord"; ECS, *Revolution* (September 17, 1868): 161–62 made clear that this was Charles M'Clintock; Bullard, "Elizabeth Cady Stanton," 613–14; Martha Wright to LCM, January 6, 1856, Garrison Papers, Smith.

29. *Report of the Woman's Rights Convention,* 8, 5. Stanton claimed credit many times for introducing this point at the convention. "I stood alone in the demand for the right of suffrage," she wrote in 1898, typescript draft of letter to 50th anniversary meeting, UR.

30. Bullard, "Elizabeth Cady Stanton," 613–14; *New York Tribune,* July 19, 1848, reported that Henry Stanton lectured in Canandaigua.

31. Interview with Charlotte Woodward Pierce, quoted in Rheta Childe Dorr, *Susan B. Anthony: The Woman Who Changed the Mind of a Nation* (1928; reprint, New York: AMS Press, 1970), 47–49. See also "Oldest Suffragist Hits Woman's Party," newspaper article, Philadelphia, June 2, [1921?], in NAWSA Papers, LC; and *Seneca County Courier,* July 18, 1848.

32. Dorr, *Anthony,* 47; ECS, SBA, and Gage, *History of Woman Suffrage,* 1: 69; ECS, "In Memoriam," 373.

33. Dorr, *Anthony,* 4; Bull, "Woman's Rights and Other 'Reforms,'" 1; ECS, SBA, and Gage, *History of Woman Suffrage,* 1: 69, noted that James Mott took the chair on the first day. The *Report of the Woman's Rights Convention,* [3], however, clearly stated that "the question was discussed throughout two entire days: the first day by women exclusively, the second day men participated in the deliberations." No men's names appeared in the minutes of the first day's meeting, but the minutes noted that James Mott assumed the chair on Thursday morning, while Thomas M'Clintock chaired in the evening.

34. Bullard, "Elizabeth Cady Stanton," 613–14; *Report of the Woman's Rights Convention,* [3].

35. *Report of the Woman's Rights Convention,* 4–6.

36. *Report of the Woman's Rights Convention,* [3–4].

37. Bull, "Woman's Rights and Other 'Reforms,'" 1; *Report of the Woman's Rights Convention,* 4.

38. *Report of the Woman's Rights Convention,* 6; ECS, SBA, and Gage, *History of Woman Suffrage,* 1: 69, noted that Martha Wright herself "read some satirical articles she had publicized in the daily papers answering the diatribes on woman's sphere." Bull, "Woman's Rights and Other 'Reforms,'" 1; Martha Wright to LCM, October 1, 1848, Garrison Papers, Smith; Sherry H. Penney and James D. Livingston, "Expectant at Seneca Falls," *New York History* 84 (Winter 2003): 33–49.

39. Bullard, "Elizabeth Cady Stanton," 614.

40. *Seneca County Courier,* July 21, 1848; LCM to ECS, July 16, 1848, Stanton Papers, LC; Eliab W. Capron, *Auburn National Reformer,* August 3, 1848, quoted in Gordon, *Selected Papers,* 1: 84.

41. *Seneca County Courier,* July 21, 1848; Foner, *Life and Writings of Frederick Douglass,* 84; *North Star,* June 30, 1848.

42. ECS, SBA, and Gage, *History of Woman Suffrage,* 1: 69; ECS, *Eighty Years, 149;* Rhoda Palmer, "Early Days of Suffrage," *Geneva Daily Times,* March 17, 1915; Bull, "Woman's Rights and Oth-

er 'Reforms,'"; Amelia Bloomer, "Bloomerism, the Lily, and Mrs. Stanton" [Letter to Editor], July 12, 1880, printed in the *Seneca Falls Reveille,* July 30, 1880.

43. Tilton, "Elizabeth Cady Stanton," 613.

44. ECS, SBA, and Gage, *History of Woman Suffrage,* 1: 69; *Report of the Woman's Rights Convention,* [3]; LCM to ECS, July 16, 1848, Stanton Papers, LC; David Wright, July 19, [1848], "Account Book, July 19, 1847–November 29, 1848," Osborne Family Papers, SyU, noted that "Martha went to Seneca Falls." Thanks to Claire Petula for this citation. Bull, "Woman's Rights and Other 'Reforms.'"

45. Bull, "Woman's Rights and Other 'Reforms."

46. ECS, SBA, and Gage, *History of Woman Suffrage,* 1: 69; *Report of the Woman's Rights Convention,* 6.

47. This version is taken from the first printing of the Declaration of Sentiments in *Report of the Woman's Rights Convention,* 7–11.

48. The Declaration of Sentiments, including these grievances, was first printed in the *Report of the Woman's Rights Convention,* 7–11. As printed, the grievances fall into sixteen paragraphs, rather than the eighteen that the women aimed for. Some of these points, however, might be divided into two, as perhaps they were originally conceived.

49. Stanton was wrong about one detail in these indictments. In New York, since the Married Woman's Property Act had passed in April 1848, married women could own property. By the time of the convention, however, the implications of this law were still not clear. And women still were not legally entitled to the wages they earned.

50. *Report of the Woman's Rights Convention,* 6–7; ECS, SBA, and Gage, *History of Woman Suffrage,* 1: 69.

51. ECS, *Eighty Years,* 149; *Report of the Woman's Rights Convention,* 6–7; Capron, *Auburn National Reformer,* August 3, 1848, quoted in Gordon, *Selected Papers,* 1: 87.

52. *Seneca County Courier,* July 21, 1848, noted that the declaration was read and adopted Thursday morning, and "it was then signed by many persons present." *Report of the Woman's Rights Convention,* 10–12. Thanks to Mary Kelly Black and to an anonymous student from Syracuse University for noting that men were not recorded as signers of the declaration itself.

53. Bull, "Woman's Rights and Other 'Reforms'"; Bloomer, "Bloomerism, the Lily, and Mrs. Stanton"; Palmer, "Early Days of Suffrage."

54. "Anniversary of Western A.S. Society—Free Soil Political Party," *Liberator,* September 22, 1848.

55. Bull, "Woman's Rights and Other 'Reforms.'"

56. *Seneca County Courier,* July 21, 1848. No copy of the letter from William Howitt has been found.

57. *Report of the Woman's Rights Convention,* 11.

58. ECS, SBA, and Gage, *History of Woman Suffrage,* 1: 73; *International Council of Women,* 323–24; Lawrence, "Elizabeth Cady Stanton," 28–19. Lawrence related a similar version of this story in "Who Was Elizabeth Cady Stanton? and Who Started Votes for Women? A Bit of Ancient History for the Girls of To-day, by Mrs. Stanton's Daughter, Margaret Stanton Lawrence," typescript, n.d., Stanton Papers, Vassar, 7–8. Waldo E. Martin Jr., in *The Mind of Frederick Douglass* (Chapel Hill: University of North Carolina Press, 1984), 147–48, argued that "no aspect of his [Douglass's] woman's rights cause meant more to him than his pivotal support of woman's right to vote at the Seneca Falls convention." Douglass, "Address before Woman Suffrage Association," 109–15. Stanton's accounts differed as to whether the convention passed the resolution unanimously or "by a small majority."

59. *Report of the Woman's Rights Convention,* 12; ECS, SBA, and Gage, *History of Woman Suffrage,* 1: 69, claimed that "Samuel Tillman read a series of the most exasperating statutes for women." The *Report* did not mention Tillman making any public speech, although his name was listed as one of the "gentlemen present in favor of the movement." For a more detailed discussion of this issue, see chapter 9 and Gordon, *Selected Papers,* 1: 94–123.

60. *Report of the Woman's Rights Convention,* 12.

61. *Report of the Woman's Rights Convention,* 12.

62. *Report of the Woman's Rights Convention,* 12.

63. ECS, [Speech on Woman's Rights], [September 1848], Stanton Papers, LC; *Report of the Woman's Rights Convention,* 12.

64. ECS, *Eighty Years,* 149; ECS, SBA, and Gage, *History of Woman Suffrage,* 1: 73.

65. *International Council of Women,* 329. In *Eighty Years,* 149, Stanton noted that "[s]o pronounced was the popular voice against us, in the parlor, press, and pulpit, that most of the ladies who had attended the convention and signed the declaration, one by one, withdrew their names and influence and joined our persecutors." *History of Woman Suffrage,* 1: 73, suggested, however, that the total number of signers was originally one hundred. "The Declaration was signed," noted *History of Woman Suffrage,* "by one hundred men, and women, many of whom withdrew their names as soon as the storm of ridicule began to break." In the absence of contrary compelling evidence, I am assuming that the list as printed in the minutes of the convention contains the names of all of the original signers, including those who later withdrew their names. It seems logical that Frederick Douglass would have printed the minutes and signatures from the notes that Mary Ann M'Clintock Jr., secretary of the Seneca Falls convention, took at the convention, with the original list of signatures. One supposes that Douglass took all this material back to Rochester with him from the convention itself and that those who withdrew their names did so only afterwards, in response, as Stanton noted, to negative press reaction. On the other hand, the *Liberator* noted that "more than an hundred names were subscribed," August, 25, 1848.

66. For a more complete description of these signers, see Wellman, "The Seneca Falls Women's Rights Convention," 9–37; "Ride of Women," *Buffalo Morning Express,* August 7, 1848, 4, quoted in Laura Schmitt, "A Study: Women and the Buffalo Press in 1848" (unpublished paper, State University of New York at Oswego, 1972).

67. Rosalyn Terborg-Penn, *African American Women in the Struggle for the Vote, 1850–1920* (Bloomington: Indiana University Press, 1998).

68. I worked on simple hand analysis to develop cross-tabulation charts for this material. Special thanks to Robert Schell, who helped analyze this data using the Statistical Package for the Social Sciences, and to John Kane, who worked with the same data sets using Limdep. In no case could we find a correlation between wealth and signing.

69. Based on hand calculations comparing the signers with a sample of one hundred nonsigners from Seneca Falls and Waterloo.

70. "Methodist Episcopal Church, Memberships, 1840–1844"; "Old Brown Book, Members 1841–1846"; "Old Brown Book, Members 1846–1849"; "Old Brown Book, Members, 1849–1859"; and "Marriages, 1840–1866." Compiled and typed from original manuscript records by Ruth Laresen Kelly and Shirley Minard and given to the SFHS on July 2, 1984.

71. "Roll of Members" [Wesleyan Methodists, n.d.], and "Book No. 1, The Property of the First Wesleyan Methodist Church, Seneca Falls, N.Y.," microfilm, Cornell.

72. Trinity Episcopal Church of Seneca Falls, N.Y., "Records, 1831–1890," and "Vestry Records, 1831–86," microfilm, Cornell; G. M. Guion, "Trinity Episcopal Church," *Papers, SFHS* (1906): 27–30.

73. Martha Wright to LCM, March 5, 1852, Garrison Papers, Smith; Cowing, "Mrs. Stanton Our Pioneer Suffragist," 12–18.

74. Ronald S. Burt, "Models of Network Structures," *Annual Review of Sociology* 6 (1980): 91n8, identified a broker as one who is "the only connection between two subgroups of actors."

75. Palmer, "Early Days of Suffrage."

76. Records of Farmington, Rochester, and Junius Monthly Meetings, FHL.

77. Records of Farmington, Rochester, and Junius Monthly Meetings, FHL.

78. I defined Free Soil advocates as anyone who signed one of three Free Soil lists in the *Seneca County Courier,* June 13, August 4, or August 18, 1848.

79. Nathan Milliken, *Seneca County Courier,* July 21, 1848.

80. *Seneca County Courier,* July 21, 1848. On August 4, 1848, the *Courier* printed the convention's resolutions.

Chapter 9: The Road from Seneca Falls, 1848–1982

1. ECS, *Eighty Years,* 149; Frederick Douglass, "The Rights of Woman," *North Star,* July 28, 1848.

2. Unknown, quoted in *Liberator,* September 15, 1848.

3. ECS, SBA, and Gage, *History of Woman Suffrage,* 1: 802–3.

4. ECS, SBA, and Gage, *History of Woman Suffrage,* 1: 804.

5. *Herkimer Freeman,* reprinted in *Liberator,* September 22, 1847 [1848]; [William C. Nell] to the *Liberator,* dated August 14, 1848, printed September 1, 1848; *Nashville Daily Centre-State American,* July 28, 1848, and August 15, 1848, and *St. Louis Daily Reveille,* August 11, 1848, quoted in Timothy Terpstra, "The 1848 Seneca Falls Woman's Rights Convention: Initial American Public Reaction" (M.A. thesis, Mississippi State University, 1975), 56–57. Thanks to staff at the National Women's Hall of Fame for finding this thesis. See also Sylvia D. Hoffert, "New York City's Penny Press and the Issue of Woman's Rights, 1848–1860," *Journalism Quarterly* 70(3) (Autumn 1993): 656–65.

6. *New York Tribune* [n.d.], quoted in Lutz, *Created Equal,* 52.

7. Terpstra, "1848," 54, 59, 60, 68–69.

8. ECS, *Eighty Years,* 149.

9. *International Council of Women,* 324.

10. ECS, "Reminiscences, No. XVII, Seneca Falls," Stanton Papers, Rutgers.

11. LCM to the M'Clintocks, July 29, 1848, WRNHP.

12. On Elizabeth M'Clintock's concerns, see *Proceedings of the Woman's Rights Convention, Held at the Unitarian Church, Rochester, N.Y., August 2, 1848, To Consider the Rights of Woman, Politically, Religiously and Industrially, Revised by Mrs. Amy Post* (New York: Robert J. Johnston, 1870), [3]. On Stanton, see ECS to Amy Post, September 24, [1848], in Gordon, *Selected Papers,* 1: 123–24.

13. *North Star,* August 11, 1848; *Rochester Daily Democrat,* August 3, 1848.

14. ECS to Amy Post, September 24, [1848], in Gordon, *Selected Papers,* 1: 123–24.

15. John Willis to Amy Kirby Post, October 15, 1848, Post Family Papers, UR.

16. "Proceedings of the Woman's Rights Convention, Held at the Unitarian Church in the City of Rochester," *Liberator,* September 15, 1848; ECS, *Eighty Years,* 152; ECS and Elizabeth M'Clintock to the Editors, *Seneca County Courier,* [after July 23, 1848] in Gordon, *Selected Papers,* 1: 88–94.

17. ECS to the *National Reformer,* September 14, 1848, Stanton Papers, Rutgers.

18. LCM to ECS, October 3, 1848, Stanton Papers, LC.

19. Martha Wright to LCM, October 1, 1848, and October 16, 1848, Garrison Papers, Smith. LCM to Webbs, September 10, 1848, Garrison Papers, BPL.

20. LCM to ECS, October 3, 1848, noted that "Richard Hunt speaks very favorably of thy maiden speech at Waterloo." See also ECS, *Eighty Years,* 151. Between 1848 and 1850, ECS used parts of this speech in several publications. Susan B. Anthony appended a note to the manuscript of this speech that "this is the earliest address written by Elizabeth Cady Stanton—at Seneca Falls, N.Y. sometime in 1848 *after* the Seneca Falls & Rochester Conventions" (SBA Scrapbook 1: 1, Stanton Papers, LC). In 1870, Robert Johnson incorrectly cited this speech as one given at Seneca Falls and Rochester (*Address Delivered at Seneca Falls and Rochester, New York* [New York: Robert J. Johnson Printers, 1870]). For a detailed analysis of this speech, see Gordon, *Selected Papers,* 1: 94–95.

21. [Address by ECS on Woman's Rights], Stanton Papers, LC, printed in Gordon, *Selected Papers,* 1: 95–123.

22. ECS, *Eighty Years,* 151; *Free Thought Magazine* 13 (1895): 49–50; Christopher Densmore, "Forty-seven Years before the Woman's Bible" (paper presented at the Woman's Bible Centennial Conference, Seneca Falls, N.Y., November 4, 1995), available at <http://ublib.buffalo.edu/libraries/units/archives/urr/WNYWHO.html>; LCM to ECS, October 3, 1848, Stanton Papers, LC.

23. Bullard, "Elizabeth Cady Stanton," 617–18.

24. LCM to George Julian, November 14, 1848; LCM to Richard and Hannah Webb, September 10, 1848, Mott Papers, FHL; Benjamin Gue, *Diary of Benjamin F. Gue in Rural New York and Pioneer Iowa, 1847–1856*, Earle D. Ross, ed. (Ames: Iowa State University Press, 1962), 40; Yearly Meeting of Congregational Friends, *Basis of Religious Association Adopted by the Conference Held at Farmington, in the State of New York, on the 6th and 7th of Tenth month, 1848* (Waterloo: Sentell and Pew Printers, 1848); Christopher Densmore, comp., "Friends of Human Progress (Waterloo, New York): Participants at Annual Meetings, 1849–1871" (n.d.). For a bibliography of the minutes of the Waterloo Congregational Friends/of Human Progress, see Christopher Densmore, comp., "Printed Proceedings of the Yearly Meeting of Congregation Friends and the Friends of Human Progress, Waterloo (Junius), 1848–1860" (n.d.).

25. ECS to Martha Wright, [c. 1852], Garrison Papers, Smith; Cowing, "Mrs. Stanton Our Pioneer Suffragist," 12–18. For a more detailed look at ECS's relationship to the Congregational Friends, see Christopher Densmore, "Forty-seven Years before the Woman's Bible." Minutes for annual meetings of the Congregational Friends in 1850, 1851, 1852, 1857, and 1858 listed ECS's name as an active participant, and this group continued to take strong stands for woman's rights at each of their annual meetings. ECS's attendance at the Episcopal Church is confirmed by Elizabeth Delevan, "Elizabeth Cady Stanton: Written for a Program of The Comment Club of Des Moines, Iowa, 1938" [based on family stories from Delevan's great-grandfather, Rev. Dr. John Marshall Guion, minister of the Episcopal Church], 12, SFHS.

26. ECS to Amy Post, September 24, [1848] in Gordon, *Selected Papers*, 1: 123–26; Phoebe Hathaway to ECS, November 11, 1848, Stanton Papers, Vassar; Benjamin Gue, *Diary*, 54, attended the lecture and signed the petition; Martha Wright to LCM, December 9, 1850, Garrison Papers, Smith.

27. Emily Collins, "Reminiscences," in ECS, SBA, and Gage, *History of Woman Suffrage*, 1: 88; Emily Collins to Sarah C. Owen, October 23, 1848, quoted in *History of Woman Suffrage*, 1: 91–92.

28. Gue, *Diary*, 45; HBS to ECS, [September? 8? 1848], and October 26, 1848, Stanton Papers, Rutgers.

29. Sewall, *Ballots for Freedom*, 152–69.

30. *National Liberty Party* [October 1852], printed pamphlet, Smith Papers, SyU; Gerrit Smith, *To the Voters of the Counties of Oswego and Madison* ([n.p.], 1852).

31. Sewall, *Ballots for Freedom*, 167–68; *Free-Soil Union* [Seneca Falls], November 9, 1848.

32. ECS to LCM, September 26, [1849], Garrison Papers, Smith. For a full discussion of Elizabeth M'Clintock as an entrepreneur, see Andrea Constantine Hawkes, "'Feeling a Strong Desire to Tread a Broader Road to Fortune': The Antebellum Evolution of Elizabeth Wilson McClintock's Entrepreneurial Consciousness" (M.A. thesis, University of Maine, Orono, 1995).

33. Edward Davis to LCM, October 10, 1849; LCM to ECS, October 25, 1849, Garrison Papers, Smith.

34. ECS to Elizabeth M'Clintock, [before November 12, 1849], Garrison Family Papers, Smith.

35. ECS to LCM, November 12, 1849, Garrison Papers, Smith.

36. Elizabeth M'Clintock to LCM, November 13, 1849, Garrison Papers, Smith.

37. LCM to Elizabeth M'Clintock and ECS, November 27, 1849, Garrison Papers, Smith.

38. Oliver Johnson to Gerrit Smith, November 22, 1841, Smith Papers, SyU; Thomas M'Clintock to *Liberator*, October 30, 1861, printed December 27, 1861, enclosing a description of a séance dated November 2, 1851; William C. Nell to William Lloyd Garrison, September 15, 1851, Garrison Papers, BPL; Dun and Bradstreet, April 6, 1853, and September 10, 1853, Baker Library, Harvard; George Willets to Isaac Post, October [?] 23, 1848, Post Family Papers, UR. For an overview of the spiritualist movement as it related to women, see Ann Braude, *Radical Spirits: Spiritualism and Women's Rights in Nineteenth-Century America* (Boston: Beacon Press, 1989).

39. Elizabeth Delevan, "Elizabeth Cady Stanton," SFHS, 6; Lillian/Lillias Mynderse to ECS/Theodore Stanton, [February 10, 1851] in Gordon, *Selected Papers*, 1: 179.

40. ECS to LCM, October 22, 1852, in Gordon, *Selected Papers*, 1: 212–13; Blatch, *Challenging Years*,

4; Stanton and Blatch, *Elizabeth Cady Stanton,* 2: xvii; Margaret Stanton Lawrence, "Reminiscences," typescript, 2 vols., Stanton Papers, Vassar, 1: 20.

41. ECS, *Eighty Years,* 209. The neighbor, "Mr. S." was probably William A. Sackett. Robert B. Stanton [ECS's nephew], "Reminiscences" [n.d.], New York Public Library. Thanks to Judy Hart for finding this citation. For further discussion of ECS's home life, see Corinne Guntzel and Paul Grebinger, "Real and Ideal in the Home Life of Elizabeth Cady Stanton: Domestic Discontent and the Origins of the Women's Rights Movement," unpublished paper, WRNHP.

42. Lawrence, "Elizabeth Cady Stanton," 32–33; ECS, *Eighty Years,* 163–64; Robert B. Stanton, "Reminiscences" [n.d.], New York Public Library.

43. "Elizabeth Cady Stanton: Some Reminiscences of Her Family Life at Seneca Falls, New York," typescript, n.d., SFHS.

44. Delevan, "Elizabeth Cady Stanton," [based on a conversation with Delevan's grandmother, born c. 1840], 10, SFHS; ECS, *Eighty Years,* 152–53; Lawrence, "Reminiscences," 1: 39; Cowing, "Mrs. Stanton Our Pioneer Suffragist," 14.

45. Lawrence, "Reminiscences," 2: 13–14, and "Elizabeth Cady Stanton, 1815–1915," 40–41.

46. Lawrence, "Reminiscences," 2: 9.

47. ECS, *Eighty Years,* 163. Garrison and Thompson stayed overnight with the M'Clintocks before going on to Port Byron on Wednesday morning. G.W.P., "Meetings in Central New York," *Liberator,* May 30, 1851.

48. ECS, *Eighty Years,* 165–66.

49. For further discussion of dress reform, see Jane B. Donegan, *"Hydropathic Highway to Health": Women and Water-Cure in Antebellum America* (Westport, Conn.: Greenwood Press, 1986).

50. Martha Wright to SBA, July 4, 1856, Garrison Papers, Smith; ECS to Mrs. James G. Birney, May 24, 1849, Stanton Papers, Rutgers.

51. For more on the signers, see the Web site for the Women's Rights National Historical Park, <http://www.nps.gov/wori/biolisting.htm>.

52. [Harrison Chamberlain?], "Jacob P. Chamberlain," 54–58; Chamberlain, "Early Flouring Mills," 12–13; Credit ratings for Jacob P. Chamberlain, New York, vol. 55, R. G. Dun and Co. Collection, Baker Library, Harvard Business School.

53. "Charles L. Hoskins," 269–70; Anna Henion, "Early Schools," *Papers, SFHS* (1903): 64; Monroe, "Seneca Falls in Earlier Days," 33–45.

54. Newspaper clipping in Gibbs's file, March 17, 1899, SFHS; Petition for Probate #2424, Seneca County Surrogate's Office, Waterloo, New York, from notes taken by Betty Auten.

55. Richard A. Seiber, ed., *Memoirs of Puget Sound: Early Seattle, 1853–1856, Letters of David and Catherine Blaine* (Fairfield, Wash.: Ye Galleon Press, 1978), from notes taken by Florence Hazzard from typescript edited by Edward Linn, Blaine Papers, University of Washington Library, Seattle, Wash.

56. "Elisha Foote," *National Cyclopedia of American Biography,* vol. 21 (New York: James T. Whit, 1931), 339–40; "Elisha Foote," *Appleton's Cyclopedia of American Biography,* vol. 2 (New York: Appleton & Co., 1887), 495–96; Abram William Foote, *Foote Family* (Baltimore: Gateway Press, [1981]), 352–53; Nathaniel Goodwin, *The Foote Family* (Hartford, Conn.: Case, Tiffany, 1849), 158–59; letter to author from Deborah Jean Warner, Smithsonian Institution, May 3, 1976.

57. Credit ratings for S. E. Woodworth, New York, vols. 58–60, 75, 85, 88, R. G. Dun and Co. Collection, Baker Library, Harvard Business School; Mary Stanley, "Grace Woodworth," in Lisa Johnson and Heather Tunis, eds., *Grace Woodworth: Photographer outside the Common Lines* (Auburn, N.Y.: Schweinfurth Memorial Art Center, 1984).

58. Petition for Probate for William Clark, #5676, Surrogate's Court, Seneca County, Waterloo, N.Y., from notes taken by Betty Auten; Marriage and Death Records, Trinity Episcopal Church, microfilm, Cornell; Conversation and correspondence with John Brady, descendent of Susan Quinn, 1980 and 1982; "Recollections of Two Eminent Members of Local Bar," typescript of article from seventy-fifth anniversary edition of the *Seneca Falls Reveille,* n.d., from files of John Brady.

59. Stebbins, *Upward Steps of Seventy Years,* 71; the *Liberator* subscription list noted that the M'Clintocks moved their subscription to Easton on July 8, 1856, Garrison Papers, BPL.

60. Hewitt, "Amy Kirby Post," 4–21; *Rochester Democrat and Chronicle,* May 10, 1872; May 13, 1872; January 30, 1889; February 1, 1889; and February 2, 1889. *Rochester Union Advertiser,* February 25, 1889; *Landmarks of Monroe County,* 154; Post, "The Underground Railway," 458–62; Lucy N. Colman, "Tribute to a Friend and Co-Laborer," [*Woman's Tribune*], n.d., clipping in scrapbook labeled "Woman's Word and Work," SFHS; "Isaac Post," *Dictionary of American Biography,* 8: 117.

61. Paul Messbarger, "Wright, Martha Coffin Pelham," in *Notable American Women,* 3: 684–85. Other sketches of Martha Coffin Wright include Eliza Wright Osborne, "Martha Wright," *Papers, SFHS, Sixtieth Anniversary* (1908): 53–54.

62. Eliza Wright Osborne, "A Recollection of Martha Coffin Wright by Her Daughter," 23, typescript copy owned by L. Devens Osborne, on file at WRNHP.

63. Martha Wright to LCM, September 4, 1848, Garrison Papers, Smith. The reference to Balaam is to the friend of Jonathan, King David's son.

64. Lithgow Osborne to Anne L. Hoblitzelle, March 22, 1974, copy at WRNHP.

65. Frederick Douglass to H. G. Warner (editor of the *Rochester Courier*), reprinted in *Liberator,* October 6, 1848; William S. McFeely, *Frederick Douglass* (New York: Norton, 1995), 223–37.

66. *International Council of Women,* 329.

67. "Frederick Douglass, Obituary," *Rochester Union and Advertiser,* February 21, 1895. For overviews of Douglass's position on woman's rights, see Foner, *Frederick Douglass on Women's Rights,* and Martin, *Mind of Frederick Douglass,* 136–64; Douglass to Josephine Griffing, September 27, 1868, in McFeely, *Frederick Douglass,* 269–70.

68. ECS to Salem Convention, April 7, 1850, in ECS, SBA, and Gage, *History of Woman Suffrage 1*: 812; "Cleveland National Convention," in *History of Woman Suffrage,* 1: 129–33, outlined a specific debate about whether to adopt the Seneca Falls Declaration of Sentiments or to write a new Declaration of Rights; John F. McClymer, *This High and Holy Moment: The First National Woman's Rights Convention, Worcester, 1850* (San Diego, Calif.: Harcourt Brace, 1999); LCM to ECS, March 16, 1855, Stanton Papers, LC.

69. For discussions of African American women and woman's rights, see Terborg-Penn, *African American Women in the Struggle for the Vote;* Ann D. Gordon with Bettye Collier-Thomas, eds., *African American Women and the Vote, 1837–1965* (Amherst: University of Massachusetts Press, 1997); and Nell Irvin Painter, "Voices of Suffrage: Sojourner Truth, Frances Watkins Harper, and the Struggle for Woman Suffrage," in Jean H. Baker, ed., *Votes for Women: The Struggle for Suffrage Revisited* (New York: Oxford University Press, 2002), 42–55.

70. Faye Dudden, "New York Strategy: The New York Woman's Movement and the Civil War," in Baker, ed., *Votes for Women,* 56–76.

71. *Seneca Falls Reveille,* October 13 and November 17, 1866; Frederick Douglass to Josephine Griffing, September 27, 1868, quoted in McFeely, *Frederick Douglass,* 268–69; Griffiths, *In Her Own Right,* 118–43.

72. Griffiths, *In Her Own Right,* 118–43.

73. Sally Roesch Wagner, *A Time of Protest: Suffragists Challenge the Republic, 1870–1887* (Sacramento: Spectrum Publications, 1987).

74. ECS to Theodore Stanton, July 28, 1878, Stanton Papers, Rutgers; Phoebe W. Couzins, November 22, 1888, "Lucretia Mott, Reminiscences by Phoebe W. Couzins," clipping, Mott Papers, FHL.

75. *International Council of Women,* 30–39; Anderson, *Joyous Greetings.*

76. Press release from Harriot Stanton Blatch, announcing her gift of these two pieces to the Smithsonian, n.d., Schlesinger.

77. *Address by Mrs. Elizabeth Cady Stanton at the Metropolitan Opera House, New York City, on her Eightieth Birthday, Nov. 12, 1895,* printed copy, Schlesinger. ECS to Theodore Roosevelt, October 22, 1902, reprinted in *Independent* 6 (1902): 2621–22.

78. For more on the *Woman's Bible,* see Kern, *Mrs. Stanton's Bible.*

79. *The Thirtieth Annual Convention of the National American Woman Suffrage Association and the Celebration of the Fiftieth Anniversary of the First Woman's Rights Convention, Columbia Theatre, Washington, D.C. Religious Service, Sunday, February 13, at 3 P.M.* (n.p., [1898]), program, Schlesinger. Matilda Joslyn Gage, "Woman's Demand for Freedom; Its Influence upon the World," Schlesinger. A note in Gage's hand identifies this as a speech given at the Columbia Theater in Washington, D.C., on February 18, 1898, but the date was undoubtedly February 13. Typescript of minutes of the Sherwood Equal Rights Association, July 20, 1898, Olin Library, Cornell.

80. ECS to Theodore Roosevelt, October 22, 1902, reprinted in *Independent* 6 (1902): 2621–22; SBA to Clara Colby, October 31, 1902, printed in *Woman's Tribune,* November 8, 1902; Ellen Carol DuBois, *The Elizabeth Cady Stanton–Susan B. Anthony Reader* (Boston: Northeastern University Press, 1981), 255–66.

81. "Anniversary Celebration of the 1848 Woman's Rights Convention, Seneca Falls, Wednesday, May 27, 1908" [printed program], SFHS; "60th Anniversary of the 1848 Woman's Rights Convention," *Papers, SFHS* (1908): 26–69; "Place Tablet in Opera House," clipping from an unidentified newspaper in SFHS, May 26, 1908; Ellen Carol DuBois, *Harriot Stanton Blatch and the Winning of Woman Suffrage* (New Haven: Yale University Press, 1997).

82. *Seneca Falls Reveille,* June 5 [?], 1908.

83. *Seneca Falls Reveille,* June 5 [?], 1908.

84. "Programme," Elizabeth Cady Stanton Centennial Luncheon Held at the Hotel Astor, October 30, 1915, Stanton Papers, Vassar; *Annual Report of the New York State Woman Suffrage Association, 47th Annual Convention, Hotel Astor, New York* (n.p., n.d.), 41–43.

85. *Annual Report of the New York State Woman Suffrage Association, 47th Annual Convention,* 41–43; *Annual Report of the New York State Woman Suffrage Party, 1917* (New York: Woman Suffrage Publishing Co., [1917]), 58–59; Betty Auten, "A Prestigious List," *Seneca County History,* 2(1) (September 1985): 6–11. For the woman suffrage movement in New York state, see Ellen Carol DuBois, "Working Women, Class Relations and Suffrage Militance: Harriot Stanton Blatch and the New York Woman Suffrage Movement, 1894–1909," in DuBois, *Woman Suffrage and Women's Rights,* 178–209; Frances Diodato Bzowski, "Spectacular Suffrage: Or, How Women Came Out of the Home and into the Streets and Theaters of New York City to Win the Vote," *New York History* (January 1995): 57–94; and David McDonald, "Organizing Womanhood: Women's Culture and the Politics of Woman Suffrage in New York State, 1865–1917" (Ph.D. dissertation, State University of New York, Stony Brook, 1987). For discussions of the suffrage movement nationally, see Kraditor, *Ideas of the Woman Suffrage Movement;* Anne Firor Scott and Andrew MacKay Scott, *One Half the People: The Fight for Woman Suffrage* (Urbana: University of Illinois Press, 1982); Terborg-Penn, *African American Women in the Struggle for the Vote;* DuBois, *Woman Suffrage and Women's Rights;* Marjorie Spruill Wheeler, ed., *One Woman, One Vote* (Troutdale, Ore.: New Sage Press, 1995); Sara Hunter Graham, *Woman Suffrage and the New Democracy* (New Haven, Conn.: Yale University Press, 1996); Gordon and Collier Thomas, *African American Women and the Vote;* Jean Baker, ed., *Votes for Women: The Struggle for Suffrage Revisited* (New York: Oxford University Press, 2002).

86. "The Declaration of Independence—1914," typescript, Schlesinger; Harriot Stanton Blatch, *Centennial of Elizabeth Cady Stanton* (n.p., [1915]); Lawrence, "Elizabeth Cady Stanton."

87. Clipping from a Waterloo newspaper, November 12, [1918], found by Betty Auten; "Miss Rhoda Palmer Gives Reminiscences," *Geneva Daily Times,* June 24, 1916; Rhoda Palmer obituary, *Geneva Daily Times,* August 11, 1919.

88. Kraditor, *Ideas of the Woman Suffrage Movement,* 5.

89. Flexner, *Century of Struggle,* 323.

90. "Oldest Suffragist Hits Woman's Party," June 2, [1921], clipping in NAWSA Papers, LC.

91. "Speech of Jane Addams, Chairman of the Ceremony," typescript of speeches by Addams, Sarah Bard Field, Frederick Gillett and others at the dedication of the Adelaide Johnson monument; typescript minutes of 1920 National Woman's Party convention, Schlesinger.

92. Letter to Harriot Stanton Blatch, October 13, 1923, NAWSA Papers, LC.

93. Catt to the Executive Council of the NAWSA, March 12, 1925, NAWSA Papers, LC.

94. Typescript minutes of the 1920 National Woman's Party convention, Schlesinger. Alice Paul, quoted in Robert Gallagher, "I Was Arrested, Of Course," *American Heritage*, (February 1974): 17–18; Amelia Fry, "Woman Suffrage and the Equal Rights Amendment," interview with Alice Paul, 1972–73, Bancroft Library Suffragists Oral History Project, University of California at Berkeley, 264–65; *Suffragist*, 10 (January–February 1921), 339, quoted in Christine A. Lunardini, *From Equal Suffrage to Equal Rights: Alice Paul and the National Woman's Party, 1910–1928* (New York: New York University Press, 1986), 158–59.

95. "Constitutional Amendment Will Be Drafted Here," *Seneca Falls Reveille*, July [?], 1923.

96. *Geneva Daily Times*, July 21, 1923, and July 23, 1923. Elizabeth Delevan was one of the local young women in the pageant. "It was at this time that my generation realized the historic importance of ECS's works and her place in history," she recalled in "Elizabeth Cady Stanton," 1–2.

97. Newspaper clipping, n.p., n.d., Johnstown Historical Society, Johnstown, N.Y.; *How Long Will Women Wait for Liberty?* (Washington, D.C.: National Woman's Party, 1937); Marianne Leslie Black to Katherine Devereux Blake, July 22, 1943, Sophia Smith Collection, Smith.

98. *Woman's Centennial Congress, November 25, 26, 27, 1940, Hotel Commodore, New York City*, minutes, Sophia Smith Collection, Smith.

99. *Declaration of Purpose Adopted by the Woman's Centennial Congress, November 25–27, 1940, New York City*, Sophia Smith Collection, Smith.

100. *Time*, December 9, 1940, 16–17.

101. Caroline Lester, a Seneca Falls writer and historian, wrote the original version of "Woman Awakened," which was adapted to incorporate pieces of a play, "One Hundred Years of Growing," from the League of Women Voters. *General Program, Woman's Rights Centennial, 1848–1948; Woman's Rights Centennial Mass Meeting, Tuesday, July, 20, 1848; Seneca Falls Pageant "Woman Awakened,"* Sophia Smith Collection, Smith. "Centennial Stamp Ceremony Attracts Thousands to Seneca Falls" and "Seneca Falls to Play Host to Hundreds during Centennial Holiday," *Seneca County Press*, July 14, 1948. "Feminists Conclude Centennial Program," *Syracuse Post-Standard*, July 20, 1948; "'Equal Rights Day' Proclaimed by Governor for July 19," *Seneca County Press*, July 14, 1848.

102. *Seneca County Press*, July 14, 1948; *Christian Science Monitor*, July 20, 1948.

103. *Geneva Daily Times*, July 19, 1948; "History Is Made again in Seneca Falls Event," *Syracuse Post-Standard*, July 20, 1948.

104. "Feminists Conclude Centennial Program," *Syracuse Post-Standard*, July 20, 1948.

105. *Declaration of the Women of 1948 to the Women of 2048*, SFHS. Handwritten note on this copy: "Read by Susan B. Anthony II at Mass Meeting of Centenary of Woman's Rights Convention, July 20th, 1948, Seneca Falls, New York."

106. Women's Bureau, Department of Labor, press release, July 19, 1948, Schlesinger.

107. "The Declaration of Seneca Falls," University of Michigan, [1948], Schlesinger; Eva Candia, "La Mujer y la Paz (Centenario de la Covencion de Seneca Falls), Division de Radio de Las Naciones Unidas [1948].

108. "CAW Celebrates the Seneca Falls Centennial," *Around the World, A Publication of the Congress of American Women . . . Affiliated with the Women's International Democratic Federation*, 1(5) (July–August, 1948). Thanks to Betty Millard for sending me a copy of this newsletter.

109. Rose Arnold Powell to Alice Stone Blackwell, n.d., noted an article in the *Journal* of the NEA (February 1948). NAWSA Papers, LC. *Ladies Home Journal*, July 1948, clipping, SFHS. The Sophia Smith Research Room, Smith College, has an excellent collection of articles relating to the 1948 centennial, including *Christian Science Monitor*, July 20, 1948; Nora Stanton Barney, "The Seneca Falls Centennial," *Los Angeles School Journal* (February 16, 1948); *Finger Lakes Topics, Equal Rights Centennial—Seneca Falls, N.Y.—July 19–20, 1948*.

110. Gordon and Collier-Thomas, *African American Women and the Vote, 1837–1965*; Terborg-Penn, *African American Women in the Struggle for the Vote*.

111. General overviews of contemporary U.S. women's movements include Buechler, *Women's Movements in the United States;* Ryan, *Feminism and the Women's Movement;* and Simon and Danziger, *Women's Movements in America.*

112. *The Spirit of Houston: The First National Women's Conference* (Washington, D.C.: National Commission on the Observance of International Women's Year, 1978), 193–203.

113. *Spirit of Houston,* 195, 138.

114. Mim Kelber, "Declaration of American Women 1977," *Spirit of Houston,* 15–16, 142.

115. *Spirit of Houston,* 170. "Boundary Expansion of Crater Lake National Park and Establishment of Women's Rights National Historical Park," *Congressional Record—House,* November 19, 1980, 30271–72.

116. Mary Frances Berry, *Why the ERA Failed* (Bloomington: Indiana University Press, 1986).

Index

JUDITH WELLMAN is the director of Historical New York Research Associates, a professor emerita of history at SUNY Oswego, and former park historian at the Women's Rights National Historical Park in Seneca Falls, New York. She is the author of *Grass Roots Reform in the Burned-over District of Upstate New York: Religion, Abolitionism, and Democracy* (2000) and the editor of *Landmarks of Oswego County* (1988).

Women in American History

Women Doctors in Gilded-Age Washington: Race, Gender, and Professionalization *Gloria Moldow*

Friends and Sisters: Letters between Lucy Stone and Antoinette Brown Blackwell, 1846–93 *Edited by Carol Lasser and Marlene Deahl Merrill*

Reform, Labor, and Feminism: Margaret Dreier Robins and the Women's Trade Union League *Elizabeth Anne Payne*

Private Matters: American Attitudes toward Childbearing and Infant Nurture in the Urban North, 1800–1860 *Sylvia D. Hoffert*

Civil Wars: Women and the Crisis of Southern Nationalism *George C. Rable*

I Came a Stranger: The Story of a Hull-House Girl *Hilda Satt Polacheck; edited by Dena J. Polacheck Epstein*

Labor's Flaming Youth: Telephone Operators and Worker Militancy, 1878–1923 *Stephen H. Norwood*

Winter Friends: Women Growing Old in the New Republic, 1785–1835 *Terri L. Premo*

Better Than Second Best: Love and Work in the Life of Helen Magill *Glenn C. Altschuler*

Dishing It Out: Waitresses and Their Unions in the Twentieth Century *Dorothy Sue Cobble*

Natural Allies: Women's Associations in American History *Anne Firor Scott*

Beyond the Typewriter: Gender, Class, and the Origins of Modern American Office Work, 1900–1930 *Sharon Hartman Strom*

The Challenge of Feminist Biography: Writing the Lives of Modern American Women *Edited by Sara Alpern, Joyce Antler, Elisabeth Israels Perry, and Ingrid Winther Scobie*

Working Women of Collar City: Gender, Class, and Community in Troy, New York, 1864–86 *Carole Turbin*

Radicals of the Worst Sort: Laboring Women in Lawrence, Massachusetts, 1860–1912 *Ardis Cameron*

Visible Women: New Essays on American Activism *Edited by Nancy A. Hewitt and Suzanne Lebsock*

Mother-Work: Women, Child Welfare, and the State, 1890–1930 *Molly Ladd-Taylor*

Babe: The Life and Legend of Babe Didrikson Zaharias *Susan E. Cayleff*

Writing Out My Heart: Selections from the Journal of Frances E. Willard, 1855–96 *Edited by Carolyn De Swarte Gifford*

U.S. Women in Struggle: A *Feminist Studies* Anthology *Edited by Claire Goldberg Moses and Heidi Hartmann*

In a Generous Spirit: A First-Person Biography of Myra Page *Christina Looper Baker*

Mining Cultures: Men, Women, and Leisure in Butte, 1914–41 *Mary Murphy*

Gendered Strife and Confusion: The Political Culture of Reconstruction *Laura F. Edwards*

The Female Economy: The Millinery and Dressmaking Trades, 1860–1930 *Wendy Gamber*

Mistresses and Slaves: Plantation Women in South Carolina, 1830–80 *Marli F. Weiner*

A Hard Fight for We: Women's Transition from Slavery to Freedom in South Carolina *Leslie A. Schwalm*

The Common Ground of Womanhood: Class, Gender, and Working Girls' Clubs, 1884–1928 *Priscilla Murolo*

Purifying America: Women, Cultural Reform, and Pro-Censorship Activism, 1873–1933 *Alison M. Parker*

Marching Together: Women of the Brotherhood of Sleeping Car Porters *Melinda Chateauvert*

Creating the New Woman: The Rise of Southern Women's Progressive Culture in Texas, 1893–1918 *Judith N. McArthur*

The Business of Charity: The Woman's Exchange Movement, 1832–1900 *Kathleen Waters Sander*

The Power and Passion of M. Carey Thomas *Helen Lefkowitz Horowitz*

For Freedom's Sake: The Life of Fannie Lou Hamer *Chana Kai Lee*

Becoming Citizens: The Emergence and Development of the California Women's Movement, 1880–1911 *Gayle Gullett*

Selected Letters of Lucretia Coffin Mott *Edited by Beverly Wilson Palmer with the assistance of Holly Byers Ochoa and Carol Faulkner*

Women and the Republican Party, 1854–1924 *Melanie Susan Gustafson*

Southern Discomfort: Women's Activism in Tampa, Florida, 1880s–1920s *Nancy A. Hewitt*

The Making of "Mammy Pleasant": A Black Entrepreneur in Nineteenth-Century San Francisco *Lynn M. Hudson*

Sex Radicals and the Quest for Women's Equality *Joanne E. Passet*

"We, Too, Are Americans": African American Women in Detroit and Richmond, 1940–54 *Megan Taylor Shockley*

The Road to Seneca Falls: Elizabeth Cady Stanton and the First Woman's Rights Convention *Judith Wellman*

The University of Illinois Press
is a founding member of the
Association of American University Presses.

Composed in 10.5/12.5 Minion
by Jim Proefrock
at the University of Illinois Press
Manufactured by Thomson-Shore, Inc.

University of Illinois Press
1325 South Oak Street
Champaign, IL 61820-6903
www.press.uillinois.edu